Embodied Gestalt Practice:

Selected Papers
of Edward W. L. Smith

EDWARD W.L. SMITH

A Publication of The Gestalt Journal Press

Published by:
The Gestalt Journal Press, Inc.
P. O. Box 278
Gouldsboro, ME 04607

ISBN # 978-0-939266-96-8

Embodied Gestalt Practice:

Selected Papers
of Edward W. L. Smith

Contents

Contents

INTRODUCTION

It is a pleasure to write an introduction to this collection of Edward Smith's writings. Over the years I have enjoyed reading Edward's articles, and his writings have never failed to stimulate my thinking and to give me a different perspective on the topic under discussion. How wonderful to have a collection of these essays in one convenient volume!

I am pleased, in part, to see these articles published because they represent the ideas of one who has thought deeply about theory for many years. These articles were published over a span of 36 years, and they represent the experiences of someone who has trained in several disciplines and integrated those disciplines into a complex overall approach. Gestalt therapy is well represented in this collection — as it should be given Edward's long devotion to that discipline. While Gestalt therapy has been dismissed by some as primarily a technique, it is, in fact, a complex and well developed theory, and it is Gestalt theory that is emphasized in Edward's writings. Gestalt theory and its philosophical underpinnings must be elucidated and elaborated if Gestalt therapy is to continue making contributions to the development of modern psychotherapy. Edward's contribution to our understanding of concepts such as retroflection, projection, and the contact and withdrawal cycle, for example, helps to bring Gestalt therapy alive for the reader and the practitioner.

Edward's writings bring out another aspect of Gestalt therapy that is important to understand: It is more than a theory — it is a way of living — a way of being-in-the-world. In this sense it is, as Perls averred, a true form of existential therapy. Gestalt may be useful for helping clients overcome problems, but it is more than that: It is a prescription for how to live well. Gestalt theory proposes that life is an active process, and it then describes a way to understand and negotiate that process. All forms of psychotherapy attempt to help clients resolve problems and issues, and Gestalt therapy can do that. However, Gestalt theory goes beyond that in pointing to a way of living that can be more fulfilling and more in line with our nature. Focus on personal process involves more than attempting to solve a particular problem; it takes us on the Dionysian path, as Edward puts it, a way of living. Perhaps the "Tao of Gestalt" would be a way to phrase it.

INTRODUCTION

A related emphasis in Edward's writing is the focus on the body. It is the body in psychotherapy, but it also is a prescription for how to live fully in one's body. Edward once remarked to me that he believed that much of Perls' genius derived from his remarkable ability to "read" the body, to understand what the body was expressing. Edward often referred to his practice as "embodied Gestalt practice," but I don't believe that it represents a mere collection of special techniques or even a particular type of Gestalt practice. I believe that all Gestalt practice is, by its nature, embodied, just as living is embodied living. To live fully is to live inside the body. Edward, like Perls, devoted years of his professional life to understanding the body, and several articles in his collection reflect the emphasis he places on working directly with the body and on finding the common ground in the work of Perls, Reich, and others. Embodied Gestalt practice helps the client to live in their bodies with full awareness, and Edward's writing helps the practitioner to focus awareness on this aspect of treatment.

James L. Pugh, Ph.D.

~

PERSONALITY GROWTH THROUGH THE
PRESENTIFICATION OF PERSONAL SYMBOLS

The "third" force in contemporary Western psychology, humanism, has given birth to a phenomenon known as the "human potentials movement," an increasing involvement of persons in organized activities which hold promise for personality growth (Howard, 1970). Although these activities come from diverse traditions and vary widely in their form (Peterson, 1971), they are related through an aspect of the humanistic ethic, the commitment to growth-oriented experiencing (Bugental, 1971).

In the present paper I describe a growth technique which is based on Jungian theory and Gestalt therapy. The process of coming to know one's self, both as individual and as a member of mankind, requires no justification. One avenue for this two-level process is the exploration of archetypes, insofar as the archetype represents a universal tendency toward a mode of experience; and, at the same time, the specific personification of the archetype is a highly personal symbolic embodiment of that archetype. For example, the "hero" archetype can be found in the mythology of all peoples. To explore "hero-ness," then, allows one to come to know something of what it is to be human, to participate in the transpersonal. At another level, one can attend to his personal symbolization of "hero" to experience something of what it is to be himself. His personal personification can be compared to others' personifications, thus highlighting his individuality as manifested in his personal symbolic activity.

The key to personal growth through the exploration of personal personifications of archetypes is *knowing* through the creation of a here-and-

---

From *International Journal of Symbology*, 3(2), 1-3 (1972).

now experience, as opposed to a more limited cognitive exercise in *knowing about*. The distinction drawn here is between the verbal world, or that world which we know about through words, and the extensional world, or that world which we know through direct experience (Hayakawa, 1941). The components of complete experiencing are four processes which Jung referred to as the ectopsychic functions — sensing, thinking, feeling, and intuiting (Jung, 1968). Sensing is the process of detecting a presence; thinking is the process of giving identity to the presence through verbal labeling, and dealing with the labeled presence through logic and inference; feeling is the process of evaluating the labeled presence in terms of affecting reactions; intuiting is, in part, the process of "knowing" from whence the labeled presence came and what its future will be. Whereas thinking is the mode of *knowing about*, the experimental Gestalt of all four ectopsychic functions is the mode of *knowing*.

In another paper I have set out in detail a workshop format for the presentification of personal personifications of "hero" and "villain" archetypes (Smith, 1972). In the present paper I will describe the essential steps of presentification which may be applied with various archetypes and used either as a workshop experience or in individual psychotherapy.

In that the archetypes have universal relevance, the specific choice of archetype is not crucial in terms of providing a potentially growthful self exploration. If, however, the subject is having difficulty in living, growth potential from the experience would be maximized by choosing archetypes which are most relevant to the individual's problem. For instance, a depressed person might do well to explore the archetypes of "god" and "demon," and an unhappily homosexual person might gain from exploring the "anima" and the "animus."

Once the choice of archetype has been made, the task of the therapist is to guide the subject in his creation of a here-and-now experience of his symbolization of that archetype. Since there is so much information involved in an archetypal personification, it is sometimes convenient to write down this material so that it can be referred back to with ease. The therapist suggests that the subject close his eyes and visualize the personification of the archetype to be explored. This needs to be done slowly and with as much vividness as possible. With some subjects the vividness can be enhanced through hypnotic techniques. The therapist then suggests that the subject write about the personification in terms of what it looks like, sounds like, smells like, tastes like, and feels like to the touch (sensing function); name it and describe what is implied by the name (thinking function); describe what emotional reactions he has to the personification (feeling function); guess about the past and future of that personification (intuiting function). Depending on the archetype chosen and the use being made of this technique, the therapist can now encourage the subject either to confront the personification by imagining it out in the room and talking to it (beginning with his telling the personification his sensations, thoughts, feelings, and intuitions about it and continuing wherever the confrontation leads), or to become the personification himself (describing himself in first person, present tense, in terms of the image he has described), thus reowning projected aspects of himself. In either case, the subject has explored a part of his inner space by confronting in the here-and-now his personal symbolic representation of a universal human theme.

The depth of this experience and the growth realized from it depends, of course, on both the involvement of the subject and the skill and sensitivity of the therapist. Like all techniques, its potential is limited by the person of the therapist through which it is given life.

~

Altered States of Consciousness
in Gestalt Therapy

I have been intrigued by a curious state of affairs within the profession of psychotherapy. The state of affairs to which I refer results from the seemingly prejudicial attitudes about hypnosis and hypnoid states. The prejudices run strongly both in support of and in opposition to the use of hypnoid states in the conduct of psychotherapy. As a result, there appear to be two camps of psychotherapists, those who support the use of hypnotic techniques and those who do not, or at least are not explicit in their use of such techniques, and these two camps maintain relative isolation from one another. The relative separateness of membership in the two camps was well illustrated to me some time ago at an annual meeting of the American Psychological Association. Being a member of both the divisions of psychotherapy (Division 29) and hypnosis (Division 30), I attended a major symposium of each. Both of the symposia, chaired and paneled by nationally known persons, included discussion of the spiritual aspects of psychotherapy. The remarkable thing was that very few people attended both the symposia. In scanning the second audience, I saw only a handful of persons whom I recognized from the first. I was struck by the obvious lack of sharing of ideas, experience, and colleagueship.

I think that the separation of the two camps is not based on empirically demonstrated differences in therapy outcome, or even important theoretical differences, but rather on historically based prejudices and perhaps certain personality factors which predispose some therapists away from

---

From *Journal of Contemporary Psychotherapy*, 7(1), 35-40 (1975).

contact with altered states of consciousness. But the analysis of the split in camps is not the purpose of the present paper. (Relevant personality factors are discussed in Gordon's work.)

The purpose of the present paper is, however, in good Gestalt fashion, a movement toward an integration of the split. Put differently, the purpose of the present paper is to suggest that certain of the techniques of Gestalt therapy sometimes involve an altered state of consciousness and in some cases may require the altered state for their potency.

Before looking at the Gestalt techniques specifically, I want to clarify and differentiate the terms "hypnosis," "hypnoid state," and "altered state of consciousness." One convenient way of differentiating the terms is through Shor's theory of hypnosis, in which he recognizes three conceptually separate dimensions. First is the dimension of hypnotic role-taking involvement, or the nonconsciously directive influence of the subject's motivational and cognitive attitudes regarding his role as a hypnotized subject. Second is the dimension of archaic involvement, or the establishment of a transference relationship with the hypnotist. Third is the dimension of trance, or the fading into nonfunctional unawareness of the usual generalized reality orientation. "Hypnosis" involves all three dimensions, and any given occurrence of hypnosis can be characterized in terms of the depth or extent of each of the separate but coexisting dimensions. Profound depth along all three dimensions would be characterized by role-enactments at a completely unconscious level, intense archaic object relations formed onto the hypnotist, and a shifted reality such that the hypnotic happenings become phenomenologically the only possible reality for that time. Shor's theory is, then, quite complex, recognizing "hypnosis" as involving the enactment of a role, a transference relationship, and a state of trance.

Trance and Hypnosis

An alternate term for "trance" is "altered state of consciousness." This term is therefore a broader term than "hypnosis," and includes trance states not necessarily involving transference or those particular roles defined within a culture as hypnosis. The third term, "hypnoid," is used to mean hypnosis-like and can be regarded as a third synonym with "trance" and "altered state of consciousness." We are actually referring, then, to two concepts: First, the trance or hypnoid state or altered state of consciousness; and second, hypnosis, defined as an altered state of consciousness along with some degree of transference and some degree of hypnotic role-enactment. Of the three synonyms, my preference is for altered state of consciousness, or ASC, since it is a descriptive term and does not carry the narrow and only sometimes correct connotations of glassy-eyed zombie-like behavior which are carried by the term "trance," and to a lesser degree, the term "hypnoid."

The term "altered state of consciousness," or ASC, implies a change from a normal or usual state of consciousness. The usual state of consciousness can be seen as that state in which one spends the major part of one's waking time, and which for that person, generally has an adaptive value in his environment. In an ASC one experiences a qualitative shift in his usual pattern of mental functioning.

In his thorough discussion of altered states of consciousness, Ludwig offers a more complete definition, saying that ASCs are "any mental states, induced by various physiological, psychological, or pharmacological maneuvers or agents, which can be recognized subjectively by the individual himself (or by an objective observer of the individual) as representing a sufficient deviation in subjective experience or psychological functioning from certain general norms for that individual during alert, waking consciousness" (p.p. 9-19).

Ludwig goes on to expand his phrase, "sufficient deviation in subjective experience," by saying that it "may be represented by a greater preoccupation than usual with internal sensations or mental processes, changes in the formal characteristics of thought, and impairment of reality testing to various degrees". ASCs may be produced, according to Ludwig, by a wide variety of agents or maneuvers which interfere with the normal level of sensory or proprioceptive input, the normal motor output, the normal emotional tone, or the normal flow and organization of cognitive processes. Although the specific conditions under which ASCs are produced are quite varied, Ludwig lists a number of similar features which to some degree tend to characterize most ASCs. These features consist of alterations in thinking, disturbed time sense, loss of control, change in emotional expression, change in body image, perceptual distortions, changes in meaning or significance, a sense of the ineffable, feelings of rejuvenation, and hypersuggestibility.

I turn now to Gestalt therapy and the ASCs which occur with some of the Gestalt techniques. But first, I feel a need for a clarification, for a putting of what follows into proper context. I will be focusing on Gestalt technique. The techniques of Gestalt therapy are cleverly conceived and, when brought to life through the person of an adept therapist, can be very powerful. But Gestalt therapy consists of a philosophy and a theory of personality, as well as a body of techniques. And, taken out of the context of that philosophy and psychological theory, the techniques can be misunderstood and misused easily. The position of Gestalt therapy is set forth in a number of books and articles, my choices being the following books: Perls' *Ego, Hunger, and Aggression, Gestalt Therapy*, and *Gestalt Therapy Verbatim* and Fagan and Shepherd's *Gestalt Therapy Now*. For the complete theory and rationale which justify the Gestalt technique, I refer you to these sources.

The Here-and-Now Experience

Basically, the Gestalt techniques are designed to further the patient toward a here-and-now experience. This general goal of the Gestalt session has roots in the psychoanalytic tradition, particularly the work of Wilhelm Reich, with whom Perls studied. Reich's rule was that remembrances, to be therapeutic, must be accompanied by the appropriate affect. This led Reich to emphasize the elicitation of powerful feelings in the therapy session. Perls, in turn, showed his strong belief in this approach by distinguishing the awareness-enhancing here-and-now experience from the emotionally avoidant, purely cognitive process of intellectualization or talking about. He went so far as to declare that dealing with anything in the therapy session which is not experienced (felt) in the here-and-now is a waste of time. In brief, the here-and-now experience is therapeutic in that it results in heightened awareness, and is the means whereby one may come to an organismic completion of one's unfinished business or neurotic "hang-ups" from the past. When the uncompleted Gestalten from one's past are allowed to be completed, they fade into perceptual ground, making possible new Gestalt formations.

One of the ways of implementing the here-and-now experience is through what Naranjo has termed "presentification." Presentification refers to making now and actual a past or fantasy happening by living that happening. The living comes through an enacting of the scenes with the appropriate words and body actions. If not prevented, the enactment often leads to strong feelings and the possibility then of organismic completion such as crying over loss, attacking the target of anger, or laughing in joy. Presentification offers the possibility of a second chance to finish what in my past, because of my phobic attitude, I left unfinished.

A second way of implementing the here-and-now experience is through concentration. (In some of his earlier work, Perls referred to his therapy as Concentration Therapy but later changed the name to Gestalt Therapy in recognition of the central role which behavioral Gestalt 'formation' played in his theory.) Concentration is single-minded and intense. Polster reports that when one's concentration is focused on internal events, one may move out of his accustomed frame of reference and be in a state comparable to those states arising out of hypnosis. This intense concentration moves one profoundly into a right here, right now experience, and thus enhanced awareness. In conjunction with concentration and to increase its likelihood of yield, Perls sometimes requested the patient to exaggerate his current feeling or action. A mild feeling or a small movement, by becoming exaggerated, made an easier target for concentration and, in turn, a more likely avenue to self-awareness. And, of course, increased awareness is the first step toward growth.

The here-and-now experience with its heightened awareness and its opportunity for finishing of unfinished business is, along with the I-Thou relationship, a cornerstone of Gestalt therapy. And the general approaches of presentification and concentration are direct avenues to the here-and-now. Perls developed a host of specific techniques which serve these two major, and sometimes coexisting, approaches. Examples are his style of dream-work, the empty chair dialogue, the awareness continuum, exaggeration, reversal of action, making the rounds, playing the projection, and so forth. My way of summarizing Gestalt technique is this: The specific Gestalt techniques are in the service of concentration and presentification, which in turn are the two major approaches to the here-and-now experience. The here-and-now experience allows the possibility of growth through enhanced awareness and the finishing of unfinished business.

Concentration and Presentification

Both concentration and presentification, when profound, involve an ASC. Turning first to concentration, Polster, as mentioned earlier, has called attention to the parallels between hypnosis and profound concentration. Another clue is offered by London in his review of methods of hypnotic induction. One of the features which he finds present in most induction methods is concentration. Through concentration one focuses strongly on some stimulus, be it internal or external, and concomitantly decreases the usual superficial scan of the environment. This is very clearly an instance of qualitatively changing the usual sensory input, which may then lead to an ASC. Considerable research in support of this notion has shown that there is a range of exteroceptive input which is necessary in order to maintain an anchoring in the consensually defined reality. Deviations above or below this range result in a fading of consensual reality or, in other words, the establishment of an ASC.

Turning to presentification, we see a situation in which the patient behaves as if a past event, dream, or fantasy is now real and present. Clearly, the intense involvement with and dramatization of such non-consensual reality requires a decreased involvement with the usual consensual reality, again lessening the anchoring in the usual state of consciousness.

I think this shows that Gestalt concentration and Gestalt presentification provide a sufficient condition for the establishment of an ASC. A second issue is the established ASC. Anyone who has experienced and observed intense Gestalt work will recognize the presence of an ASC in this work. During intense concentration or presentification there are combinations of the following features of ASCs.

Alterations in thinking — Archaic modes of thought or primary process thinking. in which the patient is re-experiencing his childhood thought patterns, may occur. Sometimes there is a dramatic recovery of forgotten material.

Disturbed time sense — A happening of a few minutes may seem like hours. It is not uncommon in Gestalt groups for patients to be concerned about having taken up an inordinate amount of time in their working.

Loss of control — A sense that one cannot stop the process until the process is complete. I have heard patients say after working that they did not plan to go so far, but once they started, they just couldn't stop until it was over.

Changes in emotional expression — Perhaps the most dramatic and therefore obvious occurrence which is sometimes present in Gestalt work is the rapid access to intense affect. Sometimes within minutes from starting to work, the patient explodes into grief, joy, or anger.

Body image change — Patients doing a dialogue often report the real feeling of being split into two people or only a part of themselves. The parts are subjectively real. Another frequent experience is of a distortion of body size or proportions.

Perceptual distortions — Things may look different; senses may be temporarily more or less acute. There may be quasi-hallucinations, such as a patient reporting after an empty-chair dialogue that he could "really" see his father in the chair.

Change in meaning or significance — Seeing of new relationships, finding of new perspectives is frequent.

Sense of the ineffable — One of the few appropriate uses of the exclamation "Wow!" is after doing heavy Gestalt work. Often the patient doesn't want to talk afterward but just wants to "sit with it." Observers are sometimes very skeptical about what they have seen. In a recent workshop which I co-led, an observer reacted with anger to some Gestalt work he had just seen and accused us, only partly in jest, of having rehearsed the whole performance the night before.

Reality-Transfer

Feelings of rejuvenation — Almost always, upon completion of Gestalt work, there is a feeling of comfort, relief, hope, and well-being.

Hypersuggestibility — Once committed and into Gestalt work, patients are often very ready to try out rather uncritically whatever the therapist suggests. In addition, the patient is often highly receptive to parent-like injunctions from the therapist.

The Gestalt techniques are aimed at the creation of a here-and-now experience which often is subjectively real and consensually unreal. For this subjective experience to be profoundly real requires, by definition, a state other than the normal state of consciousness. This condition is what Deikman has termed the "reality-transfer," when thoughts and images become real. My hypothesis is that the effectiveness of the Gestalt technique is related to the degree of realness of the subjective experience which ensues, or in other words the depth of the altered state of consciousness produced. But, very importantly, the Gestalt therapist does not assume the role of the change agent, as does the charismatic style of hypnotherapist. Rather, he is a guide or facilitator in an I-Thou encounter, and the patient is responsible for both his own being and becoming.

~

THE ROLE OF EARLY REICHIAN THEORY
IN THE DEVELOPMENT OF GESTALT THERAPY

In his development of Gestalt therapy, Fritz Perls drew upon several diverse traditions, gleaning from each those elements which he could validate in his own experience. To understand and appreciate Gestalt therapy as it is today requires a careful tracing of its past — those several streams which flowed together through the person of Perls.

It appears that Perls was primarily influenced by five traditions: Classical Psychoanalysis, Reichian Character Analysis, Existential Philosophy, Gestalt Psychology, and Eastern Religion. The present paper is focused on the second of these traditions, one which is often overlooked in discussions of Gestalt therapy.

Orthodox psychoanalysis served as the seedbed for the early growth of Gestalt therapy. Perls was trained as a Freudian analyst, being analyzed by Harnick and supervised by such eminent figures as Deutsch, Fenichel, Hirschman, Horney, and Landanner. He also knew Federn and Schilder and had "casual encounters" with Adler, Jung, and "the man himself," Freud (Perls, 1969c). But, with experience, Perls came to see the philosophy and technique of orthodox analysis as obsolete (Perls, 1969c).

An important step in Perls' move away from classical psychoanalysis came about as a result of a suggestion made by one of his supervisors, Karen Horney. She suggested that Perls become an analysand of Wilhelm Reich, a suggestion which he accepted. During 1931 and 1932 Perls was in analysis

From *Psychotherapy: Theory, Research, and Practice, 12*(3), 268-272 (1975).

with Reich, and the following year he participated in a seminar which Reich led (L. Perls, 1972).

The contributions which Reich offered to the world can be arranged conveniently into two somewhat distinct theoretical systems, corresponding to two periods in Reich's adult life. It was from the first period and system that Perls borrowed and for which he expressed appreciation. Of Reich's later period Perls' opinion was that Reich's fantasy had run wild and the man had eclipsed himself as a mad scientist (Perls, 1969c).

Although Perls did not become a Reichian, he did find what I see as perhaps eight elements in Reich's earlier position which are strongly represented in Gestalt therapy.

First, Perls found in Reich the rule of therapy that remembrances must be accompanied by the appropriate affect (Reich, 1949). This discovery of the necessity of the appropriate feelings concomitant with the thoughts in order for a therapeutic effect to occur was not original with Reich, for Freud had spoken of this finding. Freud said, with an apt metaphor, that a neurosis cannot be hanged in effigy. But Reich took an extreme position on this point, putting far more emphasis on the elicitation of powerful feelings and dealing with them in the therapy session than had the classical psychoanalysts. Perls showed his strong belief in this approach by distinguishing the awareness-enhancing experience of psychodramatically returning to the past incident (Perls, 1973) from the emotionally avoidant, purely cognitive "mind-fucking." He went so far as to declare that dealing with anything which is not experienced (felt) in the here-and-now is a waste of time (Perls, 1969a)! One point where Perls differed from Reich was in his disagreeing with Reich's view that emotions are disturbers of the peace and are to be gotten rid of. Rather than something undesirable, Perls saw emotions as a natural element in the organism's homeostatic cycles.

Perhaps the most significant contribution of Reich was his bringing the body into psychotherapy. Again, Freud and other early psychoanalysts spoke of the body and body symbolism but did not develop the idea into a central concept of therapy. Freud stated that the ego is first and foremost a body ego but then developed his whole theory of resistances in the realm of mental defenses. It remained for Reich to discover the "muscular armor" and thus introduce the notion of resistances as total organismic functions (Perls, 1969c). Reich suggested that the neurotic solution of the infantile instinctual conflict (chronic conflict between instinctual demands and counter demands of the outer world) is brought about through a generalized alteration in functioning which ultimately crystallizes into a neurotic "character" (Shapiro, 1965). Character is, then, essentially a narcissistic protective mechanism, formed for protection against actual external dangers and retained for protection against internal instinctual dangers. One aspect of the holistic character is the "armor," the muscular rigidities which serve to bind free-floating anxiety. In addition to calling attention to the resistances in the body realm, Reich broke with the classical psychoanalytic position by introducing intensive body contact into psychotherapy. Through feeling the patient's body, Reich could assess the muscular armoring, locating the focal points of bound anxiety. Perls included much of Reich's body orientation in his system, even stating that the deepest split, long ingrained in our culture, is the mind-body dichotomy. Thus, in therapy, one needs to attend to the patient's non-verbal communications — voice, posture, gestures, and "psychosomatic language" (Perls, 1969b). Perls also encouraged enhanced body awareness and bodily involvement to facilitate organismic completion of emotions, even suggesting exercises to those ends (Perls, Hefferline, and Goodman, 1951). Consistent with Reich's character armoring, Gestalt therapy includes the concept of "retroflection" as one of the major means of limiting one's awareness of self-functioning. Retroflection refers to the process of negating or blocking an impulse to action through opposing sensorimotor tension. Reich's notion of character armor amounts to a chronic state of retroflection (Enright, 1970). Body contact is sometimes also found in Gestalt therapy, although it is not emphasized or formalized into a treatment mode as it is in the neo-Reichian therapies.

    The third way in which I see a Reichian influence in Perls' work is in the latter's active, and at times frustrating, confrontive style (Perls, 1973). He stated that psychological growth comes only through frustration. Perls' (1973) way was to frustrate those expressions of the patient which reflect manipulatory techniques, neurotic patterns, and the patient's self-concept, while satisfying the patient's expression of his true self. The therapist's tools are support and frustration. In turn, the therapist's basic responsibility is to challenge all statements and behaviors which, rather than representing the patient's self, are evidence of the patient's lack of self-responsibility. There are times when it seems that the therapist must be cruel in order to be kind (Perls, 1973). The earlier position of Reich shows an extremely close similarity. Reich's view was that during resistance phases of therapy it is up to the analyst to direct the course, first interpreting that the patient is resisting, then interpreting how the resistance is taking place, and finally interpreting what is being resisted. (Reich used the term "interpretation" in a generic sense, encompassing what other writers would distinguish as reflections, interpretations, and confrontations, i.e., any therapeutic intervention.) Reich suggested that the patient be constantly confronted with his character resistance until he experiences it as something to get rid of. Or, put another way, it is important to undermine the neurosis from the cardinal resistance rather than from the detail resistance (Reich, 1949). Perhaps consistent with his therapeutic style, was a personal style for which Perls was well known — trouble making, roguish, disruptive, impolite, demanding, a "dirty old man," yet terms usually said about him with warmth (Fagan, 1971). Interestingly, he credited Reich with teaching him brazenness (Perls, 1969c).

A fourth influence comes from Reich's suggestion that the character resistance is revealed in the "how" of the patient's communications, rather than in the "what" of those communications. The idea expressed herein is that the form or style of communication reflects the character and therefore is more important than the content (Reich, 1949). Several persons can do or say the same thing, and thus individuality and uniqueness are not revealed in the content of the behavior, but each person behaves in his own consistent "style" reflecting his uniqueness. Following this line of thinking, Perls made "why" questions taboo. The patient who asks "why" is usually trying to "hook the environment for support"; he is asking someone else to think for him. The therapist who asks "why" is inviting the patient to rationalize, justify, comply, make excuses, or talk in tautology. As Perls said, there are no ultimate answers to "why." The relevant questions can be answered by "how, where, and when" (Perls, 1969a). Gestalt therapy walks on two legs, according to Perls (1969b), "now and how." In order to hear the "how," the therapist must listen to the sound, the music of the patient's communications. The appropriate focus is on the voice quality, the postures, the gestures, the psychosomatic language, and the content taking a secondary place, for Perls suggested that in therapy the patient's verbal communication (content) is usually a lie.

Another of Reich's concepts, which seems likely to have influenced the development of Perls' view, is the notion of the "phase of the breakdown of secondary narcissism." In terms of Reich's (1949) theory, the lasting frustration of primary natural needs leads to a chronic contraction of the armor. This conflict between inhibited primary impulses and the inhibiting character armor leads to the formation of a secondary narcissism (as contrasted to the primary narcissism of the infant which results from his cathecting his own body parts as part-objects of love). That is, as investment of libido in the outside is made more difficult or is withdrawn, the energy builds up within, intensifying a secondary narcissism. Reich spoke of the loosening and dissolution of the characterological protective mechanisms as bringing about a temporary condition of complete helplessness, an aspect of successful treatment which he termed the "phase of the breakdown of secondary narcissism." During the phase the patient moves into a position of strong, freed energy with a concomitant lack of "safe" neurotic controls. It is because of these two factors that this phase of treatment is stormy, often including strong feelings of negative transference. Perls seems to have included the essence of Reich's dynamic formulation of the phase of breakdown of secondary narcissism in his five-layer model of the neurosis. Perls (1969b; Levitsky & Perls, 1970) was consistent in his conceptual presentation of the layers of neurosis but was not consistent in his numbering of the layers. Disregarding, then, the arbitrary numbering, the layers emerge as follows: Neurosis is characterized by a cliché layer, or layer of tokens of meaning. Below that is the layer Perls named the Eric Berne or Sigmund Freud layer of playing games, playing roles, behaving "as if." Beneath this phony layer is the impasse, characterized by the phobic attitude. The phobic attitude results in avoidance, and in turn, the feeling of being stuck, lost, empty, confused. Beneath the impasse or phobic layer is the death layer or implosive layer. At this layer the person is paralyzed by opposing forces; he is trying to pull himself in, hold himself safely together. The implosive layer may unfold into the final layer of explosion. The explosive layer is characterized by the person's authentic experiencing and expressing of his emotions. The explosion may be into grief, if a loss had not been assimilated, orgasm, if a sexual block had been present, anger, or joy. There are striking parallels between Reich's "phase of breakdown of secondary narcissism" and Perls' progression through "impasse, implosion, and explosion." In both cases the essence is the dissolution of organismic (holistic) core defenses in order to emerge, after a "walk through hell," with an authentic (organismically appropriate) behavior. The impasse was defined by Perls (1969b) in terms which sound very much like Reich's concept, saying that the impasse is the position where environmental support or obsolete inner support is no longer adequate and authentic self-support has not yet been achieved. The important difference between the two men's concepts is that Reich limited his concern to the sexual impulse and establishment of a sex-economic regulation of energy following the "breakdown." Perls clearly developed the concept beyond the point where Reich stopped. Cohn (1970) regards Perls' explication and therapeutic use of the impasse phenomenon as his most important contribution to therapeutic practice. This contribution she described as Perls' discovery that the skillful separation of conflicts into their duality, and their subsequent re-enactment through the "Gestalt dialogue," leads to the feelings of helplessness — the impasse. Staying with the experience of the impasse, enduring the hell of confusion and helplessness, leads to organismic growth. In his later work Perls (1973) referred to such staying with one's confusion as a "withdrawal into the fertile void." If one stays with his techniques of interruption, and his confusion to the utmost, he may experience something like a hypnogogic hallucination or miniature schizophrenic experience leading to a "blinding flash of insight." This phase of therapy is not for the novice or the squeamish, as Reich warned therapists, and is equally applicable in Perls' system.

Perls (1969b) expressed misgivings about anyone calling himself a Gestalt therapist, because that often means that one is a technician, one who has learned to use techniques, but may have little sense and appreciation for the natural individualistic growth process. Perls saw his work as the promotion of the growth process, a process which requires time and a powerful personal commitment. To promote that process of growth Perls ingeniously invented techniques. But the techniques were invented for particular uses and employed only when they fit. Perhaps this is another influence Reich had on the young Perls, for Reich (1949) declared emphatically that for any given patient at any given time there is only one technique, and that technique has to be derived from the individual's circumstances. Reich denied that the therapist should ever impose any "ready-made schema" of therapy.

What is perhaps the seventh element of Reichian influence in Gestalt therapy is a pervasive political undercurrent. Reich's political controversies in his later period, with the book burnings, prosecutions, and eventual incarceration, are a matter of historical record. But, even in his earlier period, when Perls studied with him, Reich took a political stance with his character analysis. Reich (1949) declared that the therapist's work is in conflict with most of the heavily defended positions of conservative society, and, therefore, the therapist will be exposed to enmity, contempt, and slander as long as he maintains his integrity. One can escape the negative sanctions of the conservative society only by making concessions, at the expense of his theoretical and practical convictions, to a social order which is in opposition to the demands of therapy. There is no doubt but that Reich went political, believing that depth psychology requires the complement of radical politics (Rieff, 1966). Perls' life seems consistent with Reich's view. Perls left Germany in 1933 because of Hitler, left South Africa in 1948, and left the United States in 1969 because of a dominant political ethos with which he could not be comfortable. As Perls (1969b) saw it, there was a race on in the United States between facism and humanism, and fascism held the lead. He supported the rebellion which was going on (he said that it had not yet reached the proportions of a revolution). The meaning of life is that it is to be lived, not to be traded, conceptualized, and forced to fit into categories. The ultimate joys are not born of manipulation and control, but of authenticity. As Shepherd (1970) has suggested, Gestalt therapy may offer a promise of authenticity that is very difficult to achieve or maintain in this culture. The upshot of this is that as one successfully experiences Gestalt therapy, and thus becomes more fully aware and centered, he will be less tolerant of the destructive forces and conventions in our society. Those who successfully experience Gestalt therapy will likely become less fit for and less adjusted to contemporary society. Gestalt therapy is not a therapy of adjustment, but a therapy of self-actualization.

Some systems of psychotherapy focus only on the remedy of the acute situation, problem, or neurosis. Reich (1949), however, clearly distinguished the "cure" and the "immunization" as aspects of a successful treatment. By this he meant that a successful character analysis not only brings an end to the symptoms of the neurosis, but by virtue of the new character structure the patient is in a better position to resist the return to neurotic solutions when future problems are encountered. This orientation is expressed by Perls, as well. In his posthumous book, Perls (1973) states that the goal of therapy is to give the patient the means to solve his present problems and any problems which may arise later. Whereas Reich saw this goal as coming about through the dissolution of a neurotic character structure, Perls sees the same goal through the development of self-support. The idea of growing from environmental support or inadequate self-support to authentic self-support may be a step beyond Reich's concept of the establishment of a non-neurotic character structure, but the two notions share a common core.

It appears rather clear that in his development of Gestalt therapy Perls incorporated several elements from Reich's early period. Reich's views not only helped Perls to move away from the classical psychoanalytic position, but gave him a broader base from which to proceed as he added his experiences with Gestalt psychology, existentialism, and Zen.

The Impasse Phenomenon: A Gestalt Therapy Experience Involving an Altered State of Consciousness

Gestalt therapy increasingly has been recognized as a highly potent therapeutic approach. The use of the Gestalt therapy style often facilitates powerful contacts between the patient and figures from his past or his fantasies, as well as a greatly enhanced awareness of his moment-to-moment being. Such contacts and awareness reverberate within, often having far-reaching consequences on the patient's living.

In an earlier paper (Smith, 1973, 1975), I suggested that the various Gestalt techniques are in the service of presentification (Naranjo, 1970) (making now and actual a past or fantasy happening by identifying with and living that happening with one's whole organism) and concentration (intensely focusing on one's moment-to-moment organismic experience). Presentification and concentration, in turn, are the direct avenues to the here-and-now experience. It is the here-and-now experience, along with the I-Thou relationship, which forms the cornerstone of Gestalt therapy. I made the point in that earlier paper that the Gestalt techniques leading to presentification and concentration, and, in turn, to the here-and-now experience provide the sufficient condition for the establishment of an altered state of consciousness (ASC), as defined by Ludwig (1969). In addition, I presented evidence that those features which Ludwig (1969) states as criteria for established ASC's characterize the Gestalt therapy experience. My conclusion was as follows:

"The Gestalt techniques are aimed at the creation of a here-and-now experience which often is subjectively real and consensually unreal. For this

From *The Gestalt Journal,* 1(1), 88-93 (1978).

subjective experience to be profoundly real requires, by definition, a state other than the normal state of consciousness . . . . My hypothesis is that the effectiveness of the Gestalt technique is related to the degree of realness of the subjective experience which ensues, or in other words the depth of the altered state of consciousness produced" (p. 10).

More recently, in an article entitled "Dynamics of Experiential Therapy," Beahrs and Humiston (1974) make the emphatic statement that "successful experiential work almost always leads to a hypnotic trance, and that this greatly augments its therapeutic effectiveness." (p. 1) Throughout their article Beahrs and Humiston identify Gestalt therapy with Experiential therapy and draw impressive parallels between Gestalt therapy and the work of Milton Erickson.

I think that these two papers (Beahrs & Humiston, 1974; Smith, 1973, 1975) present a convincing case for the assertion that Gestalt therapy derives potency from the creation of an ASC in the patient.

In the present paper I will focus more specifically on the impasse phenomenon in Gestalt therapy. This phenomenon is the most dramatic to be seen in Gestalt therapy and certainly involves an ASC.

Perls' discovery and explication of the impasse phenomenon were guided by the earlier work of Wilhelm Reich (Smith, 1975). Two elements of Reich's work seem particularly relevant. The first element was Reich's rule of therapy that appropriate affect must accompany remembrances in order for the remembrance to be curative. This basic discovery was made by Freud, but it was Reich who took the extreme position on this point. Thus, those therapies which were influenced by Reich, including Gestalt therapy (Perls, 1969a), are characterized by elicitation of very strong emotions.

The second element in Reich's work which is relevant to the impasse phenomenon is what Reich (1949) termed the "phase of the breakdown of secondary narcissism." Reich theorized that the continual blocking of expression of primary needs results in a chronic contraction of the musculature, or body armor. As this occurs, investment of energy in outside objects becomes increasingly difficult, and sexual energy accumulates within. The result of this libidinal build-up is an intensive secondary narcissism (in contrast to the infant's primary narcissism which develops from his cathecting his own body parts as love objects). As successful therapy loosens and eventually dissolves the body armor, a temporary state of helplessness comes about. At this point, the patient's previously blocked energy is set free. Without the previously operative characterological defenses, powerful explosions may occur as this freed energy seeks expression.

In his five-layer model of neurosis, Perls has incorporated the essential theme of Reich's formulation of the "phase of the breakdown of secondary narcissism." Perls' model is as follows (Levitsky & Perls, 1970; Perls,

1969b). The first layer of neurosis is the cliché layer or layer of tokens of meaning. This is the layer of semi-ritualistic living, often justified and passed off as manners, niceness, or protocol. The second layer is that of roles and games, the living of an "as if" existence. This is the phony layer. If the neurotic allows himself beyond his phoniness, he reaches the third layer, the impasse. Through his catastrophic expectations, his fear of the consequences of his being authentic, the neurotic stops himself and feels stuck. It was this impasse layer that led Perls to see neurotics as characterized by the "phobic attitude." Beyond this layer of impasse, with the feeling of being stuck, confused, empty, lost, and scared, lies the fourth layer of implosion. The implosive layer is like a death layer wherein the neurotic tries to pull in and hold himself together. He feels paralyzed by opposing forces. The fifth layer is the conversion of the imploded energy into explosion. The explosion occurs when the patient allows authentic experiencing and expressing of his feelings. The previously blocked impulse, held in check because of catastrophic expectations, represents an interruption of a natural organismic process. The result is a residue of tension, or as Perls termed it, "unfinished business." The movement through the impasse to implosion and explosion is the tapping into and releasing of the blocked energy, the unexpressed emotion. This is an organismic completion of process or Gestalt closure.

A comparison of Reich's discussion of the "phase of the breakdown of secondary narcissism" and Perls' discussion of the progression through impasse, implosion, and explosion reveals a striking parallel. In both cases there is the recognition of a process whereby organismic core defenses are dissolved and authentic, previously blocked emotion is allowed powerful expression. Reich spoke of dissolution of chronic body armor; Perls spoke of giving up environmental support or obsolete inner support for authentic self-support.

However, Perls' conceptualization is broader than that of Reich. Whereas Reich (1949) saw the dissolution of character armor as leading to orgastic potency, and even took orgastic potency as the criterion for full organismic functioning, Perls saw several possibilities for authentic organismic release. When the impasse is dissolved and the implosion converted to explosion, the organismic expression may involve grief, joy, love, or anger. The patient may cry his grief, laugh his joy, strike out his anger, or paroxysmally thrust his love.

Cohn (1970) has stated that Perls' clarification and therapeutic *use of the impasse phenomenon* are his most significant contributions.

The skillful use of Gestalt techniques (Perls, 1951, 1969a, b, 1973) facilitates the patient's coming to his point of impasse quickly. Having gotten beyond the cliché layer with its social rituals, and the phony layer, with its attempts at manipulation, the patient will encounter his anxiety. He will experience his phobic attitude and in response will avoid making contact.

Before proceeding with the impasse phenomenon, I want to elaborate upon the notion of contact. Emergent needs can be met only through contact or interaction with the environment. All healthy contact involves both awareness and excitement, awareness of the need in the sense of recognizing and experiencing it, and the excitement of organismic activation. Awareness, being the more delicate of the two, more easily gives way to the onslaught of catastrophic expectations, leaving a state of excitation without benefit of the direction which awareness lends. This undirected or unfocused excitement is experienced as anxiety. The neurotic, in turn, attempts to control the anxiety by restricting breathing. The neurotic rule is, "When in doubt, don't breathe!"

Returning to the impasse phenomenon, *per se*, it is the lack of healthy contact which leads to the feelings of helplessness *and* confusion. The way out is not to withdraw, but to endure and experience fully the feelings of confusion, helplessness, and fear. If this is done, the organismic process will continue and implosion will be followed by explosion into powerful, healthy contact.

In his later writing Perls (1973) used the phrase "withdrawal into the fertile void" to describe this staying with feelings of helplessness, confusion, and fear. The neurotic penchant is to seek relief from these unpleasant feelings by escaping into the consensually validated normal state of consciousness. But the Gestalt approach is to facilitate the natural process, to support the total organismic going into and experiencing of the subjective reality. This approach involves an ASC, at times of great depth.

The Gestalt therapist has two basic tactics to use in facilitation of the movement through the impasse, frustration, and support. He can frustrate the patient's interruptions of the process by confronting the patient with his attempts to avoid, while supporting the patient's forward movement by encouraging and giving permission. Typical confrontations take the form of questions such as, "What are you avoiding?" "What are you afraid might happen?" or "How are you stopping yourself?" Support is conveyed by the therapist's presence and can be verbalized with statements such as "Stay with it," "Be aware of what's happening," "Let yourself feel that fully," "Let that happen," or "You don't have to stop yourself."

When one does stay with his techniques of interruption, with each interruption itself being experienced fully, with his confusion being entered to the utmost, he may suddenly have a blinding flash of awareness. This may come like a hypnotic hallucination with its peculiar special reality. Perls (1973) has termed this a "mini-satori" (p. 131). Following such experiences, patients report or give evidence of the various criteria for ASC's discussed by Ludwig (1969): alterations in thinking; disturbed time sense; loss of control; changes in emotional expression; body image change; perceptual distortions; changes in meaning or significance; a sense of the ineffable; feelings of rejuvenation; and hypersuggestibility.

The result of this process is a step towards the completion of Gestalten, or the finishing of unfinished business. I recognize two levels of Gestalt completion. The first is the "Behavioral Gestalt," or the completion of some behavior which one interrupted out of one's fear of the personal consequences of that behavior. In this case residual tension is expended in the explosion into grief, joy, anger, or orgasm.

The second level of Gestalt completion is the completion of the person's wholeness, or the "Person Gestalt." Through a series of incompleted behavioral Gestalten one has in effect denied a class of behavior or disowned a part of oneself. The explosion viewed at this level is the re-owning of the split-off part through the expression of emotion using that part.

This is my conceptual understanding of the Gestalt impasse phenomenon. The awesomeness and ineffable quality of the experience make such conceptual explanation seem flat by contrast. The experience, however, is not likely to be forgotten.

~

ANXIETY:

THE PERVERSE TRAVELING COMPANION

For most of us, anxiety is a traveling companion on our journeys into intimacy. As we move toward intimacy, the mutual exploration of our personal, private ground, we keep anxiety closely with us. We may abandon anxiety for a while, moving forward, only to turn a corner and meet it head-on.

The promise which anxiety makes is that it will warn us of, and thereby protect us from, dangers. And these dangers are presented with a certainty which makes ignoring them seem absolutely foolhardy. Anxiety demands at least a delay in the trip, a detour into "safer" (so anxiety promises) and more superficial public territory. These detours can become the itinerary of a lifetime.

So, anxiety is the tocsin and the detour guide. It scares us with the warning of imminent danger and then offers a path to safer ground. Only one catch. Anxiety lies.

Anxiety is the perverse half-sib of fear. Fear is an indispensable traveling companion on all long journeys. Without it we wouldn't survive more than a few trips. Fear is well educated. It uses its eyes, its ears, and all of its sensory equipment. It also remembers. This means that it has only to carry an alley cat home by the tail one time to learn an important lesson about alley cats. (Appreciations to Mark Twain for his insights about empiricism and caution.)

From *Voices*, 15(1), 27-29 (1979).

So fear is a protector from real dangers. It warns us of the presence of something which indeed will harm. Of course, this is within the limits of fear's education. Sometimes fear is misinformed and therefore gives warnings about things believed harmful but actually not so. But fear is honest.

To the best of its knowledge, what it says is dangerous, is. And fear is open to revising what it knows, based on new sensory information and carefully evaluated secondhand reports. Fear keeps a close watch on reality.

Not so, anxiety. Anxiety acts like fear, but with a major difference. It doesn't care at all about reality. So, where does it get its "information"?

Anxiety arrives on the scene with obsolete beliefs. These beliefs are based on what was true at one time but are no longer true. The basic theme is well known in most psychotherapy circles. The child learns by direct experience that certain things bring pain. Hence, fear. The child learns by direct experience that certain other behaviors bring another kind of pain — punishment (or a threat of punishment which may itself be a punishment) from parenting figures. And these latter behaviors involve what is natural, such as feelings and spontaneous expression of feelings. The child then learns that feeling certain feelings or certain expressions of those feelings brings punishment (pain). By avoiding these feelings or expressions new information, as time goes by, is not gathered and the old contingency is brought along through time. Hence, anxiety.

And that's how anxiety lies. It speaks with a force and certainty as strong as any fear, but it speaks of a danger that only was, and is no more. Anxiety has no regard for historical perspective. This is part of what Freud meant when he said that the neurotic suffers from his memories. And T. S. Eliot used an interesting phrase as he wrote of someone who was "nothing but a set of obsolete responses."

The half-sibs, fear and anxiety, can be recognized one from the other by a special quality which is peculiar to the latter. Anxiety derives this special quality from two factors. First, it is based on the perspective of a child who is threatened to its core by the powerful parent figures. So, anxiety is characterized by a feeling of smallness and relative helplessness. Second, the content is anachronistic. Almost as if in a time warp, old situations from a different time and place show up in a current context. (This is a clue to keeping anxiety a close companion. The rule is: to be anxious, assiduously stay in the "there and then.") These two factors give anxiety its power to escalate its warning to the level of certain catastrophe.

Just as fear warns of believed dangers and enhances the process of living, anxiety promises catastrophe based on a lie and diminishes aliveness. The original situations out of which anxiety developed were ones in which parental prohibitions carried a threat and demanded that the child not feel something or that he not express the feeling. This inhibition of feeling and expression is bio-negative, training in deadness.

The journey of intimacy takes one past the familiar and certain landmarks of protocol, manners, and mechanical rituals. Further on, the traveling companions known as roles find the terrain too unsuitable and drop out. This leaves the person and the companion anxiety. The struggle is between the person who wants to be known by showing who he or she is, feelings and expressions of feelings, and the companion anxiety who shouts warnings of imminent catastrophe. Each time the warning is heeded, a detour is taken which usually leads back to the place where the roles are waiting. Safe in the company of roles, and with anxiety now quiet, one can go on until out of the boredom and loneliness of alienation one returns to the journey.

At some point the traveler may explore a new area of intimacy by telling the other about the companion, anxiety. This might take the form, "I want you to know that I am afraid to let you see me cry." All the while anxiety is shouting threats such as, "Don't let them know you are weak, fool. They will hurt you like you've never imagined before. Hide, dummy, or you'll really get it." What will it be, another detour to the land where roles are the way to safe, alienated deadness, or straight on into the heartland of intimacy?

If I choose aliveness, then I go on in spite of a steadily mounting anxiety to intimacy's sacred ground. There I no longer speak of my anxiety; I simply do what before I only said I was afraid to do. So, I cry before you. In this sacred ground of intimacy, anxiety gives up and waits to meet me and test me later on, another place, another time.

~

Seven Decision Points

When Mark Stern first invited me to write something for this issue of *Voices* devoted to decisions, I felt nothing stir inside. The lack of inner stirrings to write about decisions is probably because of my feeling burned out with making big decisions. In the past year and a half my wife and I separated, I bought a condominium, she and I reunited, I sold the condominium, we bought a new house, we sold our old practice with my partners, we added a new partner to our practice group, and I redefined three other major relationships. Each one of these events was a concatenation of DECISIONS — Decisions — decisions. And then Mark asked me again. And this time something stirred.

For some time I have been using a particular model in my training seminars which I have put off writing about. "Decisions" is central to the model. I have been using words such as responsibility, choice, awareness, and self-interruption. The word "decision" fits well, so I can share some aspects of this model in a way that will shed light on the process of decision.

Some background to the model: During my training in Gestalt therapy I felt frustrated by the lack of a systematic or coherent model. The Gestalt material was exciting and profound to me. What I needed in addition was a model which would give me a cognitive grasp of that material. I got along without such a model until I began offering workshops and ongoing training. Without the model I could facilitate exciting and profound experiences for participants, but an element was missing for their being able to use their experience fully when they returned to their own practices. The missing part was a cognitive model which could serve as a framework for all the rich

From *Voices*, 15(3), 45-50 (1979).

Gestalt theory as well as a cognitive map to aid in negotiating the labyrinth of psychotherapy. Most of the elements of this model are either explicit or easily extrapolated from the Gestalt literature. In addition to my organizing and extrapolating from Gestalt theory, I integrated some further insights from Bioenergetics theory and Psychomotor theory. I then flavored the model with my own stylistic touches.

The context of the model— When I think of any psychotherapy system or approach, I think of several facets. First, there is an underlying philosophy or set of assumptions and values. Second, there is a theory of personality or ideas about how human beings normally function. Third, there is the theory of psychopathology or definition of what is problematic functioning and how such functioning comes about. Fourth, there is the theory of psychotherapy, or the views of what conditions lead to psychological growth and the cessation of problematic functioning. Fifth, there is a body of therapeutic techniques or the practical methods of actually making therapeutic interventions. All too often a therapy system is identified or even defined only by the fifth facet. The model I am presenting here focuses on the second and third facets, theory of normal personality functioning and theory of psychopathology.

Like any model, this model is a gross simplification. Its value lies in its describing and lending understanding to the human process which is the focus in psychotherapy. This model is concerned with the rhythms of contact and withdrawal, which characterize psychobiological existence.

A convenient starting point is the person's want. This "want" may be either a "need" or a "preference." By need, I mean those things which are necessary for survival, e.g., food, air, water, a certain range of temperature, sex, love, and so forth. A preference is what one chooses given that there are several options, any one of which meets the need. The goal, then, is the satisfaction of the want. Over a period of time the want arises again, and a lifelong series of homeostatic cycles are set up.

This situation is complicated by the fact that several wants may be operating simultaneously so that a preferential ordering must be done. A person then responds to the emergent want which becomes figural out of the array of background wants. The person who has contributed most to my understanding of needs and their interrelationships is Abraham Maslow.

Let's look at the steps that take place between the arising of a want (need or preference) and the satisfaction of that want.

When a want arises, there is a state of physiological arousal. This also can be termed "tension" or "excitement." The organism has become biochemically mobilized to a state of higher energy. This heightened energy state is differentiated and subjectively experienced as an "emotion," "affect," or "feeling." The emotion implies or calls for an "action" or movement of the energy into the musculoskeletal system. That action must become an "interaction" with someone or something if the final point of "satisfaction" is to be realized. The "contact episode" consists, then, of these several steps and is followed by a natural organismic "withdrawal episode." The first half of the contact episode (want, excitement, emotion) is a function of "awareness," i.e., being aware that I want (need or prefer) something, being aware of my excitement (arousal, tension, energy), and being aware of the emotion (affect, feeling). This awareness serves as a focusing of my energy in the second half of the contact episode, the "expression" (action, interaction, satisfaction). Satisfying contact involves both awareness and expression.

The steps in the contact-withdrawal cycle are cumulative, each step depending on all previous steps for its success. If a given step is skipped, or not allowed in full form, the proceeding steps will be less well formed and the ultimate satisfaction is diminished or missed completely. There are also feedback loops such that later steps may enhance earlier steps. For example, taking action may enhance the felt emotion or if the action is not appropriate to the emotion the action may reveal to the person what the actual emotion would be if it were allowed into awareness. It's as if there were a reverberating wave which further enhances the previous steps as each new step is taken.

As long as these contact-withdrawal cycles emerge and recede smoothly, maintaining the organism and allowing for the meeting of the ultimate need — self-actualization — there is a state of psychobiological health. Two types of problems can occur, however. One type of problem is the absence in the environment of the person or thing needed for the satisfaction of the want. This type of problem is not a psychological one, per se, but is a problem of politics, economics, technology, ecology, or such. The second type of problem, equally serious in its potential is the psychological problem of stopping myself in my contact-withdrawal cycles short of satisfaction. A simple example: If I am in a desert with no water at all available, I cannot get my need for water satisfied and I will perish in time regardless of the level of my psychological functioning. If on the other hand, I have water but choose not to drink it because a voice inside speaking for my parents or sub-culture says I will burn in hell for drinking water not blessed by an appropriate priest, I will still perish. This is a psychological problem, obviously. I define psychopathology *as any pattern of habitual self-interruptions in the contact-withdrawal cycle.* These habitual self-interruptions tend to obscure the inner voice which speaks the wisdom of the organism and leads to cumulative self-alienation. And, the self-interruption is a decision.

There are several points of decision in a contact-withdrawal cycle. First is the decision to be aware of wants or not. The person who "decides" not to know her/his wants exists in a state of unawareness of organismic needs or the preferences which give one individual style. This is the patient who is blank when asked, "What do you want?" or "What would you like?"

At each of the junctures between steps in the contact-withdrawal cycle there is the decision to allow the organismic flow toward completion or the self-interruption which is a pseudo-withdrawal. The pseudo-withdrawal is a short-circuiting, where the ongoing flow has been diverted before satisfaction has been experienced.

The second decision point, then, is between "wanting" and awareness of "excitement." In self-interruption the potential excitement can be averted or the person can keep from awareness the existing excitement. (I will describe below the techniques for clouding awareness and for quelling excitement). This is the patient who just doesn't get excited or else doesn't experience the state of excitement which can be seen objectively by physiological indicators.

Between "excitement" and "emotion" is the third decision point. In this case the choice of lack of awareness involves a failure to differentiate the body arousal into a specific affective experience. This patient reports some version of "I just feel nervous," or "I'm just tense."

These first three decisions involve awareness. Will I allow myself to know what I need and what I prefer within the context of that need? Will I allow myself to become aroused, excited, and experience that? Will I allow myself to differentiate that tension into a specific affective experience? These are organismic decisions, decisions involving my whole psychobiological self.

The fourth decision point, or the movement from awareness into expression, is of particular interest because it involves putting energy into the musculoskeletal system. In "deciding" to take the step from "emotion" to "action" a whole new realm is entered, the realm of deliberate movement. The decision to self-interrupt at this juncture and remain in the realm of pre-motion is especially common in over-socialized patients. (The expressive therapies such as Gestalt, Bioenergetics, and Psychomotor focus on this transition to action in a manner which is totally absent in the purely talking therapies.)

Once the transition to the realm of expression is made, the next decision is whether or not to make the action an "interaction" with someone or something in the environment. Obviously, without this decision to interact there cannot be satisfaction. The patient who "decides" not to move to interaction either does her/his action retroflectively, i.e., with the energy directed back toward herself/himself, or takes action toward a displaced and therefore not fully satisfying target, or takes action with no target at all. This juncture is the fifth decision point.

The sixth decision point is whether or not to allow the interaction to be satisfying after all of the previous steps have been taken appropriately. The patient who self-interrupts at this point simply does not let the experience be complete.

Whether or not to "withdraw" following satisfying "contact" is the seventh decision point. Prior to "satisfaction" the target holds a positive valence, in the sense that contact with that target is pursued. At the point of satisfaction the valence becomes neutral. If contact is forced beyond that point, and the natural withdrawal is avoided, the contact becomes noxious rather than satisfying and the target comes to have a negative valence. The patient who "decides" not to withdraw is stuck in contacts which no longer satisfy.

These seven decisions are basic existential ones. The issue is, do I allow a natural flow in energy process, or do I override the wisdom of my organism and interrupt my flow out of bionegative introjected messages? The decision to self-interrupt at any one of these seven points means leaving a need or preference unmet, and thus the accumulation of "unfinished business."

Two obvious questions at this point are why does one decide to self-interrupt, and how does one do so? Each of these questions invites a long intricate discussion. What I want to do here is offer only a brief answer to each.

First, the why of the decision to interrupt contact-withdrawal cycles. During early developmental years children are often told not to express a certain feeling in a particular way, or not to express that feeling at all, or sometimes not to feel certain feelings, or sometimes not even to have certain wants. These prohibitive messages may be either verbal or nonverbal. Because of the profound dependency of the young child, and their lack of personal experience against which to compare the parental messages, the messages are "swallowed-whole," introjected. During this phase of the socialization process, many of these introjected messages are bionegative, that is, they are socially arbitrary messages which do not support the aliveness of the person. The bionegative message is, then, a "toxic introject." There are two aspects to the toxic introject. There is the content of the message, and there is the threat that if the message is disobeyed, love will be withdrawn. An example is the statement to a little boy, "Big boys don't cry. Don't be a sissy." The content message is, "You should not cry," and the threat is, "If you cry, I won't love you." Toxic introjects such as these are usually maintained, unexamined and unchallenged, throughout one's life. This results in conflicts between natural psychobiological needs pressing for aliveness and the toxic introjected message which calls for deadness. After the toxic message has been introjected, the threat of withdrawal of love for disobeying becomes a conditioned phobic belief in imminent catastrophe any time the toxic message is not honored. The toxic introject carries, then, a "should" (or "should not") and a "catastrophic expectation." The greater the number and severity of the toxic intro-jects, the more phobic is the person's life and the less aliveness is allowed. Given the presence of toxic introjects, and therefore the internal voice which says, "You should not . . . " and the expectation that if I disobey then a catas-trophe will ensue, my "safety" lies in my limiting my aliveness. The self-interruption of a contact-withdrawal cycle is the very essence of limiting aliveness. Which kinds of contact-withdrawal cycles (based on which needs or preferences) I decide to interrupt, and at which of the seven decision points I choose to enact the interruption, is dictated by the details of the content of the toxic introject.

The "how" of self-interruption involves two methods which interact to enhance one another. Since satisfying contact involves both an energizing of the organism (excitement) and a focusing (through awareness) of that energy at the appropriate target, interfering with either energy level or organ-ismic awareness will effectively interrupt the contact-withdrawal cycle. The basic method for blocking energy is to limit breathing. By tightening the diaphragm and intercostal muscles, particularly, and by moving the locus of breathing into the upper portion of the lungs, breathing is greatly restricted and provides less oxygen for the metabolic processes. The result is a restrict-ing of available energy to the organism. Adjuncts to this restriction of energy include many factors which one can build into her/his lifestyle. Some exam-ples are smoking, use of drugs, alcohol, poor nutrition, lack of exercise, lack of adequate sleep and rest, and lack of play.

The second focus in self-interruption of contact-withdrawal cycles is on the clouding of awareness. No matter how energized the organism, with-out clear awareness (what do I want, what am I feeling, what do I need to do, and with what or with whom do I need to do it?) the likelihood of satisfac-tion is nil. The method for clouding awareness is to employ ego defenses. Several defenses are especially mentioned and focused on in Gestalt therapy theory: introjection, projection, retroflection, confluence, deflection, and desensitization. Without going into the details of each of these ego-defense mechanisms, I want to say here only that in each case there is a clouding of the awareness of what is wanted, or what is felt, or who it is that is wanting or feeling, or what is the appropriate action to be taken, or who/what is the appropriate target for that action.

In summary, I self-interrupt in a contact-withdrawal cycle whenever I come up against the voice of a toxic introject. That toxic introject declares what I "should" or "should not" and carries with it the threat of catastrophe if I don't obey. I then enact the self-interruption by de-energizing and by becoming confused (unaware). The exact point of interruption can be at one of the decision points. And so, DECISIONS — Decisions — decisions.

~

Responses from Psychotherapists
To "Life in a Glass House"

History informs us that in every society there has been a creative minority whose task was to lead and guide the other citizens through the maze of life. This minority represented the most creatively extraordinary of the populace. They have been called Shaman, Priest, Witch Doctor, Magician, Sorcerer, Zaddik, Master, Sage, Oracle, Prophet, Magus, Wizard, Counselor, and recently, Psychotherapist. In each case, the helper, healer, guide arose to meet a need which was recognized by members of the society. The helper existed on the margins of that society, empowered by an unconventional perspective. That unconventional perspective, sometimes called wisdom, is spontaneous and is given expression only through the "person" of the individual. But with each of the above named, the creative, *personal*, unconventional perspective was apprenticed, emulated, copied, and eventually institutionalized. Shortly thereafter, it was dead. Useless now as a creative and challenging guide, it had become merely the conventional.

So, friend, if you wish to grease the slide to a moribund state for psychotherapy, be conventional. Wear the uniform of the businessman, support regulation and standardization of practice, and avoid thinking or doing anything out of the ordinary. Freud was a radical, and look what he started. To say nothing of Jung, Reich, or Perls.

Psychotherapy is an exquisite art form given life through the person of the therapist. Good psychotherapy calls for highly evolved personhood.

From *Voices*, 17(2), 60-61 (1981).

The institutionalized expedients of the business ethic are anathema to the growth ethic of the psychotherapist. The HMO, the PPO, the so-called peer review, and the narrow definitions of "treatment of choice," all attempts at the institutionalization of the practice of psychotherapy, are impediments to this person-centered creative art.

As I sit here, this sultry Atlanta evening, I feel an admixture of disgust at what I see happening and thankfulness for my own situation. I am very fortunate in that almost half of my clients are other therapists. They have come to me, mostly self-referred, because of that indivisible complex of who I am/what I do. I see events which I believe are serious threats to the freedom which is essential for the practice of psychotherapy. I have been able to continue being me, doing what I do, without great disruption from those threatening events. However, I have been threatened with a malpractice suit, my life has been threatened, and I have been the target of malicious rumor (none of these involved therapist clients). These things go with the territory. And, so I go on. I intend to do psychotherapy the way I understand it as long as I enjoy it. I rarely wear a necktie. I touch frequently.

~

Characterological Styles of
Emotional Plague Behavior

In the present paper I want to explore the way that emotional plague behaviors are manifested in each of the basic pre-genital character types. As background for this focus I will first offer a model for the examination of patterns of interactional energy dynamics.

When two people interact openly, both are affected. We speak of two people impacting each other, or influencing each other. This happens in a context of openness, wherein there is an energy exchange. Two energy fields interact and both are transformed. The opposite, too, is possible. Two people can spend time together, even large amounts of time, and neither is impacted much. In this case there has not been much energy exchanged. Instead of openness there has been insularity. To insulate is the opposite of being open. The former prevents energy exchange; the latter allows the coming together of the energy fields. Both of these are necessary for richness in living, openness to take in positive energy such as support, protection, and nourishment, and insularity to keep out the opposite, negative energy.

I conceive of four modes of *energetic interaction*. Two are *open modes* and two are *insular modes*. (One can be most insular, of course, by not interacting at all.)

The open modes of energy interaction are *receiving* and *synergizing*, with the first being simple and the second more complex. The receiving

From *Energy and Character*, 15(1), 38-44 (1984).

mode involves openness to taking energy in from another. This is what is involved when one feels nourished, supported, or protected by another. The receiving mode has been used when one feels better after having been with another.

In the synergistic mode there is an openness to receiving as well, but with the addition of one's own energy. The result is that the two energy systems merge and both people are affected. The result is more than the sum of the first person's energy and the second person's energy. Each person receives from the interaction as the back-and-forth energy exchange builds. Through the synergistic mode of interaction both persons receive. Both persons join into the process, and the mutuality of the process makes for a building of the effects of both energy fields.

Rejecting energy sent is the simple form of the insular mode of interpersonal energy dynamics. Just as the receiving mode is functional when the energy is positive (nourishing, supportive, protective), the rejecting mode is appropriate when the energy is toxic (non-nourishing, critical, attacking).

The *oppositional* mode of insularity involves not just the shutting out of energy but the use of energy to stop the other energy field. The oppositional mode does not allow the other energy field to continue, but aggressively attacks it.

The functional pattern is to use the receiving and synergistic modes when positive energy is involved. It is appropriate to be open to positive energy. Furthermore, it is functional to use the rejecting mode or oppositional mode when toxic energy is being presented to one. It is life supportive to accept or magnify that which is itself biopositive and to reject, or in extreme cases oppose, that which is bionegative. Conversely, it is life negating to reject or oppose that which is biopositive or to be open to that which is bionegative. In the case of the rejecting mode, I find one of the Polsters' (1973) insights relevant. They have pointed out that the territory between where one says "no" and the point at which one ultimately wants to say "no" is a zone of waste. Relating this idea to the interactional modes, there may be energy which would be beneficial up to a point but beyond that would be detrimental. For instance, someone may approach with affectionate and erotic energy. I may be clear that I don't want to have sex with her, that to do so would not be in my best interest. But to say "no" at too great a distance from the act of sex would be to rob both of us of something which might be mutually nurturant. We might both enjoy talking, dancing, or holding hands. For asking me to assume the rejecting mode at too great a distance from being sexual would constitute a waste.

Pre-genital character dynamics call forth pathological patterns of interpersonal interaction. So, the person with such active dynamics may tend to be open to bionegative energy, assuming a receptive mode of interaction or even synergistically joining into the building of negative energy. An example of the latter would be to provide the other's anger towards one. Or the person may tend to be insular toward biopositive energy, either assuming a rejecting mode of interaction or even opposing the biopositive energy.

The chronic assumption of the oppositional mode of interaction toward biopositive energy constitutes a symptom of what Reich (1949, 1974) wrote about as the "emotional plague." This term carries no defamatory connotation, according to Reich (1949), and does not refer to any conscious malice. Rather, a person is a victim of the plague to the extent that their natural, self-regulatory life manifestations have been suppressed. So, to the extent that one does not live their body, does not embody organismic aliveness, they're manifesting some degree of the emotional plague.

Out of the fear of one's own organismic aliveness, the plagued individual is threatened by aliveness in others. So, the plagued individual won't endure free and natural expressions of life either in herself or himself or in others. Baker (1967) has informed us that to the extent that someone tries to tear down others or control their lives, they're functioning as a plagued character. He goes on to give examples of plagued behavior: cruelty, hurtful gossip, and resentment of others' good fortune.

Much of the previously published discussion of the emotional plague is focused on the level of political activity. As such, Baker (1967) has identified the plague character as one of the three "socio-political character types." The most thoroughgoing discussion of emotional plague and political institutionalization is Reich's (1974) book written sometime between 1943 and 1946, *Listen Little Men!* I refer the reader to these sources if interested. The political arena is beyond the scope of my intentions here.

As I see it, plague does not actually define any additional character type but is a description of an interpersonal dynamic which can occur in the context of any pre-genital character. As I have defined it above, *emotional plague is a term which refers to a chronic assumption of the oppositional mode of interaction with the life energy in others.* What this means is that anyone with pre-genital character dynamics operating may be threatened by the aliveness of another person, and in response may interact in an oppositional mode, trying to stifle such free and natural functioning in the other. Emotional plague behavior involves discouraging or stopping other people's aliveness.

Figure 1

MODES OF INTERACTIONAL ENERGY DYNAMICS

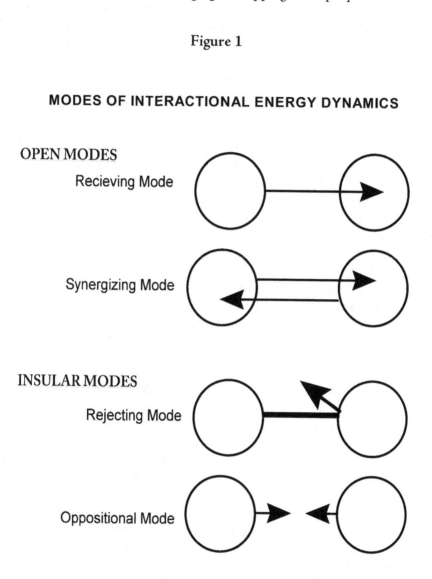

OPEN MODES

    Recieving Mode

    Synergizing Mode

INSULAR MODES

    Rejecting Mode

Oppositional Mode

With muscular armoring comes the perversion of the organismic expressions. As Reich (1949) and Baker (1967) have stated, when expression passes through muscular armor, the natural and spontaneous quality of the primary drive is converted into the unnatural, hard quality of a secondary drive. And so we have love expressed pornographically; fear expressed as paranoia; anger expressed cruelly; coldly, and sadistically; happiness packaged and consumed as a commodity; and grief expressed as bitterness and pessimism. As these perverted secondary drives become the style of one's expression, the other person, in order not to suffer must assume a rejecting mode of interaction. Too often, such perverse expressions are accepted or even interacted with synergistically. These perverse expressions are oppositional to natural biopositive expressions.

I have not read in the literature any discussion of characterological styles of manifestation of emotional plague in interpersonal interactions. It seems to me that would be useful, and so I am suggesting a style of oppositional mode of interaction for each of the primary character types. Full, rich aliveness requires mutuality in relating. Everybody needs somebody sometime, and the cycles repeat with some considerable frequency. So, to live with richness and meaning requires interrelating in transpersonal ways, ways of interdependence. This give and take transcends the myopia of selfishness and allows us to give when full, take when empty, and share the resources which you and I bring to our relationship. A common quality, however, of all pre-genital character types is myopic selfishness of vision. Remember, pre-genital character structures limit, each in its respective way, the amount of energy available for contact. In addition, the respective patterns of armoring lead to perversions of the natural expressions of emotion, these secondary or perverted urges being toxic not only for the self, but to all of those with whom one so interacts.

More specifically, then, how is each character type likely to manifest in oppositional interactional form, that is, as emotionally plagued behavior? The schizoid has a passive style of emotional plague behavior. Since the schizoid structure involves a fear of interpersonal contact, the schizoid tends not to be very available. Not only is the schizoid not very available out of her or his cautiousness, but the schizoid usually has not developed very smooth or endearing ways of relating so that they may come across as socially maladroit or even incompetent. This latter quality refers not just to the superficial layer of manners, etiquette, and protocol, but to a deeper layer at which the schizoid may not understand or be able to empathize with what the other is experiencing. In extreme, this social behavior will be bizarre. So, both from their fearfulness of contact and lack of deep relational skills, the schizoid tends not to provide much nourishing, protective, or supportive contact. The schizoid passively opposes strong interaction and contact.

The oral character also has a passive style of emotional plague behavior. This differs from the schizoid's passivity in that the oral tends towards a passive-pouting style. First, the oral may feel too tired to respond to the needs of others. The chronic low energy of the oral means a weakness of sustained contact and thus a weakness of nourishment, protection, or support for the other. In addition, the oral is needy and tends to cling. This can drain the other, and the depression of the disappointed oral character can become intolerable to those who feel the demand of that passive stance. By their clinging and demand for attention, oral characters passively oppose others' independence and moving on with their own lives.

With the psychopathic character, we find an active style of plague behavior. Whether the seducer or the bully, the psychopath is focused on controlling others. This means that compassion for the other, interest in the growth or welfare or the other is secondary, if not altogether ignored. The psychopath tends, then, to be uncaring, unfeeling, and disloyal. Taking advantage of others and setting others up for a con game are only logical ploys in the service of staying in control. An interesting behavior which I have witnessed on several occasions is the psychopath's encouraging someone beyond her or his limits and into predicaments of embarrassment or danger. To casual observation such behavior may appear as support to the other's growth or aliveness, when in fact it is the very antithesis of protection and limit-setting, two of the hallmarks of non-plague behavior. So, the psychopath actively opposes others' rising, growing, developing by controlling and to the end of being in control.

With the masochistic character we find, again, a passive emotional plague style. More specifically, it tends to be a passive-aggressive style. So, central to the masochist's character is the resistant "I won't," that influences her or his response to others' wants. Often, then, the masochist is unwilling to give the other whatever it is that they want, instead taking a stubborn position of withholding support, nurturance, or protection. Rather than responding to the wants of others, the masochist often discourages and pulls them down with a pervasive negativity. The masochist takes the stance: When in doubt, say "No." On the surface this negativity may appear to be caution and the setting of limits, in the interest of the other person. But on closer examination this behavior is revealed as a pervasive negativism, pessimism, even bitterness focused on the discouragement of the aliveness of the other person which the masochist painfully lacks. The masochist passively opposes joy, freedom, spontaneity — aliveness.

An active style of emotional plague behavior is once again met in the rigid character structures. First, the rigid female or hysteric. She, with her high energy and interpersonal orientation, often is exciting, "turning people on." But she promises by this behavior more than she follows through with; she offers a lot and delivers little, leaving the other person feeling empty after a while. Her emotions tend to be shallow, although quickly accessed, so with time she is revealed as ingenuine to a degree. The chaos of her life, brought about by her emotional lability, her disinclination toward careful or deep thought, and her tendency to use denial as a way of dealing with the unpleasant, makes her a difficult partner. The upshot of this is that genuine support, protection, and nourishment do not flow from the hysteric with any abundance. The hysteric actively opposes deep feelings and careful or deep thought.

Turning to her male counterparts, the compulsive character and the phallic-narcissistic character, we find an emotional plague behavior based on the subordination of personhood to the attainment of technical goals. There is a mechanical, inflexible quality to the rigid male. He may be hard and competitive, in the extreme, cold and ruthless in getting his goal met. Feelings are seen as inconvenient, at best, or a sign of weakness to be overcome and kept under control, at worst. This disparagement of the emotional aspects of personhood leaves the rigid male limited in his emotional sensitivity and availability. His emotional plague behavior consists of the active opposition of feelings.

The healthy alternative, what we can term the evolved person, the person of high consciousness, the actualized person, the genital character, or the person who organismically "lives" her or his body, is not bound to any great degree by the characterological fetters discussed above. Such a person exhibits minimally or not at all the emotional plague behaviors. Conversely, such a person can enjoy and even delight in the aliveness, growth, evolution of others.

Figure 2

CHARACTEROLOGICAL STYLES OF OPPOSITIONAL INTERACTION

(Characterological Styles of Emotional Plague Behavior)

Schizoid

Passive opposition to contact with others.
Weak, cautious contact means limited nourishment, support, protection, and limits offered. May not recognize or understand needs in others.

Oral

Passive/pouting opposition to others' independence.
Low energy means weakness of sustained contact and thus a weakness of nourishment, support, protection, and limits offered. Clinging, demandingness, disappointedness and depression can drain others.

Psychopath

Active opposition to others' rising in order to be in control. Compassion for others, interest in growth or welfare of others is subordinated to being in control of them. Hence, uncaring, unfeeling, disloyal taking advantage of others.

Masochist

Passive-aggressive opposition to others' joy, freedom, spontaneity. Stubborn withholding of nourishment, support, protection, limits. Negativity, pessimism, bitterness, discourage others' aliveness.

Rigid Female

Active opposition to deep feelings and deep thought.
Creates chaos through emotional lability and shallowness, and uses denial rather than coping. Turns people on to her and then fades rather than delivering nourishment, support, protection, and limits.

*Rigid Male
(Compulsive
and Phallic-
Narcissistic)*

Active opposition to feelings.
Personhood subordinated to attainment of goals.
Feelings denigrated, leaving him emotionally insensitive and unavailable.

~

The "Lived Body" as a Value in Psychotherapy

To live an abundant life requires that one not shrink or pull away, but that one embrace the world with passion and delight. By living abundantly, by embracing each new day with passion and delight one evolves. This evolution is the cosmic Dance. The important thing is to live fully where you are, now. This means neither to waste one's time ruminating about what is past, nor to waste one's time obsessively rehearsing an imagined future. What is done is done, what is not yet is not yet, what is now is what is. And one's power and ability to respond are with respect to what is. Then you will evolve.

"Life is a contact sport." Think about this.

I value aliveness. I see that which enhances aliveness as good and that which deadens as bad. Aliveness is characterized by expansion into the world and relaxed contraction into the self. This is the rhythm of life. Deadness involves anxious contraction against expansion. Aliveness evolves. First comes an organismic vibration as one experiences an urge, a wanting. The vibrating organism may pulsate, reach a state of expansion to meet the want and a relaxed contraction following an experience of satisfaction. Then comes the graceful flow or streaming in the world, where the spontaneous and unimpeded streamings of life energy within the body system are paralleled by the

From *Conhecer A Pessoa*, 4(3), 31-44 (1985) (Originally published as 'O corpo vivo como um valor em psicoterapia').

streamings of the organism in the larger system, the organism-in-the-world. The person comes to move about in the environment with a grace which identifies a freedom from fear of aliveness. Such a state of evolution is evident in a person whose gait and gestures are fluid and rhythmic, such that they appear to be dancing. This dance will tend to flow around obstacles so that this person seems to handle frustrations and hardships with aplomb.

Unfortunately, many people are phobic about life and therefore interpret anxiety as a signal to stop what they are doing or are about to do. Anxiety is a sign of blocked excitement, but is often taken as a signal to shut down. The rule for growth, that is expanded living, is to follow excitement rather than to shrink. Going with excitement rather than anxiously contracting is the essence of living passionately. In life, anxiety is a perverse traveling companion.

The above implies a relationship between being and becoming to which I want to draw attention. Being, or good living, is served by spontaneous expression of emotions. Becoming, or emotional growth is through emotional expression where it has previously not been allowed. So, growth or becoming is an amplification and deepening of being. To life, more aliveness is added.

The urge for experience is part of being alive. Experience comes from expanding into the world, from going out beyond what is familiar and known. Through experience one can become more. In discussing this facet of expansion, Naranjo states that one intuitively seeks depth or fullness of awareness. When this is not experienced, more and more environmental stimulation may be sought. So, a craving for more takes the place of the natural need for depth. As I see it, when deep experience arouses anxiety, one can take flight into high stimulation. To avoid depth, keep busy, keep distracted, keep highly stimulated. For example, if a person fears having her or his deep feelings and thoughts known, that person may avoid such intimacy by keeping a full and busy social calendar. This flurry of social contact becomes a substitute for and an avoidance of the more extended, less structured time with one or two people which would support a deepening of relationships. The difference here is between the big party and the quiet evening tête-à-tête. The choice is between superficial contact in quantity and deeper contact with fewer people which allows awareness to develop more fully. Both being (good living) and becoming (growth) have bases in emotional expression. Expression of emotion requires an embodied self. Aliveness, therefore, calls for the "body-as-subject." Dublin suggests that the "disregarded body" or "body-as-object" is a mark of pathology. In contrast, the "lived body" is the experienced body and is tied to the lived moment. The body-as-object means alienation from one's body and a diminished aliveness.

The "lived body" is the body enlivened, the "disregarded body" the body deadened. One who lives her or his body is organismically oriented, experiencing the self holistically rather than the self as a mental entity which "has" a body. Such a person feels the whole range of emotions deeply and expresses them spontaneously and fully, uses body sensations as input for cognitive and perceptual processes, has a high level of body awareness, experiences the locus of self in the body, experiences high levels of sensual and sexual pleasure, and takes care of the body, using it fully, but neither damaging it through misuse nor allowing it to deteriorate through disuse. The "lived body" is an alive body. The equating of the living of the body and an organismic/holistic experiencing of self is given scientific validation by a host of studies reviewed by Aikin. In summary, Aikin states his opinion that ". . . . empirical evidence supports the conclusion that motor activity is more than merely related to psychological activities in some parallel fashion, but emotion, perception and thinking literally *are* neuromuscular and other bodily activity."

As I look about I see many people who tend to value mind primarily or value body primarily rather than to value the organismic perspective which I equate with the "lived body." Interestingly, in both cases there tends to be an objectification of the body. The head oriented people tend to focus their growth and expansion in intellectual realms. So, such people prefer work which involves thinking, as they like rational process, planning, and cognitive understanding. These propensities tend to allow them to delay gratifications. In school settings they prefer to spend time in the class room, laboratory, and computer center. The head-oriented person tends to be, in a sense, abstract and academic. The body-oriented people, on the other hand, tend to focus their growth and expansion efforts on their physical being. They prefer work which involves physical activity, the doing of things. So, they tend in their action orientation to be impulsive or at least prefer not to delay gratification. Rather than "figure out," they would tend to "try out." In school settings they prefer to spend time in the shop, the gym, or on the field or court. The body-oriented person is concrete and practical. But both relate to the body as an object. The head-oriented person "has" a body which is downplayed and responded to mostly when it complains with aches or pains. At worst the body is ignored or even denigrated, often through disuse. The body-oriented person, too, "has" a body. It may be worked on and developed, but not "lived." At worst the body is damaged through misuse. I am writing here about two orientations which can be observed, and my descriptions are simplified by focusing on the extremes. To caricature these extremes I offer the images of the ivory tower professor, abstract to the point of being disembodied, and the professional athlete, concrete to the point of being mindless. These are the extremes of fragmentation and imbalance of the person. Less extreme is fragmentation with balance. Herein, many people think of and experience themselves as "having" a mind and "having" a body, but in this dualism they strive for a balance and value their parts equally. The position which I am valuing most highly is one which is a step beyond balanced dualism, the organismic position. That is the position of "living the body."

In conceptualizing the scripting of the body (i.e., the guidelines for the drama of one's life, based on introjected messages from childhood), I distinguish the use, disuse, and misuse ("abuse") of the body. The "lived body" is a body used. While neither disused nor abused, the body truly lived is lived with excitement, enthusiasm, and passion. Growth into deeper and fuller being means to expand and assimilate, the assimilation taking place during the relaxation into contraction into the self. And, gradually the edge of the self where growth takes place is extended. I remember Erv and Miriam Polster talking, in a seminar, about growth being the expansion of the "I boundary" to include more and more of what is experienced. In other words, one grows as more and more of the world can be encompassed and understood by one's knowing ego. The extension of this growing edge is necessary for growth. There are three attitudes which one can take concerning that growing edge. First is the *phobic attitude*. Those who assume the phobic attitude retreat in anxiety from their growing edge, afraid of pain, embarrassment, or the catastrophe of the "too muchness" threatened by their toxic introjects. This phobic attitude defines the timid and the shy, the spectators of life. Second is the *impulsive attitude* of the fool. The fool, apparently ignoring real dangers and actual limits, forces herself or himself beyond the growing edge. Such pushing and forcing of the growing edge inevitable results in injury, in some degree of self-destruction. The fool is living out a toxic script as surely as the timid and the shy. The third attitude toward the growing edge is the attitude of *respect and excitement*. Respect for the limits and the actual dangers of forcing, and excitement about the expansive possibilities make this attitude the one which allows most growth. The person with this attitude tends to be relatively free from toxic scripting, either by virtue of not having received a highly toxic script or by having gotten rid of such a script through some profound growth experience. This third attitude assumes a true "living" of the body. So, this creative participant in life "lives" the body or uses it. The fool suffers from the consequences of chronic abuse of the body. And the timid and the shy shrink into body disuse, with its pathological sequela. The choice is to participate in life creatively ("live" the body), to shrink from life (disuse the body), or to burn out or break down (misuse the body).

To be alive is to take reasonable risks. In taking reasonable risks there will sometimes be expansion far enough or frequent enough to exceed the growing edge and result in organismic injury. Surely a body totally unscarred reflects a life not fully lived. Has anyone learned to ride a bicycle or roller skate without skinned knees? I believe that honest errors of judgment can occur when one is attempting to go beyond previous limits. One of the differences between the alive person seeking growth and the fool may lie in the preparation for the expansion. The growth-oriented person is disciplined. That means that he or she assesses readiness to expand, and if the best judgment is that he or she is not ready, then he or she waits. Discipline manifests itself as delay, planning, training, setting up the right conditions, whatever preparation is judged necessary to maximize the growthfulness of the experience. So, the fool may try a dangerous expansion on impulse the growth-oriented person attends to timing, to the issue of preparation and readiness. So, the skier in playing her or his growing edge may take a fall and consequently sport some bruises or a twisted ankle. But only a foolish skier would skip the hours of body conditioning and practice and take on a downhill run well beyond her or his ability or, lacking the self-discipline of setting limits based on body feedback, push to ski when exhausted. In the latter situations, being unprepared for the expansion taken on, the foolish skier sooner or later encounters serious injury.

In the *Ultimate Athlete* George Leonard makes a convincing case for the organismically growthful possibilities of sports. He wrote of the transformational aspects of sports, in terms of human boundaries crossed, perceptions gained, and previous limits transcended. At the same time, he noted that sports share the common element of risk of injury or even death.

Sports are a way of exploring the limits. They involve the body in exploration of movement and the relationship between movement and time. Hanna has called attention to the fact that the living body is a moving body. Or, more precisely, he writes that life exists ". . . as the organized movements of an individual body." He refers to the "quick" and the "dead," seeing autonomous movement as the prime trait by which we distinguish the two. Hanna makes a case that a diminished capacity for movement corresponds to a diminished aliveness. In his teaching, Hanna has found that most adults have little ability to sense the movements of their bodies. The usual situation is for the person to reach adulthood with only a minimal development of the sensorimotor systems and then to steadily lose the abilities of body sensing and efficient body movement as they age. This impaired development of sensorimotor and proprioceptive-somesthetic faculties is seen by Hanna as the major health problem of contemporary society. In terms of full functioning, this impaired development represents a loss of human potential, a deviation from the state of "wellness." What is commonly seen is the impaired state of movement rather than efficient, graceful, unimpaired movement with proprioceptive awareness. This impaired movement can be recognized by stiff, non-rythmic, or wasteful body movements. There may be an obvious awkwardness, or perhaps just a restriction of the full range of motion of the body.

So, the "lived body" is a body moving. Sports offer the possibility of exploring, with awareness, the parameters of movement — strength, flexibility, coordination, endurance, timing. Why increase flexibility far beyond average with Hatha Yoga? Why increase strength far beyond average with weight training? Why increase endurance far beyond average with distance running? Because these expand the realm of possibility, open more options for behavior, and offer greater breadth and depth of living.

Aliveness is sometimes experienced profoundly, thus spiritually. Spiritual meaning can emerge from the awe and splendor of "lived body" awareness. Alan Watts has written that no matter how many philosophies one studies, how many spiritual exercises one practices, how many scriptures one searches, and how many spiritual teachers one consults, in the end one returns to the surprising fact of eating, sleeping, feeling, breathing, moving about, the surprising fact of being alive. This, Watts wrote, surprising fact of being alive is the "supreme experience of religion." So it is that many writers have seen deadness as the origin of all other sins.

The marvel and the mystery is to be alive.

The value called forth is life lived abundantly. This means *here* and this means *now* and this means *with awareness*. To live an abundant life requires that one not shrink or pull away but that one embrace the world with passion and delight. By living abundantly, by embracing each new day with passion and delight one evolves. This evolution is the cosmic Dance. The important thing is to live fully where you are, now. This means neither to waste one's time ruminating about what is past nor to waste one's time obsessively rehearsing an imagined future. What is done is done, what is not yet is not yet, what is now is what is. And one's power and ability to respond are with respect to what is. Then you will evolve. This lesson in the importance of experiencing fully each stage of life, each life circumstance is well portrayed by Hesse in *Siddhartha*.

Urges, those movements of desire for deep within, are life being born. To respond is to say "Yes" to life, and to tighten the muscles so as to suppress the urge is to say "No" to life and join the parade of the dead. I am not talking about the impulsive actions which a body without benefit of mind makes, but the respectful action taken by an integrated organism in response to the deep stirrings within. Any urge one feels is valid at some level. The urge is best evaluated by cognitive and affective response, and then acted out or, if the urge is thought to be or felt to be dangerous or inappropriate, not acted out. Two lines from Blake's *The Marriage of Heaven and Hell* can instruct, if not inspire:

> He who desires but acts not, breeds pestilence. . . .
> Sooner murder an infant in its cradle than nurse unacted desires.

I think in terms of two levels of awareness, the awareness of wants or needs which naturally *leads to* bodily action and interaction with the world, and awareness which *comes from* such action and interaction. I label these Level I and Level II awareness, respectively. Level II awareness comes from the experience of satisfaction or non-satisfaction following an action/interaction sequence. Wisdom accrues from this second level of awareness. But the shy and the timid are deficient in this wisdom because of their tendency toward non-action and non-interaction. Afraid of "too much" aliveness or afraid of making mistakes, the shy and the timid stay contracted. Aliveness seems "too much" whenever it approaches the limits set by toxic childhood introjects, those messages taken in by the child which restrict natural and healthy behavior. So, the timid and the shy hold back from activities and experiences which would lead to wisdom of life. Again, Blake in *The Marriage of Heaven and Hell* may be of encouragement:

> No bird soars too high, if he soars on his own wings. . . .
> If the fool would persist in his folly he would become
>   wise. . . .
> The road of excess leads to the palace of wisdom.

From the "lived body" perspective sex is more than a genital itch to be scratched every so often. "Sexual" is another word to describe and expand upon the "lived body." "Sexual" is a way of being and a way of responding to the world. It means contacting the world with passion.

To be sexual means to kiss the ground and embrace the trees, to roll on the grass and to smell deeply of the flowers. It means to feel excited when looking at a mountain peak and turned on when the breeze encircles the skin and tosses the hair. Such, by God and thank God, is passion.

To be sexual in the less encompassing sense means to relate to other people with this same passion. In its narrow sense, to be sexual means to relate to someone genitally. To be a fully sexual person involves all three of these levels of sexuality.

Turning to the genital sense of sexuality, I note that Reich, Lowen, and Perls, as well as many who have studied with them equate being alive and being sexual. As Lowen states this, "To be sexual is to be alive, and to be alive is to be sexual." The reduction of sexual feelings amounts to a psychological castration, as Lowen sees it. Not to be sexual, then, is not only an incomplete behavioral Gestalt, but it is also an incomplete body Gestalt. It is living as if one had no genitals. To be celibate is to give up the rich arena of genital life. For some, this sacrifice is important. But, would anyone deny that it is a sacrifice?

If a person is not sexual in the "lived body" sense and allows sex to be limited to the genitals, then that person will not be sexually fulfilled. There may be acts of sex, but not making love. The unfulfillment may lead to the seeking of more and more variety and greater and greater stimulation. The result — promiscuity and perversion — unless guilt holds those in check. This is the point Reich made when he wrote of secondary drives developing when primary (natural) drives are blocked. The secondary drives are hard, harsh, and a perversion of the natural primary drives. The "lived body" is alive in response to primary drives.

When one "lives" her or his body, there will be a positive regard or caring for the body. The body is identified with and included in the personal pronoun "I." This body identification implies a certain life styling. When people live their bodies, they will conduct their lives in such a manner that their bodies will be well used, and disuse and abuse will be minimal. This life style will involve a respect for and provision for the satisfaction of one's needs. One will style one's life with a value on "aliveness."

I am not proposing the "lived body" as a total guide to living or as *the* value underlying the practice of psychotherapy. What I am offering is an exploration of the "lived body" as a highly important value in psychotherapy, and one which is too often unacknowledged.

~

On Anxiety: Functions, and Re-Functions

In the Spring 1979 (Vol. 15, No. 1) issue of *Voices* I wrote about anxiety as a "perverse traveling companion" on our journeys into intimacy. I suggested that anxiety is the perverse half-sib of fear in that fear protects us from real dangers, but anxiety promises protection from that which is no longer a danger, while leading us to believe that the historical danger is still present. As uncomfortable as anxiety may be, one can come to endure and even embrace it, if one becomes familiar enough with it. Perhaps it is this embracing of the familiar, in spite of discomfort or pain, which is the re-function of anxiety. I offer a poetic statement of the dynamics of anxiety (from a Gestalt therapy perspective) for your consideration and reaction.

ANXIETUDE

Excitement growing!
Not enough support.
Imagine the worst.
Gasp! Don't breathe!
Anxiety, my old friend.

~

A GESTALT THERAPIST'S PERSPECTIVE ON GRIEF

ABSTRACT. Reflecting on Freud's approach to mourning and melancholia, the author first distinguishes grief from depression. He then suggests a three-dimensional schema involving the intensity, duration, and type of loss involved in the grieving process. Attending to the highly variable nature of this process, he describes grieving or "mourning labor" as the organism's natural healing process whereby the loss is acknowledged and the organism is made ready to go on with life, unaccompanied by that which was let go. The role of the therapist is seen as one of facilitating the natural individualized process of grieving. Help is most appropriate when the client is unable to grieve or has been grieving too long. In the first case the client is seen as refusing to enter into the experience of the labor of mourning and in the latter as refusing to finish the work. The article concludes with a description of the "empty-chair monologue" in which the client is encouraged to do the mourning labor of expressing appreciations, resentments, and regrets while the therapist attends to any inadequacy of awareness, of arousal, or of crying activity.

Sorrow comes as a welcome visitor,
moving my losses to the archives of my life.
But, depression is her monstrous half-sister
wanting to be a murderous wife.

From: *The Psychotherapy Patient*, 2(1) 65-78 (1985).

One of the frequent confusions in this bizarre realm known by the misleading name of "mental health" is the confusion of grief with depression. In the attempt to simplify, make it easy, and, in turn, popularize psychology, there is often a failure to differentiate the natural process of grieving a loss from the neurotic process, depression. The confusion is easy for the merchant of oversimplification, since, when viewed superficially, grief and depression bear resemblance. But, to consent to this superficiality is to lose the profoundly important distinction between these two human processes.

Allow me the following analogy. In the latter half of the 19th century the Augustinian monk Gregor Mendel revealed to the world the basic answers to the enigma of heredity. In his Moravian gardens Mendel was able to show predictable outcomes in his selective breeding of peas. But a riddle arose. When crossing two hybrid plants the ratio of the observable characteristics in the offspring was 3:1, not half and half, as one might expect. Through painstaking, countless trials Mendel observed until he solved the riddle. Like appearance does not reveal underlying genetic make-up. Or, phenotypic identity (same physical appearance) does not necessitate the same genotype (actual gene content). Only by getting to the level of genotype, with its 1:2:1 ratio of inheritance of a given genetically carried characteristic, was Mendel able to solve the riddle of the 3:1 ratio in the appearance of that characteristic (the phenotype). Appearances presented a riddle, and the solution came through an understanding of the underlying process.

So it is, too, for the psychotherapist. Beneath the phenotype layer of crying and said talk lie two distinct genotypes, grief and depression. These two processes are different in quite significant ways, as I will review shortly. And, to treat grieving and depression in the same manner is wasteful at best; at worst, it is of real harm to the patient. How often is the grieving patient treated as depressed, or the depressed patient treated as if grieving?

I feel concerned with the blurring of the distinction between grief and depression that I read with some frequency in the literature and hear from psychotherapists. Such blurring of categories is at variance with a basic value in Gestalt therapy. Fritz Perls studied with the Organismic theorist Kurt Goldstein, learning from him the value of care in speaking. Goldstein emphasized the importance of the ability of the person to abstract and classify, thereby engaging in "categorical thinking." He was able to demonstrate that the loss of categorical thinking by patients resulted in limitations of their orientation and of their action. Following Goldstein's lead, Perls pointed out throughout his writing the extreme importance of using the words which express the precise meaning of what one wants to convey. He encouraged the appreciation of the power in the "logos," the valuing of each word with its precise meaning and application in communication (Emerson & Smith, 1974). The study of semantics was encouraged by Perls (1947, 1969) as an excellent method of improving mental functioning and as the antidote to what he poetically referred to as "frigidity of the palate." So, once again, I want to emphasize the importance of speaking precisely when we speak of grief of depression, for both clarity of understanding and the ensuing guidelines to therapeutic practice.

Just as Mendel looked beneath appearances to understand the genotypes unrevealed through phenotype, Freud looked beneath the surface behaviors to understand the two processes referred to in the words of his time as "mourning" and "melancholia." Although there are earlier references in which the comparison of these two dynamics was made, such as that of Abraham in 1912, the classic article was published by Freud in 1917, titled simply "Mourning and Melancholia" (Freud, 1963).

Freud instructed that it was the same kinds of external events that brought about mourning or melancholia. The key to the onset of either is an experienced loss. The loss is, in Freud's words, "of a loved person, or the loss of some abstraction which has taken the place of one, such as fatherland, liberty, an ideal, and so on" (p. 164). For some, having "morbid pathological disposition," instead of mourning, a state of melancholia ensues. In both cases there is the experience of "profoundly painful dejection, abrogation of interest in the outside world, loss of the capacity of love, inhibition of all activity" (p.165). In the case of melancholia, however, there is in addition "a lowering of the self-regarding feelings to a degree that finds utterance in self-reproaches and self-revilings, and culminates in a delusional expectation of punishment" (p. 165). It is this that is *differentia specifica* at the symptomatic level, between mourning and melancholia — the fall in self-esteem.

My focus, here, is on grieving, as mourning is also called, not on melancholia, now more frequently termed depression. So I will not look further into the theories and research that have clarified the "morbid pathological disposition" which is the etiological key to depression, as opposed to grieving. I want to shift focus now to grieving, by first quoting Rycroft (1968) as saying, "All schools of psychoanalysis regard mourning as the normal analogue of DEPRESSION [*sic*]" (p. 94).

I have made a case for the importance of a differential diagnosis between grief and depression. As old as the distinction is, the boundary is often blurred or ignored even by professionals. So, how is grieving identified? Freud, as discussed above, pointed the way. In grieving, a loss has been sustained. If the grieving is progressing smoothly, the affected person will feel a level of sadness and withdrawal of interest and activity from the world that is congruent with the degree of loss. What will not be present is the loss of self-esteem that characterizes depression. There may be regrets, of course. But these regrets remain just that. In loss, I may regret that I did not go to see the deceased during his or her illness; I may regret that there are some things that I never said. But, in clean grieving I would not call myself a bad person for not having done those things. To elaborate on the recognition of grieving, there are some subtleties that I want to mention. Sadness and withdrawal of interest and activity may manifest in a rich panorama of mourning. Included may be feelings of emptiness, pessimism, and despair. There may be crying, in all degrees — from tearing up or sniffling to deep, long wailing. The person in grief may feel fatigued, with everything seeming to require great effort. With this lowered level of energy, speech and movement may be slowed, concentration may be difficult, and the person may become error-prone as attention is hard to keep. Sleep may come only with difficulty, compounding the problem of fatigue and perhaps leading to general irritability. Appetite fails. And, sexual drive usually reaches its nadir. The intensity and duration of these manifestations is dictated by the degree of experienced loss.

What, then, constitutes loss? Freud's (1963) suggestion that the loss may be of a loved person or of some abstraction which has taken the place of a loved person is, once again, an astute guide, and one deserving elaboration. The human ability to abstract the person, then abstract the abstraction, can lead to a final object with emotional attachment which is not at all apparent to the observer. So, there are grief reactions to losses which go unnoticed by those other than the one involved. A list of losses, categorized as Obvious Losses, Not So Obvious Losses, Losses Related to Age, Limbo, and Other Losses (temporary losses, losses built into successes, mini-losses), offered by Colgrove, Bloomfield, and McWilliams (1976) runs fully two pages. I will pass on to you some selected examples to give a flavor, and to bring out some of their less obvious examples: death of a loved one, divorce, break-up of an affair, loss of money, illness (loss of health), robbery, loss of a cherished ideal, loss of childhood dreams, leaving home, graduating, loss of hair or teeth, awaiting medical test reports, a loved one "missing in action," slump in business, children away at college, a dent in the new car. The point which these authors make is that these losses, whether immediate or cumulative, sudden or eventual, obvious or subtle, create an emotional wound or injury to the organism.

As I have though about loss I have envisioned a three-dimensional schema. The first dimension is twofold, representing gradual loss and sudden loss. The second dimension is fourfold, and represents the type of loss — a person, animal, object, idea. The third dimension is one of intensity and is best thought of as a continuum from slight loss to extreme loss. I want to explore these dimensions. Whereas gradual loss is itself a continuum of time, sudden loss is clearly distinct as a psychological experience. Allow me to clarify. Gradual losses are experienced over a period of time, be it years, months, weeks, days, or even shorter. But in any case, the person experiences a gradualness of the loss, or the warning of the loss over a period of time. For example, one may watch the decline of a home neighborhood over a period of years as population shifts and rezoning take their effect. Or, one may receive notice of condemnation of one's home property for the building of a new highway, the eviction date being several months hence. In each of these two cases there is a gradualness of the loss, either through a progressiveness of the loss or an advanced warning of the loss. With such gradualness of loss there may be an extended period of grieving, perhaps with periods of "time out" during which the person goes on about life as if the loss were not occurring, only to return to another episode in the overall grieving process. With prolonged gradual loss there may also be a wearing down and fatiguing of the grieved, the process which in Spanish in termed "cansar." When, on the other hand, the loss is sudden, there is a shock reaction. With shock there may be a period of disbelief or denial, and a feeling of numbness. As the shock subsides the other feelings of grief take over.

Turning, now, to the types of loss, the category of "person" includes all losses in relationship, some of which were mentioned above. The important thing to remember is that *any* relationship with another person that is subjectively felt can be lost, and with that loss grief can be experienced. "Animal" is an interesting category in that pets are treated in many respects like humans by their owners, but that private relationship may not be recognized by the outsider. And, obviously, the person and animal categories share the quality of being relationships with other life.

Relationships with nonliving objects can take on rich symbolic meaning and can be of considerable intensity. Whether the home neighborhood of the above example, a personal car, an old jacket, or a pocket knife handed down from one's father, the object may be cherished to a greater or lessor degree, and thereby become a source for the experience of loss.

The fourth category for loss, "ideas," contains several things. What is common among them is that they are nonmaterial entities with which one may relate. Oftentimes these relationships with things mentalistic are quite private, so outsiders may not recognize easily when a loss has taken place. By ideas I mean one's hopes, dreams, plans, and illusions. Whenever a hope is dashed, a dream disappears, a plan fails, or the bubble of illusion is burst by an undeniable prick of reality, a loss is sustained. As I write this a scene from my boyhood comes back vividly. I remember in fourth grade watching the boy who was believed by all of the other boys, as well as by himself, to be the fastest runner, stand in tears at the end of a race in which someone had outrun him. His myth had been shattered. From so simple an example as this, to complex examples of lifelong dreams, the losses are real and demand a proper grieving.

The third dimension of my schema is concerned with the magnitude or intensity of loss. The important thing to recognize about this dimension is that the experience of loss is highly subjective, so that what for one person might be only a slight loss, for another that loss might be devastating. The crucial factor is the degree of relationship felt. As the saying goes, you can't lose what you never had.

For clarity, a two-dimensional drawing of my schema appears in Figure 1:

The message of my three-dimensional schema is that loss comes in myriad form. The implication of that message is that the grieving process

Figure 1

SCHEMA OF LOSS

	Person	Animal	Object	Idea
Sudden				
Gradual				

which ensues is highly variable in its intensity, its duration, and its style. Although there is a set of feelings, as presented above, which are recognized as the feelings of mourning, there is not set pattern for grief.

Grieving, or as Freud called it, the "mourning labor," is the organism's natural healing process whereby the loss is acknowledged and the organism is made ready to go on with life, unaccompanied by that which was let go. The organism withdraws from the world, in grief, and into itself in order to feel keenly the loss and to access its meaning. Grief is a natural and powerful figure that can emerge with such clarity and vividness that all else is but a vague background. The everydayness of life has importance only as an irritant, distracting from the healing at hand. This process is to be respected. As Freud (1963) acknowledged, "we look upon any interference with it as inadvisable or even harmful" (p. 165).

Clearly, then, the role of the therapist is to facilitate the natural individualized process of grieving, and not to prevent it, interfere with it, or short-circuit it. There are two situations in which a therapist is of special help in grieving. One is the situation in which the person who has sustained loss seems unable to grieve. The other is the case of grief which seems to be going on too long.

When someone has obviously suffered a significant loss, and yet does not grieve, I think in terms of two dynamics which may be operating, singularly or together. The first is *pain phobia*. Perls (1969, 1975) identified the "phobic attitude" of the neurotic, and more specifically, the phobic attitude toward pain. Perls (1969) placed great emphasis on the phobic attitude, which he also termed the "avoidance" and the "flight from." In his words, "The enemy of development is the pain phobia — the unwillingness to do a tiny bit of suffering" (p. 56). In the case of deep grief, the suffering is more than "a tiny bit," of course. But, the point is that the avoidance of feeling pain is a way of trying of sidestep part of life. Losses demand grieving, a feeling of the loss, and a hurting with the loss in order to let go and move on with life. To refuse to do the hurting, to refuse to fully feel and express the sadness is to interrupt a natural organismic process and thereby create "unfinished business." I am struck with how often patients want me to take away the pain of their grief, to help them avoid the hurt and the tears. Sometimes they even believe that their sadness and their tears are evidence that they are neurotic. The pain phobia, the fear of natural psychological pain, is sometimes culturally supported and a part of the illusion that when one gets far enough along in therapy there will be no more pain. This is the "self-image actualization" myth. As Perls noted, nature has created pain in order to call attention to something important. In grief, attention is being called to the loss, the importance of the processing of that loss. By staying with the unpleasantness, rather than running from it, one can move through it and feel a completion of the process of grief.

The second dynamic which can prevent grieving fully is the "be strong" script. The wording varies, including such messages as "Don't be weak," "Don't cry," "Don't show your emotions," "Don't show you're hurt," and "Be a man." Messages such as these all have as their essential meaning, "you should be strong," and imply that to feel sad and to cry, and otherwise to express sadness, is a sign of weakness. In *The Body in Psychotherapy* (Smith, 1985, ch. 3) I described the process of taking in toxic script messages as follows:

> The treatment of the child by the parents, in general or in specific ways, encourages natural aliveness or discourages or even forbids it. During early development, most importantly the first five years or so, children are told not to express a certain feeling in a particular way, or not to express that

feeling at all, or not to feel that feeling, or not to get excited, or sometimes not even to have certain wants. These prohibitive messages may be expressed verbally or nonverbally. Due primarily to the profound dependence of the child on the parenting figures for its very survival, the prohibitive messages are "swallowed whole," introjected. Secondarily, the process of introjection is facilitated by the fact that the child has little life experience, relative to the parenting figures, against which to judge the prohibitive messages. During this phase of the socialization process, many of the introjected messages are bionegative, that is, they are socially arbitrary messages which do not support the child's aliveness. The bionegative message is, then, a Toxic Introject.

There are two components to the Toxic Introject. First, is the content, of the specific prohibition. Second, is the threat that if the Toxic Introject is not obeyed love will be denied. The threat is experienced as if something awful, terrible, even catastrophic will happen. An example is the message to a little boy, "Big boys don't cry. Don't be a sissy." The content of this message is, "You should not cry," and the threat is, "If you cry I won't love you any more." Such Toxic Introjects are usually maintained, unexamined and unchallenged, throughout one's life. The result is lifelong internal conflict between the natural urge for aliveness and the toxic, introjected message which calls for deadness. Once the toxic message has been introjected, the threat of loss of love for disobeying becomes a conditioned phobic belief in imminent catastrophe whenever the toxic message is not honored. The Toxic Introject carries a "should" or "should not" (the content) and a Catastrophic Expectation.

As an aside, I want to mention a couple of common phrases which carry the meaning of "Be strong." The existence of these as highly recognizable saying gives evidence for the pervasiveness of the "be strong" script in our culture. One phrase is "Chin up!" The other is to "Keep a stiff upper lip." The latter has been traced to John Easter in 1833 (Sperling, 1981). "What's the use of boohooin? Keep a stiff upper lip, no bones broke — don't I know?" (p. 28). The phrase "a stiff upper lip" has come to mean an unfeeling person.

Notice that both of these dynamics which prevent full grieving are based on phobic behavior. In one case there is a pain phobia, and in the other case there is a phobia of breaking an old toxic — script message. That latter phobia is what is otherwise termed the "catastrophic expectation."

The experience of loss sets up a state of tension. It is through grieving that this tension is relieved. Therefore, the absence of full grieving results in "unfinished business," an incompleted task. To the extent that the task of grieving is not complete the person suffering loss is left in a state of some degree of tension. It is a law of human nature that things don't just go away, and, contrary to the platitude, time does not heal all. What heals the wound of loss is grieving the loss. Grieving takes time, and that may be the source of the platitude. What is important, though, is what one is doing by way of mourning labor during the passage of time.

When grieving is avoided, the unfinished business remains forever. With effort the grief can be kept from awareness much of the time. But it is still there, the tension ready to break into awareness whenever the rigid vigil is not kept. The clinical evidence for this dynamic of unfinished business is compelling. A dramatic example from my own experience is a woman I worked with briefly several years ago. Her father had died twenty-some years before, and she had never grieved. In the workshop she told of how she had read comic books in the limousine on the way to the cemetery so as to keep herself away from the funeral experience and to appear to everyone as un-moved by her father's death. For all these years she had maintained her nongrieving position, of course having to rigidify her life and limit her expo-sure to reminders of "father" and of "death." In the workshop she asked for help in grieving, wanting to be able to expand her living beyond the narrowed limits which she had had to observe. My cotherapist and I created a casket from some pillows, and invited her to see her deceased father lying in state. As she imaged this scene she gradually began to weep. We encouraged her talking to him, her expressing her long-guarded feelings toward him. After a few minutes of talking to him and weeping, she exploded into deep wailing. Her crying continued for almost an hour, as we hold her. I had never before witnessed so dramatic an example of giving into the process of grieving after an extended period of the refusal to grieve.

Turning, now, to the second situation in which a therapist can be of use in the grief process, we find an undue prolongation of grieving. Whereas the absence of full grieving *creates* unfinished business, the prolonging of grieving *maintains* a condition of unfinished business. In the former case there is a refusal to fully enter into and experience the labor of mourning. The later case consists of a refusal to finish the work, to let go and move on with one's life.

There are, I believe, two dynamics which may extend the grieving period beyond what is natural. First, grief may feed an underlying depression. If one is characterologically disposed to depression, then the labor of mourning may serve to introduce the dysphoria and to set off a depressive episode. Since the symptoms of mourning match those of depression, except for the fall in self-esteem in the latter case, it is an easy transition for the predisposed person to use a loss as an entrée to depression. Tears of grief and tears of depression both are wet and salty.

The second dynamic which may extend the period of grieving is akin to the psychoanalytic concept of "secondary gain." If the labor of mourning is more exciting than the alternatives seen in one's life, then the mourning may go on indefinitely. Mourning labor has its own reason and dynamic, but secondarily, entering into the process may provide meaning to an otherwise drab existence. The increase in meaning may come from a sense of focus and importance of the mourning labor, as well as increased attention from others. So, one may make a fetish of one's grieving, and then be reluctant to allow it to come to completion.

Figure 2 summarizes these situations in which the natural process of grieving is diverted and therapeutic intervention is helpful.

Figure 2

THERAPEUTIC INTERVENTION IN GRIEVING

I. Absence of full grieving (Creates "unfinished business")

    A. Pain phobia

    B. "Be strong" script.

    C. "Be strong" script.

II. Undue prolongation of grieving (Maintains "unfinished business")

    A. Grief feeding underlying depression.

    B. Grief as a major source of meaning in life.

To emphasize the point again, grieving, appropriate to the loss experienced, is necessary for healthy living to go on. Without grieving, the person who has sustained loss is tied to the past by her or his unfinished business. As Perls (1947, 1969) wrote, "Mourning is a part of the resignation process, necessary if one is to overcome the clinging to the past. This process called 'mourning labour' is one of the most ingenious discoveries of Freud" (pp. 96-97). Interestingly, Perls observed that in the analysis of the retrospective character (the person obsessed with the past) there is always one distinct symptom — the suppression of crying. So, to suppress the labor of mourning is to invest in the past, and rob the present.

So what is the nature of grief? In Macbeth (IV. iii) Shakespeare offers us the observation, and warning:

> Give sorrow words; the grief that
> does not speak
> Whispers the o'er fraught heart and
> bids it break.

Not only is Shakespeare acknowledging the need for grieving, anticipating Freud's discussion of mourning labor and Perl's expressive methods, but he is calling attention to the "heaviness" of sorrow. Indeed, our word "grieve" derives from the Latin "gravare" meaning to burden, to oppress. That Latin verb relates to the adjective "gravis," or "heavy," from which we have evolved the word "gravity." So, we are informed etymologically that grief is heavy. It can burden and oppress with its gravity, and if not given words, as Shakespeare at once advises and warns, may break the heart. Allowing further etymological elucidation of grief, we can turn to the synonym "sorrow." Here we find the Middle English "sorwe" and the Anglo-Saxon "sorg" as roots, and a new meaning in Scottish and Irish use. In those countries "sorrow" also means the devil! Another dimension is added if we look at some names which involve the word "mourning." The "mourning widow" known also as the "mourning bride" is a garden plant having dark purple flowers. A purplish-brown wing is found on the butterfly known as the "mourning cloak." And, the "mourning warbler" has a breast of black. The darkness — purple, brown, black — earned each of these their "mourning" epithet. Those who bestowed the names recognized the relationship of darkness and grief, and by the same symbolic connection chose black as the non-color for the "mourning band" to be worn on the mourner's arm. Finally, there is the "mourning dove" which gives us a sound by which to understand the meaning of grief. Informed, then, by the sound, the color, and the logos, we know something of the nature of grief. Heavy, burdening, oppressive, grave. Brown, purple, black, dark. A sound which is low, and repeated in a slow rhythm, reaching deeply inside and pulling a sadness. An encounter with something from hell! So powerful can be the experience, that we can identify grief with God, and at the same time call upon Him. I base this on the fact of the use of the expletive "Good grief!" as a minced form of the oath "Good God!" (Espy, 1978).

I want to shift the focus, now, to the psychotherapeutic task of working with grief. Freud called professional attention to the necessity of the mourning labor; Perls offered the professional community some active methods for its facilitation. Building on Freud's observation, Perls recognized that loss without a grieving for that loss constitutes a situation of unfinished business. He then provided procedures for the completion of that process.

Basically, the Gestalt approach is to support grieving. This means, in any way needed, to facilitate the grieving process while frustrating any attempts to avoid it. (This includes the frustration of depression.) Gestalt is an active therapy, emphasizing organismic involvement.

To understand the reason for the Gestalt procedures requires a recognition of the components of grieving and of their relationships. Using the Contact/Withdrawal Model (Smith, 1979, 1985) I conceptualize the unit of grieving as follows:

Loss → Need to grieve → Organismic tension → Feeling sad → Action of crying → Relief

This unit of grieving, or grief cycle, can vary in intensity, frequency, and number of repetitions, depending on the degree of loss. In each case, however, the loss calls for grieving and that organismic need leads to a state of organismic tension or arousal. That state of tension is subjectively experienced as the emotion of sadness. The organismic action called forth by that emotion is crying. When the crying is sufficient to match the need, for that particular unit of grieving, there is a sense of relief or satisfaction. Some time may then pass during which the need to grieve again builds up to the point of once again being experienced.

Since the grief cycle requires awareness of the loss, awareness of the need to grieve, awareness and allowing of the tension or bodily arousal to build, awareness of sadness, and the activity of crying, the incompleteness of any of these decreases the amount of relief which can be experienced. So, the therapeutic focus is on any inadequacy of *awareness, arousal,* or *crying activity.*

In his classic article, "Saying Goodby," Stephen Tobin (1971, 1975) has described the use of the empty-chair dialogue in the Gestalt procedure of saying good-bye to someone not literally present. In addition to his description of the method, he has provided an instructional clinical transcript re-creating some of this work. I want to elaborate on the basic method outlined by Tobin.

The Gestalt procedure of saying good-bye is the same regardless of what is being grieved — a person, an animal, an inanimate object, or an idea. The basic guideline is to create a situation in which the patient can psychodramatically encounter the object of loss. (For heuristic purposes I will talk about a person as the object of loss.) So, I invite the patient to imagine the person sitting in the empty chair. Depending on how experienced the patient is in doing empty-chair work, I may do some preliminary work to increase the vividness of the image of the person. This can include the suggestion of seeing the person as clearly as possible, hearing that person say "hello," and even smelling that person, if smell had been a strong memory of that person. (Sometimes there are vivid memories of an odor associated with a person, such as a pipe-tobacco smoke, a perfume, or such.) Bringing the person into the here-and-now experience of the patient is the first step of the psychodrama.

When the person is experienced with an adequate degree of vividness, I move to the second step. I ask the patient to sit for a few moments and just see what it is like to be with the person. I may suggest that the patient feel whatever emotions arise.

The third step is to invite the patient to tell the person whatever he or she is feeling. This is what is sometimes stated in Gestalt therapy as the "no gossiping rule" (Levitsky & Perls, 1970). The idea is to *talk to* the person rather than to *talk about* the person. (A little experimenting with this is sufficient to demonstrate that talking to someone is far more emotionally impactful than talking about the person.) I invite the patient to say all he or she is thinking and feeling, as long as the thoughts are not avoidances of the here-and-now experience. There are three elements which are important in the expression: *appreciations, resentments,* and *regrets.* I encourage the full expression of each of these, and call attention to any element which has not been expressed spontaneously. Appreciations reflect the good memories and good feelings, the love for the person. On the other hand, resentments represent the unpleasant memories and bad feelings for the person, in extreme form, one's hatred. Regrets are the acknowledgment of things not being or not having been as one would like. A good, clean grieving seems to require the expression of all three. Otherwise, some piece of unfinished business remains.

The fourth step is making this empty chair monologue into an empty chair dialogue. This is done by inviting the patient to switch chairs, "be" the person, and respond to what the patient has said. This shuttling back and forth allows for amplification of the feelings, and a sense of completion and satisfaction. The timing of these switches is part of the artistry of an adept Gestalt therapist.

These, then, are the four steps in the Gestalt procedure for saying good-bye. I attend to the grief cycle during this saying good-bye, watching for any *avoidance of full awareness, avoidance of allowing the buildup of arousal,* or *avoidance of crying.* The points of avoidance are the points for therapeutic intervention. Often, the intervention needs only to be a calling attention to, or an encouragement of what is being avoided. Some examples are as follows: "Will you look at him when you say that?" "Stay with what you're experiencing." "Feel what you're feeling." "Tell him you know he isn't coming back." Such interventions focus on awareness. Since arousal is quelled by inadequate breathing, the avoidance of arousal may be dealt with by interventions such as: "Don't hold your breath." "Keep breathing." In order to frustrate the avoidance of crying, the therapist could say: "Let that out," "Let your tears come." "Let the sound out." "Make sound."

When simply calling attention to an avoidance, or verbally encouraging the flow of the grief cycle is not a potent enough intervention, my bias is to intervene with body work. Such work may be aimed at increasing awareness, increasing breathing, and in turn, arousal, or at softening muscular tensions which are inhibiting crying. The rationale and techniques of such body interventions are presented in detail in *The Body in Psychotherapy* (Smith, 1985).

I want to close with a quote that I take as an expression of wisdom and of hope. Hemingway (1970, p. 296) put the following words into the mouth of Thomas Hudson:

> You always feel better and you always get
> over your remorse. There's only one thing
> you don't get over and that is death.

~

RETROFLECTION: THE FORMS OF NON-ENACTMENT

When I was very young, three, perhaps four-years old, my older male cousins played a game with me. It must have looked simple, and as a brief impromptu game was never dignified with a name. The game consisted of one of my cousins taking hold of my arms just above my wrists, and lightly hitting me in the face with my own hands while playfully reproaching me with "Why are you hitting yourself?" or "Stop hitting yourself!" That game is really not as simple as it must look. As I remember, I usually laughed, being amused by the contradiction of hitting myself, but yet not hitting myself. Then, as the game sometimes continued beyond my amusement I would cry, not from pain, since I wasn't "hitting myself" hard, but from the frustration of not being in control of my own arms and hands. Even as that three or four-year old I experienced something very strange and intriguing. As I look back on that experience now, I see it as playing with retroflection; playing a game (although not always willingly) which, if totally real (it was only half real since I was "hitting myself" but I was also not hitting myself) would have been an instance of pathological retroflection. This was a case of play as an exploration of crazy living, perhaps a parody on something grownups were observed doing.

This was one of my introductions to retroflection, or more accurately, to one of the forms of retroflection, the turning of energy which is appropriately directed at the environment back toward one's self.

From: *The Gestalt Journal,* 9(1), 36-54 (1986).

The prefix "retro" is Latin for "back" or "backward." Add to this the Latin "flexus" (past participle of "flectere," to bend, to turn) and we have a word to signify "to bend or turn abruptly backward," "retroflex" The noun becomes "retroflexion" or "retroflection" In keeping with the spelling "retroflection" to designate the technical term, the word "retroflect" is the acceptable verb form.

In its earliest appearance in the Gestalt literature "Retroflection means that some function which originally is directed from the individual toward the world, changes its direction and is bent back toward the originator" (Perls, 1947, 1969a, p.p. 119-120). This implies a splitting of the self into a "doer" and part "done to." As Perls said, "A genuine retroflection is always based upon such a split personality and is composed of an active (A) and a passive (P) part" (Perls, 1947, 1969a, p. 220). In discussing this split, Perls (1969) alluded to Kierkegaard's writing on the relation of the self to the self. In his early writing, Perls (1947, 1969a) clarified that reflect actions are not retroflections.

Perls (1947, 1969a) saw self-hate, narcissism (self-love), and self-control as the three most important retroflections. In this statement, I see three *forms* of retroflection, and for conceptual clarity their differences have to be made explicit.

In the first instance, self-hate, the impulse to hurt is turned back on the self, clearly and simply in keeping with Perls' above stated definition of retroflection. The active part of the self chooses the passive part as the target of its aggression.

The second instance is different in that in self-love there are two healthy needs involved, the need to love and the need to be loved. As in the first instance of self-hate, the passive part of the self is the chosen target. In addition to this substitution of target, which leaves the need to love another unfulfilled, the passive part of the self doesn't get loved by another and this need, too, goes unfulfilled. Both active and passive parts of the self are substitutes from the perspective of the other part.

The third instance, self-control, involves a block or inhibition of action. The first two instances, self-hate and self-love, involved a substitution of target and a substitution of target and doer, respectively. But in self-control the appropriately active part of the self is held back and thus made passive (or relatively so).

These three instances of retroflection involve three different forms, as briefly delineated. The common core is the solipsism. In each instance of retroflection the self splits and engages itself rather than engaging the environment.

In order to clarify the forms of retroflection further I want to refer now to some other basic theoretical points of Gestalt therapy. The model I want to use is my version of the Contact/Withdrawal model (Smith, 1979; 1985).

The contact/withdrawal model is a model for describing and understanding psychobiological existence. It focuses on the rhythms of contacting the environment for the satisfaction of wants and withdrawing into the self for rest until dissatisfaction again arises and impels another cycle of contacting.

The starting point is the Want. The Want may be a true Need, something which is necessary for survival (food, air, water, a certain range of temperature, love, esteem, etc.), or it may be a Preference, what one would choose, given a choice of options any one of which would meet the need. Sometimes the Preference is simply what one would like, but there is no urgency to the underlying need. Several Wants may be in existence at any given moment, requiring a preferential ordering. A person then responds to the emergent Want which has become figural out of the army of background Wants.

With the emergence of a Want there is a state of physiological arousal, or tension, normally experienced as Excitement. The person has become biochemically mobilized to a state of higher energy. This heightened energy state is differentiated and subjectively experienced as an Emotion (i.e.,, affect, feeling).

The Emotion implies and calls forth an Action or movement of the energy into the musculoskeletal system. That Action must become an Interaction with someone or something in the environment in order for Satisfaction of the Want being served.

The "Contact Episode" consists of these several steps, and is followed by a natural organismic "Withdrawal Episode." The first half of the Contact Episode (Want $\rightarrow$ Excitement $\rightarrow$ Emotion) is in the realm of Awareness, i.e., being aware of what I want, being aware of my excitement (energy), and being aware of the emotion (feeling). This Awareness serves to focus my energy for the second or Expression (Action $\rightarrow$ Interaction $\rightarrow$ Satisfaction) half (actually Awareness + Expression of the Contact Episode). Thus, satisfying Contact involves both Awareness and Expression.

The steps in the Contact/Withdrawal cycle are cumulative, each step depending for its success on all of the previous steps. if any step is not allowed in full form, the proceeding steps will be less well formed and the ultimate Satisfaction will be diminished or missed completely. There are also feedback loops such that later steps may enhance earlier steps. For example, taking action may enhance the felt emotion, or if the action is not appropriate to the emotion the action may reveal to the person what the actual emotion would be if it were allowed. It's as if there were a reverberating wave which further enhances the previous steps as each new step is taken.

As long as these contact-withdrawal cycles emerge and recede smoothly, maintaining the organism and allowing for the meeting of the ultimate need — self- actualization — there is a state of psychobiological heath. Two types of problems can occur, however. One type of problem is the absence in the environment of the person or thing needed for the satisfaction of the want. This type of problem is not a psychological one, per se, but is a problem of politics, economics, technology, ecology, or such. The second type of problem, equally serious in its potential, is the psychological problem of stopping myself in my contact-withdrawal cycles short of satisfaction. A simple example: If I am in a desert with no water at all available, I cannot get my need for water satisfied and I will perish in time regardless of the level of my psychological functioning. If on the other hand, I have water but choose not to drink it because a voice inside speaking for my parents or subculture says I will burn in hell for drinking water not blessed by an appropriate priest, I will still perish. This is a psychological problem, obviously. I define *psychopathology as any pattern of habitual self-interruptions in the contact-withdrawal cycles.* These habitual self-interruptions tend to obscure the inner voice which speaks the wisdom of the organism and leads to cumulative self-alienation. (Smith, 1979, p. 47)

At each of the junctures between steps in the Contact/Withdrawal cycle there is the possibility of allowing the organismic flow, or of interrupting (see Figure 1.).

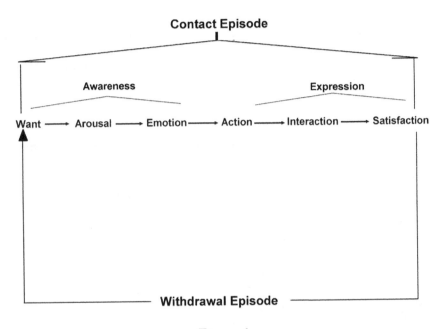

CONTACT/WITHDRAWAL MODEL

Figure 1

Such a self-interruption is a short-circuiting of the cycle and is therefore not the appropriate Withdrawal following Satisfaction, but a pseudo-withdrawal of avoidance. The pseudo-withdrawal can, then, involve avoidance of Awareness or avoidance of Expression, or avoidance of genuine Withdrawal. An avoidance can occur as a short circuit at any one of the seven arrows in Figure 1.

An avoidance of Awareness may focus on not knowing what I want (therefore staying in the realm of Withdrawal), or not experiencing my arousal (not experiencing Excitement), or not experiencing Emotion (not allowing the differentiation of excitement into a specific emotion). When the avoidance is at the juncture of Excitement → Emotion, the result is anxiety. Avoidance of Expression may focus on not taking Action (not allowing musculoskeletal movement), or not allowing the Action to be involved with the appropriate environmental target (not allowing interaction), or not allowing the interaction to be satisfying (not allowing Satisfaction). Finally, the avoidance may be of Withdrawal, which means staying in Contact beyond the point of Satisfaction and therefore feeling Revulsion. This is the "hanging on bite" (Perls, 1947, 1969a).

The question, then, is do I allow the natural flow in my energy process, or do I override the wisdom of my organism and interrupt my process with bionegative introjected messages? Any interruption of a Contact/Withdrawal Cycle means leaving a want unsatisfied, and thus the accumulation of "unfinished business."

An obvious question is "What is the purpose of self-interruptions of Contact/Withdrawal Cycles?"

During early developmental years children are often told not to express a certain feeling in a particular way, or not to express that feeling at all, or sometimes not to feel certain feelings, or sometimes not even to have certain wants. These prohibitive messages may be either verbal or nonverbal. Because of the profound dependency of the young child, and her/his lack of personal experience against which to compare the parental messages, the messages are "swallowed-whole," introjected. During this phase of the socialization process, many of these introjected messages are bionegative, that is, they are socially arbitrary messages which do not support the aliveness of the person. The bionegative message is, then, a "toxic introject." There are two aspects to the toxic introject. There is the content of the message and there is the threat that if the message is disobeyed love will be withdrawn. An example is the statement to a little boy, "Big boys don't cry. Don't be a sissy." The content message is, "You should not cry," and the threat is, "If you cry I won't love you." Toxic introjects such as these are usually maintained, unexamined and unchallenged, throughout one's life. This results in conflicts between natural psychobiological needs pressing for aliveness and the toxic introjected message which calls for deadness. After the toxic message has been introjected, the threat of withdrawal of love for disobeying becomes a conditioned phobic belief in imminent catastrophe any time the toxic message is not honored, The toxic introject carries, then, a "should" (or "should not") and a "catastrophic expectation." The greater the number and severity of the toxic introjects, the more phobic is the person's life and the less aliveness is allowed. Given the presence of toxic introjects, and therefore the internal voice which says, "You should not," and the expectation that if I disobey then a catastrophe will ensue, my "safety" lies in my limiting my aliveness. The self-interruption of a contact-withdrawal cycle is the very essence of limiting aliveness. Which kinds of contact-withdrawal cycles (based on which needs or preferences) I decide to interrupt, and at which of the seven decision points I choose to enact the interruption, is dictated by the details of the content of the toxic introject. (Smith. 1979, pp. 49-50)

At this point we have examined the normal psychobiological process of Contact/Withdrawal Cycles and introduced an explanation of the decision to interrupt the process. Once this relationship of toxic introjects (with their prohibition and their threat of catastrophe if the prohibition is not followed) to the process of contact and withdrawal is understood, the logical next question is "how?" In other words, once I make the organismic choice to self-interrupt my flow of energy and limit my aliveness, how can I do it?

The "how" of self-interruption involves the use of one or more of three related mechanisms. The mechanisms can interact in a manner such as to enhance one another. Since satisfying contact requires arousal of the organism (Excitement), focusing of that aroused energy (Awareness), and the enactment with that energy (Action, interaction guided by continuing awareness), the three mechanisms of interruption operate on these three aspects of Contact. What this means is that the voice of the toxic introject can be honored through a quelling of Excitement, a clouding of Awareness, or a non-enactment of the energy. What usually happens is a synergistic interaction of all three mechanisms. The resulting interference can be either a complete stoppage of energy flow or just a diminishing of that flow. The Polsters (1973) have suggested the term "block" for a complete stoppage of the impulse and "inhibition" for the diminished expression.

Let's look at the three mechanisms of self-interruption in more detail. The primary method for blocking or inhibiting Excitement is to limit breathing. By tightening the diaphragm and the intercostal muscles, specifically, and moving the locus of breathing into the upper portion of the lungs, the amount of oxygen provided for the metabolic process is greatly restricted. The result is a diminished level of energy. This method of blocking or inhibiting Excitement is a reflect action in response to fear, in the neurotic context of self-interruption, the fear elicited by the voice of the toxic introject, Several factors which one can build into one's lifestyle serve as adjuncts to the primary method. They include smoking, use of drugs and alcohol, poor nutrition, lack of exercise, lack of sufficient sleep and rest, and lack of play.

The second focus in self-interruption of Contact/Withdrawal Cycles is on the clouding of Awareness. No matter how energized the organism is, without the focus which Awareness provides (What do I want; What am I feeling; What do I have to do to get what I want; With whom or with what do I have to do what I have to do?), the likelihood of Satisfaction is nil. The specific mechanisms for clouding awareness include introjection, projection, confluence, deflection, and desensitization. In the case of the first three, confusion is created. In introjection I think something is mine when it is yours. Projection is the reverse, in that I attribute something to you which in fact is mine. Confluence involves a blurring of ego boundary such that what is mine I think is ours. As Perls (1973, p. 40-41) put it, "The introjector does as others would like him to do, the projector does unto others what he accuses them of doing to him, the man in pathological confluence doesn't know who is doing what to whom . . . " In the case of deflection and desensitization there is a dulling of Awareness. "Deflection is a maneuver for turning aside from direct contact with another person . . . by circumlocution, by excessive language, by laughing off what one says, by not looking at the person one is talking to, by being abstract rather than specific, by not getting the point, by coming up with bad examples or none at all, by politeness instead of directness, by stereotyped language instead of original language, by substituting mild emotions for intense ones, by talking about the past when the present is more relevant, by talking about rather than talking to, and by shrugging off the importance of what one has just said" (Polster and Polster, 1973, p. 89). "Desensitization is the sensory analog to motoric retroflection. Scotomata, visual blurring, chronic 'not hearing': sensory dullness, frigidity, etc. . . . " (Enright, 1970, p. 112). I suggest a reading of Perls, the Polsters, and Enright on these mechanisms which so effectively confuse and dull.

The third focus in the self-interruption of Contact/Withdrawal Cycles is the enactment, or the Action → Interaction sequence. The specific mechanisms are retroflections. So, in the terms of the above Contact/Withdrawal model, we can say: *Retroflection refers to the mechanisms which block or inhibit energy flow specifically at the points of Action or of Interaction in the Contact/Withdrawal Cycle.*

And now to the heart of the present writing, retroflection.

Retroflected Action

One of the forms of retroflection involves blocking or inhibiting action. This corresponds to what Perls (1947, 1969a) called "self-control." The juncture between the awareness portion and the expression portion of the contact/withdrawal cycle is of special interest because it involves the movement of energy into the musculoskeletal system. During the awareness portion most of the energy is in the vegetative system, but with the movement into the expression portion, the voluntary muscles become the main loci of energy. One retroflective task, then is to diminish or totally prevent muscular movement. This task falls under the rubric of what most people term self-control. As Perls (1947, 1969a) wrote, most people understand self-control to mean repression of spontaneous needs and the compulsion to do things without being interested in doing them. Such repression of spontaneous needs is the very perversion of self-control as a holding back in a situation where there is real danger in moving ahead.

It is exactly this form of retroflection to which Enright (1970, p. 112) was referring when he wrote, "Retroflection describes the general process of negating, holding back, or balancing the impulse tension by additional, opposing sensorimotor tension. . . . Since the net result of all this cancelled-out muscular tension is zero — no overt movement — there is no particular increase in activity at the contact boundary . . ." Enright (p. 112) went on to point out that "Reich's 'character armor' is chronic retroflection."

Perls (1947, 1969a, p. 229) had this to say about this action- deadening form of retroflection: "We repress vital functions (negative energy, as Reich calls their sum) by muscular contractions. The civil war raging in the neurotic organism is mostly waged between the motoric system and unaccepted organismic energies which strive for expression and gratification. The motoric system has to a great extent lost its function as a working, active, world-bound system and, by retroflection, has become the jailer rather than the assistant of important biological needs. Every dissolved symptom means setting free both policeman and the prisoner — motoric and 'vegetative' energies — for the common struggle of life."

Perls (and in turn, all Gestalt therapists) was strongly influenced by Reich. There are numerous points which Pals. clearly learned from Reich and adopted, sometimes with significant further theoretical or procedural development and elaboration (Smith, 1975, 1976). Perhaps Reich's major contribution to psychotherapy, and in turn to Gestalt therapy, was his focus on the body. Perls (1969b) credits Reich with discovering the "muscular armor" and thus introducing the notion of resistances as functions of the total organism (as opposed to mental events only). And, this concept of muscular armor gets translated in Gestalt theory into retroflection (of the form presently being discussed, retroflection as blocked or inhibited action).

Let's look at Reich's notion of muscular armor which predate the "retroflection" of Gestalt therapy. To begin, Reich believed that the neurotic solution of the child's chronic conflict between instinctual demands and counter social demands from the parents and other representatives of the society is brought about through a generalized alteration in functioning which ultimately crystallizes into a neurotic "character" structure. Character, then, is a narcissistic protective mechanism formed for protection against actual external danger, and retained for protection against internal instinctual danger. One aspect of the character is the "armor," or muscular rigidities which Reich (1949, p. 341) referred to as ". . . chronically fixed *muscular attitudes!"*

In Reich's (1949, p. 342) words, "The ego, the exposed part of the personality, under the continued influence of the conflict between libidinal need and threatening outer world, acquires a certain rigidity, a chronic, automatically functioning mode of reaction, that which is called 'character.' It is as if the affective personality put on an armor, a rigid shell on which the knocks from the outer world as well as the inner demands rebound." "Basically, emotion is an expressive plasmatic motion" (Reich, 1949, p. 358). And "Chronic muscular hypertension represents an inhibition of every kind of excitation" (Reich, 1949, p. 347).

The presence of this form of retroflection can be recognized by observing the body. In mild degree, the retroflection is physically manifested in a holding back, so that movement toward the environment is weakened, diminished, or awkward. This weakness of approach or awkwardness comes from the muscular ambivalence, the interplay of simultaneous reaching out and holding back. In moderate degree, this form of retroflection can be seen in tightness or stiffness of the person in certain circumstances. "In retroflection, the person tightens a part of himself, rather than using that part to express a feeling in the direction of other people" (Zinker, 1977, p. 26). In severe degree, this form of retroflection is a true muscular armor, the tightness is chronic and not limited to selected circumstances. ". . . in the case of neurotic armoring, the muscular rigidity is chronic and automatic" (Reich, 1949, p. 349). Being able to recognize retroflected action depends on one's observational skills. In order to highlight the retroflected action, the therapist may request the patient to perform certain specified movements or assume particular postures. An example would be to use a Bioenergetics stress posture (Lowen and Lowen, 1977) to make body stiffness or body armor more obvious.

Retroflected action, in its three degrees, may be revealed by the patient in the form of reported body phenomena. Enright (1970, p. 112) suggested that, ". . . perhaps, since there is increased activity at the points of muscular opposition, awareness may develop there as pain or discomfort." Consistent with this suggestion Reich (1949, p. 389) believed ". . . inhibited pleasure turns into rage, and inhibited rage into muscular spasms." And, similarly, Zinker (1977, p. 103) reported "The retroflector usually suffers physical (muscular-skeletal) symptoms which show where the energy is frozen." A working hypothesis of this view was given by Baumgardner (1975,

p. 16), "... any discomfort not induced by disease or trauma is indicative of and the result of unexpressed feeling."

There are, of course, degrees of severity of discomfort which the retroflecting patient may report. This is reflected in the following statement. "The end result of such censoring, whether recognized or not, is invariably a more or less psychosomatic dysfunction: impairment of powers of orientation or manipulation, ache, weakness, or even degeneration of tissues" (Perls, Hefferline, and Goodman, 1951, p. 162). Corresponding to the three degrees of retroflected action which I mentioned above, I am hypothesizing the following as the most probable body phenomena which the patient would report. On a continuum of increasing severity and chronicity:

(1) Weak or awkward action — Weakness, clumsiness, or hot spots. (Hot spots suggest the production of high energy in a body area without its release, and therefore conversion into static heat.)
(2) Body stiffness or tightness — Stiffness, painful areas, or cold spots. (Pain follows from the chronic tensing of muscles either as muscle fatigue or cramping. Cold spots result from a cutting off of blood supply or energy flow.)
(3) Body armor — Aches, numbness, or symptoms from tissue degeneration, e.g., the burning pain of a stomach ulcer. (With the extreme chronicity of body armor, chronic aching may be experienced in muscles, joints, or viscera. In time this may evolve into numbness. The symptoms of degenerative disease are, of course, widely varied depending on the particular organ or organ system affected.)

Not only are the physical phenomena listed with the levels of retroflected action my hypotheses, bur the allusion to mechanisms for the phenomena are hypotheses at this time. These hypotheses are consistent with my clinical experience and with the observations of others. An example of this is in Gestalt Therapy (Perls, Hefferline, and Goodman, 1951) on pages 177 and 188 in which the authors state that numbness, fogginess, or nothingness (blind spots or scotomata) are more severe than just the feeling of tightness. Another point of clarification is that the armor involves segments of the body, not just a particular muscle or muscle group. The segments, then, are functional units which include viscera. As Reich (1949, p. 371) stated this himself, "Armor segments, then, comprise those organs and muscle groups which are in functional contact with each other, which can induce each other to participate in expressive movement."

The key physiological mechanism for retroflecting action is the antagonistic action of muscles. Action can be frozen by using the antagonist to counter and balance the muscle which would be the prime mover for the action. More accurately, several antagonists would work in symphony to oppose the prime mover, and its synergistic and fixation muscles. Even though the action is stopped or diminished, work is being performed, with all of its physiological requirements. That is, the demand for oxygen and nutrients to the involved muscles is increased, as is the need for carrying away waste products. So, even with retroflected action, an increased demand is made on the cardiovascular system, the lymph system, the respiratory system, the endocrine system, and so on. At the same time, the normal movement which correlates with this increased demand on the systems is absent. A very unnatural state is created when this is the chronic state of the organism. The precise physiological mechanisms for various psychosomatic problems are not well known. Even so, this superficial view holds some considerable cogency. And, as Reich demonstrated clinically, body armor involves body segments which include visceral tissue as well as voluntary muscles.

One particular physiological mechanism which was discovered relatively recently (reported in 1974) and which may he involved in retroflected action is that of "reactive muscles." In a reactive muscle (Walther, 1976), there is weakness following the contraction of another muscle. What this means is that a strong healthy muscle may become temporarily dramatically weakened after some simple activity. What is believed to happen is that the proprioceptors associated with the first muscle get "set" incorrectly as result of trauma. The resulting incorrect information from these causes inhibition to the second or reactive muscle when it is not needed. So each time the muscle with the problem proprioceptors is used, the result is a dysfunction in the reactive muscle. This reactive weakness lasts for 20 or 30 seconds. Frequently the reactive muscle is an antagonist or works in some synergistic way with the muscle which has the involved proprioceptors. I hypothesize that the reactive muscle phenomenon is sometimes involved in the "weak or awkward" level of retroflected action.

In addition to observation of the patient's body structure, posture, and style of movement, and the patient's self-reports of body phenomena, there is a third clue to retroflected action. That is a verbal clue, the use of the reflexive personal pronoun. Examples are phrases such as stopped myself, held myself back, contained myself, quieted myself, restrained myself. (Although such phrases clearly bespeak retroflection, they may specifically be clues to types of retroflection other than retroflected action. This will become clear with the material that follows.)

Retroflected Interaction

In addition to retroflection of *action*, there are two more forms of retroflection, both involving the blocking or *interaction*. Earlier, I mentioned that Perls (1947, 1969a) saw self-hate, narcissism (self-love), and self-control as the three most important retroflections, and that these can be seen as three forms of retroflection. "Self-control" corresponds to retroflection of action as discussed above. In the following I want to explicate the two forms of retroflected interaction which correspond to Perls' "self-hate" and narcissism.

In both self-hate and self-love action is taken, The problem is that the movement from action into interaction goes awry, so that full organismic satisfaction is not possible. As Perls (1947, 1969a, p. 118) stated very early in his writing, "Aggression is at least as much object-bound as sex, and it can in the same way as love (in narcissism or in masturbation) have the 'Self' as object. They both may become 'retroflected.' " Perls (1947, 1969a) clearly sees self-hate as the most dangerous of retroflections,

The essence of retroflected interaction is the absence of any environmental object. A clear statement of this was made by the Polsters (1973, p. 71): "The *retroflector* abandons any attempt to influence his environment by becoming a separate and self-sufficient unit, reinvesting his energy back into an exclusively intrapersonal system and severely restricting the traffic between himself and the environment." In speaking of this type of retroflector, Perls, Hefferline, and Goodman (1951, p. 146) stated that, "He stops directing various energies outward in attempts to manipulate and bring about changes in the environment that will satisfy his needs; instead he redirects activity inward and *substitutes himself in place of the environment* as the target of behavior. To the extent that he does this, he splits his personality into 'doer' and 'done to!'"

Upon closer examination it becomes clear that this type of retroflection, retroflection of interaction, consists of two different forms. Early in his writing Perls made this explicit. Following a discussion of retroflected anger, Perls, Hefferline, and Goodman (1951, p. 150) noted, "Retroflections also include what one *wanted from* others but was unsuccessful in obtaining, with the outcome that now, for want of anyone else to do it, one gives it to himself."

The Polsters (1973, p. 82) were also explicit in distinguishing these two forms of retroflected interaction: "Retroflection is a hermaphroditic function wherein the individual turns back against himself what he would like *to do to someone else,* or does to himself what he would like *someone else to do to him.*"

In the latter form, wherein someone does to himself what he would like someone else to do to him, the paradigm content is love. This can be recognized verbally by self-complimenting or statements of liking or loving one's self. The physical actions include self-holding, self-patting, self-stroking, self-preening, and masturbation. (Masturbation can also be carried out as a self-rape, in which case it becomes doing to oneself what one would like to do to another — an act of aggression, not love.) The mythical representation of this form of retroflection is, of course, Narcissus. And the curse, as stated by Nemesis, goddess of righteous anger, is, "May he who loves not others love himself" (Hamilton, 1942, p. 88). Two elements are involved in retroflected love, as mentioned earlier. First is the impulse to love (the "doer" role), and second is the need to be loved (the "done to" role). By making the self the target, the "doer" fails to have the experience of loving another, and the "done to" fails to have the experience of being loved by another. The problem lies in the fact that "doer" and "done to" are only two roles played by one self.

The other type of retroflected interaction, or third form of retroflection, is the doing to oneself what one would like to do to another. The paradigm content is anger (self-hate). This can be recognized in the verbal realm by such statements as "I hate myself," "I don't like myself," "I can't stand myself," "I'm mad at myself," or "I could kick myself." More subtle than these phrases using the reflexive pronoun are the various statements which are derogatory of one's self. Examples are "I'm so dumb," "I'm so clumsy," "Dumb me," "What a klutz," and so forth. Self-hate, or retroflected anger can be identified by any act of hurting one's self: scratching one's self, hitting one's self, biting one's self, kicking one's self, cutting one's self, and so on. Often these acts of retroflected anger are performed in a diminished way and as such do not cause much pain or damage. If, however, the biting of one's lip or pounding of one's fist on one's leg is exaggerated, the meaning becomes obvious. Perls, Hefferline and Goodman (1951, p. 167) have suggested that "Repeated mistakes or acts of clumsiness are often retroflected annoyance."

This third form of retroflection can be seen in a way as a case of mistaken identity. The act may be an appropriate expression, but the substitution of the self for the other as target prevents the energy from being inter-active. An example which Perls (1947, 1969a, p. 120) offered is the following: "If a girl, disappointed by her lover, kills 'herself' she does so because her wish to kill him is retroflected by the will of her conscience. Suicide is a substitute for homicide or murder." The self becomes the substituted target, for it is always available and often seems far safer than the appropriate target. And so, in retroflection "He literally becomes his own worst enemy" (Perls, 1973, p. 41). A common result of retroflecting aggression is the experience of depression (Naranjo, 1980). To summarize, I offer Figure 2, a Typology of Retroflection.

Figure 2

TYPOLOGY OF RETROFLECTION

I. Retroflected Action

Continuum of
Increasing
Severity
and Chronicity

A. Weak or awkward action (possible hot body areas).

B. Body stiffness or tightness (possible pains, cold body areas).

C. Body armor (possible body aches, numb areas, or serious disruptions of normal body processes).

II. Retroflected Interaction

A. Do to self what self would like other to do to self.

B. Do to self what self would like to do to other.

Retroflection refers to the mechanisms of blocking or inhibiting energy flow at the point of body action or body interaction with the environment.

Each of the three forms of retroflection can be manifested in degrees. The first two (retroflected action and retroflected interaction of the form: Do to self what one would like other to do to self) even have a normal or biopositive occurrence. In the case of retroflected action, the biopositive manifestation is appropriate self-restraint. "Retroflection is healthy behavior when it constitutes holding back for the sake of caution in a situation of genuine danger" (Perls, Hefferline, and Goodman, 1951, p. 212). An elaboration of this point is offered by Perls, Hefferline, and Goodman (1951, p. 455): "Normally, retroflection is the process of reforming oneself, for instance correcting the impractical approach or reconsidering the possibilities of the emotion, making a readjustment as the grounds for further actions And more generally, any act of deliberate self-control during a difficult engagement is retroflection." And, finally, Perls, Hefferline, and Goodman (1951, p. 147) stated that "In some situations holding back is necessary, even life-saving . . . The important question is whether or not the person has *rational grounds* for presently choking off behavior in given circumstances?"

"Doing to oneself what one would like another to do to one" also can be manifested as biopositive. In healthy development the person learns to take over many of the functions which previously were done by the parents. So, in a sense, self-parenting is the appropriate level of this form of retroflection. Perls, Hefferline, and Goodman (1951, p. 150) addressed this as follows: "This, of course, is healthy, provided it does not include trying to gratify for oneself what are genuinely interpersonal needs." At times the need is present and the other person is not. At such times self-loving, self-stroking, and such self-attentions are appropriate and second preferences. Zinker (1977, p. 103) wrote insightfully about the positive and negative sides: "The price he pays — among other things — is that of using his own energy rather than being replenished by another person. His rewards are independence, self-reliance, doing better for himself than another can, privacy, and the development of his individual capacities and talents."

A recognition of the positive level of this form of retroflection is expressed in the title of Schiffman's (1971) book, *Gestalt Self Therapy*. A little thought will reveal many positive retroflections. These can be summarized and subsumed under a key Gestalt concept, that of "self-support!"

The third form of retroflection, doing to oneself what one would like to do to another seems limited to bionegative expressions. Perhaps with some considerable stretching of the mind a biopositive expression could be imagined.

The key element that defines an instance of the first two forms of retroflection as bionegative or pathological is the quality of avoidance. Avoidance of action or of interaction, as opposed to chosen restraint, is pathological. Stated in another way, "It is only when the retroflection is habitual, chronic, out of control, that it is pathological . . . " (Perls, Hefferline, and Goodman, 1951, p. 147). The result, as interpreted by the Polsters (1973, p. 84) is that "The natural rhythm between spontaneity and self-observation loses out and the loss of this rhythm divides man into self-impeding forces."

Some comparisons can be made of the three forms of retroflection. Of the three forms, retroflection of action is the most primitive. It is the most primitive in the sense that it precedes the other two forms of retroflection in the contact/withdrawal cycle. Of the three forms, retroflection of action also makes the most direct contribution to psychosomatic disorders. To use a more current term, it is retroflection of action that is a key to stress related, degenerative diseases. Reich was so keenly aware of this. ". . . the muscular armor fulfills the same function in the physiological behavior as does contactlessness and superficiality in the characterological and psychic behavior" (Reich, 1949, p. 352). "This armor makes the individual less sensitive to unpleasure but it also reduces his libidinal and aggressive motility, and, with that, his capacity for pleasure and achievement" (Reich, 1949, p. 342). The Gestalt version of this view was stated succinctly by Perls (1975, p. 98): "I believe all symptoms are a stagnation or condensation of energy or, as I call it, the excitement of the organism!"

Just as potentially lethal, *and* much less subtle in its drama is "doing to oneself what one would like to do to another." In the extreme there is self-flagellation, self-mutilation, suicide (self-murder). As I stated earlier, I see this form of retroflection as unique in having no biopositive form.

Life implies enactment. And, in the words of Black (*The Marriage of Heaven and Hell*), "He who desires but acts not, breeds pestilence."

~

ON MONOMANIA

SUMMARY. "Monomania," defined as an extreme and passionate interest or enthusiasm for some one thing, is explored as the healthy flip-side of pathological obsession. It is recognized for its contribution to two of the hallmarks of aliveness — excitement and growth. The parameters of monomania are delineated and its dynamics presented.

My purpose herein is to explore a rather neglected sector of a vast territory, that of obsession. The major part of that territory has been extensively explored and mapped. The names used in the professional literature include obsession, obsessional character, obsessional neurosis. The official psychiatric nosology has evolved, so that the terms that are most familiar to one may depend on which Diagnostic and Statistical Manual was current at the time of one's basic training. The first *Diagnostic and Statistical Manual: Mental Disorders* (DSM) (American Psychiatric Association) introduced in 1952, listed "Obsessive compulsive reaction" as one of the "Psychoneurotic Disorders" and "Compulsive personality" as one of the "trait disturbances" which come under the heading of "Personality Disorders." The definitions are important for a later point which I will make, so I quote as follows:

Obsessive compulsive reaction.
In this reaction the anxiety is associated with the persistence of unwanted ideas and of repetitive impulses to perform acts which may be considered morbid by the patient. The patient

---

From: *The Psychotherapy Patient*, 3(2), 73-83 (1986).

himself may regard his ideas and behavior as unreasonable, but nevertheless is compelled to carry out his rituals. (p. 33)

Compulsive personality
Such individuals are characterized by chronic, excessive, or obsessive concern with adherence to standards of conscience or of conformity. They may be overinhibited, overconscientious, and may have an inordinate capacity for work. Typically they are rigid and lack a normal capacity for relaxation. (p. 37)

As of the publication of the DSM-II (American Psychiatric Association) in 1968, the term "Obsessive compulsive neurosis" was listed under "Neuroses," and "Obsessive compulsive" under "Personality Disorders and certain Other Non-Psychotic Mental Disorders." It is indicated that "Obsessive compulsive personality" is equivalent to the term "Anankastic personality," which was used in the Eighth Revision of the International Classification of Diseases. Again, the definitions:

Obsessive compulsive neurosis
This disorder is characterized by the persistent intrusion of unwanted thoughts, urges, or actions that the patient is unable to stop. The thoughts may consist of single words or ideas, ruminations, or trains of thought often perceived by the patient as nonsensical. The actions vary from simple movements to complex rituals such as repeated handwashing. Anxiety and distress are often present either if the patient is prevented from completing his compulsive ritual or if he is concerned about being unable to control himself. (p. 40)

Obsessive compulsive personality
(Anankastic personality)
This behavior pattern is characterized by excessive concern with conformity and adherence to standards of conscience. Consequently, individuals in this group may be rigid, overinhibited, over-conscientious, over-dutiful, and unable to relax easily. (p. 43)

With the advent of the DSM-III (American Psychiatric Association) in 1980, "Obsessive compulsive disorder (or Obsessive compulsive neurosis)" is under the heading of "Anxiety Disorders," and is diagnosed on Axis I.

"Compulsive" is under the category "Personality Disorders" and is coded on Axis II. (Axis I is for "more florid disorders.") The DSM-III gives much longer definitions than are given in the earlier DSMs, and, in addition, introduces diagnostic criteria. I want to quote, in part, the criteria:

> *Obsessions:* recurrent, persistent ideas, thoughts, images, or impulses that are ego-dystonic, i.e., they are not experienced as voluntarily produced, but rather as thoughts that invade consciousness and are experienced as senseless or repugnant. Attempts are made to ignore or suppress them.

> *Compulsions:* repetitive and seemingly purposeful behaviors that are performed according to certain rules or in a stereotyped fashion. The behavior is not an end in itself, but is designed to produce or prevent some future event or situation. However, either the activity is not connected in a realistic way with what it is designed to produce or prevent, or may be clearly excessive. The act is performed with a sense of subjective compulsion coupled with a desire to resist the compulsion (at least initially). The individual generally recognizes the senselessness of the behavior . . . and does not derive pleasure from carrying out the activity, although it provides a release of tension. (p. 235)

> *Compulsive Personality Disorder:*
> Restricted ability to express warm and tender emotions, e.g., the individual is unduly conventional, serious and formal, and stingy . . . perfectionism that interferes with the ability to grasp "the big picture," e.g., preoccupation with trivial details, rules, order, organization, schedules, and lists . . . insistence that others submit to his or her way of doing things, and lack of awareness of the feelings elicited by this behavior . . . excessive devotion to work and productivity to the exclusion of pleasure and the value of interpersonal relationships . . . indecisiveness. (pp. 327-328)

The point I want to make from all of this is that for the past thirty-some years the term "obsession" has been linked with the realm of pathology. In point of fact, the use of obsession and its adjectival form have been associated with neurosis from Freud's time. In fact, two of Freud's classic works,

The Ego and the Id (1923/1961) and *Inhibitions, Symptoms and Anxiety* (1926) were written with obsessional neurosis in mind. In the latter, Freud wrote that "Obsessional neurosis is unquestionably the most interesting and repaying subject of analytic research" (Rycroft, 1968, p. 104). In addition, in the pre-1930 psychoanalytic literature there was already reference to the "compulsive character."

There is an abundance of material on obsession qua obsessive-compulsive neurosis and character. As suggested by what I have written, above, the topic has been central to much of the psychoanalytic literature. In addition, it is discussed at great length in the non-psychoanalytic literature, from Gestalt therapy to behavior modification. Perhaps the most ambitious handling of this topic is Leon Salzman's (1968) *The Obsessive Personality.*

Considering the plethora of material on morbid obsession, I turn to a caveat written years ago by Walter Klopfer. Klopfer warned of the "maladjustment bias," the act of looking at a phenomenon with a bias of seeing only the negative or of overemphasizing the negative. Timothy Leary offered essentially the same caveat against what he termed the "pathology error." Informed by Klopfer and Leary of the danger of over-interpreting the maladjustive or pathological aspect of a phenomenon, I want to explore the positive aspect of obsession. Just as demonstrated in the yin-yang symbol where the whole contains both dark and light, and the dark contains light and the light contains dark, a human phenomenon may contain both pathology and health. And, in every expression of pathology there is some health; in every healthy expression, some pathology.

Another way to look at this relationship between maladjustment and adjustment is through a model suggested by Andras Angyal, the "theory of universal ambiguity" (Smith, 1976). Angyal suggested that the personality has a dual organization, much like the ambiguous figures used in studies of visual perception. Just as one can look at the well-known ambiguous figure of the vase and faces and clearly see a vase, or see two faces in profile, one can look at a personality and clearly see the aspect of maladjustment or the aspect of adjustment. Both are consensually valid perceptions, with neither invalidating in other.

If we apply the model of the yin-yang or Angyal's theory of universal ambiguity to the phenomenon of obsession, one thing that becomes apparent is that the weight of perception is on the side of pathology or maladjustment. The emphasis is on obsession as a symptom or neurosis or as a hallmark of a pathological character structure.

But, what of the other aspect of obsession? It is this neglected sector of the territory that I want to explore. I chose the word "monomania" to label this terrain. Monomania has the advantage of being an obsolete term, and therefore not well known. It also reflects a degree of recognition of the point

I am making about the positive side of obsession. The Webster definitions are two, the second being "a mental disorder characterized by irrationality on one subject." The first, however, is more benign: "an excessive interest in or enthusiasm for some one thing; a craze." To label an interest or enthusiasm "excessive" is subjective and even puts the judgment in the realm of personal preference in many cases.

Note that the several DSM, DSM-II, and DSM-III definitions I gave above are laced with such phrases as "unwanted ideas," "acts which may be considered morbid by the patient," "patient himself may regard . . . as unreasonable," "unwanted thoughts, urges, or actions," "ego-dystonic," "experienced as senseless or repugnant," "desire to resist," and "does not derive pleasure from carrying out the activity." Those phrases describe the region of obsession that is widely researched and widely discussed in the literature, but not neglected sector that I propose we call monomania.

Monomania is an extreme and passionate interest or enthusiasm for some one thing. As such, the monomania becomes the focus of one's passion. With this focus of passion comes a heightened sense of aliveness and a craving for greater aliveness. So, there is no sense of those negative experiences suggested by the phrases used to describe the neurotic obsession. Instead, the monomaniacal urge is experienced as wanted, wholesome, ego-syntonic, and pleasurable. But, even these words are too mild. In monomania is heightened aliveness, passion, even ecstasy.

By its ineffable nature, monomania is misunderstood by the outsiders, those not themselves possessed. And, so the person is called crazed. Crazed, yes, but crazed as the man described by Zorba thusly —

A man needs a little madness, or else . . . he never dares cut the rope and be free.

And, therein, lies the paradox. To be free is to be possessed, but possessed by one's passion. Possessed by one's passion is the definition of monomania. "*Poco loco, sl, poco loco.*" Not to be possessed is to be dispirited!

I will rein in at this point and find calm in scholarly reference. Notice in the above the implied relationship between obsession and possession. Henri Ellenberge (1970), in exploring the ancestry of dynamic psychotherapy, has written of possession. Sprit intrusion, or possession, is one of the disease theories found in many primitive cultures. Claude Lévi-Strauss, as credited by Ellenberger, has emphasized quite forcefully the basic identity between certain aspects of primitive medicine and concepts of current dynamic psychiatry. Possession is one such example.

Let us delve into the theory of possession to see what insights that may make possible concerning the obsessed patient. According to this theory, evil spirits may penetrate the patient's body, thus taking possession of it. I note the connection, already, to the statement that may be made about the obsessed person possessed by her or his passion: "He is not quite himself," or "She is not quite herself." But who, then?

Two different types of possession are recognized in some cultures: somnambulic and lucid. In the former the individual loses consciousness during the possession and remembers nothing of it following the episode. In the later case, lucid possession, the individual remains aware of self, but with a spirit within his own spirit. Interestingly, in Catholic theology, this distinction is kept, with the terms being "possession" and "obsession," respectively (Ellenberger, 1970).

Monomania, then, bears resemblance to lucid possession, wherein the person in question maintains full sense of self, and feels the lively "spirit" within. With monomania there is often a sense of fullness, a feeling of being more than one usually feels. So, to take away the spirit would be to deprive the person of an enlivening experience, and to rob her or him of a passionate involvement. Did Ambrose Bierce (1958) have this in mind in his coverage of "Obsessed" in *The Devil's Dictionary*? He wrote that a chaplain in Cromwell's army exorcised the devil from a soldier by throwing the soldier into the water when the devil came to the surface. "The soldier, unfortunately, did not" (p. 92).

In monomania it is as if one were possessed. There is a passionate relationship set up between the possessed and that which possesses. Just as the obsessive-compulsive neurotic may go through hell with his or her "disorder," the person of the monomaniacal type of obsession may be excited, joyous, or even ecstatic in her or his focus and "order."

Monomania may mean a conversion. For in monomania one is seized, and all of one's being is focused on the object of obsession. As the object of obsession becomes the center of one's aliveness, one's energy is given clear focus, one's life organized. One's direction is determined and the desultory side trips that characterize the "everydayness" of ordinary life are curtailed in favor of single-purposed movement. And, so, the monomaniac has been converted from ordinariness to extraordinariness.

Rather than fractionated, the monomaniac is single-minded. The potency of such intense focus can be likened to the laser beam. Like the laser device, monomania provides an amplification and concentration of one's energies into a narrow and intense beam. Amplification comes about as all of one's cognitive efforts, affective responses, and conation are constellated about the object of one's monomania. Concentration results from the relegation of all else to a secondary role as the object of the monomania is given primary role. Primary role means center stage. And "concentration" captures the essence of being one with the center.

The point I am wanting to make is that the experience of monomania can be growthful and even transforming. All too often we get ensconced only to become mired in the everydayness of our lives. We go though the motions, more or less efficiently, getting accomplished the day-in day-out tasks of our lives. But, then, to those fortunate enough to seize onto and to be seized by a monomaniacal object, a quantum leap is taken. One's life is restructured. A new level of meaning and of aliveness is experienced. I am reminded of the term "metanoia" used by Joseph Chilton Pearce (1971) to label this kind of conversion, which he described as a fundamental transformation of mind. So, in monomania there can be metanoia. Monomania may bring a conversion or fundamental transformation of mind. Monomania may bring a shift in consciousness that allows a profoundly different perspective on life.

Monomania exists, of course, in degrees. Likewise, there are degrees of metanoia provided by particular experiences of monomania. I believe that we can conveniently define each particular case of monomania in terms of three basic parameters. I have derived these parameters from the two basic existential structures: space-time and embodiment (Polkinghorne, 1983). We experience, by virtue of the embodied condition of experience, that experience being constituted as spatial and temporal. Separating the spatial-temporal structure into two parameters for our purposes makes for greater clarity. So, the first two parameters of monomania are *extension* and *duration*. In defining a case of monomania we can ask, how much of a person's life space is taken up by the obsession. Does the obsession occupy only a small corner of one's life, or is it pervasive, permeating almost every inch? That is, is the obsession circumscribed like an after-hours hobby, or is it the central activity of one's life? What is its extent? And, we can ask how long the person in question has been obsessed. A few hours? Weeks? Months? Even years?

The third parameter of monomania might be termed awareness. From embodiment arises awareness. Awareness, as organismic knowing, is transforming, as has been thoroughly discussed in the Gestalt therapy literature. Metanoia, then, is ushered in by awareness. The indwelling of the obsession, the embodied awareness of the obsession may lead to that transformation and growth known as metanoia. (I am speaking, of course, of monomania, and not of neurotic obsession.) It is this third parameter of monomania that addresses the question of the degree to which the experience becomes a stepping-stone to an expanded consciousness and identity. As such, this third parameter is well labeled *metanoia*.

The *definitive dimensions of monomania are, then, extension, duration, and metanoia.* The questions to ask: What was the extent of the obsession? How long did it last? What changes in consciousness and identity did it produce?

Other things being equal, the greater the extent and duration of the monomania, the greater the possible metanoia. That is to say, the more pervasive the obsession and the longer the time spent with it, the more opportunity for the indwelling awareness to transform.

In some cases in which the monomania is extensive and enduring, and in which the object of obsession is of a higher order of good, the personal transformation may be highly dramatic. Obsessed by high social interest (in the Adlerian sense), and given sufficient extension and duration, there may be what has been called the "magnificent obsession." The magnificent obsession is characterized by a devotion of one's whole being to the doing of some good work. Often the magnificent obsession has religious overtones, if, indeed, it is not clearly a religiously guided pursuit. The prophets and the saints are the clearest examples of people so possessed. But short of being a saint, there is ample territory for the living out of a life-long devotion to an ideal.

Earlier I related awareness and embodiment. I want to return to the body as a focus in understanding the dynamics of monomania. Some need is being served by the monomania. One does not become obsessed for no reason. Rather, one becomes obsessed because the object of that obsession meets some organismic need. The object of obsession, or what is obsessed about, is, in a sense, the preference one has within the realm of choices that relate to the need. Put simply, any given need may be met by a greater or lesser number of options. The choice of option is a statement of one's preference. So, the object of one's monomania is an expression of one's preferred way of meeting some need.

With the presence of a need and the choice of a preferred object for the meeting of that need, there arises a state of organismic arousal. This arousal is experienced as tension, excitement, a "turn-on." In this state one feels enlivened and energized. If allowed a natural course, this organismic arousal will differentiate into an experience of emotion. The person so possessed will feel a raving and longing for the object of obsession. The best primary feeling word for this is love. The monomaniac is possessed with love for the object. There is a feeling of deep and passionate wanting.

A fully developed monomania involves, then, a need, a preference, a state of high arousal, and a particular feeling or love characterized by a passionate craving. It is this constellation which leads to taking action. The monomaniac, out of this *motion* of emotion, enacts motion in the service of satisfaction of the craving. But, the obsession is sustained by the high stage of arousal and emotion. As long as fulfillment is less than the need-preference-arousal-emotion constellation, the monomania is maintained. In bioenergetic terms, the monomaniac is "overcharged." That is, the charge of generated energy stays in excess of the discharge of energy. To use a term from Gestalt therapy, there is "unfinished business." And, profoundly so. For in monomania there is a perpetual state of being unfinished, as the charging function exceeds the discharging function. So, the organismic Gestalt remains incomplete. In monomania there is lack of closure, and, instead, an ongoing passionate striving.

It is this bioenergetic state of overcharge which gives the monomaniac the sense of being possessed. The state of high energy-tension-excitement may be far greater than one is accustomed to, and certainly more than one is accustomed to experiencing over any considerable period of time. So, one may feel as if taken over. The energy has presence. And, if one has a penchant for explanations more animistic, the idea of spirit possession fits nicely.

This discussion of the energetic aspects of monomania brings me to another point that distinguishes this phenomenon from obsessive-compulsive neurosis. In monomania there is a genuine need that is the source of the aroused energy. In contrast to this natural excitement in monomania, in the neurotic state of obsession there is anxiety. An educated observer has little difficulty in differentiating excitement and anxiety. And, on a theoretical level, the difference is great. Excitement is part of a natural sequence which forms a cycle of organismic contact with the world in order to satisfy needs, and organismic withdrawal following satisfaction. Anxiety, in contrast, is the experience when the natural cycle is blocked by neurotic avoidance of contact or of withdrawal. Anxiety is, in a sense, a perversion of excitement. It is the product of excitement denied and aliveness avoided. I offer an analogy:

Excitement : Monomania :: Anxiety : Obsessive-Compulsive Neurosis

(In the present context I do not want to enter into a detailed discussion of the Contact/Withdrawal Cycle. For the interested reader, I refer to chapters two and three of my 1985 book, *The Body in Psychotherapy*.)

There is an important implication for psychotherapy here. Obsessive-compulsive neurosis is a disorder, to be sure. So, it is appropriate to work toward its resolution, eradication, or cure. In the case of monomania, however, there is the potential for growth. Given the potential for an experience of metanoia, monomania is to be supported to its natural conclusion. The danger is that the therapist may misunderstand an instance of monomania to be an obsessive-compulsive neurosis, and may therefore try to cure the patient. At the very least, in this situation, the therapist is nonsupportive of a possibly powerful experience in personal transformation. At worst, he or she may stifle and short-circuit the experience.

A therapist may make the therapeutic error of interfering with monomania out of simple misunderstanding. All of us certainly misevaluate and misdiagnose at times. More serious, however, is the situation in which the therapist actively opposes the patient's monomania out of her or his own pathological process. Let us say, for heuristic purposes, that the therapist in question is fearful of her or his own natural urges for growth and transformation. To see this process begin to unfold in a patient via an experience of monomania would be most unsettling, and perhaps even quite threatening. Out of an urge to protect oneself from intimate exposure through the patient to that which one fears in oneself, the therapist may interact in such a way as to stop the patient's excursion into monomania.

The therapist dynamic discussed above is an example of what Reich (1949, 1974) termed the "emotional plague." Reich observed that a person may become victim to the plague to the extent that one's natural, self-regulatory life manifestations have been suppressed. Out of fear of one's own aliveness — excitement, growth — the plagued individual is threatened by the aliveness of others. The plagued individual won't endure free and natural expression of life in herself or himself or in others. Simply put, emotional-plague behavior involves the discouragement or the stopping of other peoples' aliveness. The manner by which this discouragement or stopping is done varies with the characterological style of the plagued individual (Smith, 1984, 1985).

Suffice it to say that the therapist who is emotionally plagued will tend to oppose excitement and growth — hallmarks of organismic aliveness — in patients. This opposition may be active or passive. The emotionally plagued therapist may state opposition to the patient's monomania, defining it as pathological, and treat the patient as if neurotically obsessed. Or, the therapist may simply ignore the patient's monomaniacal quest for growth, passively refusing to lend support or encouragement.

I believe that it is morally incumbent upon any therapist who feels threatened and oppositional to manifestations of growthful excitement in patients to seek personal therapy.

Given that one recognizes monomania in one's patients, how can one facilitate the maximizing of the potential for metanoia? The first guideline is to let the patient know that you recognize the monomania as something more than the "counting flowers on the wall" type of obsessive-compulsive neurosis. This means to *acknowledge the potential for metanoia*. Usually, it is better not to try to predict and thereby to program the nature of the potential for transformation. The direction of growth is better left to emerge as it will, guided by the "wisdom of the organism."

The second guideline is to *encourage the patient to enter fully into the experience of monomania*. This means to support the patient's "going with" the urge, the excitement, rather than holding back or resisting. This entering fully into the experience also means to be as fully aware as one can be. So, anything the therapist can do to facilitate the patient's awareness will be helpful.

The principle, here, is this: Entering into monomania fully, with awareness, will maximize the growth and transformation realized. This principle is based on a basic trust in the self-regulation of the organism. When there is an organismic urge, follow it! Not impulsively, but with benefit of awareness. So, when you feel the excitement of monomania, follow the path of that excitement as it leads, wherever it leads, as long as it leads. Don't be afraid to let yourself be taken, swept away by seemingly insatiable and excited interest. Be open to the possible living out of an experience so pervasively enlivening as to qualify as what Gordon Allport referred to as a "ruling passion."

~

BODY-FOCUSED PSYCHOTHERAPY
WITH MEN

Balanced living is found in the intermediate zone, in the territory lying between the poles of the extremes. Our attention is called to this truth in Aristotelian philosophy by the "doctrine of the mean," known more popularly as the "golden mean." Often it is easier to walk the path of the extreme. "All or nothing," "always or never." These are easier to recognize than "not too much, not too little," and "sometimes." It is easier to lean on the pole of an extreme than to find one's balance on the middle path, not wandering too far to either side. Extreme behavior lacks such balance, and is therefore the symptom and the portent of a life uncentered. This is not to say that a person who lives creatively stay on a very narrow path, never tending toward one pole or the other. Rather, it means that the person who lives creatively makes mini-swings within the middle territory, but does not swing all the way to one extreme or the other. Being centered is a flexible, dynamic process of balancing by means of such mini-swings. Polar positions are not free, but rather are rigid and static.

To make this more concrete, and specific to the psychological dynamics of males, this chapter will explore the dimension of male rigidity. This requires some basic understanding of the male rigid character structure. Character structure, as presented in the psychoanalytic and Reichian tradi-

From: Scher, M., Stevens, M., Good, G., and Eichenfield, G. (Eds.) *Handbook of Counseling and Psychotherapy with Men*, 109-118 (1987).

tion (Smith, 1985), is seen as developing from early life experiences. Character development depends on the degree of fixation at the various erogenous levels, as result of certain traumatic experiences. The result, which manifests both psychologically and physically, is a relatively fixed pattern of behavior. Although "character" is a hypothetical syndrome, and no one is a pure character type, what therapists look for is which character type is dominant and which other types may play a secondary role in the person's dynamics.

The five character types recognized in the neo-Reichian school of bioenergetics are in a development sequence. The earliest type is the schizoid, then the oral, the psychopath, the masochist, and then the rigid types. If the etiological trauma is relatively early, the probability is that the person will have difficulty developing through the successive stages as well. This makes sense, in that some of the developmental tasks of the stage of the trauma will not be mastered, leaving the child to enter the next developmental stage with a deficit. Therefore, the character types are in a descending order of complexity, as there is a partial adding of type to type, the earlier the initial trauma. In addition, as one moves higher in the developmental sequence of the character types, there is greater variety in the syndrome, since there has been more personality differentiation prior to the trauma.

Psychological issues having their etiology in a developmental stage prior to clear gender differentiation tend to manifest in quite similar ways in men and women. Several issues are the same for all children before the time they see themselves as boys and girls. The general themes are maternal rejection and schizoid character formation, maternal deprivation and oral character, parental overpowering and psychopathic character, the over-bearing mother and submissive father (who stifle the child's spontaneity and leave him or her feeling pushed, nagged, and guilty) and masochistic character formation. As these characterological styles are set before children see themselves as boys or girls, the gender issue is of only secondary influence in the formation of the pathological patterns of the adult.

With the arrival of gender identity, one's "boyness" or "girlness" becomes an integral factor in further character formation. The rigid female character, or histrionic character, is differentiated from the rigid male character even though the trauma is the same — rejection of love by the father. When the father rejects the child's love, he is rejecting an aspect of his daughter or his son. The girl is having her female love turned away by her opposite-sex parent. This means the father's rejection of her budding female sexuality, and sets the pattern for subsequent dealings with men. And so the histrionic sets upon a life-long quest for male affirmation of her childlike sexuality. This is her unfinished business, her incomplete Gestalt creating tension for closure.

For the young boy, the rejection of his love is a statement that he is not good enough. Since he experiences himself as a boy, this means he is not a good enough male, as judged by his same-sex parent. His rejection is not sexualized, but is clearly "genderized." His unfinished business is to prove himself as a boy/man.

The key element in the rigid male is the father's rejection of the son's affection and the pushing away of the boy. By being pushed away the boy feels "not good enough." At the same time the father makes the expression of his love for his son, to whatever degree he feels such, contingent on the son's performance. But, whatever his son does, it is never quite good enough. The boy never measures up to his father's standard. So, the boy grows up always believing that he has to perform. And, since his own love for his father was rejected, he gives up on reaching out with love in order not to feel frustrated and hurt anymore.

So, what is a boy to do? Residing in a man's body, and destined to live out the existential decisions come to in response to a father's rejection, how is one to live? The existential decisions become the guides.

"Dad let me know that I am not good enough for him to love me. Therefore, *I must constantly try to prove myself.* 'I will!' is my call to action, my determined declaration. I am ambitious and competitive. Under stress I am prone to take action, attending to details. I work hard, even overwork, and will keep at the job until it is done, and done perfectly. Often, therefore, I will be seen as self-confident, perhaps even arrogant, and impressive in my penchant for action. In order to reach high levels of achievement and strive for perfection I demand structure. Some would call me obsessive or compulsive.

"Dad spurned my affection, my expressions of love for him. Therefore, *I must protect myself from hurt by never reaching out, never being soft or too warm.* So, I am hard and cold. I will not surrender to soft and tender feelings.

"Perhaps you recognize me by the way I hold back in my body. You may see that I am stiff with pride. My body reflects the rigidity that my inflexible existential choices demand. Sometimes, as I walk or otherwise move about, it becomes painfully obvious that I am all too literally 'tight-assed.'

"In my relationships I can offer several appealing qualities. I will get fairly close, and bring a lot of energy to a relationship. I will be strong and active, quite dependable, and one to rely on to solve external problems. But, be warned. I will not relate on an emotional level. In fact, I will actively oppose the expression of feelings. As I denigrate feelings, you may find me emotionally insensitive and unavailable. My pattern of overwork, and obsessive compulsive task orientation bespeak my subordination of personhood to the attainment of goals. You will find my beliefs, opinions, and values as inflexible and unyielding as the postural muscles of my body" (Smith, 1984, 1985).

What has been described is the man who is "too hard." This is the hypermasculine man — active, forceful, arrogantly competitive, and unfeeling. If this man is "too hard," there must be a polar opposite who is "too soft."

The man who is "too soft" is interesting characterologically in that he represents a mixed type. Ironically, he too is rigid. However, that characterological rigidity is mixed with oral character structure. Therefore, he shows many of the characteristics that follow from pre-genital oral deprivation. *The outstanding characteristic of the "too soft" male is his passive-receptive attitude.*

"Having a passive-receptive way of being in the world, how am I to behave? I lack aggressiveness, and find self-assertion very difficult. My tendency is to be gentle and humble, perhaps overly polite and considerate. I am fearful. Life is scary to me, so I avoid risks and conflicts. At times I am paralyzed with fear. Since my aggression is blocked, I often feel helpless and hopeless.

"My way of being in the world is clearly reflected in my body structure and bodily movements. My voice is soft and modulated, lacking in resonance and sharpness. Not only does my voice sound boyish, but I have a boyish look to my face. My face is soft, as is my whole body, on the surface. My hands are soft and have a weak quality about them. My muscles stay underdeveloped. My shoulders and hips are narrow. So, overall, I may remind you of a preadolescent boy. My movements are not brusque or forceful. Instead, my actions have a quality of caution and softness, perhaps even weakness. At times people label my movements and gestures as effeminate. What they don't understand is that I am masculine, but passive, paralyzed with fear. My maternal deprivation is reflected in my underdeveloped, boyish body. Orally deprived, as I was, I carry the scar, and am terrified of abandonment. So, I must tread lightly and move softly. My deeper muscles are tense. This severe tension reflects my response to my father's rejection, as surely as my surface softness reflects my mother's unavailability. So, here I am, 'undernourished' and 'not good enough.'

"Relating to women is difficult for me. I find myself being dependent and mothered when the woman is inclined toward such a role. At times I can play father to a younger woman. But, a man to woman peer relationship eludes me."

In contrast to the hypermasculine man described earlier, his opposite on the dimension of rigidity is the man who is "too soft." The latter is overly sensitive, fearful, and passive, a caricature of what has traditionally been described as the hysterical woman. He has, indeed, been identified in the clinical literature as the male hysteric.

In the idiom of the East, the too-soft male is too yin and too-hard male is too yang. The soft male embodies an excess of yin force and tends to lack a balancing yang energy. This leaves him vulnerable to being hurt through his overly sensitive nature. It also means he will shy away from much of life, lacking the healthy aggressiveness necessary to reach out and take hold of life. His opposite, the too-hard male, embodies an excess of yang force, and lacks the yin energy necessary for balance. Through his forcefulness and willfulness he may hurt others and be unfeeling. In addition, this rigid stance prevents him from an openness to receiving tenderness and finding the joy of soft emotions.

The Eastern symbol for unity, the T'ai gi, better known as the yin-yang, graphically illustrates the balanced composition of the yin and the yang forces. The circle is equally divided by a smoothly flowing "S" curve, forming a white half and black half. Within the white half is a dot of black, and within the black half is a dot of white. Unity, wholeness, balance. The marriage of yin and yang. This is not a blend, a mixing of black and white into a uniform gray. Rather it is black space and white space within the whole, each interpenetrated by its contrasting opposite.

The T'ai gi is a suitable symbol to aid in the understanding of the problem and the resolution of the problem of the too-soft and too-hard male. The idea is to introduce yin energy or yang energy where it is deficient. This task is guided by an insight emphasized by Jung (1963). To shift now to the language of Jungian theory, the too-soft male is denying his animus, while the too-hard male is repressing his anima. Animus and anima, as masculine and feminine principles, respectively, can be allowed to manifest or not. The too-hard male represses his anima, allowing only the masculine principle to guide his thoughts and actions. But as Jung instructed us, the energy repressed is present in the unconscious, and will press for expression. Our therapeutic task, then, for the too-soft male is to support his expression of his latent masculine hardness. In the case of the too-hard male, our task is to facilitate the uncovering of his repressed anima or soft feminine principle.

In Figure 7.1 I have summarized the characteristics of the too-soft and the too-hard male. These form the two poles within the dimension of male rigidity.

The Dimension of Male Rigidity

Too soft ◄————————————► **Too hard**

Overly sensitive	Unfeeling
Gets hurt easily	Hurts others
Denies animus	Represses anima
Too Yin	Too Yang
Passive-receptive	Active-forceful
Caricature of the Feminine	Hyper-masculine
"I can't"	"I will!"

FIGURE 7.1 THE DIMENSION OF MALE RIGIDITY

The too-soft male and the too-hard male are incomplete in their manifest being. In both cases their way of being in the world is out of balance. Rather than creatively living in the intermediate zone of the "golden mean," making mini-swings toward one pole at times, the other at times, each tends to stay at one pole. Therapy for each can be thought of as an Hegelian dialectical process. The pole at which the client is rigidly in place forms a manifestly lived "thesis," the opposite pole the "antithesis." By supporting the living of the antithesis the therapist may facilitate a creative "synthesis."

Examining the specifics of the therapeutic task first, consider the too-soft male. The task is to toughen the man who is too soft. Since this client is fearful, he must not be pushed too fast, but rather he is to be given adequate support and encouragement in his movements toward toughness.

Since the too-soft male's tendency is to be passive, shy, and quiet, emphasize with him experiencing in the therapy room what it is like to be active, bold, and loud. To this end, Smith (1985) suggested body postures, movements, and sounds. Such exercises allow a dramatic enactment of emotionally laden material. These exercises must be graded so that they match the growing edge of the client. In other words, if the exercise is not advanced enough for the client, little or nothing of value will be gained.

If, on the other hand, the exercise is too advanced, the client will not feel safe enough to enter into it fully, and will again gain little or nothing. Worse still, he may scare himself, reinforcing his timid, passive style. This is the "boomerang effect" that occurs when the exercise is graded too high. *The idea is to provide a psychodramatic experience through which the client successfully transports himself beyond his previously assumed limits.* The too-soft male is living out a script that prohibits his masculine-assertive expression. Each time he is able to break his script he weakens its power and relaxes his rigid adherence to that way of being.

A good way to move into the psychodramatic exercise is to listen to the client's story as he tells it. Watch and listen for manifestations of the "be soft" script. Notice the lack of animation, the cautious, inhibited gesture, the effeminate mannerism, the shy posture. Hear the guarded, soft voice, and hear the language designed to avoid confrontation. Any of these can be noted and pointed out to the client. Any characterological manifestation can be productively used in this way.

The therapist's two tools are "support" and "frustration." His job is one of supporting any of the client's honest attempts at expression of his best self, and frustrating the client's attempts to continue his characterological script. Pointing out characterological manifestations, as mentioned above, is a way of frustrating the client's unchallenged continuation of his script. In order to support his expressions of his best self, encouragement can be offered and acknowledgment given when such expression is in evidence. The psychodramatic exercise is an event, designed from the story material given by the client and for the purpose of giving him the opportunity to break from his script there in the counseling room. The consulting room is a safe place to experiment with new behavior.

There is much artistry that goes into the creation of the psychodramatic experiment. It is learned through practice and, most important, apprenticeship with a skilled practitioner. All that can be offered here are some guidelines. Once a characterological manifestation is noted and commented on, the client can be invited to experiment with it, transforming it into a harder, more forceful, bolder expression. This may mean changing a constricted posture into a more open, expansive one. It may mean speaking more loudly and breathing more deeply. And it may mean to imagine someone is present and to speak directly *to* that person with clearly assertive language, rather than only to talk *about* her or him.

The idea is to recognize the "soft scenario" and invite the client to redo it as a "hard scenario." It is these excursions into bold expression that bring forth the heretofore denied animus. On the way to these more active, forceful expressions, the client may get scared. It is as if the original authors of the "be soft" script (various parenting figures) come forth with their greatest force to stop the client from extricating himself from their life-long grip. When this happens, those voices are to be identified and confronted psychodramatically, with the therapist's support.

Since the purpose is not to practice a performance that is to be presented at a later time but rather to facilitate a characterological shift, the expressions to be worked toward are extreme. Remember, the synthesis comes about only after the thesis is opposed by its *anti*-thesis. This is the law of the human dialectical process. Years of dwelling at one extreme requires many excursions to the other extreme before the golden mean can be recognized. So, in working with the too-soft male, we need to persist in the psychodrama of the "hard scenario" over time, session after session, until the client has grown comfortable with stomping his feet, waving his fists, kicking the cushions, screaming, laughing from his belly until the room echoes. He has known shyness; now he must know boldness.

In addition to this therapy work in the consulting room, carefully assigned homework is useful in working with the too-soft male. This falls into two categories. First, the client can be invited to practice more assertive, active, forceful ways of being in his social life. Sometimes specific anticipated events can be discussed and a particular course of action can be decided upon in the therapy session. The carrying out of that course of action is then the homework assignment. Just as the psychodramatic work done in the counseling room needs to be graded to the client's level, so it is too with the homework to be carried out in the literal world.

The second type of homework involves some ongoing activity outside therapy that brings forth the expression of the animus energy. The therapist may suggest that the client find such an activity, but it is usually better if the client himself shops around and chooses the particular one. Any martial art, outdoor survival training, or vigorous physical discipline will potentially be of value for the too-soft male in his growth toward freeing his animus. The key, once again, is in the activity's being graded to the client's progressing level. Unfortunately, many too-soft men have had their characterological position only reinforced when they have been discouraged or even humiliated by an activity beyond their level or an instructor who was "too hard."

Consider now the treatment of that instructor, or one of his cohorts in the Society of the Too Hard, assuming that he comes for therapy. And that is quite an assumption; as numerous as the "too hard" men are in our culture, they are among the least likely to approach psychotherapy willingly. They may be coerced or ordered into therapy with some frequency, but are not so frequent volunteers, and this makes sense. After all, the hypermasculine image does not find peace with asking for help with one's life, let alone one's emotions. What is addressed here is the body-oriented psychotherapy of the too-hard male who has come to the point of voluntary participation. The task question, of course, is how does the therapist soften the male who is too hard?

Whereas the task of toughening the too-soft male is one of disinhibiting his pent-up animus energies, the task of softening the too-hard male is one of inviting out a repressed anima. In the former case the technique, as discussed above, is to exaggerate the shy animus expressions into their full-blown form. The technique is different in the case of bringing forth latent anima energy.

The too-hard male is likely to exhibit considerable muscular tension throughout his body. Stiff with pride, and ready for action, his back side, including hips, back, neck, and shoulder, may be tight and hard. At the same time, his front side, including chest and abdomen, will be tense in order to protect his vulnerability to soft feelings.

The major focus of body work with the too-hard male is on his front side, since this is the major body locus of tender emotion. This psychobiological fact is reflected in our lived language by such phrases as "letting your heart melt," being "broken hearted," being "love sick," which includes loss of appetite and "butterflies in my stomach," and feeling deep feelings in the "pit of my stomach." In the kinesic communication of some animals, submission is shown by the animal's exposing its "soft underbelly." In yoga, the chest region is known as the "heart chakra," and is associated with the experience of love.

Before entering into this body work designed to melt the body armor of the chest and abdomen, it is usually necessary to do some cognitive framing for the client. The too-hard male is a "thinking type," in contrast with a "feeling type," to use a distinction from Jung. This means that he leads with his thinking, and wants to understand. Once the client has committed himself to therapy and understands the rationale for this body work, it can be undertaken.

The specific procedure is to have the client lie on his back. If he is not too threatened by this, it is preferable for him to be unclothed from the waist up. The skin to skin contact is more powerful. Then offer the following instructions:

> Relax as much as you can. I want you to breathe deeply, through your mouth, and make an "aaahhh" sound as you exhale. I am going to place my hand on your chest and leave it there for awhile. Let whatever wants to happen, happen. Allow any body sensations, memories, or emotions that want to come, come. Let me know when something important happens.

Maintain this static contact for up to ten or fifteen minutes, unless something important happens sooner. Break the silence only to restate part of the instructions, if needed, or ask what he is aware of, if you see something happen (a tear, a change in posture, a tremble, or such) and he does not speak of it within a reasonable amount of time.

Over a series of therapy sessions one might try hand placements on the client's upper chest, along the sternum, upper abdomen (between rib cage and navel), and lower abdomen (between navel and public bone). One might work in this way to invite a softening or letting go of the muscular tension by which the client binds his tender feelings. As he allows his armor to melt, he will begin to get in touch with his softer emotions. As he allows the therapist *to touch* his tender parts, the touch invites him *to get in touch* with his tender feelings. (Demonstration and supervised practice are strongly advised before undertaking hands-on body work.)

As memories and feelings emerge, that material can then be processed using a variety of therapeutic procedures. One particular way of processing this body-accessed material is to set up a dramatic enactment, the basics of which were presented earlier while discussing the treatment of the too-soft man. In the case of the too-hard man, the emphasis will be on his psychodramatic expression of his tender feelings — sadness, hurt, disappointment, love, caring. From his feelings and memories brought forward by the body work, a scenario can be envisioned that can then be acted out in the here-and-now context, allowing the client to express fully his feelings to the imagined appropriate target.

When this work is far enough along and when the client has reached a point of significantly reduced armoring in his chest and abdomen, work on his back armoring can begin. If the work on his back is undertaken prior to the chest and abdominal softening, the client will resist mightily, presenting a concrete-like back, almost impermeable to any touch.

When the client is ready for body work on his back, two procedures can be used: soft technique and hard technique (Smith, 1985). Soft technique has been described, the only change now being that the therapist would place his hands on various points of the back, wherever he can find tension or where the client reports tension. The instructions are the same as before, but obviously the client needs to be lying face down. A variation in the work is to have the client lie on his back while the therapist simultaneously contacts a point on the client's front and back. This usually works best if the touch is applied to points directly opposite each other on the chest or abdomen and the back. An exception is the holding of the nape of the neck and some chest or abdominal point.

Some of the hard techniques absolutely require demonstration and supervised practice, so they will not be described here. A hard technique is deep muscle massage on the back. Instructions similar to those used with the soft technique can be used, substituting "I am going to massage the muscles of your back," where appropriate. Again, emergent feelings and memories can then be processed through a mutually created psychodrama.

Difficult as it is to capture the richness of psychotherapy by writing about it, it is even more difficult when part of the therapeutic technique is nonverbal. Body work needs to be studied experientially in order to get a real feel for it. This chapter describes the basics of working with too-soft and too-hard men. It provides information for recognizing the too-soft and the too-hard male, understanding their core dynamics, and understanding some of the basic guidelines of a body-oriented psychotherapeutic treatment. Elaboration of this material can be found in *The Body in Psychotherapy* (Smith, 1985). So, in either case, therapy seeks attainment of a dynamic balance for the client. The more extreme the client's skew toward too soft or too hard, the more extreme his experience of the opposite needs to be. The more extreme the poles, the more powerful their synthesis. The more powerful the synthesis, the more powerfully whole the man.

Gestalt Lessons from Nature

On Assimilation

The tiger hunts,
stalking, watching, waiting.
At just the right moment!
I emulate your power!

On Deflection

The wolf makes its bloody kill.
The she-wolf licks her cubs.
I turn from the sight.
Is this really too much?

On Support and Frustration

The mighty eagle returns.
A fresh fish for the nestling.
One day the eaglet will go hungry.
Behold, a new eagle soars!

What Is, Is

Oh, unicorns and dragons.
Alas! Where are you?
Are not the rhinoceros and the crocodile
quite enough to contend with?

From: *Pilgrimage,* 13(2), 10 (1987).

~

THERAPISTS IN SEARCH OF THE HOLY GRAIL

A tenth anniversary is an apt time for reflection. As I think of *The Gestalt Journal's* reaching the decade mark in its existence, my associations are about the relationships among breadth of experience, depth of experience and time. In the following paragraphs I want to share with you some of these associations, hopefully organized with due regard for coherence.

From a starting point, we can think of the two basic existential structures; space-time and embodiment. Experience is constituted as spatial and as temporal. That is, I experience events as either "there" or "here." Also, as either "then" or "now." The "then" may be the remembered past, fondly held as a pleasant reminiscence or as a painful regret. Or, the "then" may be a fantasized future, dreaded or anticipated with joy. "Now" is the moment of actuality and power. Tolstoy told us of this through the voice of the hermit in *Three Question* (quoted by Barry Stevens, 1970, p. 219):

> Remember then: there is only one time that
> is important — *Now!* It is the most impor-
> tant time because it is the only time when
> we have any power.

The moment of "now" is the balance point between the receding past and the arriving future.

From: *The Gestalt Journal,* 10(1), 115-124 (1987).

"There," "here," "then," "now." These are in reference to my embodied, experiencing self. Extension and duration are relative to me. Something is experienced as to my left or my right, above me or below me, far from me or near to me, but always in relation to my physical, organic being. Likewise, "now" has physical co-existence, whereas "then" is not physically, actually with me. My experience is formed through my self, embodied.

Fritz (Perls, 1947, 1969) called attention to an interesting relationship between the body and time. He related the anus to the past and the mouth to the future. As I see it, the anus is the body's exit, the organ located on one's "behind" and whose function it is to leave behind that which is no longer of value to that organism. The mouth, located at the opposite end of the body from the "behind," opens or closes tightly as it anticipates that arrival of nurturing or toxic material. The mouth opens to approach and take in the new.

In Gestalt circles, the existential structures of space-time and embodiment are usually acknowledged through a simpler and more functional set of terms, namely, *here, now* and *awareness*. (Since awareness is based in bodily sensation, we can easily shift from the more structural term "embodiment" to the more functional term "awareness.") The relevant questions which are implied by these terms are *where, when* and *how*, respectively.

Unlike most therapy systems which have a content focus, Gestalt therapy focuses on process. Gestalt therapy asks, in various ways: Where? When? How? By asking these questions at many levels, awareness is invited, and the process of growth is served. The techniques which are created and employed all have as a purpose the creation of the here-and-now, awareness-enhancing experience. With increasing awareness comes growth.

Growth, as I think if it, happens when one successfully goes to where one has not successfully gone before. Stated somewhat differently, growth accrues from extending one's growing edge, by risking going beyond previous limits and thus expanding the experienced self. The Polsters (1973) have written of growth as the extension of one's "I-boundary," so that more of one's experience can be encompassed within the boundaries of one's "I." The idea is the same. What I am talking about is opening to allow more of the world to become one's experienced world. As this happens one becomes bigger and contains more. Growth takes place as one opens to heightened awareness.

Awareness takes time to develop. At times there may be an "aha!" experience, an illuminating moment of insight. Usually such an insight is but the final step in an unfolding of awareness through time.

The word awareness, as has been implied, can be used to designate both the unfolding process which is "growing" and the level reached in one's growth at a particular point in time. Thus, we can say that growth comes about through exposure to the world under conditions of heightened awareness. Or, we can speak of one's level of awareness. Interestingly when doing so we use seemingly opposite adjectives. The result is this equation: heightened awareness = deepened awareness = deep understanding = higher consciousness. (This is a reflection of the fact that the Latin "altus" means both high and deep. This was recognized by Freud (1963) in his 1910 essay on "The Antithetical Sense of Primal Words," being a review of an 1884 pamphlet published by Karl Abel.)

In *Gestalt Therapy Verbatim*, Fritz Perls wrote:

> We are here to promote the growth process and develop the human potential. We do not talk of instant joy, instant sensory awareness, instant cure. The growth process is a process that takes time. (Perls, 1969, p. 2)

Of course! Growth takes time. You can't grow more quickly that you can grow. But, you can grow more slowly than you can grow.

This brings me to the heart of this paper, the growth of the therapist. I see the therapist's growth as including both development of personhood and the development of technical skill. In a highly functioning therapist the techniques flow out of her or his person such that it is difficult to distinguish who the person is from what the person does. "Techniques . . . are given life and meaning through the person of the therapist" (Smith, 1985, p. 148). Nevertheless, it is useful at times to distinguish between the person of the therapist and the technical approach used. Techniques which are not enlivened through deeply developed personhood lack humanness and tend to be mechanical. Such a therapist is a technician, performing a series of maneuvers from her or his bag of tricks. At best, he or she is shallow and fades as her or his gimmicks lose their novelty. At worst, he or she is manipulative for self-serving ends. On the other hand, the therapist without technical skills tends not to be very potent. He or she may be a good person, well-meaning and caring, but without effective procedures has little to offer in the facilitation of the growth process of another.

I think, again, of the ten year anniversary theme. The therapist's growth, both growth in personhood and growth in technical skill, takes time. For some, ten years of experience means ten years of deepening experience, for others it means one year's experience repeated ten times.

I remember Jim Simkin's musing that a person could spend a lifetime studying and living Gestalt, and still not exhaust what is there to be understood. Originally, I planned to title my first book "Beyond Gestalt Therapy." It was Jim who opened my eyes, in his inimical style, by declaring, "What right do you have to write about 'Beyond Gestalt Therapy' until you have proven that you know all there is to know about the Gestalt therapy that exists!" He refused to contribute to my edited book. I heard him, and changed to title to *The Growing Edge of Gestalt Therapy* (Smith, 1976).

I come across quite a few people who tell me that they have trained in Gestalt therapy, but their behavior and their lack of theoretical sophistication bespeak their neophyte status. Often, these people go on to list the many other approaches in which they have been "trained." The picture, here, is one of rampant eclecticism, born of a never ending search for the right and true system. They are in search of the Holy Grail. Being, perhaps, impatient, greedy for instant enlightenment, they introject the vocabulary and a few techniques from their introductory Gestalt training. Not yet enlightened, and perhaps a bit disillusioned, they are ready to grab for the next system to come along. The hunger for understanding and growth is natural and laudable. The mistake is to confuse breadth of exposure with depth, one year's experience repeated ten times, with ten years' experience.

In introjection one swallows whole, without really getting one's teeth into the material. Without benefit of mastication, the material cannot be assimilated, made part of one. The result is indigestion, perhaps regurgitation, and an unmet hunger. So, the introjector doesn't grow from what he or she swallows. The introjector, rather than becoming a ruminator, in the best sense, moves on to new material, to introject again. The ruminator, on the other had will chew the hunks of material later, and again, and again, until what remains is assimilable. Gestalt, I believe, is a cud to be chewed for years.

The number of therapy fads extant is a reflection of the hunger for growth coupled with the penchant for introjection, in our society. Many therapists are impatient with "rumination," many want instant growth. So, we see how many therapists are constantly searching for what is new, looking for the enlightened system in instant form, rather than developing greater depth.

To some degree Gestalt therapy has flowed into the mainstream of psychotherapy and so, although strongly preset, is not always clearly visible or easily recognized. In addition, however, Gestalt has lost some of its newsworthy status by virtue of not being new. Not any longer new, it doesn't hold fad appeal. And, not being new, it is less appealing to the searchers for the newly revealed magical system. Those in search of the Holy Grail, having stopped off in the land of Gestalt, have moved on.

It is important to survey what school or systems of psychotherapy are available, to sample, and to see what is a fit for one's person. In writing about some of the ethical considerations in being a psychotherapist, I named the "ego-syntonic imperative" (Smith, 1985). By this, I meant that it is ethically imperative that a therapist relate only to a patient in ways which are congruent with who that therapist is. In other words, techniques need to be syntonic with the person of the therapist. To find the techniques and the system or systems which are ego-syntonic means to experience several and selectively retain those which are a fit. Once a fit is discovered, then the task is to deepen understanding.

A convenient model for helping to describe and understand the growth of the therapist is the classic learning curve. This is, as I said, a convenient model. It is only that. Bear with me. The classical learning curve is approximated by the data generated in a simple learning task such as those traditionally studied in experimental psychology (e.g., reaction time, nonsense syllables learned, and maze learning). Plotted with time or trials on the horizontal axis and correct performance units on the vertical axis, the curve shows negative acceleration with an asymptote. In other words, the curve becomes less steep over time of practice (negative acceleration) and reaches a point at which much more practice is required to show any gain in learning (asymptote). In actual practice the learning curves produced in the experimental laboratory are not smooth, but show the ups and downs of erratic performance which characterizes human beings. So the curve actually looks more like the blade of a curved saw, with the teeth pointing up. Often times these cycles of progression-regression in learning tasks are caused by factors extraneous to the learning task *per se* (e.g., worry, loss of sleep the night before, an environmental distraction, etc., so the curve is smoothed by averaging adjacent peaks and valleys. So, the classical learning curve emerges thus: (*see figure 1, next page*)

FIGURE 1

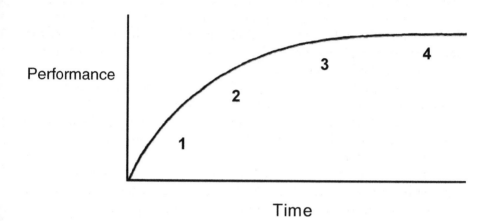

Using this model, let us go back to the specific issue of the growth of the therapist. Let the learning curve represent the level of growth of the therapist over time. Note that I have designated five points on the growth curve.

Point 1 represents the point of beginning, no time yet invested and no growth in and with the new system. The area of the curve from point 0 to point 1 represents the zone of growth of the *neophyte therapist.* The curve is steep, here, which means that the rate of growth is rapid. Starting from a zero point, the neophyte enjoys a large return from the time invested. During this time the neophyte learns about the *basics* of the system — basic vocabulary, basic concepts, basic therapeutic procedures. The rate of growth is exciting, and the early gain of basics can give a strong sense of accomplishment. The danger is that the neophyte does not know how much he or she does *not* know. Some of this early learning, perhaps the major portion, is more introjection than assimilation. So, the material has not become a part of the neophyte therapist, but it is available for rumination and potential assimilation. During this neophyte state the therapist will probably develop some sense of whether or not this system is a fit, whether to pursue further study or to move on to another system.

The area of the curve between points 1 and 2 is the area of the *journeyman therapist*. Notice that the curve continues to be steep, so growth continues to be rapid. During the journeyman phase of development, the basic material, which was in large part introjected as the neophyte phase, is ruminated on and made suitable for assimilation. By gradually experiencing the basics over and over again, and contemplating their meaning, they become the possession of the journeyman therapist. The danger at this stage of development is that the clarity gained may give birth to an illusion of expertise. The journeyman has experienced enough to have some genuine understanding, but not enough experience to have a seasoned perspective. The journeyman therapist has the common elements, the usual manifestations of the therapeutic trade, but not yet the rare elements, the unusual manifestations.

The *dilettante therapist* is the therapist who moves from system to system without ever becoming a journeyman therapist in any one. So, he or she is stuffed with unassimilated material from many sources. Perhaps he or she reveals himself or herself by announcing a workshop which is based on "Gestalt, reality therapy, massage, behavior modification, Bach flower remedies and Christian mysticism." Just as certain chemical elements may join to form compounds, but other combinations, not having affinity or "valence" for each other remain only mixtures, the introjected elements of psychotherapy systems can only be mixtures. The dilettante is a neophyte several times over.

Some therapists are content with a journeyman level of understanding, and prefer breadth of perspective to greater depth. Accordingly, the *generalist therapist* is born. The generalist is a journeyman several times over. As a journeyman he or she will be less likely to try to put together elements of different therapy systems which become but an incompatible mixture. The generalist may, in fact, create some workable compounds. These compounds, although workable, still may offend the expert who remains pure, in pursuit of higher levels of understanding within her or his chosen system.

The *expert therapist* is in the area of the growth curve between points two and three. The slope of the curve has shifted to a less steep climb. Further growth for the expert therapist is much slower than it was for her or him at the journeyman stage. More time and more practice is required for the experience of the less common events of the craft. This is the stage of advanced growth, growth into expertise. The danger which comes with expertise is the temptation of arrogance. Oftentimes the expert, out of her or his very real power as a therapist, becomes arrogant. This temptation toward arrogance can be offset by self-discipline, which then may provide passage of the last stage of growth.

The point on the growth curve designated by the 3 is the asymptote of the curve. From this point on, growth is very slow, with much time and experience being required for the realization of further increments. True, the therapist may never stop growing, but the yield from additional experience is preciously small. The esoteric elements of therapy are now learned. The phase from point 3 to point 4, the point of death, is the stage of the *master therapist*. For the master therapist further growth is stopped only by her or his dying.

The Gestalt literature, interestingly, can be viewed in terms of how far along the growth curve it is of value. Some of the books and articles lend themselves well to introjection of the basics, and therefore are of most value to the neophyte therapist. Others are of great value of the journeyman therapist as they give cognitive resonance to the growing therapeutic experience of the journeyman. Still others require the understanding gleaned by the expert or even the master before they can be fully understood.

The question sometimes asked, of how long it takes to become a Gestalt therapist, might be made more specific by asking how long it takes to become a journeyman, an expert and a master Gestalt therapist. The answer, of course, is "It depends." In the martial arts there are certain techniques traditionally known as "Twenty-year techniques." Mind you, that does not mean it takes twenty years to master the art; it means it takes twenty years to master that particular technique! We in the West tend, as a culture, not to be so patient. Somehow, we think we ought to get "it" quickly. When "it" does not come quickly, some move on to try another system. And, so, arise the dilettantes, those in search of the Holy Grail.

Fritz (Perls, 1969, p. 2) said it well when he wrote:

You don't have to be on a couch or in a Zendo for twenty or thirty years, but you have to invest yourself, and it takes time to grow.

~

The Training of Gestalt Therapists: A Symposium

George Brown, Elizabeth Mintz,
     Sonia March Nevis, Edward W.L. Smith — Participants

Robert Harman —Moderator

BOB HARMAN: Good morning. For those of you who were here last year for my presentation of "The Case of Rose: or Will She Fit in a Toyota" [A transcription appeared in the spring, 1986, issue of *The Gestalt Journal* (Vol. IX, No. 1)] Rose sends her regards. She knew that I was coming and wants the people who are familiar with her to know that she's doing well and much better according to her self report.

Today's panel will discuss training and the training of Gestalt therapists — a topic that I've been interested in for a long time. I've done some quick adding in my head about how many years of experience with Gestalt therapy and Gestalt therapy training there are up here and I think it comes close to a hundred years.

I am not going to say a lot about these people. They are well known. George Brown is on my immediate left. He's an author, an educator, and an administrator. Next will be Sonia Nevis, who's been involved in training at the Gestalt Institute of Cleveland for many years and was the Director of Training there for several years. Following her will be Edward Smith from Atlanta who is active in training and has authored two books. Finally will be Elizabeth (Betsy) Mintz, a noted therapist, trainer, and author.

We'll begin this morning with George Brown.

From *The Gestalt Journal*, 10(2), 73-106 (1987).

GEORGE BROWN: Thank you. I guess I'm an idiosyncratic deviant, and I'm not sure I should be up here, because I'm not involved in traditional training of therapists. We don't have an institute, and that's not one of my primary goals. I'm involved in two settings: The first is at the University of California Santa Barbara. I teach in a program called "Confluent Education" which started out by focusing on the integration of the affective and the cognitive domains, affective feelings, emotions, values and cognitive thinking, intellectual activity. That has developed and become more sophisticated; essentially what we're doing there is applying a systems approach to education. (When I say "education" I mean this in the broadest sense because we have people from a whole variety of occupations including industry.)

"Confluent Education" conceptualizes what happens within the individual (intrapersonal) and interpersonal and small group activities, the organizational context, and various instructional methodologies. And sometimes we design curriculum. I especially like that we see these things not as isolated components but all interacting. My major focus is on the intrapersonal and this is where I do the Gestalt work. I train, systematically, my graduate students — it's a graduate school I work in — in Gestalt therapy, making it very clear that this training is not for them to be used as therapists. Occasionally some of them, relatively few, do continue on and become therapists, but in order to do that in the state of California there are all kinds of requirements that they have to meet. So I don't have to worry that with the brief training that they get with me, people are going to go out and stamp themselves as Gestalt therapists.

What I am concerned with is how they can apply the principles, methodology and theory of Gestalt therapy to their own particular professional contexts, and those of you who are familiar with some of my books know that I've done a couple of books in education relative to that and I have one coming out, published by the Gestalt Institute of Cleveland, dealing with a Gestalt approach to organizations. Actually it's a way of conceptualizing organizations and working in organizations from a Gestalt point of view. It's an exciting, promising and rewarding approach and I encourage any of you who move in fields other than therapy to make use of what Gestalt has to offer.

That's one thing that I do. The second thing I do is train people in Europe in Gestalt therapy with my wife Judith. We work with people who are therapists, as well as social workers, teachers, medical doctors, etc., who want to have some familiarity with Gestalt and incorporate Gestalt in their own work.

I'd like to sketch an overview of the sequence of activities that we go through, touching here and there on some of the things we do in our training.

We start talking about Gestalt as in Fritz Perls' terms — both of us were trained by Fritz and worked with Fritz — we talk about Gestalt therapists essentially doing nothing more than stating the obvious and making the implicit, explicit. Then we build a sequence of training experiences around that. We begin with learning to see. We do this in a nonverbal way through use of mirroring activities. Then we add hearing so that people learn to give voice feedback without words, like "dada dada" to catch the sound of the voice and to get out of listening to the content, for the time being. Then we put these two things together by adding language and focusing on stating the obvious: What do you see and what do you hear? We combine these. Then we add personal response. We build these sequences cumulatively. Then we usually emphasize basic Gestalt questions: What are you doing now? What are you experiencing now? What are you feeling now? What's happening with you now? Later on: What are you avoiding? What are you wanting? But not at this time. Those last two, we've found, tend to put people up in their heads. At this stage we don't want that. Then we do things like working with "top dog, under dog." We work with resentments, demands, and appreciations. This pretty much covers the first stage.

This goes on at my training at the University, but when we work with people in Europe we usually run a five-day workshop. The format is usually that Judith and I work in the morning with clients in a demonstration context. Then we talk about what we're doing as we work and relate it to the particular things that we're focusing on as we move through the sequence. We run mini-labs later on in the day where they have a chance to practice these things.

In the second stage of our training, we have something we call "pick a patient." We have a couple of chairs in the middle of the room and one person's a therapist and one person's a client, and we work on four themes. We work on the now, and that's to help recapitulate the first sequence that we've developed, because these usually don't run consecutively. (Usually people come and then come back next year or six months later, that sort of thing.) So we focus on the now, which again is related to stating the obvious. Then mobilizing energy, and we do experiments, like exaggeration, polarities, using your whole body, getting out of a chair and moving around, using sound, the voice, a variety of things.

Then we move into learning to work with the total Gestalt, the big picture as you look at someone: What's the message you get? This relates to the last particular theme, trusting your intuition, where we help people to get in touch with various ways of knowing: learning to listen to phrases that come up, e.g., learning to listen to song titles. One of the things that happens with me when I'm doing Gestalt is I start to hear music and songs, and usually these songs have some connection with what's going on. Other people don't respond that way. They get pictures. They get images, metaphors, whatever. You learn it's O.K. to have these things, how to use them judiciously. Related to trusting your intuition we have a line that we say, "If I had the courage right now, what would I do?"

You learn how to become more creative as you use these particular things.

Then we move into something that we call "mass Gestalt." We put the group in two circles facing each other (the inside circle facing out and the outside circle facing them) and we run a sequence of Gestalt sessions, some lasting a minute or a couple of minutes. In the first one we have the people on the inside become patients and they make some kind of statement about how they are at the moment. The person on the outside is the therapist and responds using all the things that he or she has learned up to that time. We give them a minute. We stop. The therapists move on. The patient begins again with the same statement said the same way and gets another response . . . so both the clients get an opportunity to see how different people are responding to them and the therapists learn how to respond immediately to whatever is going on. It breaks the old, going into your head kind of thing and interpreting, analyzing. Then we have two or three other kinds of things we focus on using that same format. It's very exciting. We also do some co-therapists, conjoint therapists work. We do a lot of processing as we go along. One of the exciting things that we've added in the last four or five years is what we call "the Cleveland approach": working in Gestalt from a group context.

People respond to this training with enthusiasm and with . . . we get lots of reports about how useful it is for those whose work is different from therapy. For those who are already therapists it adds a whole new dimension to their work.

One of the things that bothers me is the so-called "confrontive approach" to Gestalt. To me it's antithetical to what Gestalt is really about. Any therapist who assumes, even in an implicit way, to know better about what's happening with the client than the client, and this leaks out, especially in the quality of the voice, "I don't believe you," — that kind of stuff — when you do that it is antithetical because you immediately place yourself in a "top dog" role and we all know what happens with "under dogs," right? So we also spend a lot of time on developing a nonjudgmental attitude and values. That's all I have to say.

SONIA NEVIS: I tried to figure out what would answer this question, what was being asked of us, what I could tell you about training that would be interesting. I remembered that about twenty-five years ago we had Carl Whittaker came to Cleveland to talk about training a therapist. He said he had the same dilemma we are having: How do you train a therapist? He thought and thought about it. What he came up with is: You read the poets and the novelists and you go to concerts and you travel and you learn to play musical instruments and, if you work with adults you work with children for a while, and, if you work with children you work with adults for a while, and so on. He was talking about people that we all, I assume, would like to train. People who are lively. People who have interests. People who care about what is going on in the world and therefore are going to care about what's going on with someone else. If we talk about selection, we would probably agree that that's what we would look for. I believe that he was right — if training doesn't end up with everyone being excited and interested in what's going on then the training didn't take.

I've picked out three training issues of the many that we could talk about. All three have to do with what feels very important at the Cleveland Institute. Now I'm talking for myself — I'm sure that if I talked to each person at the Cleveland Institute everybody would come up with a different three. But I think it does represent something very real there at the Institute.

The first thing important for training at Cleveland is it's history of some thirty years of articulating Gestalt theory, of talking about it, writing about it, developing exercises in it, extending it into working with the body, extending it into working with couples, families, groups, extending it into many other professions: working with the administration of public health and mental health agencies, organizations. There's been encouragement and support at the Institute for people to follow their own interests, so there's a body of well thought out information, well thought out theory, well thought out exercises.

However, that's not training — that is the ground for training. The training that goes on has to do with the practicum or the practice. The training has to do with taking all of that information and making it into muscle and glands and blood — well chewed and assimilated.

The practicum, starting the first week of training and going on again and again consists of people working as therapist, client and observers. The trainees expect to be looked at; expect to be talked about; expect to talk; you expect to question; they do not expect to be good. There's an easy-going ambience around practicum work that goes on for years. We remind our students that it takes a long time to take theory and make it a part of themselves so that they're not working from theory. (It's no different than learning to play a musical instrument.) When you first start you're doing scales, and you're counting, and you've got the notes, and you don't really make music for years. There is the discipline of practicing five finger exercises, and eventually arriving at the place where they're making music, where it's assimilated into them. So in that sense the training is a process that goes on over time.

The second important issue at the Institute is that we do everything we can, and have from the time we started, to make sure that introjection doesn't happen, that a trainee does not decide that one style or one person's way of working is the right way and therefore they are trying to imitate it. It's been very important for us to have a staff whose styles vary widely. We all talk about what we do exactly the same way, but our styles of what is apt to become figural, and the way we do our work is different. We've always tried to teach with more than one faculty present, and tried to get teams of people who are different enough so the minute a trainee thinks that one person's style is wonderful they see another one work that's very different and that's also wonderful. We downplay demonstrations because demonstration can be seen as the way one should work. We've even tried to keep the didactic presentations ever-changing — I don't think I've given a lecture yet that said the same thing.

We use at the Cleveland Institute a diagrammatic way to describe psychological process called the "experience cycle." It's been noted at the Institute — every time you hear the "experience cycle" described, it is described differently. It's simply not a fixed concept and our aim is to make sure that it isn't. We're not talking about introjecting concepts but genuinely grappling with them and assimilating them.

The third training issue is hard for me to say simply. It seemed important enough to struggle with how to say it, but I haven't been satisfied up to now. It has something to do with the general atmosphere at the Cleveland Institute, an atmosphere that makes learning, experimenting, trying things, lively and open. For example our own staff takes each other's programs. Everybody is into something new at all times. There is no sense that you can succeed or that you can fail. I don't think that exists there. There is both rigidity and anarchy, maybe because Ohio is middle America, we find we can go between being rigid (in the sense that the programs are laid out and one knows what the schedules are, and the curriculum, and things like that) and within that there's total anarchy. I think there's an atmosphere that supports learning there that is not easy for me to put into words but I think it's an essential ingredient of training. I think that's what George was talking about when he was talking about the nonjudgmental climate — it's a welcoming atmosphere for learning.

EDWARD SMITH: The training which I'm doing now differs considerably from the training which I started doing in the early 1970's so I want to say a little bit about this evolution. When I first started doing Gestalt training, I did it through The Pine River Center in Atlanta. This was a group of psychologists and I was one of the junior members of that group. In the beginning we started with Gestalt training. Then we got caught up in all of these integrations with Gestalt. That was one of the periods in the evolution of Gestalt therapy. For a while it was transactional analysis and Gestalt, bioenergetics and Gestalt, whatever and Gestalt. That made sense, was exciting, and we thought we were right on the leading edge of what was happening.

Then I started hearing Laura Perls talk about the umbrella, how big the umbrella of Gestalt is. Then I was confronted by Jim Simkin. He challenged me for not having proven that I knew everything about Gestalt first, and asked what right I had to integrate anything until I knew all about Gestalt. So I thought about that. I didn't change much, but I thought about it.

I did learn something in the middle years of Pine River: we were overly inclusive. We were trying to teach too much, too many things. For a while we had three programs running simultaneously. We had a paraprofessional program for people who were not professional people, but were helpers of various kinds. We had a second track which was an introductory professional training program. And then we had an advanced training program for people who had already completed the second one. And, in both the introductory and the advanced programs we tried to teach Gestalt, transactional analysis, psychomotor and bioenergetics. That was in a nine-month program! Each quarter we changed leaders (there were nine leaders) in each group, with one leader having two consecutive quarters. So there was the continuity of one leader carrying over each time, and one new leader each time. We got a mixture of orientations (the thing Sonia was talking about) — giving people exposure to a number of orientations and working styles. But it became a hodgepodge from trying to be overly inclusive of content. The trainees said it was interesting, it was exciting, sort of like going to the circus, but they came out it not feeling enough depth in any one approach to feel competent and confident.

The next stage at Pine River was to stop doing training for a while. For several years we didn't offer any training. Then I started training again and did a program by myself. I narrowed the content considerably which worked much better. The difficulty I had was putting a label on it to describe it to people, to announce it ahead of time, because what it was was what I did. It was my style of working which I think of as coming under the broad umbrella of Gestalt, but my particular excitement for the last few years has been very heavily body focused. So I called it "The Body in Psychotherapy." The training I do now has taken a turn, again, because I left Pine River in July of 1985 and now have one partner, Suzanne Imes.

So this has been an overview of the kinds of programs that I've offered. In preparing for this morning's presentation, I remembered a paper that I had written several years ago. This was an invited paper. It was to be a chapter in a book on training and supervision that was published several years ago. But when I finished the chapter and sent it to the editor, he wanted me to do some rather extensive revisions. He wanted me to include some material on the American Psychological Association's guidelines for supervision, and things like that in which I was not the least bit interested. So I didn't revise it, and consequently it wasn't published. That's a funny quirk about me. I've found I don't like revising anything I write. I love writing, but once I've written something, I feel finished and I want to move on. I don't want to go back and rework it and rework it. So I would rather give it one shot and get published, and if it doesn't go, stick it in a drawer and go on to something else. So I welcome the opportunity to now present this chapter. It's just been lying there dormant, just waiting for today.

What I put into this chapter were some guidelines that I have learned from the several years I have been doing training. These are rules of thumb. These are not, certainly, absolute rules. These are the things that seem to have worked for me, the things that I have come to understand about the kind of training that I do.

The first guideline is that *the doing of psychotherapy is best learned by apprenticeship.* As I look at psychotherapy, I think of it as an exquisite art form. I think of it as a performing art. And as such, to learn the doing of psychotherapy, one must apprentice to someone who does it. One must watch and listen and begin doing it, practicing it, polishing it. We can be scientific about psychotherapy. We can theorize about it, do research about it, study about it, talk about it, all of which I believe are valuable, all of which I'm interested in. But the actual doing of psychotherapy, as opposed to studying about it, I think is an art form. So that's the main guideline for the training that I do: I think of people who want to train with me as apprenticing and learning about an art form.

The second guideline is that *in order for someone to really learn a particular way of therapy, a particular general approach to therapy, and to be able to perform it masterfully, that form must be egosyntonic for that person.* That way of therapy must fit with who that person is, must fit with that person because any therapy system, any school of therapy is given life, is brought to life, through the person of the therapist. This is another way of saying what Carl Whittaker was talking about. That is, the person of the therapist grows and develops by playing a musical instrument, going to concerts, reading the great writers, traveling, experiencing, living. I don't believe that the Gestalt approach to therapy is for everyone. There are some people who just don't find a resonance with it. It's not egosyntonic for them. And it's a mistake for them to try to do it, because if they try to do it they are going to be doing something that doesn't come from their souls. If it isn't egosyntonic, then that body of material is going to be introjected, and the product will be similar to the product of introjected food. And you know what happens when you don't chew your food. From time to time I hear people identifying Gestalt therapy by the techniques, by particular, specific techniques that particular Gestalt therapists have used or have popularized. I remember the story, Bob, you were telling me over lunch a couple of days ago about some people saying that what you did wasn't Gestalt therapy because you didn't use a hot seat, you didn't have an empty chair there, so it wasn't Gestalt. Gestalt is certainly much more than techniques. It does include a body of techniques which have evolved, which have been developed. But that's not a closed list. That list goes on, hopefully. In addition to a body of techniques, Gestalt therapy involves a particular organismic theory of personality, which has roots in quite a number of people. And the part that is most often overlooked is that Gestalt therapy also has a particular philosophical underpinning. Gestalt therapy makes sense only in the context of that philosophy. It is, basically, a humanistic existential philosophy with a little oriental flavoring thrown in. Now if a person does not believe, does not have as a basic philosophical position something that fits with existentialism, some basic appreciation for such things as choice, responsibility, experience, then the techniques of Gestalt therapy make no sense. They are mechanical. I have found that sometimes I have trainees who do not go on to do Gestalt therapy, that the most valuable thing they learn in the training program is that this is not for them. And I am very satisfied when that happens. I think that's an important discovery and they go with my blessings.

The third guideline that I have stated is *I can teach only what I know. I can teach only what I want to learn.* The first half of that is a truism. Obviously I can't teach anything that I don't know. I have to be pretty well grounded in something before I am able to demonstrate it, convey it, show it, talk about it, in a way that is interesting, in a way that's alive, in a way that people can take hold of, chew on, and hopefully assimilate. The second half of this seeming paradox is that I can only teach what I want to learn more about. I think that one of the most important functions of a teacher, not just in Gestalt therapy, but a teacher of anything, is to be inspiring. There are two meanings of inspiration. One is getting excited, getting turned on to something. The other is, of course, (breathes) that kind of inspiration. That's the one we worked with yesterday. Breathing. And they're connected. Not just etymologically, but they are connected experientially. To be inspired is to be excited, turned on. And to be turned on, you have to breathe, you have to take in, you have to breathe in. And that's the way I try to teach. I like to teach. When I am on, when I am centered, that's what I do. I like to turn people on and get them excited, because out of that excitement people will move. Excitement leads to activity, to action, to movement, to interaction, to dealing with the environment. Now if there is something I am teaching that

I want to learn more about, I will be excited, and then I will be more inspiring. If it's something that I have taught over and over and over in the same way then it's going to be dull for me. I am going to be dull, and my presentation is going to be dull. I perked up my ears when you were talking, Sonia, about "the experience cycle," how it's different every time it's taught. There's a basic core of information there, but the teaching of it is done differently every time. I call my version of that cycle "the contact-withdrawal cycle" in my book, *The Body in Psychotherapy*, and I have had that experience, both of teaching it differently at times and being excited and people really liking it. And there have been times when I haven't felt like doing it and I was scheduled to do it, and I would do it like I did it last year, and the performance lacked luster. So I want to teach whatever is exciting to me, wherever my growing edge is, and something that I can be excited about and turned on about. So that's going to be changing, that's going to be developing from time to time. Over the years there have been trainees who have repeated the program and I believe their repeating was more for the inspiration than for the information. The information itself evolves slowly, but the inspiration is fresh with each training program.

A fourth guideline. This one is one which I think has been talked about a lot and yet sometimes gets forgotten or neglected and that is that *experiential learning is of primary importance*. In our culture, the western culture, at least as far back as the time of John Dewey and his writings, we have known that experiential learning is more efficient, is more interesting. People learn better by experiencing things than by being told about things. So the main part of my training programs, the main emphasis, the main devotion of time, is to create experiences, to set up situations where experiences can develop.

Closely related to that is a fifth guideline. This is almost a corollary to the previous guideline. And that is that *experiential learning is enhanced by cognitive structuring, cognitive framing*. In terms of the teaching model, what I learn best from and what I prefer to use in my teaching is to do the experiential work first and then a cognitive framing of that work. There are a couple of reasons for this. One is that if you do a cognitive structure first, a didactic presentation, and then try to follow it up with experiences, people don't always follow the rules. People may not have the experience you just told them they're going to have. I remember this in a training program with the Polsters in La Jolla. They laughed and chuckled about this. They would do a lecture in the morning, about an hour's lecture, and then they would try to demonstrate those phenomena, but they would always preface their demonstration by saying, "Now this demonstration may turn out to have nothing to do with what we've been talking about." And, that was true about half the time. So if you do the didactics first, then the experiential may not follow; it may not connect. Conversely, by doing the didactic work first, you may be programming what's going to happen. You may give people the hint that this is what they should do. You may be inadvertently giving them a should in that and programming the experience. So by programming some of the spontaneity, some of the aliveness is lost. Just as importantly, doing the experiential work first then makes the didactic material personally relevant. And that's how we all learn best. We learn about that which is personally relevant. That may be the biggest problem in public education, in those years and years of school. I'm hearing it now from my kids. I have a daughter in high school and I have a son in grammar school, and they both hate school. And when I ask them about school, what they hate is that they are studying things, they are memorizing things, that have, as far as they can see, no personal relevance whatsoever. Now I learn very quickly, I feel very bright, very smart, when there is something I'm interested in and I read about it, or some experience I've had that I then go read about. Right now I'm turned onto whales. I went whale watching yesterday, and when I get home I'm going to read about whales. And I imagine I will feel very smart as I read that material. I'll really take it in because it will have some personal relevance, some relevance because I have experienced something now with the whales and I feel inspired. So if you can do some experiential work and then talk about that work specifically and relate that to theory there will be a personal relevance, and a connection can be made. If you do too much experiential work without cognitive framing, it's difficult for the person to transfer that experience into a new situation. The model is concrete work, concrete experience which then gets abstracted and filed away through cognitive framing. That abstract cognitive framing allows, then, a coming back down to, bringing that back down to the next experience, making the connection.

One more guideline. This is a practical one, and that is I have learned it is extremely important to *keep the training contract explicit*, to be very clear at the outset what it is that I'm offering. In the early days of Gestalt demonstrations, a lot of times very little structuring was done. I remember the first Gestalt workshop I was ever in was with Jim Simkin, and I didn't know what in Hell was going on. I walked into this room and there was a circle of chairs where people sat. He was out in the middle and he had a chair with nobody in it and a box of Kleenex. We walked in and sat down and there was silence. Nothing happened. We sat and sat and sat. It seemed like ten or fifteen minutes. It probably wasn't, but we just sat. I didn't know what was going on. There was so little structuring. I think that's a mistake in a training program. I think in a training program it's important to tell people what you have in mind, what it is you think you're offering, so when people pay their money they have some agreement with you as to what they're going to get from that.

I think that's respectful. I talked a little bit in my workshop yesterday about respect. Several people were asking questions about doing body work in psychotherapy and some of the possible dangers of that: legal dangers, ethical dangers, what not. And one of the things I said is that the major thing, the major safeguard is to work respectfully, to be respectful of the personhood of each person with whom you work. And I think having an explicit contract for training is part of that respectfulness. That way people don't get disappointed. The explicit contract is a way of minimizing some of those implicit expectations. Remember what Fritz said about expectations. That can get very heavy in a training group when someone has paid several hundred dollars and spent several months with you, and at the end said, but I thought I was going to learn such and such. I thought we were going to do so and so.

BETSY MINTZ: What I'm going to do here is to tell you about some techniques which I have developed to help therapists — and also sometimes to help myself — develop empathy with their clients. Now as you know, empathy is not the same as sympathy. It does not mean feeling sorry for the client. Nor does it mean getting your own feelings all mixed up with the client's feelings, which of course is what we call confluence. Indeed, it is my hope that the techniques which I will present to you can enable a therapist to separate his own feelings from those of his client, while at the same time understanding and accepting the client's emotional experience.

Now, as we know, therapy walks on two legs. One is the intellectual, cognitive, technical aspect, which we learn from books and instructors and our own experience and which we may then try to teach. We can't dispense with this, but probably it is the less important aspect of our work and the more important aspect is our awareness, which I think is based on intuition as well as conscious observation, of what the client is experiencing at the moment. And technique alone is by no means enough to help the client himself become more fully aware of this experience. At any given point in therapy, it is always possible to use the empty chair, or say "Keep doing that," or say "What is your bodily experience now?" or say "Notice your breathing." Usually there are perhaps half a dozen interventions at any given time which may be useful, and perhaps a hundred interventions which may be useless or even damaging, like the example (which I liked) given by George, "I don't believe you," which I thought would almost always be non-productive or even counter-therapeutic. Our task, then is to choose which intervention out of many may be best, and this must be done in a split second of time, and the choice cannot be wise unless we are in empathic attunement with the client.

My techniques for fostering this kind of empathy have been developed in small supervisory groups of three to five working therapists, whom I see in private practice, since I am not associated with a training institute. In supervision, the most effective approach which I have ever found appears to be simple but very often — in fact, *usually* — has rather remarkable results. This is role-playing.

Let me describe this. Your supervisee introduces the client, usually beginning with elementary data — age, gender, how long in treatment, and perhaps the client's presenting complaint. And if the therapist goes on, describing sessions with the client, it is perilously likely to approach what Fritz used to call gossip — that is, we are hearing *about* what happened, and nobody is experiencing anything.

So I say something like, "Go out of the room and enter again as Joe, or as Susie, or whatever the client's name is. Be Joe-or-Susie. Feel like him, walk like him, speak with his voice and feel his feelings. And — this is important — don't necessarily try to imitate him but try to feel the way he feels. And whatever you do, don't break role. Don't give us little asides to explain your imitation. Just be the client, and I'll be the therapist." And I also explain that, in roleplaying a therapist, I am by no means trying to give an example of absolutely perfect therapy, setting myself up as a role-model of how this client "ought" to be treated. I am simply re-creating the therapeutic situation in order to give the therapist an opportunity to role-play his client.

Chairs are now arranged facing one another, as in a therapeutic situation, and I sit opposite a chair reserved for the client. Role-playing his client, the supervisee is asked to leave the room and reenter in role. And when the supervisee comes in, I say "Hi, " which is my usual way of greeting my clients, and await his first statement.

Now, very often, something really extraordinary happens, and never do I cease to marvel at it. The supervisee becomes somebody else. His voice is different, his manner and gait are different, he even seems to be wearing his clothes differently, he has completely different mannerisms. Even the liniments of his face (or, of course, her face if the supervisee is a woman) seem to be different. You have seen photographs of great actors and actresses playing various roles? They look different in every role, and this is by no means entirely a matter of different costumes and make-up and hairdo, but also a matter of facial expression. The actual liniments of the face seem to change. I am constantly amazed by the dramatic talent shown by supervisees who, probably, have never seen themselves as having any special histrionic gift.

However, this does not necessarily happen at once. Very often, despite my explicit directions, the supervisee will break off and explain to me and the group, "I forgot to tell you, she just got a divorce" — or something like that. In this case, I say something like, "I want to hear it from the client. Go out of the room, come back as the client, and maybe you'll tell us about the divorce better that way." Or, perhaps, instead of identifying with the client, the supervisee will caricature the client, indirectly poking fun at the client, imitating in an exaggerated way the speech and mannerisms which obviously irritate him.

If this happens, we have already found out something — namely, that the client is irritating to the supervisee — but my practice is to put this aside temporarily and simply say, "I don't think you're really identifying. Please go out of the room again and really be your client and come in again." By now, of course, we are not using the word "client" but are saying Joe, or Mary, or whatever the supervisee calls this particular client. And, in role-playing the therapist, I am careful to use the name of my supervisee's client as often as may be appropriate, to facilitate identification.

Perhaps before we go further I should add that, in taking the role of the therapist, I confine myself to very general remarks designed to further the identification process. For instance, I would not suggest the use of the empty chair, which as we know often taps the deep unconscious. A couple of times I did try to get my therapist-supervisee to use the empty chair when role-playing the client, but we got such a mixed-up jumble of supervisee and client with this very powerful technique for tapping the unconscious that now I restrict myself to remarks which are designed simply to keep the situation going and to facilitate identification.

Now here's an example of the way this supervisory technique works, an example taken from my actual experience. Let's say that we have a client, a woman who is working with one of my supervisees in my small supervisory group, who is very compliant and does everything the therapist suggests. And the therapist could say almost nothing except "I'm really scared!" but reported later that he had experienced a slight trembling and an actual chill, a physical terror.

Now, what happened in the next therapeutic interaction with Sally?

Very little, in fact, that was really dramatic. Certainly the therapist, my supervisee, was too skillful to announce to Sally, "I understand you now, you're really scared" which would have been absurd. But there were subtle differences in his interaction with Sally, and in his choice of therapeutic interventions.

Within a few sessions Sally had acknowledged the underlying terror of abandoning what Fritz would have called the "phony layer" and what psychoanalysts would call "defenses," and to experience and express her authentic feelings. This was not dramatic, but it did mark the beginning of real and rewarding therapy. Dramatic moments do occur in therapy, but as we know they are few and far between.

We may speculate as to how and why this breakthrough of the therapist's understanding of his client occurred in the role-playing, a breakthrough which usually occurs — though not often so impressively — when the therapist drops his therapeutic stance, or in some instances perhaps his therapeutic mask, and identifies with the client. In this situation, I believe, a deeper knowledge of the client comes to the surface, but in my opinion this knowledge really was always there, though not available, In my opinion, we all know more about one another, including people whom we meet socially and not in the therapeutic situation, than we are aware of, a knowledge which comes in part through subtle subliminal clues — body language, tone of voice, and so on — and in part, I believe personally, through telepathic awareness. But this is a controversial point which we need not discuss here and which in any case is not directly relevant to supervision. Role-playing, then, is simply a method by which we can get our own selves out of the way and obtain access to our knowledge of the client's experience.

The example of Sally is one of many examples which I could offer you if time permitted, but it is by no means unique. Role-playing usually works. It taps direct experience, it's rewarding, and it's fun. Also, you can use it for yourself as a therapist. If you have a client who bores you, irritates you, frustrates you — and who among us does not have at least one such client? — you may be able to break the deadlock simply by imagining how it must feel to be that client. You can even go into an empty room and role-play the client all by yourself, although it does go better if you're with a colleague or a trusted friend.

You may find some interesting surprises awaiting you, and you may find your work with the client less frustrating in the future.

Now I'll go on to share another of my favorite supervisory techniques, although I like this one less well than roleplaying. It's called, "Say what you really want to say." Here the therapist-supervisee remains himself, puts the client in the empty chair in his imagination, and tries to follow the instructions which I offer:

"Say what you'd really like to say to the client. Forget your professional responsibility. Forget that you're supposed to fill a therapeutic role. Just let yourself go, say what you really want to say."

Usually the therapist finds it difficult to abandon his therapeutic stance even for a few minutes. He will still try to "help" the client but will talk louder and be more directive. It takes several efforts on my part, usually, before the inner feelings really come out. Here's one example:

The client, Judy, was working with one of my therapist-supervisees who was irritated by her, and understandably so. She had inherited a little trust fund which gave her barely enough money to live on, but not to live comfortably, and because her income was so low she had persuaded the therapist to accept her at a very minimal fee. Incidentally, I think that the importance of the fee, be it high or low, is often minimized in supervision, whether therapy is carried on in private practice or in a clinic.

Anyhow, Judy had some secretarial skills and she was young and healthy and reasonably personable, but she just couldn't seem to muster up the energy to find a job. She thought she ought to find a job. She really thought she ought to do something. But somehow or other, she didn't seem to get around to it. She slept late, went to movies, went to beauty parlors. And her therapist, my supervisee, worked very hard for what was almost a token fee, with endless dialogues between lazy-Judy and Judy-who-wants-to-work, but nothing happened. So I asked him to put an imaginary Judy in the empty chair, with instructions to let himself go and tell her how he really felt about her.

At first, as usually happens, he was like most young therapists — older ones also — in finding it difficult to abandon the therapeutic stance. He exhorted Judy to get a job, scolded her for not doing so, almost pleaded with her — but he was still a therapist and had not really expressed his feelings. Finally we did have a real breakthrough and it went like this:

"Judy, you are a lazy bum. You are a drone. You are a pimple on the face of society. You lie in bed half the day, you go to the beauty parlors to get your hair done when you could perfectly well do it at home — I notice you can afford beauty parlors — and here I am working my ass off to help you at practically no money whatsoever!"

The therapist changed chairs, became Judy and said in a soft, pathetic voice, "Oh, but I have so little money, I can't afford to pay you any more."

At this fantasized reply (probably just what Judy would really have said) the therapist lost his temper and shouted "Okay, enough already! Either you pay a decent fee or no more therapy, get it?"

There was a long silence. Then the young therapist looked at us, half-grinning, half-embarrassed. "My God, am I mad at that woman! And to think I've been letting her string me along all this time!"

We now discussed what should be done, and agreed that Judy should have a reasonable time — perhaps a month — to find a job and pay an appropriate fee, and that otherwise the therapist would not continue to see her. He left the supervisory session feeling relieved and exhilarated, and reported at our next meeting that he had indeed been able to confront Judy, and that she was looking for a job.

Was there a sudden miraculous change in Judy? Regrettably, no. She delayed a serious effort to find work, and dropped out of treatment. She did, however, return to the same therapist seven months later, with a rather good job as a receptionist, paid an appropriate fee, and settled down to work. The dynamics of this therapeutic achievement are beyond the scope of this presentation, but it is my conviction that if we had approached the problem only in terms of Judy's laziness (presumably compounded of a wish to be cared for and a wish to control the therapeutic situation) the therapist would not have been able to confront Judy effectively. He was able to do so only after expressing and assimilating his intense irritation in the supervisory group. Because of his completely genuine wish to be helpful, and his starry-eyed belief that a therapist should not be concerned with money, he had been helping Judy avoid the real question which underlaid her job problem, the question "What shall I do with my life'" His confrontation, eventually, helped her to face this question.

Let me describe one more technique, which is less useful and less dramatic than the ones I've just described, but still I think it's worth knowing. It's a modification of a little-known projective technique called "Eavesdropping," which probably should be better known because it's easy and useful.

Here's the original projective technique; you might enjoy trying it with yourself first. Imagine that you are in one of those old-fashioned restaurants with high-walled wooden booths, so that you cannot see who's sitting behind you, but you can hear their voices. And they are talking about you. They know you, they are friends or acquaintances or perhaps just people who know you by reputation. What would you most like to hear these people say about you? Do this part of the technique first, or else your client may be too upset to do the other part. And of course the second part is, "What would you least like to hear said about yourself?"

Okay, now here's how it can be used in supervision when you wish to explore the therapist-client relationship with your supervisee. You say, "Imagine that you're sitting in a high-walled restaurant booth. Behind you, out of sight but not out of earshot, is your client and a close friend, a confidant. And your client is talking about his work with you, and the confidant asks, 'Well, but what kind of a person is your therapist?' And your client answers. What would you most like to hear him say, what would you least like to hear him say, and what do you think he might actually, really say?" This little technique often gives the young therapist new insight into his relationship with his client and into the therapeutic relationship in general.

It's pretty clear, I think, that my techniques, my games, do not offer my therapist-supervisees any new knowledge about their clients. In formal supervision, the supervisor might diagnose the client, formulate the client's psychodynamics, and tell the therapist what he should do. It is better, I believe, to help the therapist become aware of what he already knows about the client, which is usually more than he is able to recognize and use. Nor does this approach rule out the more conventional form of supervision, which can be used alongside my games if it seems necessary. The games are fun, they make the supervisory sessions come alive — and aliveness, of course, is what we're after in Gestalt work.

GEORGE BROWN: I just want to say, Betsy, how much I enjoyed what you had to say, how much I support what you say. One thing that I thought about, Ed, when you were talking, was this whole issue of inspiration. It sometimes concerns me. Those of you who have watched Judith and me work know we tend to be inspirational. One of the things I'm worried about when we do training, is that this may give a magical quality to our work so that people think, "Oh, what you guys are doing is — you know it's great, creative, and so forth; I could never do that." And I don't want that and we try very much to talk about, not only individual styles, which is something very important, but the fact that *you can do this.* You'll do it in your own way, but there's nothing magical about any of this. You know, it's basic stuff. There's a sound theory for it. You can learn it. That's one dimension of it. The second dimension of it is when people look at me as if I'm some kind of charismatic or inspirational leader, it puts a great deal of distance between them and me, and I don't like it. And so we intentionally (I don't think in a manipulative way), when we do workshops, (most of these are residential) we are with our people and we talk about ourselves the way they talk about themselves. So that they will see us as like everybody else. I think that's important.

BOB HARMAN: Sonia, would you like to respond?

SONIA NEVIS: When we were coming in from the hallway, we were talking about whether there was going to be controversy here and were we going to say different things? Well what stood out for me was how different we are, and how similar. Certainly you're not going to mistake one of us for the other. Our styles are different. We pick different things to talk about. Things that were important to one weren't important to the other, but there is no mistaking that we are all saying the same thing. There's just no mistaking that we're coming from a common ground in terms of a stance we take with other people, in terms of how we expect to treat and be treated, that the theory . . . obviously there was nothing said here that jarred me, that I would not say, "Well, of course."

EDWARD SMITH: I was thinking that the "time of the Guru" is over. I think that may have been an important phase of the development of Gestalt therapy. That was an exciting time in our country. And I have some nostalgia for that period with the flower children and all that. But that's over. That doesn't fit now.

GEORGE BROWN: I don't think it fit then.

EDWARD SMITH: It was fun at any rate. And I don't know of or see very often that kind of charismatic therapist. I don't think there is much of a place for the kind of charismatic, turn-on therapist that we saw in the sixties.

GEORGE BROWN: That's a problem in Europe, though, because there are some over there. I don't know about too many in the States, because of the nature of my work. But I know in Europe there are some and it really bothers me. Especially confrontive Gestalt which you find a lot in Europe, especially in Germany.

BOB HARMAN: Before we begin answering the audience's questions, I have a few responses of my own. There was a lot of agreement among the panelists and I was thinking how Gestalt therapy sometimes gets over-identified with techniques and people miss the real essence of the therapy. There are some powerful techniques. I believe the first time Fritz Perls said to someone, "Put your mother in the empty chair," was probably one of the most creative moments in the history of psychotherapy. The second time he did it, it was technique. And because we're smart people, and we see things work for others, we tend to pick up on that. People who study Gestalt therapy need to learn a sense of timing, they need to learn in their training that there are times when techniques go out the window and you are with a person in the empathic way that Betsy was speaking about this morning, and for me that's what distinguishes a trained Gestalt therapist from someone who has picked up a few techniques. There are Gestalt therapists who are willing and able to be with the client in such a way that the techniques are gone and they are with that person, responding to them out of their own personhood and out of a strong background of theory. For me that's what training is all about.

I was impressed with what the panel spoke about. I was also impressed with some of the things that were not said. For example, when do we decide, as trainers, to ask someone to leave a program? What criteria do we use to evaluate trainees' progress? Might we ask a trainee to repeat a year or, as I heard Jim Simkin say, "Take a year off and then have your therapist write to me about what you're doing?"

I would like to ask the panel members, before we get some more audience participation to respond some to these issues about when is a person trained, how do we decide that a person isn't suitable for training, how do we select people to come into training?

GEORGE BROWN: I'd like to comment on that. First I'd like to comment on your comment. I can't remember whether Fritz said this or wrote this, and because I'd spent time with him and also read his stuff I can't remember. It's all one big, amorphous Gestalt. I think he said that using techniques is the last resort.

SONIA NEVIS: . . . when I don't know what else to do.

GEORGE BROWN: When I don't know what else to do. In terms of having someone leave the group or . . . this used to happen a lot more with me than it does. I don't know whether I'm becoming more mellow or what. I usually am pretty clear in terms of my response to that person that there's a lot of pathology there. If I had the time and the energy I could do it. But I don't have the time and energy. And it's not fair to the other people in the group and so it's very clear for me and I do it with . . . feeling a little badly for the person, but clear and clean, and I say to them, "You're not ready."

This is mostly in the university situation. I had a case recently of a professor from a European country who came to be in our training, in our work, and in all four of our classes that were going on that quarter he was wanting to teach the class. And that manifested all kinds of strange and bizarre behavior. And I remember telling him to leave, with pleasure.

EDWARD SMITH: I think there's a prior issue to asking people to leave, and that's the issue of screening or "deselecting" in the first place. "Deselecting." That's a word I learned from the Peace Corp. I worked for the Peace Corp some years ago as a field assessment counselor and we "deselected" people.

In a training program you have the option of deselecting at the technique level — deselecting or slowing someone down in the program if they are just catching onto techniques. Or, if, as I was saying earlier, the approach is not egosyntonic for someone.

I think there are two issues here: There is the issue of technique — do the trainees resonate with what you're teaching or do they just not catch on, just not get the message because it doesn't fit with who they are? And the other issue is one more of ethics and morality. There are people who have a relatively neglected sense of respect for other people, and some of them want to be therapists. Over the years I can only remember our deselecting one person on that basis who was already in the program. There may have been some others . . . this person may be outstanding because we had a lot of trouble with him. He was a social psychologist who wanted to retrain in clinical and was taking Gestalt training but seemed to have a lack of a sense of appropriateness. And so we asked him not to continue the program. We told him he could not continue the program and suggested that he seek some individual therapy and begin exploring himself in that way.

BETSY MINTZ: The big controversy in a number of organizations that I'm familiar with is a topic on which I have no opinion — which is kind of unusual for me — and that is whether or not we should accept for training people with no background in one of the relevant disciplines (psychology, psychiatry, social work, nursing). I feel there is so much to be said on both sides of this issue. It's a very hot topic. It has practical implications because of the insurance situation and the malpractice situation and I think this has to be recognized.

SONIA NEVIS: I'm not sure I have anything new to say except that it's an issue that has been batted about over the years at the Institute and that we go back and forth between total anarchy and total rigidity. I remember a whole day when the staff got together to try to deal with selection issues and we divided into two groups, those who were "elite" and those who were "slobs." I was in the "slob" category. So I don't know. Selection is talked about — not decided about. There are things to be said on all sides. I agree with what you're saying, Ed, in terms of selection. I don't imagine that anybody comes to the Institute without somebody having known them previously, trained with other people that were known, or known other students. For people who are slower learners it's the responsibility of the staff to continually tell them that they are learning slowly and tell them what we think and tell them what we think they need. I don't think it's our job to control what they do and how they do it, but to stay honest to what we see and think. Thinking back over all the years, I can remember two people we asked to leave. Two.

BOB HARMAN: I'd like now to open the floor for questions from the audience.

QUESTION: I wonder if there's any ethical or legal problems in a university setting when a student is matriculated and already accepted into the program and performing adequately on papers and tests and so forth — I believe you can't flunk them out of the program or give a bad grade for having a bad personality . . .

GEORGE BROWN: In my university that is true. You can't kick someone out of a program, but each instructor has the authority to not take anybody in his or her class that he or she doesn't want. So, in effect, if they don't want to leave, we'll say fine, hang around, but you're not going to be allowed into any other of the classes.

QUESTION: I wonder if you'd deal with the issue of certifying or not certifying as a result of going through an institute training program? Why not have certificates for people who have reached a certain point in Gestalt training? What might that communicate to the public?

BETSY MINTZ: Well, I am unable to take a firm stance on this whole question of training. There's really no question but what some awfully challenging people may be lost to us if we require formal academic preparation and yet I have actually seen people who have never been able to do anything that worked out for them and they think to themselves: "Well, I may as well be a therapist." I've never been able to think this through thoroughly. I would like somebody to help me think it through clearly.

SONIA NEVIS: I have a strong bias. I'm very much against certification. I was against it all those years ago when they first began licensing laws in Ohio. Things change. Shapes change. I don't know what people are going to do and what direction they are going to take. I can't predict into the future who's going to develop in what way. And, I don't see that licensing has done us any good anyway. So I'm against it.

QUESTION: I've been hearing all weekend about how we as trainers and therapists have been evolving and the rules won't work and it's past. We seem to be implying that there is something new about trainees today that wasn't true before. I don't think that's been clearly articulated as yet.

SONIA NEVIS: I'll start. I'll start on the guru side and then get to how the trainee side is different. I think there are no gurus now because the very things that we are teaching are not mysterious. That's what a guru is — mystery. Therefore, all the power is invested in the person that's doing this mysterious thing. I don't think that what we do is mysterious anymore. I think those years have gone and that many of the things that we teach are now in the general culture. I think we've had a tremendous impact. So here we are. You know what I know when you're my trainee. Obviously I know more if you're my trainee because I've had many more years of experience and I've put a lot of energy into finding ways to talk about it and finding ways to teach it, but you're not coming to me for some mysterious things. You know very well that therapy comes from a certain frame or theory, a certain set of practices. We, the trainers, have some idea of what people can learn, how they learn, how much they learn. They know they're not going to be transformed. So, I think trainees today are different. They're very sophisticated compared to twenty-five years ago. It's dramatically different and the questions that are asked make teaching much more interesting and more challenging.

BETSY MINTZ: I'm very impressed with what Sonia just said — that the guru is now obsolete because we are no longer mysterious. I like that concept very much. But I think we must recognize at the same time that there are always unexplored frontiers and that if you ever believe that you have codified your approach to your patients and your knowledge of theory and your knowledge of techniques to the point where you just have to push a little computer button and out comes the right technique, you're dead. You have to rely to some extent upon your mysterious wisdom and upon the mysterious wisdom of your client and your trainee.

QUESTION: Should training require and/or involve Gestalt therapy for the trainee? Also, what's the difference between training and therapy?

SONIA NEVIS: Therapy has to be part of the training or else the training is nothing.

EDWARD SMITH: Yes.

BETSY MINTZ: You know, you could make a case for their being similar. I see therapy, or I like to see therapy, as helping someone grow up and develop, rather than us fixing up symptoms or problems, and certainly training is also not only the imparting of knowledge but the stimulus, the provision of an optimum climate for self development. And here there's a lot of overlap. I always resented having come originally from the psychoanalytic background. I was always infuriated by the assumption that if an analyst in training had any countertransference problems, back to the couch. You're not supposed to have any feelings for your patient. I recall when I was doing supervision ages back, my first supervisor said, "I think I have a problem with this patient. I like him." Now that's a little too far of a spin off of are they the same, but I think you are dealing either in therapy or in training with a whole, entire human being including both the feelings and the intellect, and if you emphasize only the intellect in training and only the feelings in therapy you're off.

SONIA NEVIS: I see it the same way. For me, they're totally different, and yet you can't take them apart. The image I sometimes have is of playing the piano with two hands. With the left hand you're keeping the beat. That's what you're doing in training. You're teaching people what the beat is and what to be aware of and what to watch and to get that sense of timing and rhythm. But with the right hand, the melody, you're being more authentically there, which has to do with therapy and of course what makes therapy so hard is that you've got to play with two hands. They come together and I can't imagine any training program that doesn't pay attention to both, all the time, side by side.

BETSY MINTZ: I would like to mention that I think it is almost always a bad idea to have the same therapist serve later as supervisor, that you get so imbued with a particular approach that you become narrow or perhaps you introject in the sense of swallowing without chewing. I'm always distressed when I hear that a therapist has been in treatment with so and so for so many years and then supervision with the same person for so and so many years. It seems to me this is deadening.

QUESTION: I'd like to bring up the issue of confrontation again. I was disturbed by the ease with which it was decided that confrontation is a bad thing to do.

BOB HARMAN: I don't believe we decided that.

QUESTION: Well, that was my sense. And I'm a little struck by the absence of controversy, argument, disagreement here. I'd like to know in your teaching how you handle the issue of aggression. To me, a healthy part of my experience at the New York Institute for Gestalt Therapy was dealing with argument and disagreement and restructuring, and rebuilding. And I really haven't heard much discussion about how you handle that in your training.

BOB HARMAN: I personally welcome disagreements and aggression and differences when it's done respectfully. I encourage that.

QUESTION: What is respectful aggression?

BOB HARMAN: It's when a person is searching for information or making a point or expressing themselves fully in such way that they are not trying to annihilate me.

SONIA NEVIS: Aggression and confrontation are not the same thing. Aggression in the sense of lively differences or aggression in terms of being very interested in something and pursuing that interest and mobilizing oneself and mobilizing other people seems to be just so central to Gestalt therapy that I can't imagine a training program or an institution without it.

I joke that in Cleveland there are as many views of an issue as there are people viewing the issue. There's never agreement at one level even though there may be agreement at another level. As for confrontation, I called it the other day "cowboy psychology." Confrontation is coming at somebody aiming to surprise and startle and to get them off their center when they're not ready. It's not that I don't know the advantages of startling and surprising and not even that I don't do it when I'm in the mood to be mean — but those are not my proudest moments. I don't think it's intrinsic to Gestalt therapy at all, that kind of shocking, startling, surprising thing that I call confrontation. Again that has nothing to do with disagreement. There's plenty. There's plenty here on the panel.

BOB HARMAN: I would like to thank the panel for being here. I think your contributions have been excellent.

This article was edited from a transcription of a panel presentation at The Gestalt Journal's Eighth Annual Conference on the Theory and Practice of Gestalt Therapy which met in Provincetown, Massachusetts, on May 16, 17, and 18, 1986. The individual participants edited their own sections and Journal Editor Joe Wysong edited the question and answer section and assembled the final version.

~

STAGES OF THE
THERAPEUTIC CRAFT

A few months ago I sat with Sol and Bernice Rosenberg and twelve or so other psychotherapists in a small room of the Plaza del Mar, a few miles north of Ensenada. A couple of doors down the walkway, Steve McQueen had spent some of his last days, seeking assistance from a drug not legally available in his homeland. We talked about him and we talked about how we came to be psychotherapists. Two trends emerged as we conversed well into the night. One was reflected in the number of us who were firstborn or only children. The second was reflected in the number who had at least one psychologically suffering parent. The pattern for many of us was to have taken a responsible and helping role early in life vis-à-vis a psychologically dependent parent. Most of us had been set up to be helpers, to help the troubled parent or parents. The high cliffs overlooking "el Océano Pacifica" are a good place to walk and contemplate such things. I walked in the mist and dampness.

I'm sure, for me, and believe it is true for most others who do not merely dabble in psychotherapy but give long-term devotion to its pursuit, that the first stage in the therapist's development is a "setting of the stage." Being the only child, as was my case, or a firstborn child, and having a parent looking to one for help, sets the stage for one to become a therapist. Childhood, then, is the unrecognized internship. Much longer and much more intense it is than the recognized one to be formally entered into many years

From: *Voices*, 23(4), 49-55 (1988).

later. If not overwhelmed or burned out by the familial internship, the child has the stage set, waiting until, now grown and formally trained, the adult child can step upon it to enact the role of psychotherapist. The residues and continuations of the familial internship often form the bulk of the budding therapist's personal therapy.

For the past several months, since that evening at the Plaza del Mar, I have been thinking about the stages of the adult therapist's growth. What are the steps gone through as one plays out the role for which the stage was long ago set? These stages have emerged in my thinking as I have reviewed my own training process from Ph.D. at twenty-six to established, recognized therapist at forty-five.

The therapist's development includes both personal growth and technical growth. That is the therapist grows both in fullness of personhood and in skills of therapeutic technique. So, the therapist's development is two-faceted. The relationship between these two facets is an interesting one. Techniques that are not brought to life through the deeply developed person-hood of the therapist lack humanness and tend to be mechanical. This thera-pist is a therapeutic technician, performing certain practiced maneuvers from her or his set repertoire. At best, he or she is shallow and fades as the novelty of her or his gimmicks is lost through over-use. At worst, such a therapist is manipulative for self-serving ends. The therapist who is lacking in technical skills, on the other hand, tends not to be very potent. He or she may be a good human being, compassionate and understanding, yet without effective procedures this therapist has little to offer in the facilitation of the growth process of another.

In a highly functioning therapist, techniques flow out of her or his person such that it is difficult to differentiate *who the person is* from *what the person does*. The techniques are enlivened and given meaning through the person of the therapist. He or she knows *how to be* and *what to do* in the authentic enactment of the therapeutic role.

There is an ethical principle that can be derived from this relation-ship between "person" and "technique." In *the Body in Psychotherapy* (Smith, 1985), the chapter on ethics, I wrote:

> The first ethical duty which I see is what I term the "ego-syntonic imperative." By this term I mean that for one to function optimally in the therapeutic role it is essential that he or she relate to the patient only in ways that are congru-

ent with who that therapist is . . . It is imperative, then, that the therapist only interact with the patient through techniques which are consistent with the therapist's person. To use ego-dystonic techniques is to be mechanical and inauthentic. So, if a therapist feels like herself or himself in using a technique, if that technique seems to flow out of her or him, then it is an appropriate technique to keep in one's repertoire. (p. 148)

It may be of interest to note that John Warkentin, a founder of the Atlanta Psychiatric Clinic style of Experiential Psychotherapy, referred to his supervision group which I was in as his "technique seminar."

The integrated growth of personhood and technical skill takes time, much time, years. The path to mastery requires decades to traverse.

A useful model for describing and understanding the therapist's growth is the classical learning curve (Smith, 1987). For those readers whose roots are not in experimental psychology, I will describe briefly the nature of the learning curve. For those of you who do have roots in experimental psychology, but developed distaste for things statistical, just bear with me.

The classical learning curve is derived in approximate form by the data generated in a simple learning task such as those traditionally studied in experimental psychology (e.g., maze running, memorization of nonsense syllables, reaction times, motor coordination tasks, and discriminate learning). Conventionally plotted with number of trials of time spent in practice on the horizontal axis and number of correct performance units on the vertical axis, the curve shows negative acceleration with an asymptote. That is, the curve becomes less steep across trials or amount of time of practice (negative acceleration) and reaches a point after which the amount of practice required for an increment of improvement in performance becomes much greater than before (the asymptote). Spoken in the vernacular this is "the point of diminishing returns." In actual practice, the learning curves generated in the laboratory are not smooth, but show the ups and downs of erratic performance. An actual learning curve looks more like a curved saw blade, teeth pointing up. Oftentimes these cycles of progression and repression in learning tasks are the result of factors extraneous to the learning task *per se* (e.g., an environmental distraction, anxiety, loss of sleep, preoccupation with something else), so the curve is mathematically smoothed by averaging adjacent peaks and valleys. So, the classical learning curve emerges thus (see Figure 1):

Now, to relate this model to the growth and development of the therapist. Note that I have designated five points on the growth curve, labeled, 0, 1, 2, 3 and 4.

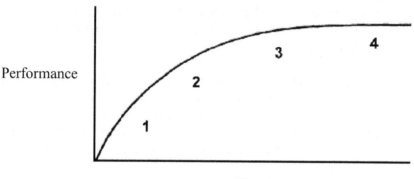

Performance

Time

The point designated 0 represents a beginning point of professional investment, no time yet invested and no professional development in evidence.

The area under the curve from point 0 to point 1 represents the state of the *neophyte therapist*. The curve is very steep here, which means that there is a rapid rate of growth during this stage. Beginning with a zero point, the neophyte enjoys a large return of learning from the time invested. This rapid rate of growth is usually exhilarating, lending the novice a strong sense of accomplishment. What is learned during this stage are the basics of the therapy system: basic vocabulary, basic concepts, basic therapeutic procedures. Much of this learning of the basics is more through introjection than through assimilation. In other words, the new material is swallowed more or less whole, not having been chewed thoroughly. Therefore, the new material is in the neophyte therapist, but it is not a part of her or him. It has not been digested and assimilated, mentally speaking. The telltale indication of this introjection is that the neophyte therapist is prone to confusion (mental indigestion) and to rote behaviors, copied from reading or from mentors (mental regurgitation). Having introjected this material, the neophyte often either lacks confidence or has a false sense of confidence. The danger, at this stage of development, is that the novice does not know how much he or she does not know.

The second stage, that of the *journeyman therapist*, is represented by the area under the curve between points 1 and 2. Note that the curve continues to be steep, although not as steep as it is in the neophyte stage. This reflects that learning continues to be fairly rapid. The journeyman stage is the stage of the therapist's development in which the basics of the system, introjected during the neophyte stage, are ruminated on and thus made assimilable. By reexperiencing the basic vocabulary, concepts, and techniques, again and again, and contemplating their meaning, they get assimilated. They become part of the substance of the therapist. Having assimilated the basics, the journeyman therapist is afforded a certain clarity. The danger for the journeyman therapist is that the clarity gained may give birth to an illusion of expertise. At this state of development the therapist has enough experience to have some genuine understanding of the therapy process, but not enough experience to have a seasoned perspective. The journeyman therapist has seen the basic elements, the usual manifestations of her or his therapy trade, but not yet those rare elements, the unusual manifestations of the system.

Most therapists, I have come to believe, do not develop beyond the journeyman stage. Many do not even reach the journeyman stage, but spend their professional careers at the stage of the neophyte. This is the case of the *dilettante therapist*. Moving from therapy system to therapy system, without ever investing enough time in any one system to reach the stage of journeyman, the dilettante therapist is full of unassimilated material from many sources. Remember, the type of learning which characterizes the neophyte stage is introjection, and the content is the basics of the system. So, the dilettante knows, in the sense of introjection, the basics of several systems, but lacks the genuine understanding which is afforded in the journeyman stage. For integration to take place, the material must first be assimilated, truly understood. Only then can the elements be connected in a manner that yields something new in the blend. By analogy, certain chemical elements may join to form compounds, while other combinations of elements, not having "valence" or affinity for each other, remain only mixtures. A neophyte chemist can mix chemicals together, but a journeyman chemist, one who understands "valence" (oxidation states), can create compounds. The dilettante therapist identifies herself or himself when he or she announces a workshop on "Neo-Reichian therapy, Cognitive Behaviorism, Bach Flower Remedies, Gestalt Techniques, and Sufism." To swallow that is to insure mental indigestion. The dilettante therapist is the product of rampant eclecticism.

The dilettante therapist chooses breadth of exposure over depth of exposure. Two factors illuminate this choice for me, and make it more understandable. The first factor involves the dynamic of introjection. Remember, in introjection one swallows whole, not really getting one's teeth into the material. Without benefit of mastication the material cannot be assimilated, cannot be made part of one. Not only does this result in mental indigestion, as discussed above, but it leaves an unmet hunger. Impatient, the introjector doesn't get filled in any lasting, satisfying way. So, the dilettante therapist, rather than becoming a ruminator, in the best sense, keeps moving on to new material in response to her or his hunger, only to introject again.

The second factor which makes dilettantism understandable is found in the nature of the classical learning curve which we have been using as our model. As we saw, the learning curve is steepest at the beginning. Learning is at a faster pace and is more exciting during that phase of the curve than at any other. Perhaps this is part of the reason that youth is such an exciting time of life; there is a continual beginning of new growth curves. Each facet of life presents another start on a course of growth and learning. The dilettante therapist seems to abandon the further pursuit of a therapy system when the excitement of the steep initial phase of the learning curve begins to wane. He or she then moves on to start with another system, to once again feel the excitement of a beginning. So, out of a chronic hunger to know, coupled with a fondness for the excitement of beginnings, the dilettante therapist moves lightly from system to system, candidate for the next therapy fad.

Some therapists, more patient with rumination than the dilettante, prefer breadth of perspective to greater depth of perspective, so reach the journeyman level before moving to learn another therapy system. Thereby, the *generalist therapist* is born. The generalist is a journeyman therapist several times over. Whereas the dilettante is eclectic in a superficial sense, the generalist is eclectic with a true understanding, developed through rumination and assimilation. As a journeyman, he or she is less likely to combine incompatible elements of different therapy systems into mixtures. The generalist may, actually, make some creative and workable compounds.

Those therapists who crave great depth of understanding of a therapy system continue their development into that stage which is represented by the area under the growth curve between points two and three. I am labeling such a person an *expert therapist*. The slope of the curve is less steep now, a reflection of the fact that further growth for the expert therapist is much slower than it was for her or him at the journeyman stage. Much time and practice are required for experiencing the less common events of the craft. This is the stage of advanced growth, the growth into expertise. With the attainment of such expertise, the therapist has much to offer as a teacher of neophytes and journeymen. The temptation for the expert therapist is to become arrogant. Oftentimes, the expert therapist, out of the experience of her of his very real power, becomes arrogant. This temptation can be offset by self-discipline, which may then provide passage to the last stage of growth.

The point on the learning curve designated by the 3 is the asymptote. Beyond this point, growth is very slow, with much time and experience being required for the realization of further increments of growth. The therapist may never stop growing, but the yield from additional experience from this point on is preciously small. During this stage it is the truly esoteric elements of the therapy system which are learned. I have named this stage, from point 3 to point 4, the point of death, the stage of the *master therapist*. The master therapist is stopped from further growth as a therapist only by her or his dying. It is these master therapists who sometimes are known for developing therapy systems. It is they who are the true luminaries of the craft of psychotherapy.

The growth curve can represent the entire lifetime of the master therapist. For others, there may be two or three or several growth curves, each ending short of the master stage, the expert stage, or, as we have seen in the case of the dilettante, even the journeyman stage. If the master therapists develop the systems of psychotherapy and train the trainers, and the expert therapists train the journeyman therapists, it is the journeyman therapists who deliver most of the good psychotherapy to nonprofessional patients. The neophyte stage is a necessary, even desirable one. At this stage, the tyro therapist may wish to be exposed to several therapy systems, sampling and introjecting the rudiments of each system until he or she recognizes a fit. Recognizing a fit means recognizing a system that is ego-syntonic. That system may then be learned to a journeyman level, or perhaps even beyond. The problem, as I have shown, is when the neophyte therapist remains a perpetual neophyte by moving from system to system, without ever investing in the rumination necessary to assimilate the material and thereby enter the realm of the journeyman.

These, then, are the stages as I see them — neophyte, journeyman, expert, and master. An eclectic therapist may be a neophyte many times over, and thus a dilettante; or a journeyman several times over, and thus a generalist. By virtue of the time required, it is very rare for an eclectic therapist to be an expert in more than one system; and almost by definition, there are not eclectic masters. Of course, it is possible to be an expert or even a master in a system and to have neophyte or even journeyman knowledge in another. (The evaluations of other systems which experts and masters sometimes offer bespeak their neophyte status relative to those systems. Their remarks lack the depth of understanding which characterizes assimilated material, and evidence, instead, an introjected corpus of basics.)

The model which I have presented seems, even in its simplification of a complex topic, to me to be useful. In the same vein of simplication, but in the medium of poetry, Delacroix wrote:

> To be a poet at twenty
> is to be twenty.
> But to be a poet at forty
> is to be a poet.

I offer a paraphrase:

> To be a therapist at thirty
> is to be an imitator of technique.
> But to be a therapist at fifty
> is to be a therapist.

~

SELF-INTERRUPTIONS IN THE RHYTHM OF
CONTACT AND WITHDRAWAL

I eagerly accepted the invitation to respond to the article "Boundary Processes and Boundary States." I welcome the opportunity to focus on the issues raised therein, and hopefully offer some clarification through my perspective. (At the time of this writing I did not know the identity of the author of the article.)

I want to demonstrate the development of my perspective and thereby show how I came to the explication of the Contact/Withdrawal Cycle. In so doing, I make no attempt to be exhaustive of the references to the Gestalt literature. That literature is large and rich. I will use only some of the possible references, leaving it to the interested reader to make further connections with other Gestalt writing.

As a starting point, we can take Perls' (1947, 1969, p. 7) statement "that the central conception is the theory that the organism is striving for the maintenance of a balance which is continuously disturbed by its needs, and regained through their gratification or elimination." We have, here, the basis for a dynamic process, a process of needs arising and needs being dealt with, in a rhythm.

To elaborate, I quote from *The Body in Psychotherapy*, (Smith, 1985, p. 29):

> Psychobiological existence is based on need cycles, the cycles of contacting other people and other things in one's world for the satisfaction of needs and the withdrawal that follows. There is a rhythm to the process: a periodicity as needs arise, are satisfied, giving way to other needs, and arise again after

---

From: *The Gestalt Journal*, 11(2), 37-57 (1988).

a while. The cycle of contact-satisfaction-withdrawal has a certain integrity and can be seen as a "unit of living." Each unit emerges as a particular need becomes prepotent, and an organismically lived figure takes shape within the context of the environmental background. This is a Gestalt, forming, dynamically playing out, and de-forming. From the organ-ism-in-environment background a dynamic organism-in-living emerges and recedes in figure-ground formations. The choice of which need is to be given prepotency at any given moment is based on the "wisdom of the organism."

We can gain considerable conceptual clarity by doing a more fine grained analysis of the contact-satisfaction-withdrawal cycle. When a need arises, the organism becomes mobilized to a state of higher energy. This is a state of arousal or excitement. Perls placed strong emphasis on this arousal, referring to ". . . the basic energy in us, on the basic being of the human organism, namely, to be excited. You can either be bored (or indifferent) or excited" (Perls, 1978a, p. 60).

Excitement naturally differentiates into a subjective experience of emotion. "Now, this excitement is not always there as excitement. You see, it changes. It changes mostly into emotions" (Perls, 1978a, p. 60). "In primi-tive undifferentiated form, emotion is simply excitement, the heightened metabolic activity and increased energy mobilization . . ." (Perls, Hefferline, and Goodman, 1951, p. 95). Emotion serves as the organism's direct evalua-tive experience of the organism/environment field.

Contained in the word "e-motion" is the implication and call for action. Action means a movement of energy into the musculoskeletal system. Action is concrete movement of parts of the body or even the whole body. The step from emotion to action is a transition from more sensory events to events more motoric.

Meaningful action must, in turn, become interactional. It must in-volve an *inter-action* with someone or something in the environment that is appropriate to the fulfillment of the need in question.

If all has gone well, a point of satisfaction is reached, the need is met. Prior to satisfaction, the potentially satisfying person or thing is regarded with interest, and given positive valence. With satisfaction comes a shift to disinterest and a neutral valence (with respect to the immediately satisfied need). The natural movement is then to withdrawal.

What I have described is a Contact/Withdrawal Cycle. *The Contact Episode* involves several stages:

Need → Excitement → Emotion → Action →
→ Interaction → Satisfaction

Following the experience of satisfaction is the *Withdrawal Episode.*

"The steps in the contact/withdrawal cycle are cumulative, each one depending for its success on the full and effective development of all previous steps. If a given step is not allowed to develop in full form, the proceeding steps will be less well formed and the ultimate satisfaction will be diminished or missed completely. There are also feedback loops such that later steps may enhance earlier steps. For example, taking action may enhance the felt emotion ..." (Smith, 1985, p. 31).

The contact/withdrawal cycle which I have developed is based on "The Transformation Theory" which Perls introduced in "Psychiatry in a New Key." The gist of the theory is that "Excitement is transformed into specific emotions, and emotions are transformed into sensoric and motoric actions" (Perls, 1978b, p. 52). In this same manuscript Perls referred to the "contact/withdrawal rhythm."

With the contact/withdrawal cycle as a conceptual tool, we can proceed now to an analysis of the self-interruptions, referred to variously, in "Boundary Processes and Boundary States," as neurotic mechanisms, boundary disturbances, major channels of resistant interaction, psychological mechanisms, and contact/ boundary interference.

Perls, Hefferline, and Goodman (1951, p. 118) stated that "Every healthy contact involves awareness ... and excitement (increased energy mobilization). Every block conversely necessitates the performance of actual work to prevent contact." Yes, healthy contact, meaning satisfying contact, requires awareness and excitement, and it also requires, as we see in the contact/withdrawal cycle, expression. To awareness and excitement we must add expression, that is, action and interaction. *The probability of satisfying contact is maximized by clear awareness, excitement, and an action-interaction sequence guided by that awareness and energized by that excitement.*

"Neurosis is characterized by many forms of avoidance, mainly the avoidance of contact" (Perls, 1947, 1969, p. 7). "The neurotic has a diminished contact with reality" (Perls, 1979, p. 14). This diminished contact with reality can be brought about by an avoidance of any of the steps in the contact/withdrawal cycle. So, one can avoid being aware of one's need, avoid becoming excited, avoid being aware of emotion, avoid taking action, avoid making the action an appropriate interaction, avoid being aware of satisfaction, or avoid withdrawal. I see, then, seven loci of avoidance or self-interruption. "At each of the junctures between steps in the Contact/Withdrawal cycle there is the possibility of allowing the organismic flow, or of interrupting. ... Such a self-interruption is a short-circuiting of

the cycle . . . a pseudo-withdrawal of avoidance" (Smith, 1986, p. 39-40).
Following from this, psychopathology could be defined as ". . . any pattern of
habitual self-interruptions in the contact/withdrawal cycles" (Smith, 1979,
p. 47). (*See Figure 1, next page.*)

Having defined "what" psychopathology is, in terms of the con-
tact/withdrawal cycle, two questions logically arise. They are the questions
of "why" and "how." Why does one choose to self-interrupt, and how can one
self-interrupt?

Let's address the question of "why," first. The answer lies in the
dynamic of the toxic introject. Certainly, anyone even superficially conversant
with the Gestalt literature is familiar with the "toxic introject." For this reason, I will be brief in my discussion and emphasize the relationship of the
toxic introject to the cycle of contact and withdrawal.

> To the basic patterning set in utero and in the birth process,
> there is then added the early learning history of the child.
> The treatment of the child by the parents, again, in general
> or in specific ways, encourages natural aliveness or discour-
> ages or even forbids it. During early development, most im-
> portantly the first five years or so, children are told not to
> express a certain feeling in a particular way, or not to express
> that feeling at all, or not to feel that feeling, or not to get
> excited, or sometimes not even to have certain wants. These
> prohibitive messages may be expressed verbally or
> non-verbally. Due primarily to the profound dependence of
> the child on the parenting figures for its very survival, the
> prohibitive messages are "swallowed-whole," introjected . . . .
> During this phase of the socialization process, many of the
> introjected messages are bionegative, that is, they are socially
> arbitrary messages which do not support the child's alive-
> ness. The bionegative message is, then, a toxic introject.
> There are two components to the toxic introject.
> First, is the content, or the specific prohibition. Second, is
> the threat that if the toxic introject is not obeyed love will be
> denied. The threat is experienced as if something awful,
> terrible, even catastrophic will happen. . . . Such toxic intro-
> jects are usually maintained, unexamined and unchallenged,
> throughout one's life. The result is lifelong internal conflict
> between the natural urge for aliveness and the toxic,
> introjected message which calls for deadness. Once the toxic
> message has been introjected, the threat of loss of love for
> disobeying becomes a conditioned phobic belief in imminent

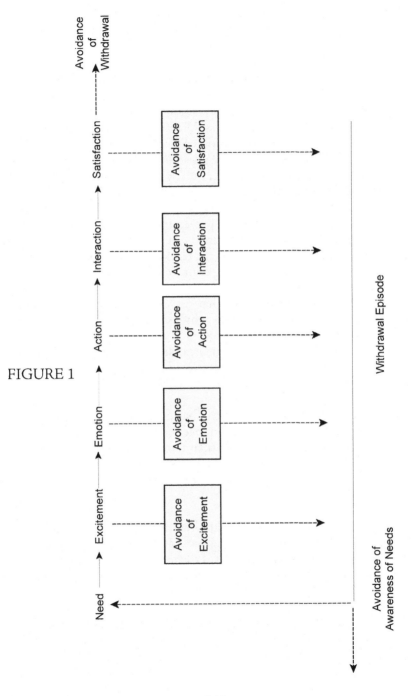

FIGURE 1

catastrophe whenever the toxic message is not honored. The toxic introject carries a "should" or "should not" (the content) and a catastrophic expectation.

The greater the number and severity of toxic introjects the more phobic the person is, and the less aliveness the person allows. The self-interruption of contact/withdrawal cycles is the essence of limiting aliveness. Which contact/withdrawal cycles (based on which needs or preferences) I interrupt, and at which of the seven points of possible avoidance I choose to enact the interruption, are dictated by the details of the content of the toxic introject. (Smith, 1985, pp. 37-38)

Introjection, therefore, has a pre-eminent position. It is the process which allows for the creation of neurosis. It is the process whereby toxic messages are incorporated, leading to the choke to interrupt one's rhythm of flow through cycles of need satisfying contact and withdrawal.

This brings us to the question of the "how" of self-interruption. Having answered the questions of "what" psychopathology is, in the context of the contact/withdrawal cycle, and "why" one would choose to self-interrupt, we can now address the processes whereby one can effect the self-interruptions, the avoidance of the next stage of contact or withdrawal.

Once again, Perls' early work provides an orientation. In a lecture delivered in 1946 or 1947, Perls (1979, p. 12-13) said:

As my theory assumes that the basic human functions are orientation and manipulation, every interference with the biological instinct cycles will maintain the specific dissociation by diminishing awareness or disturbing the free use of the motor system. Our patients are desensitized or awkward or both.

The point Perls made is that there are two distinct categories of processes for self-interruption. The two categories are: (1) diminishing awareness; (2) disturbing the free use of the motor system. The first is in the sensory realm, the second in the motor realm.

Perls (1979, p. 13) continued:

The figure/background/formation can be interfered with by deliberately changing one's attention, recognition of one's needs by blotting out awareness, for instance, by amnesia, scotomization, frigidity, semantic blockage, and so on, expression and gratification by linguistic and other motoric blockages, such as paralysis, and, more often, muscular spasms.

In *Ego, Hunger and Aggression*, Perls (1947, 1969, pp. 65-66) attempted a comprehensive and systematic listing of the "means of avoidance," admitting, however, that "The means of avoidance are so manifold that it is hardly possible to bring them into any kind of order, yet it might be worthwhile to approach the problem dialectically." In a scheme (though incomplete) we can put down:

(a) The means which tend toward annihilation, which have a subtractive function:
   (1) Scotoma.
   (2) Selectivity.
   (3) Inhibition.
   (4) Repression.
   (5) Flight.

(b) The hypertrophic growths or additions:
   (6) Over-compensation.
   (7) Armor.
   (8) Obsessions.
   (9) Permanent projection.
   (10) Hallucinations.
   (11) Complaints.
   (12) Intellectualism.
   (13) Mal-coordination.

(c) Changes and distortions:
   (14) Displacement.
   (15) Sublimation.
   (16) Many character features.
   (17) Symptoms.
   (18) Feelings of guilt and anxiety
   (19) Projection.
   (20) Fixation.
   (21) Indecisiveness.
   (22) Retroflection.

Obviously, chaos is created by Perls' combining processes with outcomes, combining different levels of abstraction, and combining specific concepts with more general concepts. I leave it to the reader to sort through these twenty-two categories and come to the reduction reported by Perls, Hefferline, and Goodman in *Gestalt Therapy* (1951, p. 451). Their reduction yielded five processes, namely Introjection, Projection, Retroflection, Confluence, and Egotism.

Perls, himself emandated his list in his later writing. Several other Gestalt theorists have had their own ideas of the list. Among these, starting with Perls, are the following:

(1) Perls, F. (1973): "Four mechanisms of boundary disturbances," introjection, projection, confluence, and retroflection.

(2) Enright, J. (1970): "Ways in which areas of self-functioning are kept out of awareness," introjection, projection, retroflection, and desensitization.

(3) Harman, R. (1982): "Boundary Disturbances," introjection, projection, confluence, retroflection, and deflection.

(4) Latner, J. (1982): "Contact boundary disturbances," introjection, projection, confluence, retroflection, and egotism.

(5) Polster, E. and Polster, M. (1973): "Major channels of resistant interaction," introjection, projection, retroflection, confluence, and deflection.

Combining these lists, we find introjection, projection, and retroflection in common. With the exception of Enright, confluence is also in common. The disagreements are with regard to desensitization (Enright), deflection (Harman, following the Polsters), and egotism (Latner). Crocker's (1981) suggestion of an additional process which she termed "proflection" completes the current list.

All of these currently used concepts can serve to effect a self-interruption in contact/withdrawal cycles. *I believe that much of the disagreement among theorists as to what are the basic boundary processes can be resolved by systematically differentiating the locus of self-interruption and the primary organismic system involved, with reference to the contact, withdrawal cycle.* As I have shown, there are seven loci of possible self-interruption, namely, avoidance of awareness of a need, avoidance of excitement, avoidance of awareness of emotion, avoidance of action, avoidance of interaction, avoidance of satisfaction, and avoidance of withdrawal. There are specific organismic processes which are utilized at these several loci to effect the avoidance.

Earlier in the present paper I stated that satisfying contact is served by clear awareness, excitement, action, and interaction. Any processes which, therefore, interfere with clear awareness, excitement, action, or interaction will be effective in diminishing satisfying contact. At one level, then, we can say that there are four general processes of self-interruption: clouding awareness, quelling excitement, diminishing action, and inappropriate interaction. At a more exact level, we can speak of the specific processes involved at each of the seven loci of avoidance.

In the cycle of contact and withdrawal, the stages of need, emotion, satisfaction, and withdrawal are basically awareness oriented stages. To move into each of those stages, successfully, requires clear awareness. The general process for avoiding any of these steps is, then, the clouding of awareness. Awareness is at the very heart of contact and withdrawal, for it is the orienting function which focuses and guides one's energy, one's behavior. As such, the specific processes involved in clouding awareness are in a sense the most basic of disturbed psychological functioning. (My focus in the present paper is on disturbed functioning, so I will not discuss the healthy use of these processes or any of the processes which are dealt with later.)

Clear awareness means sharp awareness, perceptually speaking, and certainty of one's identity as the perceiving agent. So, by interfering with perceptual clarity or with self-identity, awareness becomes clouded. Taking these in reversed order, identity as the perceiving self can be confused through at least three processes, namely, introjection, projection, and confluence. There is adequate consensus in the Gestalt literature as to the primary and key roles of introjection and projection in disturbed contact. And, they have been discussed sufficiently that I will not be redundant.

Although confluence was not mentioned by Enright (1970) as one of the "ways in which areas of self-functioning are kept out of awareness," it has been included in most Gestalt theorists' lists of basic processes of disrupted contact. The author of "Boundary Processes and Boundary States" declared that he did not believe that confluence belongs on the list of boundary processes. The author's point was that while introjection and projection can appear in present participle and gerund forms, we do not speak of "confluencing." True enough, though it misses the point. There is an experientially verifiable process which leads to what that author correctly calls a state of confluence. But the state of confluence is not reach via introjection or projection. In introjection and projection there is a confusion of ownership, believing that what is yours (psychologically) is mine or that what is mine (psychologically) is yours, respectively. In both cases, however, there is no confusion that I am I and you are you. Only the ownership of the need, the emotion, the satisfaction is the point of confusion. In confluence there is a loss of ego boundary, a failure to differentiate "me" as the perceiving self from "you," an experience only of an "us." Again, careful introspection will yield the experiential data to confirm this process and this state.

Although I have preferred to retain the term "confluence," because of its widespread familiarity in the Gestalt community, there is a grammatically more cooperative term which has common historical roots with Gestalt therapy. The infinitive form of the term is "to fuse," the established state, one of "fusion." Circa 1933, Perls and Hellmuth Kaiser were in an ongoing seminar led by Wilhelm Reich (Smith, 1976). In *In and Out the Garbage Pail*, Perls (1969) referred to Kaiser as a lovely person and acknowledged him as a good therapist. Kaiser's central thesis was that the neurotic communicates in a way such as to give himself the feeling that he is not responsible for his words and actions. Everyone creates some degree of the "illusion of fusion," but to the extent that one's aloneness is intolerable and one tries to make the illusion real, he or she is neurotic (Fierman, 1965). So, we could speak of "fusing" and of "fusion," as the process and the state of that phenomenon whereby in the I-You-Us interplay, the I and You disappear and only the Us remains.

Awareness can be dulled by the processes of deflection and desensitization. I believe it is useful to distinguish the two closely related phenomena. In the literature the two processes have usually not been differentiated and have sometimes been subsumed under one heading.

Deflection, as introduced by the Polsters (1973, p. 89) is "a maneuver for turning aside from direct contact with another person ... by circumlocution, by excessive language, by laughing off what one says, by not looking at the person one is talking to, by being abstract rather than specific, by not getting the point, by coming up with bad examples or none at all, by politeness instead of directness, by stereotyped language instead of original language, by substituting mild emotions for intense ones, by talking about rather than talking to, and by shrugging off the importance of what one has just said." Deflection can be used either by the sender of a message or by the receiver. In either case the message is diluted.

Desensitization as explained by Enright (1970, p. 112), can take the form of "Scotomata, visual blurring, chronic 'not hearing,' sensory dullness, frigidity, etc ...." The essence, here, is the dulling of awareness by decreasing the acuity of a sensory modality. In Perls' early writing he used the word "scotomata." In *Ego, Hunger and Aggression* Perls (1947, 1969, p. 155) stated "Of the sensoric resistances, the most frequent is scotomization, a minus or a deficient function by which the perception of certain things is avoided." Four paragraphs later, Perls used the term "de-sensitivization" [sic], referring to a "hypo-anesthesia, a kind of dimming." He continued by discussing genital frigidity and oral frigidity — numbness of taste, lack of appetite. In *Ges-*

talt Therapy (Perls, et al., 1951, pp. 177-178) we find a statement that "scoto-mata" develop through having "desensitized." In that case, you may find . . . sensations of numbness, fogginess, nothingness."

Desensitization pertains both to exteroperceptions and proprioceptions. For those who do nor want to develop skills of desensitization, breweries, distilleries, and pharmaceuticals houses offer products which can be put to this use quite effectively.

To summarize, the processes of introjection, projection, and confluence lead to a state of confused awareness concerning the self as perceiving agent. Deflection and desensitization create a dulled awareness, a lack of perceptual sharpness. Confused awareness and dulled awareness are sub-categories of clouded awareness.

Turning, now, to the second general process of avoidance, the restricting of breathing, we enter the realm of motor activity. By means of tightening the diaphragm and/or the muscles of the rib cage, breathing becomes shallow, the result being a diminished oxygen supply. This leads directly to a lowered energy level, to a quelling of excitement. In response to a toxic introject which forbids the mounting excitement, breathing, which ordinarily proceeds automatically, is restricted. The muscular holding back of breathing is, of course, a retroflection of energy, a self-restraint. For a detailed discussion of the mechanics and psychodynamics of breathing I recommend *The Body in Psychotherapy* (Smith, 1985, pp. 39, 119-122, 129-131) and *Sexual Aliveness* (Smith, 1987, pp. 45-50).

In the immediately preceding paragraph I opened the discussion of retroflection, as a process of self-interruption. Not only can this process operate at the juncture between want and excitement, but it also is the primary process of avoidance of action and one of the primary processes of avoidance of interaction.

Retroflection is better understood if it is seen in the context of the contact/withdrawal cycle, since the basic process takes quite different forms. In an earlier article, "Retroflection: The Forms of Non-Enactment" (Smith, 1986), I made a case for three forms of retroflection, based on a suggestion in Perls' early writing. Perls (1947, 1969) saw self-hate, narcissism (self-love), and self-control as the three most important retroflections. "A genuine retroflection is always based upon such a split personality and is composed of an active (A) and a passive (B) part" (Perls, 1947, 1969, p. 220).

In the first instance, self-hate, the impulse to hurt is turned back on the self. The active part of the self chooses the passive part as the target of its aggression. This is the paradigm for one type of retroflected interaction, namely, doing to myself what I would like to do to you.

The second instance is different in that in self-love there are two healthy needs involved, the need to love and the need to be loved. As in the first instance of self-hate, the passive part of the self is the chosen target. In addition to this substitution of target, which leaves the need to love another unfulfilled, the passive part of the self doesn't get loved by another and this need, too, goes unfulfilled. Both active and passive parts of the self are substitutes from the perspective of the other part.

"In both self-hate and self-love action is taken. The problem is that the movement from action into interaction goes awry, so that full organismic satisfaction is not possible (Smith, 1986 p. 48). As Perls (1947, 1969, p. 118) stated, "Aggression is at least as much object-bound as sex, and it can in the same way as love (in narcissism or in masturbation) have the 'Self' as object. They both may become 'retroflected.'"

The essence of retroflected interaction is the absence of any environmental object. This has been stated dearly by Perls, Hefferline, and Goodman (1951) and by the Polsters (1973). These same writers were explicit in their recognition of the two forms of retroflected interaction. As the Polsters (1973, p. 82) stated, "Retroflection is a hermaphroditic function wherein the individual turns back against himself what he would like to *do to someone else*, or does to himself what he would like *someone else to do to him.*"

The third instance, self-control, involves a diminishing or stopping of action. Earlier, I showed how retroflection can be used to quell excitement through the tensing of the muscles of breathing. Similarly, action can be frozen by tensing those muscles which are the antagonists to those muscles which would perform the act forbidden by the toxic introject. Enright (1970, p. 112) described this retroflection of action when he wrote, "Retroflection describes the general process of negating, holding back, or balancing the impulse tension by additional opposing sensorimotor tension .... Since the net result of all this cancelled-out muscular tension is zero — no overt movement — there is no particular increase in activity at the contact boundary ...." Enright continued, to point out that "Reich's 'character armor' is chronic retroflection." Perls (1947, 1969, p. 229) put an interesting slant on this when he wrote:

> We repress vital functions (negative energy, as Reich calls their sum) by muscular contractions. The civil war raging in the neurotic organism is mostly waged between the motoric system and unaccepted organismic energies which strive for expression and gratification. The motoric system has to a great extent lost its function as a working, active, world-bound system and, by retroflection, has become the jailer rather than the assistant of important biological needs.

Thus, the retroflections, as basic processes for self-interruption in the contact/withdrawal cycle, operate to quell excitement, diminish action, and interfere with potentially satisfying interaction, in two forms. Retroflection of breathing and retroflection of action involve muscle tensing, whereas the two forms of retroflection of interaction involve a solipsism, a targeting of one's self for one's interaction. Underlying a retroflection is a toxic introject.

Proflection, as identified and named by Crocker (1981), is also a process for self-interrupting at the point of interaction. "Proflection is a kind of *reverse of retroflection* in that the proflector does something to the other instead of, as in retroflection, doing something to or for himself . . . " (Crocker, 1981, p. 19). "Proflection and deflection have in common the fact that each is an interpersonal disturbance" (Crocker, 1982, p. 86). When I first read Crocker's description of proflection, I thought, "of course!" This was a phenomenon which I had recognized often. It is, in my experience, a common occurrence in therapy groups, and Crocker has made a major contribution by labeling and explicating it.

I want to make three more points concerning the dynamics of the contact/withdrawal cycle. First, as is implied by the entire discussion above, the processes of self-interruption work in synergistic combination. Second, following a distinction made by the Polsters (1973), a self-interruption may be either a block or an inhibition. A block means a complete avoidance of the next stage of contact or of withdrawal, whereas an inhibition means a partial avoidance. In blocking, all energy flow stops. In the case of an inhibition, there is a reduced energy flow, and the possibility of further inhibitions and/or a block farther "downstream" in the contact/withdrawal cycle. And, third, to the extent that inhibitions or blocks are present, the tension from the partially or totally unmet need remains as "unfinished business."

Summary

Much of the disagreement as to what are the basic processes of disturbance at the contact boundary result from a lack of clear differentiation between predominately sensory processes and predominately motor processes, and among the possible points of self-interruption in the stages of the contact/withdrawal cycle. Different processes are primary in the avoidance of awareness (sensory), the avoidance of excitement (motor), and the avoidance of the action (motor) and interaction (motor) which are guided by that awareness and fueled by that excitement. The processes of self-interruption are summarized in *Figure 2 (overleaf)*. I invite the reader to study the figure carefully exploring the relationships stated.

FIGURE 2.

PROCESSES OF SELF INTERRUPTION IN THE CONTACT/WITHDRAWAL CYCLE

Stages of the Cycle	Primary System of Avoidance	General Process of Avoidance	Specific Process of Avoidance
Need	Sensory	Clouding Awareness	Confused Awareness (Introjection) (Projection) (Confluence
			Dulled Awareness (Deflection) (Desensitization)
Excitement	Motor	Quelling Excitement	Retroflection of breathing
Emotion	Sensory	Clouding Awareness	Confused awareness (Introjection) (Projection) (Confluence)
			Dulled Awareness (Deflection) (Desensitization)
Action	Motor	Diminishing Action	Retroflection of Action
Interaction	Motor	Lack of Appropriate Interaction	Retroflection of interaction and Proflection
Satisfaction	Sensory	Clouding Awareness	Confused awareness (Introjection) (Projection) (Confluence)
Withdrawal	Sensory	Clouding Awareness	Confused awareness (Introjection) (Projection) (Confluence) Dulled Awareness (Deflection) (Desensitization)

~

THE SWING OF THE PENDULUM,

THE TURN OF THE SPIRAL

My experiential perspective on psychotherapy is one of twenty-three years. I sat down with my first patient and my first therapist in the middle of the 1960s. Eventually, the therapist shot and killed himself. I have kept on.

Informed by these years of experience, and by the secondhand knowledge coming from the words of those whom I have listened to and read, I discern a pattern in the evolution of psychotherapy. I speak of the core practice of psychotherapy — its philosophy, theory, and procedures — not its accoutrements. But, allow me to say something about the latter before turning to my primary focus.

The most obvious change I have seen in psychotherapy is the proliferation of therapists. The yellow pages are full! With this growth in numbers have come various nomothetic means of handling therapists — more credentialing, more credentialing boards, more laws governing practice, more ethics committees. What this reflects is an increased bureaucratization of the practice of psychotherapy. The *practice* of psychotherapy has become increasingly controlled and monitored.

At the same time, it has become much more business oriented. Hardly a convention is held in the field without workshops on "how to generate more referrals," "how to computerize your billing," "how to market your practice," "how to insure your future."

From *Voices,* 25(1/2), 130-133 (1989).

Many practitioners have also become more image conscious. This intent on an image of respectability is reflected in many of the articles in current professional publications. For example, comments on "how a psychotherapist should dress" graced the pages of a major psychotherapy newsletter a few issues ago.

As I see it, the *degree* of increased emphasis on bureaucratizing the practice of psychotherapy, making it a better business, and making it look respectable has detracted from its core — the development of the therapist and the practice of the art. Too many workshops on the appurtenances spell a de-emphasis on matters which I see as more important. My hunch is that there is a curvilinear relationship between competence and commitment to the art, and competence and commitment to the appurtenances. Either a total lack of interest or a very high level of interest in these accoutrements probably accompanies a lesser development of therapeutic wisdom and skill. I do not believe that belonging to many organizations and serving on many committees, or having an M.B.A., or wearing a business suit with wing-tip shoes or high heels makes one a better therapist.

I now turn my attention to the core of the practice of psychotherapy: its philosophy, theory, and procedures. Many theoretical orientations have come into prominence and then faded. Some of them have enjoyed a resurgence. In some cases the prefix "neo" has acknowledged the second wave of interest, as in neo-Freudian and neo-Reichian. In other cases, a new name has accompanied the rebirth and reflected a particular theoretical emphasis in the new position. An example is "object-relations theory." An interesting feature of this is the cycle of waxing and waning of interest. For some theoretical positions the time has been too short to discern a pattern. Some may have had their moment. For others, it was a season. And, for others, what we may call major theoretical positions, it is a cycle of waxing and waning prominence.

The originators of each position offered a philosophy; a theory; and a procedure which was fresh, radical enough to be noticed, but not radical enough to be dismissed summarily. Each position, then, offered something effective for a given context: a given time, place, and consciousness. In time, the freshness and creative radicalness is lost, as second- and third-generation practitioners institutionalize the system. As they popularize and dilute the original position, they trivialize and rob it of its liveliness. In time, if it still holds recognizable wisdom, it may be born again with the help of an energetic and creative midwife. Some aspect of that nascent wisdom is elaborated, restated in current terminology, brought to the fore; and once again there is a position which speaks for a time, a place, and a level of consciousness.

There are two graphic models which have been used to describe such evolution. One is the pendulum, the other the circle. The pendulum model speaks to the trend, swinging from one extreme to the other. For example, we can see evidence for a move from liberal to moderate to conservative to moderate to liberal attitudes.

Using the physical analogy of the pendulum, one can predict that when the extreme of either liberalism or conservatism is reached, a move toward the other extreme will soon commence.

The circle model is but another way to present a graphic analogy for repeatability. We can think of various theoretical and procedural issues of psychotherapy. It seems that we keep coming back to these issues. Like points on the circumference of the circle, as we move around the circle, we continue to return to the same points. A variation on this model is to make the circle into a spiral. The opening of the circle in this manner allows a depiction of movement through time. Now, as we move around the cylindrical spiral, we come to the same points (as seen in the two dimensional projection of the spiral, i.e., the circle), but it is never quite the same. It is the same issue, but at a new point in time, and, therefore, with the benefit of the wisdom gained in each other instance of addressing that issue. The same point is reached at a new level.

Capra (1984) has shown that the circle phenomenon and the pendulum phenomenon can be related as follows: Turn the circle so that its edge is toward the observer and shine a light on it. A point moving around the circle will then project onto a screen as a point oscillating between two extremes, appearing as a swinging pendulum. I suggest the conversion of the circle into a spiral, thus acknowledging the evolving of time. The projection of that spiral now becomes a wave. This wave model, I believe, may be of use in describing and understanding the evolution of the theory and practice of psychotherapy. It combines the analogies of the circle and of the pendulum, while also taking time into account. It is, then, in a sense, a historical, dynamic model for the evolution of psychotherapy, its values, attitudes, theoretical interests, and procedural trends. It is a graphic resolution of the paradoxical relationship between the following two statements: "History repeats itself," and "Nothing stays the same." So it is that both statements are true, in the evolution of psychotherapy. The consistency of psychotherapy and the constant change of psychotherapy become understandable, by analogy, with the consideration of the spiral-projection wave model.

The concept which I have expressed with the spiral-projection wave is not only a central concept of Eastern mystical thought, but is a central experience of the mystic. Consider, for instance:

Life on its way returns into a mist,
Its quickness is its quietness again.
(Bynner, 1962, p. 51)

To the Eastern mystic, all developments of the world, both the physical world and the social world, proceed in cyclic patterns. The world is one of continuous flow and change. And, for the Taoist, all change in nature arises as a manifestation of the dynamic interplay of polar opposites. Thus, in speaking of the Tao:

> Being great, it flows.
> It flows far away.
> Having gone far, it returns.
> (Feng, 1972, chapter 25)

This is the swing of the pendulum, the turn of the circle. It is the spiral-projection wave form. And, it is Chapter Forty of the *Tao Te Ching* (Feng, 1972):

> Returning is the motion of the Tao.
> Yielding is the way of the Tao.
> The ten thousand things are born of being.
> Being is born of not being.

Perhaps, then, we can understand where psychotherapy has been and where it is going as a dynamic interplay of opposites. Opposites of attitude, value, theory, technique. Yielding and returning. The ten thousand things of psychotherapy.

~

EXPLORING CONFLUENCE

ABSTRACT. Healthy coupling, defined as coupling which supports the growth of the personhood of both partners, is explored herein. Healthy coupling is viewed as being based on a rhythm of *confluence* (formation of a "We" from the "I" and the "Thou") and *difluence* (clear differentiation of an "I" and a "Thou" from the "We"). Criteria for the recognition of natural, flexible confluence and difluence are contrasted with those of an unnatural, rigid pattern.

Healthy coupling, as I conceive of it and as I observe it, is coupling which supports the unfolding of the humanness of both persons. That means that the personhood of each develops. Each of the two explores, experiences, and grows as is urged by that inner voice, that voice which comes from a most private realm of the self. This voice speaks the "wisdom of the organism," not the words of the social system, swallowed whole and regurgitated as so much cud, incompletely chewed. As one goes more deeply into one's self, the organismic self, as opposed to one's intellectualized slogans, clichés, and phony roles, one finds the urge for becoming and being. Following that urge, personhood evolves.

Paradoxically, the unfolding of full personhood is supported by, and even requires, at times, the temporary merger of the self with the other. Paradoxically, selfhood develops through certain experiences of loss of self, the giving up of self for the experience of being a couple. In terms of Eastern philosophy, this is the paradox of "investing in loss."

So, in a healthy coupling, there is stimulation for both individuals to grow. And the "couple" is the context. From my vantage point there are you,

---

From: *Journal of Couples Therapy*, 1(1), 21-27 (1990).

I, and we. The "we" is a supra-being. It cannot exist other than through the cooperative wills of you and of me. But, given my will for relationship with you, and your will for relationship with me, we can establish and maintain the supra- "we."

Readers conversant with existential thought may be reminded of Martin Buber's distinction of the I-Thou and the I-It relationship. The I-Thou is a subjective relationship, wherein the I and the Thou are known through their relating. The I-It relationship is objective. The "I" is experienced as separate from the "It," which is an object. Objectified, the "It" is fair game for being manipulated and being used. Even in this simplified version, the terms and concepts of these two types of relationship add a dimension to the understanding of healthy coupling. Let us shift our terminology, accordingly, and proceed to develop the theme.

In healthy coupling, there is a flowing together of the I and the Thou to create a We at the supra-level, without the sacrifice of either the I or the Thou. The creation of the We at the supra-level serves, in turn, as a growthful context for the I and the Thou, a context of support and stimulation for the unfoldment of the two personhoods. In contrast, unhealthy coupling involves the sacrifice of the I and the Thou in the creation of the We. Rather than an I and a Thou existing in the context of the We at the supra-level, what exists is an It and an It, two objects, deadened and diminished.

At this point I can offer a graphic model to contrast healthy and unhealthy coupling (see Figure 1).

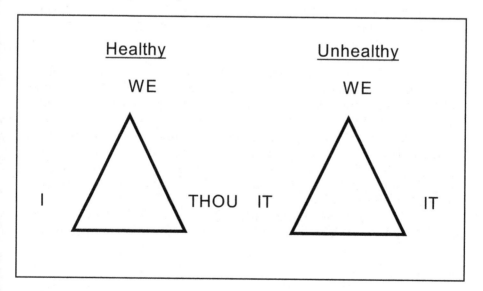

Without the creation of a We, there is not a coupling. There may be ongoing social interaction, but not coupling in the psychological sense.

The key to the creation of the We at the supra-level is the *flowing together* of the I and the Thou. Gestalt therapy has given the term *confluence* to this phenomenon. In terms of denotation, confluence means a "flowing together," from the Late Latin "confluentia."

Regard confluence, then, as a process, a fluid phenomenon.

Confluence is the process of the flowing together of the I and the Thou in the creation of the We at the supra-level. In healthy coupling, or to use the process word confluence, there is a context of recognition of the I and Thou. Even if, for a time, the focus is on the We, the I and Thou are always potential. The We is pregnant with the possibility, always, of re-birthing an I and a Thou. A new term may be useful, here, to identify this latter process. I will suggest *difluence*. So, through a flowing together of I and Thou, a We is created. This we call *confluence*. And, through a flowing apart from the We, an I and Thou are stimulated and supported. This we can call *difluence*.

Healthy coupling is based on a good rhythm of confluence and difluence. There is a shift in emphasis in this rhythm from I and Thou, to We, and back. But, if this rhythm is not natural and flexible, a system of unhealthy confluence is created and thus, an unhealthy relationship.

Unhealthy or pathological confluence lacks the flexibility of smooth flow from the level of I and Thou to the meta-level of We and back. In Gestalt psychology terms, the We becomes too fixed a figure. This rigid figure of We exists while there is an inadequate energy charge at the level of the I and the Thou. Therefore, rather than the I and Thou ever emerging as figure, they remain as background to the rigid We figure. The I and the Thou are lost. They become, then, a background of an It and an It. In this situation the meaning of the couple relationship derives almost entirely from the figural We. As dim background figures, the two people involved have lost most of their personal meaning. They now exist for the We.

So, in pathological confluence there is a loss of self, a loss of personal identity. This involves a confusion of personal identity with coupled identity. Gestalt therapy has provided some very useful theory concerning confused awareness of identity. The triumvirate of confused awareness of identity are introjection, projection, and confluence. I have summarized this as follows (Smith, 1985, p. 39):

> In the case of introjection I believe something is mine when it is really yours. That is, I have taken your idea, value, belief, moral guideline, whatever, and act on it without having examined it thoroughly and decided if I really wanted to incor-

porate it into my overall system. Projection is the opposite process in that I attribute something (idea, belief, value, feeling, or the like) to you when it is really mine. Confluence involves a blurring of the ego boundary so that I do not differentiate "you" and "me," and recognize only "us."

As Perls (1973, p. 40-41) wrote, "The introjector does as others would like him to do, the projector does unto others what he accuses them of doing to him, the man in pathological confluence doesn't know who is doing what to whom . . ."

In terms of specific effects of pathological confluence, the confusion of awareness of self becomes manifest in several important ways. It can affect the recognition of one's needs, recognition of one's emotional state, recognition of when and to what degree one's needs are satisfied, and recognition of when withdrawal from contact is appropriate. By interfering with each of these contents, confluence can present a major problem in the rhythm of organismically based contact with and withdrawal from the physical and social world. (For a detailed discussion of this, see Smith, 1988.)

Confluence can be identified both through verbal and nonverbal patterns. Verbally, confluence is reflected by the use of the subject pronoun "we," the possessive pronoun "our," and the object pronoun "us." In each case — "We feel . . . ," "Our feeling . . . ," " . . . made us feel . . ." — the pronoun reflects joint ownership. This reflects a pathological confluence when the appropriate meaning is conveyed by the singular pronoun — "I," "my," "me," "you," "your." I invite the reader, at the end of the present paragraph, to put this reading aside for a few minutes and experiment with this linguistic reflection of confluence. Make a statement about a belief, value, or feeling that is true for both you and someone else, beginning the statement with "We." Repeat the statement aloud, several times. Listen carefully, and be aware of how you feel inside as you speak. Repeat the statement aloud, several times, but now beginning with "I." Again, listen carefully. Be aware of your feelings inside. You may want to say the sentence first with the plural subject pronoun, then with the singular, to highlight the contrast. Experiment with this until you can feel the difference, until you can appreciate the experience of individuality and of confluence as reflected in the logos. If you wish, you can repeat the experiment, contrasting "our" with "my" and "us" with "me."

In addition to these linguistic signs of confluence, I have observed in my working with couples two conversational patterns which reflect pathological confluence. The first when one of the couple speaks for the other. For instance, I may ask one of the couple speaks for the other. For instance, I may ask one of the couple how she feels about something, only to have her partner speak up, offering, "She feels angry about that." It is as if the two have become as Siamese twins, having only one vocal apparatus between them.

The second conversational pattern reflecting pathological confluence is more subtle. This is the pattern of taking what is my personal issue and making it our issue, or less commonly, taking your issue and making it ours. The subtle aspect of this is recognizing when the line of personal openness is surpassed, and the sharing becomes a confusion of what is more appropriate for me to deal with myself, rather than make into our issue. What I am saying is that it is naïve to believe that *all* interpersonal processing of psychological material is healthy in a couple. Sometimes, neither growth of the person nor growth of the relationship is served by "sharing" certain issues. Therapists, all too often, accept blindly that for couples to open up and share every feeling is good, and to not "share" is bad. This is naïve. I have seen so many examples of how this "sharing" has become an unnecessary burden and has left one or both of the couple worn down and burned-out. *When, chronically, more time is spent on processing what has gone on between a couple than is spent being together in other ways, this suggests a pathological confluence.* This may not be the only pathology in evidence, to be sure. But, it does show that too much has been put into the realm of joint ownership or joint responsibility.

I have seen this overprocessing most frequently in couples where one is a psychotherapist. In couples where both are psychotherapists, as they have come to me for couples therapy, it is almost the rule. As I said, this is subtle. Is not the processing of feelings a major part of what therapy is about? And, is not the processing of feelings a major part of what "working on a relationship" is about? Of course. The question is, at what point does processing become dysfunctional? At what point are the couple worn down and in need of a respite? And, at what point is the processing an attempt to shift *my* responsibility to one of *our* responsibility, thus creating a pathological confluence?

A clear example is hard to give because of the subtlety, which I have mentioned. The entire context of the couple must be considered. Sometimes, the confession of a misdeed is an attempt to shirk personal responsibility and shift the onus to the supra-level of *our* responsibility, done under the guise of that purported panacea, "openness." Even an apology *can* be so used. The question there is whether I am truly sorry, accept my full responsibility, and let you know that, or am I asking for you to forgive me, thus relieving me of the burden of consequences for my action and that task of revising my behavior accordingly. In the latter case I am making my issue of growth our issue of smoothing over or denying the consequences of my behavior.

Confluence is also reflected in non-verbal ways. Shared gestures is one way. Sometimes when a couple is together one can observe their making an identical movement or using an identical mannerism. Another way is shared dress. From time to time couples may be seen wearing matching or coordinating outfits, a non-verbal statement that "we are a set." "Sympathy pains" is another possible way, when one of a couple has a pain due to an injury or illness and the partner begins feeling a pain in the same body location. Remember, although these are suggestions of confluence, they do not necessarily reflect a pathological confluence. The determination of that requires deeper evaluation of the nature of the relationship.

Healthy confluence requires a strong sense of self to return to; unhealthy confluence involves a loss of self. The loss of self means that the I and the Thou each become an It, mere objects to be manipulated and used by the Us. In *The Devil's Dictionary* Ambrose Bierce (1958, p. 86) captures this in his definition of marriage:

> The state or condition of a community consisting of a
> master, a mistress and two slaves, making in all, two.

Good *contact* involves the appreciation of differences, while the condemnation of differences brings *alienation*. *Confluence* involves the appreciation of similarity. The healthy couple flow between confluence and good contact when together.

In closing, I invite you to feel yourself into the following words:

On Confluence

Small creeks join.
Tributaries unite to form rivers.
Many empty into a vast sea.
When does the sea say "We"?

On Difluence

Sea mists rise.
Clouds blow in, heavy rains begin to fall.
Trickles swell to become small creeks.
Each creek takes its own name.

~

EMBODIED GESTALT PSYCHOTHERAPY

Definition

Psychotherapy in the Embodied Gestalt practice is a way of personal growth. As a path of growth it focuses on the embodiment of experience, the living out of that embodied experience, and the choice for growth through a change in the way one has embodied an experience. This is existential phenomenology applied. It is also applied Taoism. Personhood is highly respected, as the subtle, delicate process of awareness is facilitated in its unfolding in the here-and-now.

Qualification Statement

The philosophical underpinnings of Embodied Gestalt practice are existentialism and its Eastern analogue, Taoism. Both address basic ontological issues — the experience of the lived moment, freedom, choice, meaning, responsibility, value. Existentialism suggests the "I-Thou" relationship for the psychotherapy encounter. Taoism suggests the discovery of "what is" as the starting point for change. It also emphasizes the coming into harmony with what is natural by removing impediments and allowing the flow that is intrinsic.

From: Zeig, J. and Munion, W. (Eds.) *What is Psychotherapy?* (pp. 107-111) (1990).

Gestalt and Reichian therapy provide the theoretical underpinnings. The basic idea is that the human being functions through homeostatic need cycles. There is a natural rhythm whereby a need arises from the background of needs and the person proceeds to satisfy that figural need, then letting it recede again to ground and allowing a new figure to emerge. Thus, there is a cycle of contact and withdrawal. A *contact episode* involves several states of development:

Embodied Gestalt

Need —> Excitement —> Emotion —> Action —> Interaction —> Satisfaction

Following satisfaction comes the *withdrawal episode*

Personal dysfunction can be viewed as self-interruption in the natural flow through the contact withdrawal cycle. Because of "toxic introjects" (verbal and nonverbal messages received in childhood that prohibit natural aliveness), a person may choose to avoid allowing the next step in the cycle to develop. These avoidances (or inhibitions) are existential choices of diminished aliveness, and they may occur at any combination of the seven junctures of the cycle, with specific mechanisms that operate at each of these loci. Thus, by clouding, dulling, and/or confusing awareness, one may avoid awareness of a need, of a differentiated emotion, of satisfaction, and of appropriate withdrawal. One may avoid organismic excitement by means of restricted breathing (through tension in respiratory muscles). Action may be avoided by chronic contractions in those muscles that are antagonistic to the muscles that would perform the action forbidden by the toxic introject. Potentially satisfying interaction can be avoided by several tactics.

The main goal is to facilitate clients' awareness of *where* in the cycle they self-interrupt, *how* they do so, and *what* the underlying toxic introject is that demands this. A second goal is to support their taking responsibility for their choice. By confronting the toxic introject in a psychodramatic manner, an organismic choice may be made to reinstate a natural contact/withdrawal cycle. The toxic introject is embodied in a manner that diminishes natural flow and aliveness; thus, the psychodramatic acting out of the new choice is the quintessence of a change in that embodiment. Growth occurs through experiences under conditions of heightened awareness.

As arcane as the philosophy may seem, and as complex as the theory, the methods are simple. The procedure is to observe phenomenologically,

tracking the client through the cycle. At the point of self-interruption, the client is facilitated in awareness and choice. The methods include role playing, experimenting with postures and movements, direct body contact, focused breathing, sensory awakening techniques, and functional questions (for example, What are you aware of? How are you doing that?). The dictum is "Be aware, experience, express."

Critique Statement

It is both its advantage and its limitation that Embodied Gestalt practice is growth-oriented. As its advantage, this allows the practice to focus keenly on the development of the human potential. Thus the practice is suitable for facilitating movement from an ordinary level of functioning to an extraordinary level, as well as from a level of dysfunction to the level of ordinary functioning. Growth, in this approach, involves awareness both as a method and as a criterion. However, awareness takes time to develop. In some situations symptomatic cure and behavioral change may be accomplished more quickly by other means. In some other therapies, awareness is not required for effective outcome with symptoms and undesirable behaviors.

In Embodied Gestalt practice issues of transference and countertransference often are left in the background. By the nature of the practice, attention tends to be on the client's personal process, with the practitioner as facilitator at points of self-interruption. This does not tend to bring forth transference and countertransference in as obvious or blatant a manner as is the case with certain therapies. Many would see this as a frequently lost opportunity in this practice.

A related limitation is that this practice does not encourage client regression for reparenting. Regressive reparenting may be a procedure of choice in the case of some severe characterological disorders. In this practice the role is more that of a guru than that of a parent.

In the group format, this practice focuses on the individual-in-environment process rather than on group process. Group process remains ground, unless a group issue reaches the threshold of interruption to the individual process. Thus, the potential benefits of group process work and analysis of group dynamics often are lost.

Embodied Gestalt practice is noncoercive. It may be confrontational, at times, but only in terms of firmly pointing out an avoidance. It does not offer either the pressure for change or the powerful backup that is needed in many cases of criminal behavior and substance addiction. If someone needs a period of external locus of control, this practice is not a good choice.

It does not offer a high degree of structure.

This practice requires a commitment to growth-oriented experiencing. The client who benefits most is one who has at least a modicum of self-curiosity, values intraception, and enjoys working on herself or himself through experiments and disciplined activities. When these qualities are not present in the client, this practice will be of limited value.

Embodied Gestalt practice eschews advice giving, interpretation, and strategic manipulation. To many this would be seen as severely limiting. Learning is viewed in the practice as self-discovery. To paraphrase Fritz Perls, personal truth can best be tolerated if you discover it yourself, because then the pride of discovery makes the truth palatable.

~

EVIL FOR GOOD, GOOD FOR EVIL

Black hat. Black boots. Black shirt and pants. Black gunbelt and holsters. White, wavy hair. White horse. Guns with pearly-white grips. Black and white, that was Hopalong Cassidy. The dust of World War II was still in the air. The Allied Nations had defeated the Axis Powers. "Good" had triumphed over "evil." "Hoppy" was a timely and representative symbol, his formula B-Westerns a vivid Saturday afternoon lesson in the dichotomy of good and evil, and the certain victory of the former over the latter. When my first book was published in 1976, I dedicated it, in part, to my childhood hero, Hopalong Cassidy. He died on my twenty-ninth birthday. For me, the days of black and white were over.

Such clear demarcation of good and evil, such dichotomy tends to be the perspective of monotheistic societies. William Boyd's role as Hopalong Cassidy is certainly an expression of a premise of a monotheistic mythology. Through such a mythology one is oriented to judge the foci of one's experience as either good or evil. Thereby, everything, every event tends to be identified as of god (good) or of the devil (evil). Monotheistic orthodoxy tends, then, to offer a certain moral clarity for those who embrace it. How comforting it can be to see the events in one's world as clearly good or clearly evil. Such clarity, such certainty can have a stabilizing effect on the psyche as experience is organized thusly. Perhaps, this makes for a strong ego, just as it encourages powerful and grandly elaborated ethical and legal systems.

From: *Voices*, 27(3), 5-9 (1991).

If monotheistic orthodoxy exerts a strong organizing and stabilizing effect on the psyche, polytheistic orthodoxy is open to more psychic complexity and fluidity. Distinctions between good and evil are less clear and the psyche can be mercurial in its perception of events. The door is then open to polymorphous perversity.

An example of the polytheistic orthodoxy, and one that nicely illustrates the relativity of good and evil, is the old Norse religion. Eclipsed by a swordwielding Christianity, the old religion was believed dead and was relegated to the scholars, to be studied only as an interesting, but ancient mythology. (This attitude illustrates Joseph Campbell's well known remark that myth is "other people's religion.") But, the fact that it has remained of interest to the scholars, the fact that it is currently in resurgence as a viable religion for the second time this century, and the fact that remnants of it * have been manifest continuously since its being driven underground by the missionaries of a "jealous god," give evidence that it manifests important archetypal message through an idiom still understood. That is, it is a compelling expression of the *mysterium tremendum et fascinans*.

Allow me to call attention to several examples of how the problem of good and evil is handled in the Norse *mundis archetypes*. A primary dynamic of life is represented by the struggle between the gods and the giants. They have been at odds since the beginning of their mutual existence, and will be until the end of the Great Cycle, the day of Ragnarok. But, the dynamic is not so simple as to be just good (gods) versus evil (giants). The situation is not nearly so clear-cut. For instance, we find in the Norse cosmogony that Odin, leader of the Norse pantheon, was born of the union of a proto-god and a giantess. Odin, along with his two siblings, then slew Ymir, the first of the frost giants, and from his body parts created the nine worlds. So, we see the interpenetration of gods and giants both in Odin's heritage and in the fact that the worlds, including the worlds of the gods, are created from the material corporeal of Ymir, a giant. This is to say, the leader of the gods is half of giant lineage, and the gods dwell in the body, though reorganized and redistributed, of a giant.

True, the gods and goddesses, in a general way, represent forces of good. Of two races, the Aesir are the warrior gods and goddesses, and the Vanir are the fertility gods and goddesses. So, the gods and goddesses em-

---

* Living vestiges of the Norse religion are found in the English names for the days of the week, the dates, in some cases the deeper level of meaning of the major Christian holidays, and in many folk beliefs and customs in both the United States and northern Europe.

body creative and defensive energies, energies for bringing into being and for preserving that which has been brought into being.

At the mystical core of the Norse religion is the view that all of nature is in constant flux, flowing through cycles of arising, being, and passing away. Just as the Vanir embody the force of creating-arising-birth and the Aesir the force of defense-being-maintenance, the giants embody forces of destruction. So the dynamic interplay of gods *and* giants is required in the playing out of the cosmic rhythms of arising, being, and passing away. As agents of chaos, the giants seek to destroy through nonconsciousness, fiery overactivity, and ice-cold entropy. The paradox is, however, that destruction is necessary for the next cycle of arising. And, so it is that the gods create and then hold at bay the destructive giants. But only as the giants win are the gods allowed to continue. Thus is the mystery of the cycle of arising, being, and passing away. Thus is the dynamic interdependency of gods and giants.

If we were to take as a beginning premise that the gods are good and the giants are evil, we would have to admit that there is some evil in the good and some good in the evil. For example, as shown already, giant blood pulses in the arteries of Odin. And, as is also true of others of the Norse gods, Odin is a complex, multifaceted character. He is referred to by many "heiti" or nicknames, among them "Bölverker," the worker of evil! Another example of evil within the good is found in the character of Loki, the trickster god. As the trickster, he plays pranks, some benign, others more serious or even deadly. But, consider that it is he who will betray the gods, leading the giants against them on the day of Ragnarok. So, not only is Loki an example of evil within the good (a god who does evil), but of transformation of good (a member of a race of gods) into evil (joining the side of the giants and monsters against the gods and heroes). Many more examples of evil within the good can be drawn from the Norse myths. An example of good within evil, also mentioned above, is the dwelling of the gods within worlds created from the disassembled body of Ymir the frost giant. Thus, both Asgard and Vanaheim, the respective homes of the Aesir and Vanir, are of Ymir's body. Symbolically this can be seen as good (gods) contained within evil (a giant). Again, many more examples can be found in the myths.

Looking still further into the handling of good and evil in Norse mythology, we find that it is said that in Midgard, the world of humankind, good and evil exist in equal quantities. For it is that this Middle Earth lies on Irminsul (the Cosmic Axis), suspended betwixt Asgard (world of the Aesir deities) and Alfheim (home of the elves) above and Svartalfheim (home of the dwarfs or black elves) and Hel below. And it is, too, that Midgard lies between Niflheim (home of ice) to the north and Muspellheim (home of fire) to the south, and between Jotunheim (home of the giants) to the east and Vanaheim (home of the Vanir deities) to the west. Here it is, in Midgard, that we humans dwell, and here it is that we find the point of balance of all other realms found within Yggdrasill (the World Tree). The energy of each realm is balanced by the energy found in the opposite realm — Asgard and Hel, Alfheim and Svartalfheim, Niflheim and Muspellheim, Jotunheim and Vanaheim. The point of dynamic balance for all of these energies is in Midgard.

The Mysteries, themselves, are summarized in the runic symbols. Each rune expresses a cosmic truth, a Gestalt of existence and consciousness, the understanding of which is a step into "heill hugr" (higher consciousness of enlightenment). And, the runes can present themselves either as "myrk-runar" or as "heidhrunar," that is, in their dark aspect or their light aspect. The myrkrunar mean either cataclysm or obstruction, the destructive energies of the giants (fiery overactivity or ice-cold entropy).

These examples illustrate the core of Norse mysticism — all of nature is in flux (arising, being, passing away), everything is connected to everything else in this dynamism, and every polar field contains a seed of its opposite. (This core, given life so vividly in the Norse mythology, is the "perennial philosophy," and is found in all mystical traditions.)

Applied to the problem of good and evil, Norse mythology illustrates, then, the relativity of these two concepts. For, at the very root of the Odinic archetype is the notion of wholeness within twofoldness. So it is, good and evil are inextricably joined. Consider this metaphor: Try to imagine a wave that has a crest but no trough. Crest is crest only in dynamic relation to the trough. The crest arises from the level water, as the trough recedes, its being, being relative to its opposite. The crest then passes away by receding to meet the rising of the trough. Each is recognized, in its time-limited existence, only in relation to its opposite. It is the rising and falling of the same substance, the water, that is identified as the arising, being, and passing away of the wave. It is only in its dynamic movement relative to itself that the water comes to be called wave.

The Norse mystics taught that true knowledge is gained through careful observation of nature. A modern Norseman might use the expression "se na godt etter (see, now, well after)!" So, we "see well after" the wave. In doing so, we see that water is the predifferentiated stuff of crests and troughs. It is only in its transient relationship relative to itself that it is crest and trough. Underlying both is water. Water is predifferent. So, too, there is a predifferentiated stuff that forms in transient relationship to itself that which we label good and evil.

There is a consonant theme found in Gestalt therapy. Fritz Perls taught about "creative indifference," a term and concept borrowed from Friedlander, a German philosopher. There is a movement of consciousness to a meta-dimension when one can suspend the usual judgmental labeling of the polar opposites and contact instead the predifferent level from which both arise. We haven't a word for that stuff that in our judgment we differentiate and polarize into good and evil. But to do so, in spite of not having a quick and handy word, is surely a consciousness builder. Perls noted that good and bad are not facts of nature, but are tendentious judgments that we make of nature. This is not to say that it is evil, or bad, or even dysfunctional to label experienced objects or events as good and evil. Rather, it is a caution against moving too quickly into making such judgment. It is an invitation to expand awareness by first seeing the predifferent dimension and by seeing the process of differentiation, including a recognition of the bias that one opts to employ. This is a position of creative indifference.

Jung has suggested that one's entire reality orientation hinges on one's religious outlook. And, of course, that religious orientation is learned from the sacred literature, that is, the mythology that one has assimilated. Personality imitates myth and, thereby, one comes to be oriented in a moral system. Should we, then, harken to the plangent sounds of the Norse myths, we might admit to seeds of evil in all good and seeds of good in all evil. Furthermore, we might admit that one cannot exist except in relationship to the other and that both are necessary in the cosmic drama. We might, then, no longer say "for good" when we mean "forever," recognizing that it is the stuff of the evil — good substratum that goes on and on, with its polarized forms (good and evil) having their turns in ascendency. Perhaps we would more willingly be with the flow, and perhaps we could discourage the stagnation of either extreme.

> A young lamb lies fresh slain.
> The she-wolf licks blood from its throat.
> This same tongue licks her cubs.
> Where is the evil? Where is the good?

GESTALT, A DIONYSIAN PATH

> ... and Fritz was a shaman in more than his role: in his reliance on intuition, in his scientific-artistic orientation, his combination of power and ordinariness, his unconventional way and defiance of tradition, his familiarity with heavens and hells, and perhaps most importantly, his Dionysian-mindedness and appreciation of surrender. (Claudio Naranjo, 1978, p. 81)

Gestalt continues to be a largely misunderstood approach. As I travel about, teaching Gestalt therapy, I find two major distortions in people's thinking about it. First is the distortion of regarding it as a type of cognitive-behavioral therapy. Those who distort Gestalt therapy in this way tend to ignore its existential and Taoist-Zen philosophical underpinnings, and to minimize its organismic theoretical position. Further, they violate its spontaneous, intuitive approach to technique and, instead, grab on to demonstrated techniques as standard Gestalt therapy procedure. This standardized set of techniques is then related back to a cognitive-behavioral theoretical and philosophical rationale. The artistry, richness, and profundity of the Gestalt therapy approach will suffer through this distortion.

The second distortion which I find is the belief that Gestalt therapy is wild, uncontrolled, undisciplined — in a word, dangerous. Those who hold this belief tend to dismiss Gestalt therapy summarily. Given that persons who come to my workshops are self-selected, I seldom meet face to face those who are most extreme in this type of distortion. Those whom I do see tend to be overly cautious and distrustful of the Gestalt Way.

From: *The Gestalt Journal,* 14(2), 61-69 (1991).

Consistent with my observation that Gestalt therapy *continues to be a largely misunderstood approach* is the fact that Gestalt therapy has remained a minority position. *This is understandable if one recognizes Gestalt therapy as a Dionysian manifestation. This deserves elaboration.*

There are two alternate visions which appear across cultures. Although the terminology used to describe these two competing world views differs, the elements are consistent. As Sam Keen (1974) put it, in modern times the majority of people have followed a vision which is represented by the Greek god Apollo. The minority have followed an alternative vision identified with the Greek god Dionysus.

It is precisely this Dionysian-Apollonian split which not only makes the Gestalt therapy approach difficult for the majority to understand, but makes it seem dangerous to some. In order to elucidate this phenomenon, we need to delve at some depth into the nature and meaning of the Dionysian and Apollonian visions.

These two alternate world views are clearly represented in the deified personalities of Dionysus and Apollo. Turning to the latter first, Apollo was the god of reason, truth, order, balance, moderation, light, and boundaries. Dionysus, in contrast, was the god of wine, of excess, fantasy, and metamorphosis. He was unique in that he was the only Greek god whose parents were not both divine. Dionysus could confer blessings or a curse upon humankind, as he offered freedom and ecstasy on the one hand, savage brutality on the other. For example, Dionysus was known, on at least one occasion, to take the form of an angry lion. In one story the god of wine made a group of women mad, causing them to attack and devour their own children.

Dionysus could make people merry, quicken their courage, and banish their fear. And he could bring people to destruction through drunkenness. But he taught the world about metamorphosis. In the winter his vines were dark and withered, but with spring his vines sprouted forth green, spreading and growing, eventually yielding the summer and fall harvests of his grapes. This metamorphosis was dramatic, from apparent deadness to exuberant aliveness and abundance. Then, too, the grape became the wine, another dramatic demonstration of metamorphosis.

Karen Horney (Shostrom, 1967), seeing both the Apollonian and Dionysian leanings as natural human "tendencies," stressed the emphasis of mastery and molding in the former and surrender and drift in the latter. Neither, then, is better than the other, and a given person is not totally of either vision. Most people tend to exhibit tendencies in one direction or the other at different times. When a person exhibits the Apollonian tendency, he or she will wish to be in charge, to take control and make things happen. The goal is to bring the world into congruence with one's will. It is just the opposite when one-exhibits the Dionysian tendency. Rather than exerting her or his will in order to control the world, the person disposed toward a Dionysian approach will give in to "what is," and allow the world to sweep her or him away. This is a surrender of one's personal will to the will of the world. In summary, the Apollonian tendency is to conquer the universe, tame the wilds, improve upon nature, and make the world as one wants it to be. The Dionysian tendency, in contrast, is to get in harmony with the universe, experience the wilds, understand nature, and come to a relaxed acceptance of the world as it is.

Less poetic than these terms used by Nietzsche and by Horney are the plain terms "scientist" and "artist." But these balder terms, too, add some perspective on the two world views. The scientist, of course, is more Apollonian in her or his view and approach to life. For the pure scientist the goals are description, understanding, and prediction of the world and its manifestations. Using the insights of the pure scientist in order to control the various phenomena of the world is the goal of the applied scientist. In contrast to the scientist, the artist is oriented around appreciative observation and pleasing representation of the world through various media. Rather than control and change the world, the artist tries to illuminate and reflect it in an esthetic light. So, whereas the scientist wants to effect change in the world, the artist wants to create an esthetic experience of the world.

Paralleling the terms Apollonian and Dionysian, Jung (1970) spoke of the principles of "logos" and "eros." The logos principle is one of objective interest in the world. One operates in accord with this principle when one takes an objective view of something, putting aside emotional and personal subjective considerations. Historically, in the West, this has been identified with the "masculine" orientation. The eros principle, on the other hand, is one of psychic relatedness. This principle is expressed in the subjective emotional experience in relating to the world. This more personal intimate mode of experiencing can involve one's relating to other people, animals, ideas, and even the inanimate. Jung noted that such psychic relatedness is usually seen as "feminine" in the West. Clearly, then, the logos principle corresponds to an Apollonian orientation, while the eros principle is consistent with a Dionysian orientation.

These two opposing world views are discussed in a particularly intriguing way by Robert Pirsig (1974) in his unusual book *Zen and the Art of Motorcycle Maintenance*. The subtitle of his book, "an inquiry into values," offers an important insight, for these two world views which we are exploring are positions of rather basic values. Pirsig's terms for the two world views are "classical understanding" and "romantic understanding." From the classical position, underlying form is what is seen in the world. But, from the romantic position, the world is seen in terms of immediate experience. These abstract notions beg for clarification, so allow me an example. Imagine showing a blueprint to two people, one of them classically inclined, the other a romantic. Seeing it as a thing in itself, the romantic would see lines, geometric shapes, numbers, and symbols. It would probably seem rather uninteresting. However, for the person of classical bent, interest would likely be aroused. He or she would recognize that the blueprint is representational. The lines, the geometrical forms, the numbers, and the symbols all reflect some underlying form. Simply put, the romantic sees a blueprint, the classicist sees a representation of a house.

Pirsig offered elaboration of this difference between the person of classical and the person of romantic inclination. The mode of the romantic tends to be inspirational, imaginative, creative, and intuitive. Feelings are given priority over facts, and esthetic considerations rate highly.

The person in the classical mode proceeds in orderly fashion based on reason and lawful principles. More intellectual than emotional in orientation, this person gives priority to facts, downgrading esthetic considerations. The classical mode is one of control, not merely the intuition of the meaning of things.

Pirsig identified that not only do persons tend to orient themselves through one of these two modes, but that then they often have difficulty appreciating people who have chosen the other mode. This difference in orientation contributes to people's misunderstanding of each other. This may well be the case when someone says with perplexity, "I can't understand why anyone would want to do that!" The fact is that "although motorcycle riding is romantic, motorcycle maintenance is purely classic" (Pirsig, 1974, p. 67). The romantic mode is Dionysian; the classical mode is Apollonian.

Sam Keen (1974) has offered some additional insights into the Apollonian-Dionysian split. Referring to the former as the "rational" view and the latter as the "cosmic" view, he identifies them as left-brain and right-brain functions, respectively. (Simply stated, the studies of hemispheric specialization have suggested that the left lobe processes data by sequential analysis of abstract, symbolic "bits." This process involves a logical, temporal, cause-and-effect approach. In contrast, the right lobe processes data in a holistic, integrative way, providing recognition of patterns. It may have primary involvement in imaging and emotional expression.) In the rational view work is valued above play, whereas, in the cosmic view there is the opposite priority. If work and play are the contents which differ, respectively, within the value system of the rational view and the cosmic view, then the styles are also different. The rational view seeks efficiency. For the cosmic view it is ecstasy which is sought. So it is that efficient work and ecstatic play define the poles of the rational view/cosmic view continuum.

For those readers who are of the Apollonian world view, I hope I have provided an accurate, precise, and efficient intellectual understanding of the Apollonian and Dionysian orientations. For those of a more Dionysian persuasion, I hope to have provided an esthetically pleasing image and inspirational picture with which you can feel yourself relate. A summary is offered in *Figure 1*.

APOLLONIAN VERSUS DIONYSIAN VISION	
APOLLONIAN	**DIONYSIAN**
Mastery and molding	Surrender and drift
Scientist	Artist
Logos	Eros
Objective interest "Masculine"	Psychic relatedness "Feminine"
Classical	Romantic
Order Reason Law Control Underlying form Facts predominate Unadorned Intellectual	Inspiration Imagination Creativity Intuition Immediate experience Feelings predominate Esthetic Emotional
Rational	Cosmic
Efficiency Work Left-brain	Ecstasy Play Right-brain

Figure 1

Anyone conversant with the Path of Gestalt will surely agree, at this point, that it is of the Dionysian. Therapies of the Apollonian bent strive for cure, solution of problems, and the achievement of goals. In true Dionysian spirit, Gestalt therapy is a Way of personal transformation. On the continuum of cognitive to emotional-expressive therapy it is past center, leaning toward the latter pole. With cogent evidence, Joen Fagan (1976) has argued this last point in her presentation of "The Gestalt Approach as 'Right Lobe' Therapy." Clearly, in its philosophy, in its theory, and in its techniques, Gestalt therapy represents the Dionysian world view in the land of the psychotherapies.

Seeing Gestalt therapy as a Dionysian manifestation, then, opens one to understand the two major distortions which I introduced earlier. The first can be thought of as the Apollonian distortion. To one who is Apollonian of view, Gestalt therapy would be seen through that template. Hence, Gestalt therapy is interpreted and judged as a cognitive-behavioral therapy, as discussed in my opening paragraph.

In order to understand the second distortion of Gestalt therapy, we need to mention the Roman reinterpretation of the Greek god Dionysus. Sheldon Kopp (1971, p. 74) summarized this transition beautifully when he wrote, "Later, when this cult of the Mad God appeared in Rome, it became debased into celebration by orgies of debauchery, rather than simple revelry. . . . Bacchanalia . . . " Dionysus was a vital counterpoint of Apollo for the Greeks. Again, to quote Kopp (1971, p. 74), "If Apollo brought reassuring reason, order, and objectivity to the Greeks, Dionysus brought the divine madness of inspired creativity, the freedom of blessed ecstasy, and the deliverance of lusty sexuality. He turned the people he inspired toward the life of the flesh, of free expression, of pleasure touched with madness." But, in Rome the Bacchanalia became a debased form of the Greek Dionysia. What had been a mystery cult of profound meaning became a ceremony marked by hysteria and self-destructive abandon. A large element of violence and a domination of sexual frenzy characterized these festivals of Bacchus. (A thorough account of this transition from Dionysia to Bacchanalia is given by Burgo Partridge [1960] in A History of Orgies.)

The second distortion of understanding of Gestalt therapy can be seen as a Bacchanalian distortion. The Bacchanalia were, truly, debased and dangerous. Those who see Gestalt therapy as dangerous, perhaps even debased, are viewing it as Bacchanalian, not as the vitally important Dionysian expression that it is. Those who distort Gestalt therapy in this way are quick to summon evidence of irresponsibility and harm based on the behaviors of some Gestalt therapists. True, Gestalt therapy debased is Bacchanalian. But, the true spirit of Gestalt therapy as I know it, is decidedly Dionysian. It is of the minority position which dynamically balances and guards against the extremes of Apollonian self-control, moderation, and order. As a modern Greek reminds us:

> A man needs a little madness, or else ... he
> never dares cut the rope and be free.
> (Zorba)

~

THE EGO-SYNTONIC IMPERATIVE

Nearly a century ago, William James made a case for the justification of religious belief on experiential grounds. He stressed that neither philosophical argument nor reductionistic scientific explanation proves adequate. Philosophy cannot justify religious belief, for it can circle itself and argue the other side equally as glibly.

Scientific explanations cannot justify religious belief since they reduce it to events of brain physiology, or, at best, the dynamics of psychological hypothetical constructs. Deep religious belief (what today we might refer to as spiritual knowing) is born of profound personal experience, and it is this experience in itself which is adequate justification for that belief.

Is it not the same with psychotherapy? Here, too, there are volumes of philosophical debate about psychotherapy — arguments about whether it works or about the superiority of one type of therapy over another. Added to this is another literature of scientific explanations and research findings. The theoretical explanations, again, offer fertile ground for debate after debate. Mind games. The research findings, often the bane of graduate students and an embarrassment to conscientious practitioners, remain for the most part tentative, inconclusive, and self-disclaiming in their cry that "further research is needed." So, what is one to do with "one-third greatly improved, one-third somewhat improved, one-third not helped" results, repeated across therapies and time?

From: *Voices*, 28(2), 9-10 (1992).

I believe that the justification for belief in psychotherapy, like the justification of religious belief, lies in the personal experience of it. Neither philosophizing about psychotherapy nor scientific researching about it provides adequate justifications for it. If the enterprise of psychotherapy depended on those latter justifications, surely it would be dead by now.

There are many fine testimonials in the literature of psychotherapy that highlight belief based on personal experience. An excellent example, from a patient's perspective, is Orson Bean's *Me and the Orgone* (1971). I mention this example because it shows so clearly the justification of belief through personal experience in contrast to disbelief in the therapy system, in this case Reichian Orgonomy, based on lack of adequate scientific support

It is personal belief, justified by firsthand experience, that accounts for the existence of the many varieties of psychotherapy. How many patients or therapists engage in psychotherapy, or in a specific style of therapy, because of the philosophical discourses about it or the research findings supporting it? Very few, I believe. It may have been some reading that first attracted them, but it is surely their personal experience that is the basis for their decision to remain engaged. Both therapists and patients shop until they either find the therapy that suits them or give up the pursuit as a lost cause. Over a period of time various selections may be made as circumstances, both internal and external, change.

Psychotherapy is an interpersonal event. It is only through the personhood of the therapist that a therapy is breathed life. Paradoxically, we still speak of a style of psychotherapy as if such existed apart from the persons of those who practice it. Nowhere is this point better illustrated and explored than by Jim Dublin in "Gestalt Therapy, Existential-Gestalt Therapy and/versus 'Perls-ism'" (1976). It has been said that there are as many Gestalt therapies as there are Gestalt therapists. The same could be said of other therapies, as well. What a patient experiences is a particular therapist/artist's version, rendition or interpretation of a style of therapy.

All of this leads to an important implication for the therapist. He or she may sample therapies, gleaning what feels like a personal fit. It is the personal expression of this fit that is the best that the therapist has to offer. *I believe that for a therapist to function optimally, it is essential that he or she relate to the patient only in ways that are congruent with who that therapist is. This is the "ego-syntonic imperative."* To work in any other way is to be mechanical and inauthentic. And, it is in the recognition of this that A.A.P. is dedicated to the nurturance and growth of the person of the therapist.

Without benefit of either philosophical or scientific certainty, we have but our belief. That belief, though, neither capricious nor random, is grounded in personal experience.

~

THE SWEAT LODGE EXPERIENCE
FROM A GESTALT NEO-REICHIAN PERSPECTIVE

My first Inipi (Lakota for "sweat lodge") was a profound experience. Subsequent Inipi experiences have proved to be very powerful also, each being different. I want, now, to translate the experience of the Inipi into the language of psychology, more specifically, the language of Gestalt and neo-Reichian therapy. Before doing so, I want to emphasize strongly that the *experience* was primary. My interpretation of that experience through a theoretical framework is not meant in any way to diminish, let alone trivialize the experience through reductionistic explanation. Rather, I wish to enhance the lasting meaning of the experience by adding a cognitive understanding.

A quote from *The Many Colored Buffalo* (Taegel, 1990, p. 116) serves as a segue for the psychological: "A most impressive feature of these Native American myths and ceremonies is that they deliberately lead the seeker into the vulnerable." Vulnerable — open to attack, to being wounded. Herein lies the key. In psychotherapy terms this means to reach below the ego defenses and contact the authentic self.

A model that I find useful is that of Fritz Perls' layers of the personality. Most certainly derived from the earlier model suggested by his mentor, Wilhelm Reich, Perls' model is less political and more detailed. To appreciate the model more fully, let us begin with that of Reich, in his own words:

From: *Voices*, 28(4), 37-43 (1992).

The patriarchal, authoritarian era of human history has attempted to hold the asocial impulses in check by means of compulsive moralistic prohibitions. It is in this way that civilized man ... developed a psychic structure consisting of three layers. On the surface, he wears an artificial mask of self-control, compulsive insincere politeness and pseudo-sociality. This mask conceals the second layer, the Freudian "unconscious," in which sadism, avarice, lasciviousness, envy, perversion of all kind, etc., are held in check without, however, being deprived of the slightest amount of energy. This second layer is the artificial product of a sex-negating culture and is usually experienced consciously as a gaping inner emptiness and desolation. Beneath it, in the depth, natural sociality and sexuality, spontaneous joy in work, the capacity for love, exist and operate. This third and deepest layer, which represents the biological core of the human structure, is unconscious, and it is feared. (Reich, 1973, p. 233)

In addition to being stated in less political terms, Perls' model is more dynamic in form. His discussions of the model (Levitsky & Perls, 1970; Perls, 1969) are inconsistent in the way he numbered the layers, but the essence is the same. Neurosis is characterized by a cliché layer, a layer that manifests only tokens of meaning, the semi-ritualistic living through "manners," "protocol," and "niceness." Below this is a phony later consisting of set roles and interpersonal games which creates an "as if" existence. Third is the impasse. The impasse is a level at which one, out of fear of the consequences of being authentic, stops oneself and feels stuck. The impasse layer is, then, the phobic layer, created by catastrophic expectations and characterized by a sense of being stuck, confused, empty, sacred or lost. At the next layer, the implosive, there is a pulling in or holding together, a deadness. The implosion is characterized by the paralysis from opposing forces. The fifth layer is created by the conversion of the implosion into an explosion. The explosion occurs when one allows authentic experiencing and expression of feeling. In summary, Perls' model consists of five-layers: Cliché layer, Phony layer, Impasse (Phobic layer), Implosive layer, and Explosive layer.

Not only does Perls' model seem to derive from Reich's, but Perls' discussion of the dynamic of working through the levels to the explosion into authenticity shows many parallels to Reich's earlier writing on the "phase of the breakdown of secondary narcissism" (Smith, 1975, 1978, 1985). Let us turn, once again, to Reich. In terms of Reich's (1949) theory, the lasting frustration of primary natural needs through societal inhibitions leads to chronic muscular contraction or "armor." This conflict between inhibited primary impulses and the inhibiting character armor results in a "secondary narcissism" (as distinct from the "primary narcissism" of the infant, which results from her or his cathecting its own body parts as part-objects of love). That is, as investment of libido in the outside world is made more difficult or is withdrawn, the energy accumulates within, intensifying a secondary narcissism. Reich described the loosening and dissolution of the characterological protective mechanism as bringing about a temporary condition of complete helplessness, an aspect of successful treatment that he termed the "phase of the breakdown of secondary narcissism." During this phase the patient is in a position of powerful, freed energy with a concomitant lack of "safe" neurotic controls. Because of these two factors, Reich reported that this phase of treatment is often stormy.

There are striking parallels between Reich's description of the phase of the breakdown of secondary narcissism in orgonomic therapy and Perls' discussion of the progression through the impasse and implosive layers to the explosive layer, as experienced in Gestalt therapy. In both cases, the essence is the dissolution of organismic core defenses in order to emerge into an authentic (organismically appropriate) behavior. Perls described the impasse as the position where environmental support or obsolete inner support is no longer adequate and authentic self-support has not yet been achieved. Staying with the experience of the impasse, enduring the confusion and helplessness, referred to as "withdrawal into the fertile void" (Perls, 1973), can lead to something akin to a hypnogogic hallucination, a "blinding flash of insight." Although sometimes dramatic, the explosion is not always so. It may be a relatively quiet explosion, depending on the amount of affect previously inhibited or blocked.

The impasse phenomenon with the attendant five-layer model of personality, along with its roots, seems to me a useful template of meaning to place on the Inipi experience. To wit: The Inipi experience began with my decision to take part in it and with my preparatory fast. As I fasted, I was enacting my commitment to the process, not just committing with words, but living out the choice by an intentional interruption of my usual pattern of eating. My fast was a chosen non-action with decided bodily involvement. Impacted both physiologically and psychologically by my not eating, I spent a period of 36 hours intending toward the ceremony to come. Knowing that others were probably doing the same, I felt already a joining with them.

My feeling of joining was greatly magnified when we assembled at dawn, speaking for myself, sleepy, hungry, curious and excited. The drive, then even more, the walk into the woods allowed me the feeling of being on a wondrous adventure, together with a column of pilgrims. This was an occasion for personal exploration and growth, and opportunity for spiritual expansion. With the building of the lodge, I felt a continuation and expansion of these feelings. The structure and timing of the events attracted my attention and made it easy for me to concentrate. I find some of Perls' words apropos:

> There seems to be, in all human beings, an inborn tendency towards ritual, which can be defined as an expression of man's sense of social identification, his need for contact with a group. (Perls, 1973, p. 28)

The silence from unnecessary talk and the focused activities of lodge building had already cast, for me, an air of reverence. Entering the lodge and participating in the ceremony enhanced this reverent feeling immensely. Again, let me evoke the words of Perls:

> If at an important occasion there were no ritual . . . the whole thing would seem meaningless and flat. The ritual seems to give such experience order, form and purpose. In Gestalt terms, we could say that it makes the Gestalt clearer, makes the figure stand out more sharply. (Perls, 1973, p. 29)

Once inside the lodge and engaged in the ceremony, the silence from extraneous taking and the atmosphere of reverence carried us rapidly beyond the Cliché layer. This was not absolute, as for instance when the flap was opened between rituals. But, for the most part the Cliché layer was quickly passed. To me, the vestige of cliché seemed more than irrelevant, more than out of place. It seemed profane.

These same factors quickly eroded whatever phoniness was being expressed. The participation in the very rituals themselves made the playing out of habitual roles and interpersonal games difficult, if not untenable.

What I am suggesting is that the agreement to participate in the ritual activities of the Inipi — preparatory fasting, group walking to the site, constructing the lodge, chanting, and particularly, the ceremony inside the lodge — in large part require one to pass beyond of Cliché layer and the Phony later of functioning. These two layers are manifested in interpersonal interaction, that is, they are superficial social layers. The instructions for participation in the Inipi "rule" them out, so to speak.

The impasse phenomenon is, in contrast to the Cliché and Phony layers of social interaction, more an *intra*personal arena. The dynamic is one between the introjected toxic voices that threaten catastrophe as the consequence of authenticity and the genuine self in wish for authenticity. It is difficult to impact at this level with prose. A social statement that rules out certain behaviors has not sufficient force. In the psychotherapy realm, here is the point of body involvement. So, Gestalt body work, Reichian, Bioenergetics or other neo-Reichian work is enlisted. The Inipi is, itself, "body work."

After a while of sitting I reached the threshold of my pain. My legs, hips, back, shoulders and neck ached and, finally, cried for relief. My muscles were stretched and stressed as much as they have ever been in Bioenergetics stress postures. Add to this the darkness, taking away visual scanning and social orienting. And, most powerful of the manipulations, the intense damp heat. I suggest that this combination of extreme wet heat, postural stress, and darkness maintained long enough fairly pulls one past any vestiges of the Cliché layer and Phony layer and forces one into a core confrontation. The known, the habitual ways of being socially present break down in the Inipi. And, as these customary defense-ridden ways are stripped away, what is left is the core, that is, the genuine self and the toxic introjects.

I felt layers fall away as in a sort of regression to an unsophisticated, unsocialized, primitive state. My urges came — anger, joy, sadness, love — only to run headlong into confusion and anxiety prompted by old voices of catastrophic threats. But the muscular pains grew. The heat increased. I thought I couldn't breath. My heart pounded. I thought I might have a heart attack and die right there. Terror! The voices of catastrophe were winning.

Perls is oft quoted as saying, in the terms of the 1960s, "Lose your mind and come to your senses." This is precisely what I experienced in the Inipi. The demand characteristics of the situation were so strong, that usual thinking became extremely difficult. The here-and-now experience was so impelling that my controlled, defense-laden thought patterns were disrupted. With cliché and phoniness stripped away first by rules, then devastated by the stark here-and-now sensory experience of over-heated wet darkness, I huddled with my inside pressures. My brothers and sisters and I shared in eruptions from within, at times mild, at times dramatic. Quietly I would huddle in hesitation, feeling empty, scared, at "impasse." I would tighten to endure, implode. And, again, an explosion into tears, laughing, curses, and pounding or meltings of love. Sometimes visual images of people in my past would come to me with my feelings, but not always. Out of a background of emotional unfinished business, emotional figures would emerge and explode into expression. Each time I chose as if I could not tolerate any other choice but that of expression.

Important to the Inipi is the fact that it is so sensorially compelling. The strength of the hot, wet, dark, rule-guided, socially shared stimulus situation is so great, that one is hard pressed not to concentrate on it. Thus, the pull of the here-and-now. The rule of talking in turn (with the exception of the ritual to the West) prevented the interruption of anyone's concentration on her or his own process by others. Thus, was there both social support by virtue of the shared participation and prevention of social intrusion on personal emotional process.

Turning, again, to Perls' words:

> Magic . . . serves to enhance the value of the group as a tool of the achievement of goals. It is used to evoke the support of beneficial powers and to annihilate dreaded powers. . . . Once engaged in ritual, all other activity is disesteemed as profane. The highest concentration . . . is demanded and achieved with solemnity and awe. Only a full participation of the entire personality will result in that religious feeling of intensified existence, of exaltation, of integration, without diminishing the full awareness of both the individual and the group. (Perls, 1973, pp. 29-30)

The Inipi brought together the group in shared purpose, and the group became a tool, to echo Perls' phrase. The group was a tool in the sense that it offered powerful support for the personal process to be undertaken. The group ritual became an environmental support that facilitated each person in allowing the energies, both internal and external, to take her or him to the brink. The demand characteristics of the Inipi, both social and physical, pull strongly for the "full participation of the entire personality." And, certainly, I felt profoundly "that religious feeling of intensified existence, of exaltation, of integration." My experience was at once, then, deeply personal and transpersonal. I experienced both myself and the group, and even more, I had a glimpse of the "humanity" that transcended our personal natures.

If the Reichian-derived five-layer Gestalt model of personality addresses the vertical dimension, then the Bioenergetics model of Charge → Ground → Discharge (Lowen, 1975) addresses the horizontal dimension. The latter model describes the dynamics of body energy, defining three crucial issues. First is the issue of energy production or charging. This is regulated by the rate and depth of breathing. Grounding, the second energetic issue, refers to the literal experience of being connected to the ground (i.e., supported). As expressed by Alexander Lowen (1975, p. 196), ". . . the more a person can feel his contact with the ground . . . the more charge he can tolerate and the more feeling he can handle." The third energetic issue, discharging, refers to the expression of feeling. This basic Bioenergetics model has clear utility in understanding the Inipi. Allow me to explain.

The act of sitting on the ground is *de facto* "grounding." This grounding is enhanced in the Inipi in two ways. First, the sitting is extended in time, uninterrupted by standing or moving about. Second, the sitting is made intimate between the person and the earth by virtue of bringing bare skin (recall that we wore only bathing suits) in touch with the soil (remember, we removed the sod). (Although some of us began by sitting on towels, soon the towels were sweat soaked and disarrayed, making skin to soil contact the rule.) Being thus so grounded gave support for the experience and containment of high charge of energy. It is also worth noting that we grounded in a sitting or at times half-lying position. In neo-Reichian terms, this approaches "horizontal grounding" as opposed to the "vertical grounding" that occurs in the standing position. Based on clinical evidence, horizontal grounding tends to invite regressive experience, a tapping into deeper, more child-like feelings than is true for vertical grounding. I believe, then, that the extended, mostly unclothed sitting or lying on the bare earth provided both the grounding that allowed for the toleration and containment of high feeling states (until the breakthrough into focused expression) and the pull for regressive feelings.

The intense moist heat is also interesting, bioenergetically. I found myself breathing more rapidly and my heart beating at an accelerated pace in response to the heat. Without exerting physically, without even moving about, my physiological response was one of charging. My energy-feeling charge would build and build to a point that would have been an "overcharge" had it not been for the strong grounding.

Having emerged from the lodge, lying prone on the grass, I enjoyed wages of spasms. I recognized these as the "orgastic reflex" that Reich identified as the evidence for the dissolution of armor. I felt loose, relaxed. For now, my armor was melted. The work had been effective, as judged by this Reichian criterion.

I suggest, then, from my experience that the Inipi creates a very effective arena for personal and transpersonal growth, understandable in terms of bioenergetics and of Gestalt therapy. Bioenergetically speaking, the structure of the Inipi offers strong grounding, high energy charging and the opportunity for focused energy discharge. It can be seen, then, in light of bioenergetics, as a ritual of energy attunement. In Gestalt terms, the Inipi, both through the social demand characteristics and the physical demand characteristics of its ceremonies provides the support and compelling invitation to work through the personality layers to the explosion into authentic being. It strips away the superficial social layers of cliché and phoniness and pushes one powerfully into a here-and-now confrontation with the conflicts within.

As I emerged from that womb into the fresh coolness, I was filled with awe and wonder. There is much more to the Inipi than I have understood through my Gestalt and neo-Reichian grids. Beyond the practical, and in tension with it, lies the mystery.

~

The Camel, the Lion, and the Child

Embedded in the recondite speeches of Zarathustra (Nietzsche, 1982) lies a metaphor most relevant to the understanding of the "psychotherapist as revolutionary." It is in "On the Three Metamorphoses" that Zarathustra speaks of how the spirit becomes a camel, the camel a lion, and the lion, finally, a child. There is much that is difficult for the spirit, he begins. The spirit that would bear much takes on the most difficult things and, like a camel, speeds into its desert. But in the loneliest desert the spirit can become the lion who would be master of its own desert. The camel can become the lion if it seeks out its last master and defeats him. Who is this last master, this dragon that must be slain? Zarathustra answers, "'Thou shalt' is the name of the great dragon. But the spirit of the lion says, 'I will.' 'Thou shalt' lies in his way, sparking like gold, an animal covered with scales; and on every scale shines a golden 'thou shalt'" (Nietzsche, 1982, pp.138-139). The dragon reflects the values long ago created and claims to be all created value. The dragon speaks, verily there shall be no more "I will."

Zarathustra asks why there is need for the spirit of the lion, why the beast of burden that renounces and is reverent is not enough. In answer, Zarathustra speaks. "The creation of freedom for oneself and a sacred 'No' even to duty —for that . . . the lion is needed. . . . He once loved 'thou shalt' as most sacred: now he must find illusion and caprice even in the most sacred, that freedom from his love may become his prey: the lion is needed for such prey" (Nietzsche, 1982, p.139).

But there is more. Even after the leonine "No!" to all of the "thou shalts," there is something more, which the child can do. "The child is inno-

---

From: *Voices*, 30(1), 21-24 (1994).

cence and forgetting, a new beginning, a game, a self-propelled wheel, a first movement, a sacred 'Yes'" (Nietzsche, 1982, p. 139). It is only through the sacred "Yes" that the spirit wills its own will and conquers its own world. Zarathustra tells us that the game of creation requires this sacred "Yes."

The traditional virtues, constituted of the "thou shalts," consecrate stereotyped mediocrity, but seduce with the offer of sound sleep. As Zarathustra spoke, "Now I understand clearly what was once sought above all when teachers of virtue were sought. Good sleep was sought, and opiate virtues for it. For all these much praised sages who were teachers of virtue, wisdom was the sleep without dreams: they knew no better meaning of life" (Nietzsche, 1982, p.142). Thus are we instructed, where sleep is the goal, life lacks meaning. The camel plods on through its desert.

In its two aspects, revolution means a complete or drastic change and it means a complete cycle of events. The revolutionary, then, is one who introduces radical change and at the same time begins or ends a cycle (a defined point of beginning or ending of a cycle is, of course, an arbitrary choice). The revolution can be seen in psychotherapy in light of the camel to lion to child metaphor. It is as if there are camels, lions, and children dominating at certain times or periods of the cycle. Allow me to elaborate.

The child, to pick a convenient starting point in the cycle, is the revolutionary. The child brings innocence, as a guiltlessness and guilelessness. The child is neither guilty of the sins (neglect and violation) that harbinger the demise of the creative phases of the previous cycle nor guileful (deceitful and treacherous) in maintaining the adherence to the old order. The child brings forth a new beginning, invites participation in a new game and says "Yes" to the inchoate form. Freud and Reich may be seen as such children of revolutionary creativity.

If the child is the revolutionary, then the lion is the evolutionary. The lion with its reactive "No" is less creative than the child with its more proactive "Yes." But, importantly, the evolutionary integrates the forces by juxtaposing a ferocious "No" with the established "thou shalts" of the latter phases of the previous cycle. In this reaction and juxtaposition, the evolutionary polishes and further develops the inchoate form into its fullness. An example might be Fritz Perls.

The camel represents the third phase of the cycle, that of the conservative. Just as the camel trods on, bearing and accepting the burden of its "thou shalts," the conservative tends not to question, but to preserve what has been established. Disposed to maintain the existing views, the conservative says neither "Yes" nor "No" to them, but goes over them, reciting them again and again. Remember, the camel, beast of burden that it is, is also a ruminant.

If I may play a bit with Zarathustra's metaphor, I willpoint out that the camel is often found with another animal, the ass. The ass, reputed for obstinacy and stupidity might well represent the reactionary. Farther right even than the conservative is this asinine figure.

To be discreet, I have not suggested any names of the conservatives or the reactionaries, the camels and the asses of psychotherapy. In addition to discretion the listing of recognizable names becomes more difficult because the ranks swell in the later phases of the cycle. Few, indeed, are the evolutionaries, the lions, and fewer still the revolutionaries or children of psychotherapy. One might argue my choice of psychotherapist examples, or might find other examples that seem more apt. The point, however, is that in psychotherapy there are cycles, introduced by revolutionaries and developed further by evolutionaries, only to be maintained in an established, diluted, rigid form by the conservatives. These three stages of the cycle correspond to the child, the lion, and the camel metaphor as presented by Nietzsche. We can add to this the reactionary, symbolized by the ass, who resists the emergence of the next phase of revolution. (See diagram)

Revolutionary ➡ Evolutionary ➡ Conservative ➡ Reactionary ➡ Revolutionary

(CHILD)	(LION)	(CAMEL)	(ASS)
("YES" TO ONE'S OWN WILL)	("NO" TO THE "THOU SHALTS")	(CONFORMS TO THE "THOU SHALTS")	(STUBBORNLY DEFENDS THE "THOU SHALTS")

If psychotherapy is in the service of the creation and development of the individual, if the struggle is for the assertion of personhood, then the cycle of child, lion, camel (as ass) takes on clear meaning and dimension. In Nietzsche's ethic we find this theme central. "Become who you are!" exhorts Zarathustra (Nietzsche, 1982, p. 351). "But only man is a grave burden for himself! That is because he carries on his shoulders too much that is alien to him. Like a camel, he kneels down and lets himself be well loaded. . . . He loads too many *alien* grave words and values on himself, and then life seems a desert to him" (Nietzsche, 1982, p. 305).

Nietzsche's theme is echoed by Freud throughout much of his writing. Again and again, Freud posits the biological urge of the individual against the restrictive forces of society, the id in conflict with the superego. Freud spoke out in that Victorian climate, gave voice to the id while the society was champion of a strict and rigid superego. More political in his style, his student, Reich, railed against the societal restrictions and distortions of natural libidinous forces. In turn, Reich's student, Perls, continued the evolution by further developing and popularizing this essential Freudian message. Thus, we can trace Nietzsche's message of ""This is *my* good and evil'; with that he has reduced to silence the mole and dwarf who say, 'Good for all, evil for all'" (Nietzsche, 1982, p. 370). More polite was Freud, in his translation of Nietzsche's philosophy into scientific revolution. But, then spoke Reich with the arrogance of a true revolutionary in his *Listen Little Man!* (Reich, 1974). "Your slave driver is you yourself" (p.7). "Only you yourself can be your liberator" (p.8). "You know Hitler better than Nietzsche, Napoleon better than Pestalozzi. A king means more to you than Sigmund Freud" (p.11). "I know, I know, you want your 'geniuses' and you're ready to honor them. But you want *nice* geniuses, well-behaved, moderate geniuses with no nonsense about them, and not the untamed variety who break through all barriers and limitations" (p.45). "I know you have your 'great moments,' your 'flights of enthusiasm' and 'exaltation.' But you lack the perseverance to let your enthusiasm soar, to let your exaltation carry you higher and higher. You're afraid to soar, afraid of heights and depths. Neitzsche told you that long ago, far better than I can" (p.26). "Take your destiny into your own hands and build your life on rock" (p.68). "Trust the quiet inner voice that tells you what to do . . . **BE YOURSELF!**" (p.70).

With Nietzsche it was "Hear it well, little boys!" and "Become who you are!" And with Reich. "Listen, little man!" and "Be yourself!" For Perls it was *In and Out the Garbage Pail* (1969b) and "I do my thing and you do your thing. I am not in this world to live up to your expectations. And you are not in this world to live up to mine" (Perls, 1969a, p.4). See the common thread as it develops. "There is a race on between fascism and humanism. At this moment it seems to me that the race is about lost to the fascists" (Perls, 1969a, p.3). Perls' predications have been summarized thusly: "Listen to yourself, the stirrings, the movements inside; not to the words in your head: other people's words, your parents' words, society's words. . . . Be aware of you, where you are, what you're doing; not the shoulds, the commands, the expectations. . . . Don't give yourself away. . . . Hear the important messages inside you. . . . Find your rhythm; find your base; find your support. . . . Dare. Risk, Discover. Enjoy" (Fagan, 1992, pp.331-332).

Nietzsche's message is clearly a Dionysian one. It is a message of "Become who you are!" (Nietzsche, 1982, p.351). And, it is a message of eternal recurrence. "Alas, man recurs eternally! The small man recurs eternally!" (p.331). It is a revolutionary message in two senses.

So, in the history of psychotherapy, as in all creative cycles, we are visited by the genius of the revolutionaries, a Freud and a Reich, and the genius of the evolutionaries, a Perls. Following this creative period comes the period of rigidifying the teachings, making them into a set of "thou shalts" and preserving their form, now pale or lacking of spirit, intact. This lends security. But, warned Zarathustra, "Beware lest a narrow faith imprison you . . . . For whatever is narrow and solid seduces and tempts you now" (Nietzsche, 1982, p. 387).

"Laughing lions must come!" (Nietzsche, 1982, p. 395). Thus spoke Zarathustra, and having heard, thus spoke Freud, Reich, and Perls.

~

THE EMBODIED COUPLE:
POSTURE CHANGE AS AN ASSESSMENT TOOL

SUMMARY. Herein is described the use of a specific physical posture for couples to assume for the purpose of assessing the dynamics of their relationship. Its careful and artful use creates a microcosm of the couple's interactive style, revealing significant behaviors and feelings in the therapist's presence.

Any psychotherapy which does not attend to the body is incomplete. It is attention to the whole person — the irreducible, indivisible psyche-in-body—which is the mark of a complete psychotherapeutic approach. To me, this is a self-evident truth, made obvious to anyone of sagacious bent who has the opportunity to witness the growth process of psychotherapy.

I have shared my phenomenological method, my theoretical rationale and some of my clinical techniques for focusing on the body as both locus for understanding the person and locus for therapeutic intervention in *The Body in Psychotherapy* (1985) and its sequel *Sexual Aliveness* (1987). In these two volumes I addressed psychotherapy of the individual, primarily. But what of couples' work? What of the *embodied couple?*

In an article on confluence which appeared in *Journal of Couples Therapy* (1990), I used the conceptual model of the couple as represented by a triangle with the points standing for the "I," the "Thou" and the "We." In no way can this "I-Thou-We" relationship and its dynamics be more clearly

From: *Journal of Couples Therapy*, 6(1/2), 175-178 (1996).

presented in the therapy office than by having the couple assume certain structured postures together. It is in these postures that the couple embodies not only the "I" and the "Thou" (or its objectified "I-It" or "It-It" forms), but the couple embodies also the "We." By *experiencing* their embodied coupling, the two can come to know more of how they relate. But, this is only a first step. Ultimately, and of more importance, the couple invite transformation of the relationship through living the experience together. To do the posture is to inform, and to do the posture is to transform.

The postures which I use are highly structured and derive from several sources, including not only psychology, but the sacred traditions. Some of the postures are complex and best shown rather than described. Likewise, the clinical use of some of the postures is difficult to describe. The use of these postures is best learned experientially in a workshop or other supervised situation.

For now, I will limit my presentation to just one posture. I have chosen it because of its relative simplicity and because of its great usefulness as a tool in assessing the dynamics of a couple's relationship. This is the "back-to-back" posture. I introduce it thusly:

> I would like for you to try an experiment. In a few moments I am going to ask the two of you to assume a particular position together. The purpose of doing this experiment is to see what you can discover about yourselves and your relationship with each other and what I might observe which I can then share with you. So when I invite you to assume the posture, stay as aware as you can of how the two of you do the posture and how you feel as you do it. Just breathe and be aware of all of the body sensations, emotions, memories and thoughts which you have. In order to focus on these, it's better that you not talk while you do this. In a few minutes I will call time and we can discuss what each of you has discovered and what I have observed. Ready? (Clarify any questions.) Now, stand back-to-back, with your backs touching. Allow whatever wants to happen, to happen.

While the couple stand, I remind them not to talk if they begin doing so, and I remind them to breathe if they begin restricting their breathing. Sometimes it becomes apparent that a lot is happening and I judge it appropriate to stop soon in order to process what has occurred. This is especially the case when there is obvious emotion drawn forth by the experiment, for example, if there is crying. At other times, I may see little happening, and let the experiment go on longer, at least ten minutes. During this time I may repeat part of the instructions, such as:

> Just stand and breathe. Let whatever wants to happen, happen — body sensations, emotions, memories, thoughts, whatever.

After I call time, I invite the couple to sit with me and share whatever they wish to of their discoveries. If I have observations which seem congruent or otherwise relevant to something one of the couple shares, I may interject it then. Otherwise, I prefer to save my observations until they have done their sharing.

What fascinates me about the use of this posture is that, simple as the experiment seems, the discoveries are almost always of great value. Often profound, frequently emotionally laden, and sometimes surprising, the discoveries reflect the significant aspects of the couple's dynamics. This back-to-back posture tends to be an embodied microcosm of the couple's relationship. The couple may discover boredom (not allowing anything existing to happen), playfulness (enjoyable movements together, as a back-to-back free-style dance), competitiveness (pushing against each other), dependency (leaning against the partner), being burdened (being leaned on), co-dependency (accepting being leaned on), longing or sadness (the return of touch which has been absent), sexual desires or frustrations, cooperation or trust (mutual leaning or taking turns leaning) or lack thereof. The list could go on, much further. The point is, that whatever is going on of importance in the couple's relationship, it is highly likely to go on when the couple assumes this posture. Their experience in the posture echoes their experience in their relationship.

An advantage of the use of postures as assessment tools in working with a couple is that the couple's *behavior* becomes apparent. The behavior becomes manifest in this micro-cosmic event in the presence of the therapist, for all parties to observe. The manifest behavior cannot be denied, and often the meaning of that behavior is so clearly implied or inferred that the couple's issue is laid bare before the eyes of all present. Another advantage is that the couple are actively participatory in the assessment process — acting, describing their own and their partner's and joining into the discussion of how the emerging meanings are manifested in the macrocosm of their lives together. Such active participation in the assessment of their relationship introduces an active set which may help in their being more actively participatory in the therapy itself. In a very real way the therapy is underway as the assessment tool is being used.

I have two special suggestions for the therapist. First, begin observing very carefully from the moment you invite the couple to stand together. The manner in which the couple come into the posture and first adjust to it may be especially revealing and significant. Second, I suggest that the therapist share mostly, if not entirely, phenomenological observations, leaving the meaning to emerge from the couple as the processing continues. Statements such as, "I saw you stand still, while he walked over to you and turned his back to yours," "I saw tears in your eyes," "I saw you clench your teeth and hold your breath," "I noticed your face flush," "Your were leaning at more of an angle with only your shoulders touching him," can lead to useful exploration and emergent meaning by the couple.

As with any technique, this postural assessment will come alive only through artful use. It is the skill, sensitivity and grace of the therapist which can make this seemingly simple experiment potentially rich.

~

'PERLS-ISM,' GESTALT THERAPY AND THE CONCENTRATION
ON PERSONAL PROCESS

The present paper is based on an invited address presented
at the Centennial Convention of the American Psychological
Association. The question of the future of Gestalt therapy is
approached by distinguishing three manifestations of what
the author sees as the core of Gestalt — the concentration
on personal process. At the most general level, this process is
identifiable not only in Gestalt therapy, but in other systems
as well (e.g. T'ai Chi Chu'an, yoga, Zen etc.). Gestalt therapy
is one particular form of this process, peculiar to a
socio-political-historical context, namely, contemporary
Western psychotherapy, but through the person of Fritz
Perls and his close colleagues. These three levels — a process, a particular contextual form of that process and a specific personal interpretation of that process-in-context — are
explicated and the fate of each estimated.

Gestalt focuses on personal process unfolding moment-to-moment.
Consider this very carefully. In this definition I experience a coruscation and
an opening to esoteric understanding, in Gestalt terms, an "Aha!" experience.
The term "personal process" may require explication. It refers to one's psychological process, that is, the immediate experience of the person embedded

From: *British Gestalt Journal,* 5(1), 3-6 (1996).

in her or his environment. This would include sensory processes, intuition, emotion, fantasy and other cognitive processes. This in-the-moment uniquely personal process evolves as the here-and-now moment ineluctably emerges in an ongoing way. The method for focusing on personal process is awareness. Various specific techniques are invented, repeated and modified in the service of enhancing awareness. Like the Uroboros which circles itself and bites its own tail, awareness is both the method and the goal.

Taking the intentional focus on personal process as the core of Gestalt, we can then address the question of the future of Gestalt in an interesting way. I find this interesting in that this core can be recognized manifest on three levels. In good Gestalt pedagogical style, I will begin with the whole and differentiate two increasingly specific levels from that.

In graphic and succinct form Barry Stevens (1984, p.73) wrote:

> T'ai chi is zen is dhana is meditation is yoga is Gestalt is awareness is t'ai chi is zen — and I have to put them all in a circle and start anywhere to know that.

That's it! In this equation, in this statement of redundancy Barry Stevens has acknowledged the supra-system. She has alluded to the focus on personal process which is held in common by these systems of personal or spiritual growth and which thereby lies beyond them. Each system is a particular manifestation and together they echo the core process. We could, of course, add the names of other systems of personal or spiritual growth to her list. Her allusion is brought into clear focus by something which she wrote several years earlier (Stevens, 1970, p.14):

> Awareness. Noticing. That's gestalt. It's also Gestalt. And Indian — in the old way.

I want to mention a definition that is sometimes given of Zen. It is as follows, "Common things, uncommonly done." The "uncommonly done" phrase translates into the less poetic phrase "done with mindfulness." So Zen is doing the ordinary but with mindfulness. All of this can be tied back into the above discussion through the following analogy:

Mindfulness : Zen : : Awareness : Gestalt

In a philosophical vein James Bugental (1971) wrote of this core process, calling it "growth-oriented experiencing." Describing it as a major point of the humanistic ethic, he said that people who have incorporated the humanistic ethic tend to seek "growth- facilitating experiences." The specific "technique" or particular system could vary.

Turning to the mythological corpus, we do not have to search far to find examples of the core process being discussed. This is well represented in the "mundis archetypus." Intentional, disciplined practice leading to personal transformation is portrayed in the religion of my ancestors most clearly through the Odinic archetype. In *The Poetic Edda* (Hollander, 1962) we read:

> I wot that I hung on the wind-tossed tree
> > all of nights nine,
> wounded by spear, bespoken to Othin,
> > bespoken myself to myself,
> upon that tree of which none telleth
> > from what roots it doth rise.
> Neither horn they upheld nor handed me bread;
> I looked below me — aloud I cried -
> caught up the runes, caught them up wailing,
> > thence to the ground fell again.

And thus, through shamanic initiation did Odin become the God of Personal Transformation. And, as the one who delivered the runes to humankind, he became the God of Poetry.

The connection between poetry and transformation is made in the Odinic archetype and it can easily be seen in many of the systems of personal process. Consider, for example, the poetics of the body in t'ai chi, the Zen koan or the mantra of a yogic meditation.

Before leaving Odin let us look at yet another of his aspects. Odin's intriguing and allegorical adventures were guided by his consultations with his two ravens Huginn (Thought) and Muninn (Memory). Each day he would send his ravens forth to fly throughout the nine worlds. When they returned they would report all which they had observed. Thus informed by thought and memory could Odin act. Hear the refrain of "common things uncommonly done." We are instructed in the use of awareness, mindfulness, focus on personal process through the Odinic archetype. In honor of this process we have named a day of the week Odin's day. In Danish, Norwegian and Swedish it is Onsdag, in Dutch Woensdag and, of course, in English it is Wednesday.

In *Transformations of Myth through Time* Joseph Campbell (1990) calls attention to a difference between the approach to personal transformation in the Near Eastern traditions and the Western European traditions. In the Near East, he explains, one's membership in the community is what counts. One is regarded as a member of a society, primarily, not as an individual. The respect for the individual path is typically European. This is strongly in evidence in the four powerful pre-Christian traditions: Classical Greek, Classical Italic or Roman, Celtic and Germanic.

This emphasis on the individual and the necessity for the person to discern her or his unique path is beautifully revealed in one of the versions of the Grail legend, *La Queste del Saint Graal*. As quoted by Campbell concerning the taking leave of the Knights,

> They agreed that all would go on this quest, but they thought it would be a disgrace to go forth in a group, so each entered the forest at a point that he, himself had chosen, where it was darkest and there was no path. (Campbell, 1990, p.211)

Campbell (1990, p.212) interprets this passage poignantly and succinctly when he adds, "If there is a path, it is someone else's path, and you are not on the adventure."

The theme of the Grail legend is one of bringing life into what was "the waste land." In terms less poetic we can say that the theme is the bringing to life of the deadened individual through focus on personal process.

From this more general level we can now shift our focus to a more specific level of manifestation of focus on personal process, that of Gestalt therapy. In so doing, we immediately encounter a paradox. It is this: a therapy system is brought to life only through the person of a therapist, and yet we can conceptualize the system. It is much like a song which exists, but does not exist except when it is sung. At the present level of discourse I will focus on the abstract system, Gestalt therapy.

Gestalt therapy is one particular form of concentration on personal process peculiar to a certain socio-politico-historical context, namely Western psychotherapy. This context provides much of the form in which the core process becomes manifest. Briefly, this includes the roles of psychotherapist and of patient or client, as these are defined by our society, as well as the economics of the endeavor.

In a previous article (Smith, 1978) I addressed what in my view are the underlying philosophy, theory of personality and style of work which characterize and identify Gestalt as a distinct therapeutic system. Having discussed this at some length I summarized as follows:

> I consider this blend of existential and Zen philosophy, this organismic personality theory, and this phenomenological experiential style of working to be the necessary and sufficient conditions to define the Gestalt approach. I don't define the Gestalt approach by techniques. (Smith, 1978, p.46).

The purpose here is not to elaborate, but briefly to call attention to Gestalt therapy as a particular manifestation of the focus on personal process. To the above summary statement, I now will add that in working on personal process Gestalt emphasizes the identification of "unfinished business" or "incompletely formed Gestalten" from one's distant or more immediate past which in pressing for completion interfere with the spontaneous figure-ground formations of here-and-how behaviors and perceptions. Otherwise said, Gestalt emphasizes the identification and resolution of blocks and inhibitions, caused by toxic introjects, in the spontaneous flow of contact-withdrawal cycles (Smith, 1985).

From Gestalt therapy we can differentiate an even more specific level, shifting our focus to "Perls-ism." Reverberating with the statement of paradox made earlier, we are now at the level of the Gestalt therapy developed and given lived expression by Fritz Perls and some of his close colleagues. This specific personal form of Gestalt therapy was named "Perls-ism" by Jim Dublin (1976) and carefully explicated by him.

In the interests of brevity and to help keep the present aim on the levels of manifestation of focus on personal process, I will offer only a sketch of the particular theoretical and stylistic elements of "Perls-ism".

Perls evolved in his work format from individual therapy to the workshop model and eventually to the commune model. The "hot seat" procedure is, at least in large part, an artefact of the workshop model. Perls emphasized oral aggression in his exposition of theory, developing a model of oral stages, analogous to Freud's psychosexual stages. Consistent with his theoretical stance, Perls demonstrated a good deal of oral aggression in his personal style. He is well remembered for at times being harshly confrontational. His value on authenticity found expression in an interpersonal openness to the point of often being socially offensive. In his strong emphasis on maturity as self-support he left out, at the very least through de-emphasis, relatedness in love, the true "I- Thou" of Buber. This translated into a radically frustrating therapeutic style. Perls was for the most part a non-supportive therapist. In spite of the fact that Perls' early writings are cogent and sagacious, in the style of the European scholar, his later work, written and orally expressed, showed a decided anti-intellectual bias. Consider, for instance, his favored terms "top-dog," "under-dog," "elephant-shit," "chicken-shit" and "mind-fucking." Perls' brand of existentialism was a biological hedonistic one. This left little room for consideration of the spiritual or transpersonal. He was radically individual centered. Seeing the therapist's function as the facilitation of awareness, as he did, Perls left change strictly up to the patient. This led to a relatively non-nurturing, non- protective, non-limit setting, non-supportive style which may well fail to address the question of the patient's genuine developmental level.

In the above sketch my purpose is not to challenge or critique either Perls' theories or his personal style. Rather, I wish to call attention to the flavor of "Perls- ism" as a specific lived form of Gestalt therapy. The elements I mention are relative, not absolute, and certainly not exhaustive. I leave it to the individual reader to agree or to disagree with the bold stand which Perls took. In addition to Jim Dublin's (1976) chapter I recommend a paper by Joen Fagan (1971) entitled "The Importance of Fritz Perls Having Been" for an elaboration of "Perls-ism."

Thus are the three levels of manifestation: a process, a particular contextual form of that process and a specific personal interpretation of that process-in-context. Each of these levels of focus on personal process is, of course, time bound. Their durability is in inverse order. "Perls-ism" will surely continue to fade insofar as Perls was very much a person of the decade or so of his prominence, basically the 1960s. Psychotherapy will no doubt evolve, continuing to weave aspects of Gestalt philosophy, theory and technique into its broadening fabric until "Gestalt" will no longer be identified as such. And, with the passage of more time, psychotherapy may itself disappear. The core process will no doubt continue, as it has for centuries, manifesting under the cloak of contemporary contexts and structures and expressed through the persons of emergent leaders.

I close on a wistful note from Barry Stevens:

Sometimes I prefer Zen even if it does take twenty years. (Pause) I'm not sure that Gestalt doesn't take twenty years to reach the same place. (Stevens, 1970, p.9)

~

ENTHEOS: TOWARD A BIO-EXISTENTIAL
RATIONAL THEOLOGY

Only one thing matters: live a good life. Do your heart's
bidding, even when it leads you on paths that timid souls
would avoid. Even when life is a torment, don't let it harden
you.

—Wilhelm Reich

To some, the juxtaposition of the words "rational" and "theology"
would appear oxymoronic. I think not, however. What I want to do is set
forth a statement of my *personal* theology. Neither a revealed theology, born
of divine or Biblical revelation, nor a dogmatic theology, put forth by an
authoritative church body, this is a rational theology. Rather simple in form,
it builds point by point on reason. It is ultimately just my opinion, of course,
but bolstered up by the opinions and thoughts of a great many others. The
ideas are from many sources — only the arrangement is mine. Most importantly, this theology offers a spiritual foundation for my understanding and
praxis of psychotherapy.

In setting forth my personal theology I will proceed in good Gestalt
fashion by beginning at the most general level and differentiating, step-wise,
increasingly specific elements. In order to keep this step-wise process of
differentiation as a structural figure, I will introduce each successive level with

From: *Voices*, 32(4), 46-50 (1996).

the word "Therefore." I will quote liberally, giving citations when I can. (Many of the quotes are contained in my personal journal, which I have kept for several years as a source of inspiration, and not always are the complete citations available.)

To begin, I accept that I exist, I live, life is. Life came into being. Whatever force, power or spirit which was involved I can call God, Yahweh, Great Spirit, or as Wilhelm Reich (1948) did, "primal cosmic energy," or any number of names which have been suggested. The many names are but cultural inflections of the god archetype offered up at a particular time in a particular place. I will use the word "God." Now I can take as the beginning of my statement of my theology: *God created life.* This statement is a bald one. I do not mean, necessarily, a personal God, an entity or any sort of quasi-personified being. I mean simply that power or energy or principle by which life came to be and is. "Life is the self-creating energy creature we call God" (Williams, 1973, p. 148).

Therefore, to affirm life is to be in harmony with God. If life is from God of God, Godly, then to affirm life is in keeping with the Way of God Ergo, not to affirm life or to disaffirm life is to be out of harmony with God. Non-affirmation of life can be seen, then, in degrees. In milder forms it may be more passive, failure to affirm, while in more extreme forms, it is constituted of acts of disaffirmation.

Being in harmony with God may be called "being in God's grace," in the sense of being in God's favor. With God considered not as a personal God of judgment, but rather as a force, then this becomes clearer. If I live, for me to affirm life (that which I am) is in my favor, because it is consistent with God's creation.

Therefore, the ultimate worship of God is a life abundantly lived. What better way could there be to honor the source of life but to live fully? In his simple words and straightforward manner, Hemingway said that "life is short and the years run away and you must do everything you really want to" (Hotchner, 1983, p. 99), and, continuing on a more personal note, added that he never regretted anything he ever did, only things he didn't do (Hotchner, 1983).

But the life lived abundantly is a life of pain as well as joy. So, too, must pain be experienced and not run from as if it were an evil. James Bugenthal (1971) gave place to this idea in his statement of a "humanistic ethic" by making the valuing of non-hedonic emotion a tenet alongside the tenet of commitment to growth-oriented experiencing. So it is that Paul Williams (1973) stated that "The affirmation of one's life — the acceptance of one's destiny as it manifests itself in each moment — is the supreme act of faith" (p. 80). And, in a more exuberant tone, he continues with, "Open yourself to absolutely anything that gets thrown at you — including death, and life" (Williams, 1973, p. 119).

Theodore Roosevelt has been immortalized by these words: "Far better it is to dare mighty things, to win glorious triumphs, even though checkered by failure, than to take rank with those poor spirits who neither enjoy much nor suffer much, because they live in the gray twilight that knows not victory nor defeat." But lest this appear all too easy, Fritz Perls (1969) solemnly warned, "To suffer one's death and to be reborn is not easy" (back cover). To be reborn to a life lived abundantly requires a willingness to take reasonable risks, to experiment and try out, to allow a natural rhythm of expansion into the world and relaxation into self, and to be undaunted by frustrations. Misfortune must not be cause for shrinking from life. The challenge, as Fritz Perls (1969) suggests — "But to *realize* that it's just an inconvenience, that it's not a catastrophe, but just an unpleasantness, is part of coming into your own, part of waking up" (p. 33).

Therefore, the ultimate praise of God is to embrace life joyously. If living life fully is the ultimate act of worship, then, surely, to embrace life with alacrity is the ultimate of praise. Hugh Prather (1977) reminds us, "There is another way to go through life besides being pulled through it kicking and screaming" (no page number). And that way is, as Horace said, "*Carpe Diem.*" Centuries later, Goethe echoed Horace when he stated, "He who seizes the moment is the right man." Taking their lead, Claudio Naranjo (1970) wrote at some length about an archetype consisting of present-centeredness, the view that the present is a gift of pleasure, and the awareness of death and decay. Taken as an archetype, this triad can be a profound guide of life.

Naranjo (1970) has made explicit the implicit moral injunctions of the Gestalt approach: "Live now" (be concerned with the present rather than the past or future); "Live here." Taken together we have the phrase so commonly found in the Gestalt literature: Here-and-now. "*Hic et nunc.*" But, to continue with Naranjo's injunctions, "Stop imagining" (experience the real); "Stop unnecessary thinking"; "Express rather than manipulate, explain, justify or judge"; "Give in to unpleasantness and pain just as to pleasure"; "Accept no *should* or *ought* other than your own"; "Take full responsibility for your actions, feelings and thoughts"; "Surrender to being as you are."

Perhaps the last injunction is the most difficult of all. And, it is basic. The Sages of ancient Greece offered as one of their three guiding principles the succinct charge "Know thyself." At once, vital and difficult. This is well reflected in Blackham's rendering of Heidegger (1959): "A man is possibility, he has the power to be. His existence is in his choice of the possibilities which are open to him, and since his choice is never final, once for all, his existence is indeterminate . . ." (p.88). He continues by explicating ". . . two decisively opposed modes of being: authentic being rooted in the explicit sense of my situation . . . ; and inauthentic being, moving automatically in the established ruts and routes of the organized world" (pp. 92-93). Perhaps e.e. cummings has expressed the struggle to be oneself most poignantly: "To be nobody — but yourself — in a world which is doing its best, night and day, to make you everybody else means to fight the hardest battle which any human being can fight; and never stop fighting." Similarly, but stated with brevity, are Ortega y Gasset's words, "The will to be oneself is heroism."

Therefore, that which one does which diminishes one's own life (or that of others) constitutes sin. Anything which one chooses which detracts from aliveness misses the mark. Clearly, then, we are, as Sheldon Kopp (1974) suggested, punished not for our sins, but by them! In *The Marriage of Heaven and Hell*, Blake (Schoen, 1994) instructs us by saying on the one hand, "No bird soars too high, if he soars with his own wings" (p. 24). Not to do so, on the other hand, would be a pity, a sin. As Blake put it, "He who desires but acts not, breeds pestilence." With greater acerbity, and equally to the point he wrote, "Sooner murder an infant in its cradle than nurse unacted desires" (Schoen, 1994, p. 32). So, what of the "rules"? Saint Augustine, not a man unfamiliar with the lusty life, said, "Love God, and do what thou wilt!" Later, Martin Luther (using a different definition of the term from mine) declared, "Sin bravely" (Kopp, 1974, p. 48). Summarized by Sheldon Kopp (1974), we have the advice, "Never mind the rules! Forget conventional wisdom and morality if you would be healed, saved, made free!" (p. 48). Finally, in *Wandering in Eden*. Michael Adam (1976) suggests ". . . deadlines as the origin of all other 'sins'" (p. 3).

Therefore, one's spiritual practice is to recognize and eschew that which one does which is deadening. If deadening oneself is sin, then letting go of such is surely the highest of spiritual practices. By "practice" I mean consistent, disciplined, ongoing working on oneself. This means being self-vigilant, becoming aware of one's means of self-deadening, whatever those means may be, and actively changing from those patterns. Fritz Perls (1969) said simply, "Everything is grounded in *awareness. Awareness* is the only basis of knowledge . . ." (p. 48). And, as Barry Stevens (1984) expressed, "What is it but awareness and acting in accord with circumstances?" (p. 4). "Be aware, alert and sensing, living and moving in harmony . . ." (p. 73). Ram Dass (1974), then, reminds us, "So, you see that the only option is to work on yourself" (p. 41).

Most, if not all psychotherapies would embrace aliveness as a value. Some, however, are more explicit in acknowledging this and even make it a focus. We see this especially in the tradition of the body-oriented therapies which have their philosophical origins in Nietzsche. Thus, we see "aliveness" as a focus in the works of Wilhelm Reich, his student Fritz Perls and their colleagues and professional descendants, the neo-Reichians and Gestalt therapists. It was this focus which I wished to emphasize by my choice of *Sexual Aliveness: A Reichian Gestalt Perspective* for the title of my book on the psychology of human sexuality (Smith, 1987). And, it is this focus which is reflected in Barry Stevens' paradoxical declaration (1970) that for her "It is more important . . . to bring someone to life than to be moral" (p. 231).

A theology based on the value of life itself, a bio-existential theology, can be a grounding for psychotherapy. It is for me. (It has become a ground out of which my therapy and most of my writing come.) And it is in the development of aliveness of the therapist herself or himself, the enthusiastic embracing of life, that the therapist is best prepared for the role. This is made clear by Ram Dass (1974): "Work on yourself, see, because your 'patients' will be as free as you are. That's why I come back to the statement that therapy is as high as the therapist is" (p. 28). So, affirming life, living life abundantly, embracing life joyously, eschewing all that diminishes life is the way of harmony, worship, praise and spiritual practice. It a way to be inspired, possessed by God — *en theos*.

~

AT THE CUSP OF BEING AND BECOMING:
THE GROWING EDGE PHENOMENON

Be with this phrase, "the growing edge." Think about it. Feel about it. Intuit it. The growing edge is on the boundary between what is actual and what is potential, between that which is realized and that which is not yet real. It is the apical meristem of the organism expanding into the world. As with embryonic tissue, the growing edge is a zone of rapid change. Paradoxically, it is a region at once both robust and fragile. This is demonstrated when the tender new shoot cracks a sidewalk of concrete in its ascent to fullness.

I view personal growth as a multifarious activity, involving the physical, mental, social, emotional and spiritual facets of the person. On each of these planes one can grow, and only when the growth is balanced does one become full in development.

One of the standard definitions of growth is to increase in size by assimilation of new matter. In personal growth, one extends one's growing edge such that the self becomes larger. The growing edge encompasses more, so the self is expanded. More of the world becomes contained within the self boundary. The person becomes a container of more experience. The growing edge expands into the world in order to contain more of the world.

From: *The Gestalt Journal*, 21(2), 9-19 (1998).

The key to growth is this. *Growth takes place through here-and-now emergence under conditions of heightened awareness.* This means that growth is a lived experience, entered into and actively participated in, by the organism. If not organismically experienced, the event does not become a part of the person. So, the less awareness of the event, the less the experienced vividness, the less growth.

The urge for self-actualization, the making real and actual what is potential in the individual, motivates one towards growth. But, unmet needs lower on the need hierarchy can take priority over self-actualization (Maslow, 1968). Self-actualization, therefore, is not an ubiquitous driving force.

There is an important paradox to be understood in self-actualization. The paradox is that growth comes through accepting one's nature, not through the attempt to make oneself different.

This has been termed "the paradoxical theory of change." Stated thus, "change occurs when one becomes what he is, not when he tries to become what he is not" (Beisser, 1970, p. 77). The journey of growth must always begin with where one is. Natural urges can be trusted to lead from there.

Not understanding this paradox, one may create an image of what one "should" be. Pursuing such an artificial and false image is an act of placating the voice of a "should," not an act of actualization of the authentic self. I cannot be other than what it is my nature to be. To try to do so is to violate my integrity.

Allow me an example through metaphor. Picture a young antelope and a young elephant. If the antelope rejects its nature and aspires to develop the brute strength of the elephant, or if the elephant rejects its nature and decides to grow up to be as fast and as graceful as the antelope, jumping just as high, then both animals will live lives of abject frustration and, ultimately, defeat. And, as they strive to become as their false image, they will become increasingly alienated from their genuine nature. Neither beast is more noble than the other. Both have the potential for great beauty.

The differentiation which I am drawing is between self-actualization and "self-image actualization" (Perls, 1992). Self-actualization, understood as the unfolding of one's genuine self, is what I am assuming in my exploration of the growing edge phenomenon.

Now, with this contextual background in mind, let us explore the growing edge phenomenon. In any facet of growth — physical, mental, social, emotional, spiritual — we can think in terms of the next growth step, the step which would take the person beyond where he or she has been. The growing edge is at the limit to be extended. It is at the cusp of being and becoming.

There are several principles which characterize the growing edge phenomenon. I have come to discern these principles through my work on myself and my work with others — mainly in two contexts. The first is psychotherapy, where I have watched the growing edge of my clients and of myself as client. The second is the realm of lifting weights where, again, I have watched my own growing edge over many years of lifting and the growing edge of others as I have served as weightlifting instructor, weightlifting coach, and workout partner. Although the principles which characterize the growing edge phenomenon hold true in any realm, the physical facet offers perhaps the most concrete, if not the clearest example. *In Not Just Pumping Iron: On the Psychology of Lifting Weights* (Smith, 1989), I wrote of lifting weights as a microcosm through which the growing edge phenomenon can be explored. I share, here, some of that material.

Imagine a lifter whose maximum bench press is X pounds. His growing edge, with respect to his bench press is, then, the boundary between X pounds and X+ pounds. He will grow in his bench press as he gradually adds weight. I want to emphasize the gradual addition of weight in the lift. Growth in muscular strength is based on the "over-load principle," the principle that the body will overcompensate for a particular lifting stress by muscular growth. Rather than simply adapting to a particular stress, the body grows from the level of that muscular stress to the point of being able to handle that plus a little more. The over-load principle dictates that increases in strength develop incrementally. So, by bench pressing X pounds over a period of several training sessions, our lifter will extend his growing edge to X+Y pounds, where X was his previous best and Y is a small enough increment to allow success. (I will not complicate the example with considerations of nutrition, spacing of training sessions, or training routines.)

If our lifter does not push his growing edge by "overloading" his muscles, his bench press will not increase. In this case he would be working too far behind his growing edge. Some technical information is needed at this point for clarification. The research suggests that growth in strength is maximized by performing three sets of four to six repetitions with 80 to 90 percent of one's best lift. Veteran lifters also know the importance of lifting their maximum, or "maxing out" periodically. The implication here is that lifting with less than .8X will not lead to the extension of our lifter's growing edge in the bench press.

The next principle of the growing edge phenomenon is one which I first learned about in my own lifting, so I will use that as my example. Very early in my lifting career, I read a report in *Science Digest* on some research which supported the claim that maximum growth in strength in a lift would accrue from warming up and then doing one lift with one's current maximum weight every day. I experimented with this with my Olympic press, and indeed showed remarkable progress for one week. After seven days my steady progress halted. Applying this strategy to our lifter, it would be that he would warm up and then do a maximum bench press every day. He would bench press X or X+ pounds every workout. Although this may work for a short period of time to stimulate a growth spurt, or to get beyond a sticking point in one's growing edge, it does not work as a regular routine. Too much time spent at one's growing edge, without respite, results in an arrest in progress and a feeling of staleness. There is a stagnation.

Physiologically there is not sufficient time for tissues to grow in response to such frequent overload, and psychologically there is not enough recovery time to allow for such all out effort.

The growing edge is a boundary to be played with, with a rhythm of pushing it, then moving back to the 80 to 90 percent maximum range. If forced, by attempting too large an incremental step, there may be a backlash. The growing edge may actually recede, with previous gains being lost. If the lifter in our example tries to make too large of an increase in his poundage, he will fail at the lift, at least. At worst, he may sustain injury. So, if he attempts X+Y+ pounds, rather than the more prudent X+Y pounds, he may tear a pectoral muscle or injure a rotator cuff.

The growing edge does not progress constantly, but shows retrogressive movement as well. In other words, the growing edge evolves by two steps ahead and one back. That is to say, growth is not linear. If the lifter in our example were to make a graph of his bench press, with time on the abscissa and maximum lifts on the ordinate, the growth line would look like an inverted saw. Imagine a carpenter's hand saw turned cutting side up with the handle on your right. The over-all trend is upward, but within any short segment along the blade there are ups and downs. Thus, our lifter, on successive days of "maxing out," may bench press Xlb., X+5lb., X+10lb., X+5lb., X+10lb., X+15lb., X+10 .... The magnitude of increases and decreases will probably not be regular, but there will be a mix of progressions and regressions.

One more refinement of the "inverted saw" model of the growing edge is needed. Imagine that the saw has a curved blade, more like a saber than the carpenter's saw. Imagine that it is curved such that the curve is greatest near the tip of the blade (on your left, as you look at it) and decreases as the blade approaches the handle (on your right, as you look at it). What this model is reflecting is but a second way in which the progress of the growing edge is not linear. Not only does it include regressive movements, but it is, overall curvilinear. And, the line is decelerating in its degree of curve. In technical language we are dealing with a negatively accelerated curvilinear growth function. In practical terms, this means that growth is most rapid early in the process and gets slower as one has progressed farther. The growing edge is rapidly moving when one sets out on the path of growth, slowing as one progresses. Our lifter, for instance, may move from X pounds to X+50 pounds in his bench press during his first few months of training. By the time he has become a world-class bench presser, several years later, he may move from X pounds to X+5 pounds over several months training, and be ecstatic over his progress!

At times, there may be plateaus, periods during which no further growth accrues. These plateaus may be experienced as times of "being stuck." The movement following a plateau is often in response to a new approach, a new strategy, a new insight. With this fresh approach may come a growth spurt. It is these spurts following a plateau that are subjectively felt as moments of "turning a corner" or "making a major shift." These are the expansive leaps of growth. For our lifter it manifests as a twenty-pound increase in his bench press after a six-week plateau. The growth spurt may be ushered in by a week's respite from training followed by a new training routine.

I have used the example of the weight lifter because of the elegant clarity which the example affords. I believe, however, that the growing edge phenomenon is universal to growth, be it physical, mental, social, emotional, or spiritual. The characteristics which I have discussed have been demonstrated countless times in the physical and mental realms — the realms most amenable to scientific scrutiny. So, whether one quantifies the growth of physical strength, endurance, speed, flexibility or coordination, or mental tasks such as foreign language acquisition, the learning of mathematical theory and operations, or any such complex body of material, the growth curves emerge with common characteristic themes and explicable, if not predictable variations: Not quite so easy to measure and plot are growth in the social and emotional realms. But, by clever and judicious use of psychological tests, even this can sometimes be done. Often this requires subtle instruments of measurement which give indirect or inferred reflection of growth. In the realm of the spiritual, the task is greatest.

An interesting feature of life is that growth takes time. Only "pop psychologists" and "pop evangelists" promise instant attainment of lofty states. Instant awareness, instant salvation, instant cure, and instant enlightenment are the devil's own promise. Growth requires time. And growth requires involvement. Growth requires a lived, here-and-now experience embedded in awareness. Thus, growth comes, incrementally. The other side of this interesting feature of life is that tragedy, destruction, and defeat often rush upon us, not in increments, but with amazing and horrendous suddenness. That which has taken years to build or develop can be totally annihilated in an instant! Our lifter might build a strong body over years of training, but with one misguided attempt for a personal record, tear muscle, tendons, and ligaments, leaving his shoulder weaker than that of someone totally untrained. Injury, psychological trauma and death can manifest in a moment.

Preparation for the overt manifestation of growth is sometimes not acknowledged or given appropriate consideration. Sometimes the overt manifestation is so dramatic that the preparation for that moment is forgotten or discounted. This is particularly likely in the case of discontinuing a negative activity. For the person who has quit smoking, after years of being a smoker, there is that moment when the last cigarette was put down. Many ex-smokers can tell of that dramatic instant of throwing away a half pack of cigarettes and never picking up another. Behind that dramatic moment, however, are two other stories, less dramatic, but crucial. First is the story of the preparation for that moment. Second is the story of the ongoing, consistent choice of not picking up a cigarette. The moment of stopping smoking for good is a fragile thing, made valid only in retrospect, and only valid as long as the decision not to smoke is an actively continued choice. I cannot decide at this moment never to smoke again. Not really. I can only decide not to smoke now and to state my intention now to persist in this choice.

In his outlining of a humanistic ethic, Bugental (1971) suggested as one of his ethical points the commitment to growth-oriented experiencing. What this means is that if one lives the humanistic ethic he or she will seek out experiences which hold promise for growth. One will see opportunities for expanding oneself and take them. Sometimes the choice for growth seems frightening. It is at such a time that one must choose between doing what would likely further her or his growth or shying away out of fear. This has been identified by Maslow as the growth choice versus the fear choice.

The idea in making the growth choice is to recognize those experiences which are likely to further one's growth, and, even if afraid, to say "yes" to those experiences. To recognize such experiences is to know one's growing edge. If I know where my growing edge is, then I will recognize what for me is likely to be a growthful experience.

Part of the task of the psychotherapist, the teacher, the guru is to provide experience for the client, the student, the follower which is at the growing edge. I believe that one of the reasons that psychotherapy sometimes goes on for long periods of time without the client's changing is because what is happening in therapy is not at the client's growing edge. The experiences are pale, not the exciting, risky experiences which stretch one and let one know that he or she is working at the growing edge.

Homework in psychotherapy is one way of assisting a client to stay on her or his growing edge. The usual and customary psychotherapy format is one hour per week. That is one hour out of the 168 hours of the week, indeed a small ratio. And, even that hour is typically of only fifty minutes. Homework is a way to keep that fifty minute hour more alive during some of the other 167 hours. Look at an example from music. Consider the progress which a student would make by taking a one-hour piano lesson once a week — but never practicing. Compare that student to one who goes home and practices what was covered in that lesson every day for an hour. In an analogous way, the insights, the healing, the expansion which one obtains in the therapy hour can be consolidated, assimilated, and integrated by putting them into practice between sessions. A wise therapist can facilitate the client in recognizing just where the client's growing edge is, and in designing the "practice" to bring life to that growing edge during the therapy session to therapy session interim. Whatever the issue is with the client, some "practice" can be designed for working on that issue. Understanding the characteristics of the growing edge phenomenon serves as a cadre for the creation of homework "practice."

The "practice" may come from yoga or T'ai Chi, meditation or jogging, introducing oneself to three strangers or exploring solitude for a weekend in the mountains, saying "no" to one's mother or asking one's boss for a raise, fasting for twenty-four hours or eating everything one wants for a week, speaking every thought aloud or maintaining a twenty-four hour silence, going to a nudist camp or dressing in conservative business clothes, keeping a daily money log or tolerating the anxiety of not double checking to see if the door is locked, breathing three breaths before replying to one's husband or keeping a dream diary.... The list is endless. The key is that the "practice" be designed to address precisely one's growing edge.

With a commitment to growth-oriented experiencing, some choose a formal growth "path," such as psychotherapy, yoga, Zen, or an organized growth group. The variety of these is multitudinous. The key to the usefulness of any of these systems is the degree to which it addresses one's evolving growing edge.

For review and reference I have summarized the characteristics of the growing edge phenomenon. This can serve as a guide, a reminder of several principles important in the task of "working on one's self."

Figure 1

The Growing Edge Phenomenon

Principle 1: The growing edge is at the boundary between that which is actual and that which is potential.

Principle 2: Growth occurs by extending the edge by small increments into the realm of the potential and possible.

Principle 3: Working too far behind the growing edge results in a lack of growth.

Principle 4: Spending too much time working at the growing edge without respite results in stagnation (arrest of progress).

Principle 5: Forcing beyond the growing edge (attempting increments which are too large) results in a backlash (loss of previous growth).

Principle 6: Progress at the growing edge is non-linear (a curvilinear function containing retrogressions and plateaus).

Principle 7: Resumption of growth following a plateau usually reflects a fresh strategy or a new insight. This may appear as a sudden expansive leap in growth.

~

ENACTMENT AND AWARENESS

IN THE GESTALT APPROACH

In 1936, Karl Mannheim (Atwood & Stolorow, 1993) astutely recognized that there are two quite different perspectives or ways of understanding an ideology or an intellectual system. He differentiated the *extrinsic* from the *immanent*. Distinct, each holds advantage and disadvantage relative to the other. In the former, the extrinsic mode of understanding, the person observes from the outside, thereby maintaining a separation and a relatively detached objectivity. In contrast, the immanent mode requires a joining of that which is studied, assuming a subjective perspective from the inside. Mannheim's distinction is lent clarity when one extends it to the different styles of the quintessential social psychologist and anthropologist. The social psychologist has valued the "objectivity" of an outside observation and measurement, while the anthropologist, on the other hand, has "gone native," moved in with the people studied and experienced the culture from the inside. If this extension of Mannheim's distinction seems forced, it is to make a conceptual point. The point is that one can explore something by observing from the outside or by experiencing from the inside.

Mannheim's distinction of these two perspectives may be applied, I believe, not only to the molar level of ideologies and intellectual systems, as he suggested, but to the molecular level of the therapy dyad and even to the

From: *Voices*, 35(4), 74-77 (1999).

atomic level of the person in therapy herself or himself. Just as our social psychologist and our anthropologist use an extrinsic and an immanent approach, respectively, a therapy may be oriented toward one or the other approach. In the former, the therapist observes and analyzes, defining the therapy as a relatively objective study from without. In the latter, however, the therapist facilitates the aware expression of the person in therapy, defining the therapy as a subjective study from within. The person in therapy contributes to the dyad by remembering and reporting as accurately as possible in the former case. In the latter, he or she experiences from within and expresses, perhaps, psychodramatically. At the molecular level, then, the therapist and person in therapy cooperate in the creation of an event relatively more extrinsic or immanent, while at the atomic level, the person in therapy manifests herself or himself in a relatively more extrinsic or immanent manner.

The significant contribution of the expressive psychotherapies is their emphasis on this immanent mode. Among the expressive therapies, the Gestalt approach is exemplary in this emphasis.

I have been reading *Voices* since 1966. One article stands out for me as being extremely important because of its explication of the possibility for growth on the part of the person in therapy through the experience of aware enactment of her or his growth issue in the therapy session. The article to which I refer appeared in the Winter, 1968 issue of *Voices* (Volume 4, Number 4, pp. 66-73) and is titled "Acting Out vs. Acting Through: An Interview with Frederick Perls, M.D., Ph.D." This interview was conducted by one of our academy members, the late Cooper C. Clements, Ph.D.

Being an interview, the Perls/Clements article lacks the eloquence of polished prose. It does, however, have a quality of unrehearsed exuberance and unpredictable direction in its flow. These latter qualities may compensate for its literary weaknesses.

That the Perls/Clements article has been seen as of great value is attested to by the decision of John O. Stevens to reprint the interview in the book which he edited under the title *Gestalt is* [sic] (Stevens, 1975). My own valuing of the interview is in small part reflected in my choosing it for inclusion in *Gestalt Voices*, a book which I edited, drawing on Gestalt material from the first twenty-five years of *Voices* (Smith, 1992).

I would like, now, briefly to discuss the cogent points of this interview which have influenced me in my living and in my therapeutic work.

First, the ground of classical psychoanalysis is *analysis*. The purpose of psychoanalytic work is to analyze a person's life, making connections between childhood events and current feelings, experiences, and behaviors. With *analysis* comes *insight*. Thus, Freud wanted analysands to *remember*, not escape from the unpleasantness of painful memories or the hard work of analysis by "acting out" their issues. Perls' departure was to stress *becoming aware through here-and-now experience* rather than remembering. Thus, Perls developed methods for psychodramatic enactment for the purpose of facilitating awareness and completion of unfinished situations from one's past.

The unfinished situation from one's past remains unfinished because one is avoiding something and is unaware of the avoidance. This view is more functional than Freud's view of repetition compulsion.

Second, the view of the layers of the personality which Perls introduces provides a very useful map for finding one's way from an inauthenticity born of avoidance of anxiety to an expressed authenticity. (It should be noted that Perls revised the names of the layers of personality in his later writing, but he remained true to the gist of this model.)

Third, Perls clarifies the limits of therapist responsibility, calling attention to the danger of a distorted view of oneself as omnipotent, if this limit is exceeded. By doing so, he empowers persons in therapy with their own responsibility. He does, also, acknowledge the importance of the therapist's taking some precautions for the safety of the therapist and the person in therapy.

These three points which I have touched on briefly, when explored in depth, define an approach to psychotherapy which is radically focused on awareness as guide for and emergent from here-and-now experience. Enactment is guided by awareness and awareness emerges as the enactment unfolds moment by moment.

With the evolution of psychotherapy, and especially with the evolution of psychoanalysis, refinements of theory and methods have accrued. Underlying all of these developments, however, remains the distinction of emphasis — insight through interpretive analysis or awareness through enactment. This, I believe, is a fundamental difference in therapeutic approaches. All therapies can be understood better if viewed in terms of this distinction. (If taken in their broader meaning, and not restricted to their technical psychoanalytic meaning, insight, interpretation and analysis describe much of cognitive therapy as well as the myriad of psychodynamic therapies. The essence is that the therapist is an external translator, tracing things to their source and explaining to the person in therapy. Depending on the proclivities of the therapist, the problems of living reported by the person in therapy may be traced to [i.e., analyzed] childhood events or to irrational beliefs and negative cognitive schemas. Even if seen as not *sufficient* for successful therapy, such analysis and explanation is seen as *necessary* by psychodynamic and cognitive therapists alike.) This distinction, as I have tried to show, is a derivative, specific to psychotherapy, of Mannheim's extrinsic and immanent ways to understanding. And, this distinction is the major thrust of the Perls/Clements interview of 1968. It is the ground of the Gestalt approach.

Athough I seem to have a long standing tendency to try to integrate, and take an eclectic stance in psychotherapy, I keep coming back to the Gestalt approach, with its refined and exquisite attention to immediate lived experience, as my base. When I am at my best, this approach produces through me, and in me, a feeling of excitement, a vividness of perception, and a richness of being which is self-validating. I know by the event which I am co-producing with the person in therapy, and at the same time experiencing and witnessing, that something at once real and vitally important is happening. The intensity of this knowing, with the attending immediate self-validation, keeps me alive as a therapist.

In contrast, I soon become bored and tired when I work from the outside, assuming the extrinsic position. Even sooner, I become bored when the person in therapy assumes such extrinsic orientation to the endeavor in which we are mutually engaged.

This, then, is how I was influenced by the article which I have discussed. It called my attention to a possibility of experience. It articulated a "way" of therapy, giving it cognitive expression and, in a sense, legitimacy. Having experienced and adopted the "way," I have found this article to be a reminder, at times, a much needed reminder. When drawn to experiment with something more extrinsic, I have re-oriented by drawing forth this article from the back of my mind, along with memories which exemplify its message. So, to Fritz and Cooper, thank you. You pointed the "way" for me. I am still following it.

~

Toward the Meaning
of "The Person of the Therapist"

SUMMARY. Too often, in discussions of psychotherapy, the techniques are given undue emphasis. Research suggests that the same techniques are differentially effective when used by equally trained and supervised therapists. Not only are some therapists more effective, irrespective of the type of therapy they practice, but some, because of their personal qualities, may actually harm those with whom they work. This research reflects the vast importance of the ubiquitous element in therapy, that of the "person" of the therapist. The question, then, follows, how may personhood be developed? This question is explored as it relates to both breadth and depth of life experience.

Intrigued by a certain mystique which attended it, I was drawn to membership in the American Academy of Psychotherapists in the early 1970s. That mystique was, for me, summarized and at the same time enhanced by the credo which I heard: "The Academy is dedicated to the continued development of the person of the therapist." This concept fascinated me and my fascination was increased by the odd phrasing, "the person of the therapist." This phrase begs expatiation, so to that end I offer what follows.

One has only to read the psychotherapy research reported and summarized during the decade of the nineties to conclude that psychotherapy is,

From: *Journal of Couples Therapy*, 9(3/4), 43-49 (2000).

in general, effective. (For quick and easy reference, see the Lambert and Bergin [1994] chapter on "The Effectiveness of Psychotherapy.") But too often, perhaps, we tend to overemphasize the techniques, the procedures, the methods. In fact, it is by its techniques, oftentimes, that a therapeutic system is most readily identified. This is a simplification which loses the richness of understanding afforded only when the philosophical underpinnings and the whole body of theory — developmental theory, theory of natural personality functioning, theory of psychopathology, theory of psychotherapy — are considered.

But beyond the philosophy, the theory, and the body of techniques, there is something more, something of a different plane. Techniques, as well as philosophies and theories, are abstractions. As abstractions, techniques are made concrete only through the work of the therapist. That is, technique is given life through the person of the therapist. The technique only becomes a lived event as it is brought to life through the therapist's personal expression.

In the words of Lambert and Bergin (1994, p. 167), "The complexity and subtlety of psychotherapeutic processes cannot be reduced to a set of disembodied techniques because techniques gain their meaning and, in turn, their effectiveness from the particular interaction of the individuals involved." With their characteristic attention to research evidence, they report that "... despite careful selection, training, monitoring, and supervision, therapists offering the same treatments can have highly divergent results" (Lambert & Bergin, 1994, p. 174). The conclusion to be drawn, then, is that the same techniques have differential effectiveness through the personal expression of equally trained and supervised therapists! Lambert and Bergin (1994, p. 182) go on to state that "the therapist factor, as a contributor to outcome, is looming large in the assessment of outcomes." Furthermore, based on compelling evidence, a portion of those whom therapy "... is intended to help are actually harmed by ... negative therapist characteristics," among other factors (Lambert & Bergin, 1994, p. 182).

Perhaps it would be good to emphasize, here, that "That individual therapist can play a surprisingly large role in treatment outcome even when treatment is being offered within the stipulations of manual-guided therapy" (Lambert & Bergin, 1994, p. 181). So, even when therapy is done "by the book," as verified through training, supervision, and monitoring, different therapists evidence different levels of effectiveness.

The intriguing conclusion which Lambert and Bergin (1994, p. 181) draw from their review of the relevant research is "... that training programs should emphasize the *development of the therapist as a person* in parity with the acquisition of therapeutic techniques" (italics mine).

It may be interesting to consider the placement of different psychotherapies on a continuum of relationship and techniquefulness. At one pole would be found the approach developed by the early Atlanta Psychiatric Clinic (Felder, Malone, Warkentin, Whitaker), Helmuth Kaiser, and some of the experiential therapies. The antipole would represent behavior therapy. In its extremity, the former pole could be summarized by the belief that "relationship is everything." The antipole, then, could be summarized as "technique is everything."

These antipodes are perhaps a bit forced, but do call attention to the fact that therapists of various theoretical persuasions disagree as to the relative importance of personhoods interacting or technical manipulations. One would have us believe that it is relationship, the other that it is technique alone which carries the day. With respect to personhood, obviously those at the pole of relationship would embrace the belief in its importance. Those at the antipode may need reminder of the research evidence concerning the importance of personal qualities in therapy outcome. Most therapies fall somewhere between the antipodes and reveal the fact that no matter what the therapy, there cannot be disembodied technique in the consulting room, nor can there be a therapist present who does not fill the time and space with her or his presence.

And, now, for the crux of the matter. What is "the person of the therapist?"

Irma Lee Shepard (1992) has expressed doubt that psychotherapy can be taught, just as being an artist cannot be taught. It is personal resources which are crucial and must be developed in order or a therapist to transcend artificially applied techniques. (Shepard, 1992, p. 239) calls forth the "power and authenticity of the person" as that which is needed for one to *be* a therapist and not just *do* therapy.

Growth in personhood accrues, I believe, through experience under conditions of heightened awareness. But to appreciate this, we must first understand both the meaning of the term "experience" and the term "heightened awareness."

"Experience" derives from the Latin *experiri*, meaning "to try, to test." Through its Latin root, "experience" is etymologically related to the word "experiment." By "experience," then, is meant trying things out, testing things, finding out about the world and about oneself in the world. As one experiments more with the world, with life, one gains in knowledge and in understanding. As knowledge and understanding accrue, one can account for more and more of that to which one is exposed. Such knowing of things and about things and understanding of the relationships among things accumulates with continued trying and testing. But such accumulation is not limited to the realm of thought or idea. It involves the realm of feeling or emotional learning and the realm of action. Aristotle acknowledged these three as the realms of human experience — cognition, affect, conation.

Considering experience, then, as cognitive, affective and conative we begin to appreciate the meaning of breadth of experience. To have broad experience implicates all of the realms of experience and also implies a wide range of exposure to life and the world. Such a view was captured by Michael Adam (1976, p. 18) when he stated that Hindus believed that ". . . a man should grow to maturity by way of experiences that left no dark corners in him, no 'unlived lives." Wide exposure is implicated.

Yet, exposure to some things seems richer than exposure to certain other things. In his explication of a humanistic ethic, James Bugenthal (1971) listed as one of its points a commitment to growth-oriented experiencing. Here is evidence of a recognition that some types of experiencing are richer in the sense that they hold higher potential for growth. Perhaps only the individual, himself or herself, so involved can judge the richness of growth from a particular experience. Perhaps, too, that judgement can only be meaningfully made through a time perspective allowed only well after the experience.

Breadth of exposure to life and even exposure to events high in growth potential is impactful only if one is open to such. Lack of personal openness limits the effects. For exposure to be real experience, there must be an openness to taking it in, and without that there can be no personal growth or transformation. Such openness implies presence, or to use the Buddhist term, mindfulness. Being mindful, being aware, is an opening to the world and events to which one is exposed.

Awareness can be diminished by the several organismic choices we refer to variously as defense mechanisms of the ego in the psychodynamic theories or contact boundary disturbances in Gestalt therapy theory. By means of these we may limit our openness to experience, shutting out and distorting that which our egos deem too threatening. Thus we may dull our awareness by deflecting that which seems too intense to receive more directly or by desensitizing our perceptive systems. And, too, we may confuse our awareness through introjections, projections, and confluence when the responsibility of our being a genuine and authentic person feels too great an existential risk. The list of such awareness clouding maneuvers is long and the dynamics of these maneuvers varied enough to invite considerable study. Used individually or in synergistic combinations, their efficiency in denying and distorting reality bespeaks their effectiveness in creating mindlessness or clouded awareness and, in turn, a diminished impact from one's exposure to the world.

It should be clear, then, that breadth of experience has meaning for growth in personhood only insofar as that experience is not denied depth. If kept superficial through the insulating effect of clouded awareness, experience is superficial and of little impact on the person. Awareness, then, is the nexus between breadth of experience and depth of experience. Or, to be more precise, one could say that it is a certain critical level of awareness that allows mere exposure to become growthful experience.

Often, as in the case of a job application or interview, experience is evaluated only in terms of the number of times interviewees have been exposed to some situation or the length of time spent exposed to the situation. Questions such as "How many times have you done that?" or "How many years of experience do you have doing that?" are inadequate to the extent that they fail to take into consideration the depth of the experience.

But, just as some attend primarily or exclusively to the dimension of breadth in considering experience, others may attend to depth to a more or less exclusion of breadth. Take, for example the view expressed by Kafka (quoted in Schoen, 1994, p. 82).

> You do not need to leave the room. Remain sitting at your table and listen. Do not even listen, simply wait. Do not even wait, be quite still and solitary. The world will freely offer itself to you to be unmasked, it has no choice, it will roll in ecstasy at your feet.

Clearly, awareness is a necessary condition for meaningful and growthful experience. Without awareness there is only exposure. So important is awareness that in Kafka's view, richness can emerge even from exposure to the simple and prosaic. He came close to implying that awareness is all that is necessary, that awareness is both necessary and sufficient for deep experience.

If great depth of experience can follow from awareness of relatively ordinary exposure, consider, then, what can emerge when such mindfulness is brought to bear on a rich sampling of the world and life events. Together, such breadth and depth result surely in a life abundantly lived. And such a life surely results in enhanced personhood.

Living life abundantly requires a certain courage and boldness. Not only does it mean to eschew the use of the awareness clouding defense mechanisms, but it means to try out life, to experiment. It means to take reasonable risks and allow for the expansiveness which is part of the natural rhythm of contact with the world and withdrawal into self (Smith, 1985).

Richness and fullness of personhood is, then, a reflection of breadth and depth of experience. This personhood represents a certain consciousness, and as Ram Dass (1973, p. 28) has suggested, ". . . therapy is as high as the therapist is." If, as he suggested, one's patients will only be as free as one is himself or herself, then one would do well to work on oneself. To quote Ram Dass (1973, p. 6) once more, ". . . the only thing you have to offer another human being, ever, is your own state of being . . . you are only doing your own being, you're only manifesting how evolved a consciousness you are . . . That's the only dance there is!"

And that is the dance of *the person of the therapist.*

~

Shamanism, Psychoanalysis, and Gestalt Therapy: An Integrative Paradigm

"If a therapist doesn't dive down to meet the Wild Man or Wild Woman, he or she will try to heal with words."
— Robert Bly in *Iron John* (1990)

I am delighted to have the opportunity to share something of my current psychotherapy practice with my friends and colleagues in GPA. What I want to share is an eclectic paradigm which I have been using for several years for facilitating growth and healing. This paradigm represents a theoretical integration, bringing together theory from shamanism, psychoanalysis, and Gestalt therapy, and technical procedures from both shamanism and Gestalt therapy.

In *Guru*, Sheldon Kopp (1971) makes a compelling case that in all cultures at all times there has been a special role taken on by designated persons to whom others turn for guidance and healing. "The earliest spiritual guide, the Shaman, is the central helper-healer in the hunting and gathering societies" (p. 25). Mircea Eliade (1951/1964), in his erudite work addresses the methods used by shamans. "The preeminently shamanic technique is the passage from one cosmic region to another . . . the universe in general is conceived as having three levels — sky, earth, underworld — connected by a

From: *Georgia Psychologist*, 55(1), 26-27 (2001).

central axis" (p. 259). This passage is most often accomplished by "riding" a drum. Carried into a state of ecstasy by the shamanic drum beat, the shaman "journeys" to the other levels to commune with the spirits of those worlds, returning with guidance for the tribe. (The "shamanic beat" seems constant across shamanic societies, whether drummed, which is most usual, or beat out with sticks or stones or emitted by a rattle.) "What for the rest of the community remains a cosmological ideogram, for the shamans . . . becomes a mystical itinerary" (p. 265).

The archetype of the three-level universe, the empyrean trilogy, finds representation in many cultures, but with specific cultural inflections. In contemporary times, in the culture of psychotherapy, Sigmund Freud (1923/1962) offered a well known example when he explicated his structural model of the psyche. In his structural model, the id represents the under-world, the ego the middle world where we live our conscious lives, and the superego represents the upper-world. The core activity of Freud's "depth" psychology is to explore the lower region (and less often the upper region) in order better to understand existence on the conscious plane of the ego and to reconcile the intra-psychic conflicts. It is these conflicts among the three "worlds" which constitute "psychodynamics." To paraphrase Freud, where Id was, then there shall Ego be.

Rollo May (1991, p. 9) has suggested that "The fact that Western society has all but lost its myths was the main reason for the birth and development of psychoanalysis in the first place." I suggest that we can understand psychoanalysis, not as a societal atavism, but as a contemporary inflection of an archetypal theme.

Each particular mythology contains a sacred technology which instructs its followers in how to enter an altered state of consciousness. For a shamanic culture, the instruction is in how to "journey." This is in addition to the story itself, written mytho-poetically (i.e., in the metaphors of parable, allegory, and kenning). One purpose of this mythopoesis is to provide a conceptual container for the experience of altered consciousness, rendering it more understandable and less likely overwhelming. In the context of shamanism, the story is the myth itself, the sacred technology focuses on drumming (or its variations as noted above). In the context of classical psychoanalysis, the "myth" is psychoanalytic theory, the "sacred technology" focuses on free-association applied to dream images, the dream itself being recognized as the royal road to the unconscious. In both the case of shamanism and of psycho-analysis, there are, of course, other techniques as well, and in both cases interpretation of the generated material plays a significant role. But in purest form, we must recognize drumming and free association as the respective technologies.

I have found that shamanic drumming usually elicits dream-like images in those persons for whom I drum, be they psychotherapists, non-therapist clients, or students. Although visual images are most common, the drumming often evokes auditory, kinesthetic and other proprioceptive, images as well. The procedure can be done one-on-one or in a group, with all of the group members journeying, each on his or her unique journey.

If there is a focal issue that the person wants to explore, I help the person to formulate the issue, perhaps in the form of a question. Sometimes we proceed without a consciously articulated issue. With the person lying in a comfortable position, I give instructions such as the following. (Depending on the purpose of the journey and the person involved, I may invite the person to assume one of the "sacred postures" which have been used by traditional shamans. Discussion of these postures can be found in the work of Felicitas Goodman [1990].) "Take a few slow, deep breaths and relax. In a few moments I will begin to drum. Listen to the drum, and allow whatever wants to happen to happen." I then drum for ten to fifteen minutes. "Review what has come to you during the drumming. Note what you may have seen, heard, or felt."

Understood from a shamanic perspective, the person has journeyed to another world, seeing, hearing, or feeling messages from the spirits of that world. If a question had been posed, then the message of the spirits was in response to that question. Placed in a psychoanalytic framework, the person's experience can be understood as an accessing of unconscious material, relevant to the question if such was posed.

Dream-like, but not a dream, the material holds potential for guidance and for personal growth. In exploring this potential meaning, I prefer to proceed not with interpretation, but with experiential exploration of the imagery. My way of doing this is to facilitate the creation of a here-and-now experience through a psychodramatic acting out of the journey. In the Gestalt style, I invite the person to re-experience the journey by assuming the role of each element which emerged in the imagery, acting out that element with concrete body positions, movements, sound, and dialogue. The element could be the person himself or herself, another person either real or fictitious, an animal, either real or mythic, a body sensation, an emotion, whatever appeared in the journey. (Sometimes, due to time or energy constraints we do not explore every element.) This procedure is born of my belief that growth takes place through lived experience, under conditions of heightened awareness.

The forté of Gestalt work is the creation of here-and-now experience with full presence. It's techniques all focus on either bringing memories (past) or anticipatory fantasies (future) into the here-and-now ("presentification"), or on enhancing the vividness of experience ("concentration"). It is the care with which this detailed focus on the *process* of experience is carried out that distinguishes the Gestalt approach.

I have found that this work almost always yields growth and understanding. The issue presented, the questioned posed is often clarified, a direction is often suggested. One of the most interesting, and not uncommon course of events, is that the person reports upon completing the journey that nothing happened. My experience has taught me not to take this response at face value. When I ask what *did* happen, sometimes suggesting that "nothing" can not happen, the person goes on to report having heard a voice or having had a strong emotion or a vivid body sensation. What the person dismissed merely as not what was "supposed" to happen, quite typically upon further Gestalt guided exploration yields unexpected or even shocking richness.

Often, too, the images with their emergent meaning take the person into a transpersonal realm. The experience may be recognized as going beyond personal meaning and reflecting something more universal. For the essence of ecstasy, when it occurs, is to become "un-stable" (from the Latin "ecstasis," "a being put out of place") with respect to the ordinary and personal. If the person feels such a pull from his or her journey and our psychodramatic work with it's images, I may suggest a search for the image or the theme of the journey in world mythology. What has been encountered may then be made more understandable by an envelope of mythopoesis, drawn from the "mundus archetypus."

A caveat is in order. Given that shamanic drumming is a powerful invitation to make contact with other worlds, or shall I say a powerful invitation for unconscious material to be come forth into consciousness, the procedure should not be taken lightly. As with psychotherapy in general, supervised practice is essential for learning the responsible application of this paradigm.

~

Awe and Terror in the Living of the Resolution of the Polarity of Insight and Expression

SUMMARY. Insight and Expression, two polar emphases in psychotherapy, are approached as inflections of the competing Apollonian and Dionysian world views. Having explored this in depth, a case is made that an embodied Gestalt approach to therapy, while decidedly Dionysian in emphasis, provides a resolution of the polarity of Insight and Expression. The resolution is through an experienced Gestalt which is constituted of Awareness *and* Expression. The Dionysian emphasis, however, brings with it potential awe and terror.

> Passion without precision — chaos.
> — Jack Nicholson
> ("The Witches of Eastwick")

> He who desires but acts not, breeds pestilence.
> — William Blake
> ("The Marriage of Heaven and Hell")

Not operating under the constraints of a psychotherapy patois, Jack Nicholson, with that inimitable look in his eyes, summarized the relationship

---

From: *The Psychotherapy Patient*, 11(3/4), 99-121 (2001).

between passion and precision. His proclamation can be taken as a tocsin, a warning of what may happen when passion is not guided precisely, when action fueled by passion is not given benefit of insightful guidance. The result is chaos, a word meaning, in both its Greek and Latin origins, confusion and the formlessness preceding order. In his role as the Devil in "The Witches of Eastwick," Nicholson has no dearth of passion. Filled with passion, emotion, eros, he is ripe for action, ever ready for spontaneous expression. So, coming from this side, he is well advised to call for precision, to invoke the logos.

Another Devil, C. S. Lewis' Screwtape, writing to his devil nephew on how to prevent human salvation, advised "Keep everything hazy in his mind now, and you will have all eternity wherein to amuse yourself by producing in him the peculiar kind of clarity which Hell affords" (Lewis, C. S., 1996, p. 23). So here we have another warning of the fate that can result from lack of insight, that clarity of mind, which is required for precision of action.

William Blake is coming from the other side. His cause is that of passion and the encouragement of action. If I read Blake correctly, he meant pestilence not just as harmful or dangerous, but in its most severe meaning of virulent or fatal. Thus comes his serious warning about passion not expressed.

Kierkegaard, too, applauds the side of passionate action. He saw all about him people professing beliefs which they did not embody and live out. With sardonic tone he wrote in his diary, "Stuff and nonsense and balderdash instead of action, that is what people want," and further, "The secret of life, if one wants to get on well, is: plenty of chit-chat about what one intends to do and how one is kept from doing it — and no action" (Kierkegaard, 1993, p. 108). Kierkegaard emphasizes the doing, the existential choice to live out into the world. "What a person can understand he must also be able to force himself to *will*. Between understanding and willing is where excuses and evasions have their being" (Kierkegaard, 1993, p. 126). Knowing, believing, understanding, those things which are the ground for precision in guiding action, are of little value if not acted upon. For, "If a person does not become what he understands, he does not really understand it" (Kierkegaard, 1993, p. 126). ". . . the Highest, after all, is not to *comprehend* the Highest, but to do it" (Kierkegaard, 1993, p. 146). In all of his discussion of "willing to action," there is the implication of underlying passion. Kierkegaard posits "the leap," as opposed to a process of slow personal evolution, as the momentum that may explain the motion of our existence. And, "the leap" assumes passion (Kierkegaard, 1993, p. 226).

In the following century, we find Paul Tillich echoing Kierkegaard in his discussion of the "existential attitude." For Tillich, "The existential attitude is one of involvement in contrast to a merely theoretical or detached attitude. 'Existentialism' in this sense can be defined as participating in a situation ... with the whole of one's existence" (Tillich, 1962, p. 652). And participation, of course, implies and includes passionate action.

In the context set by Blake, Kierkegaard, and Tillich, in which living out one's passion is highly valued, thinking, knowing, understanding — *insight* — is of little value when detached from action. In fact, such "ratiocination" may be an avoidance of action and even of feeling. Screwtape, again, instructs us, saying "The more often he feels without acting, the less he will be able ever to act, and, in the long run, the less he will be able to feel" (Lewis, 1996, p. 57). Put most tersely, in this context "Thinking is a symptom" (Prather, 1972, no page number).

Apollonian and Dionysian World Views

These two emphases, one on the control and insightful guidance of passion and desire and the other on the expression of passion itself, can be related to two alternative visions which appear across cultures. These competing world views have been labeled in various ways, but their elements are consistent. The first has been related to Apollo, Greek god of light, moderation, reason, truth, order, balance and boundaries. The second vision has been related to the Greek god of excess, fantasy and metamorphosis, Dionysus the god of wine.

Dionysus seems the more complex figure, and the symbolism of this god more mysterious. Even his origin offers complex and intriguing symbolism. Zeus was so madly in love with the Theban princess Semele that he promised he would do anything she asked of him, swearing by the river Styx, an oath unbreakable even for the supreme god. Semele said she wanted above all to see Zeus in his full splendor as King of Heaven and Lord of the Thunderbolt. Knowing that no mortal could behold him as such and survive, but being bound by his oath, he appeared to Semele as she had asked. She perished in the glory of burning light. As she died, Zeus snatched from her their unborn child. He hid the child in his side until time for it to be born so that Hera, wife and sister to him, would not know. For it was she, who, in her jealousy, had put the fatal wish into the heart of Semele. When Dionysus was born, Zeus entrusted his care to the nymphs of the loveliest of the earth's valleys, a valley never seen by a mortal. These nymphs are believed by some to be the stars which bring rain when near the horizon, the Hyades. "So the God of the Vine was born of fire and nursed by rain, the hard burning heat that ripens the grapes and the water that keeps the plant alive" (Hamilton, 1942, p. 55).

Dionysus, as the only god not born of two divine parents, presents even in his origin a promise of mystery, perhaps even danger. Just as he sprang from two sides, one divine and one mortal, he himself shows two sides. As God of wine, fantasy, and metamorphosis, he inspires toward freeing the soul to dream, imagine, and to transform. Think of his vines, themselves. In winter they are black and withered and appear dead, but in spring they send forth their green shoots, coming into a full verdant splendor with the summer, and with summer and autumn are heavy with grapes. The metamorphosis is striking and the symbolism powerful. In addition, the grape to grape juice to wine transformation offers an equally striking and powerful symbolization of metamorphosis.

The other side of Dionysus is shown in his being the god of wine and excess. Just as wine used in moderation can lift and inspire, used immoderately it can lead to behavior of terrible excess. In one story, Dionysus, who was on a ship, took the form of an angry lion, causing the sailors to jump overboard (and to be transformed into dolphins). In another, he drove a group of women mad, causing them to attack and dismember the child of one of them (Hamilton, 1942). (This is still a problem today, as alcohol abusing parents may terrorize their children, sometimes resulting in the children's "jumping ship.")

The gods of Olympus tended to love order and beauty in their worship and in their temples, following the way of Apollo. But the followers of Dionysus had no temples, preferring to "worship under the open sky and the ecstasy of joy it brought in the wild beauty of the world" (Hamilton, 1942, p. 57). "Frenzied with wine . . . they rushed through woods and mountains uttering sharp cries . . ., swept away in a fierce ecstasy" (Hamilton, 1942, p. 56).

While Apollo remained for the Romans what he had been for the Greeks, Dionysus became the Roman god Bacchus and the side of excess became emphasized (Partridge, 1960). Sheldon Kopp (1971, p. 74) summarized the transition in this way. "Later, when this cult of the Mad God appeared in Rome, it became debased into celebration of orgies of debauchery, rather than simple revelry. . . . Bacchanalia . . . " In the words of Milton (Sabin, 1940, p. 38), "Bacchus, that first from out the purple grape, crushed the sweet poison of misused wine." There is even a theory that the word "tragedy" may have its origin in "the goat-song" which was used in the worship of Bacchus. Only later, this theory purports, did the word become associated with drama (Sabin, 1940, p. 39).

The complexity of the two sided nature of Dionysus is subtly, yet powerfully revealed, again, in the mythopoesis. We are told (Hamilton,

1942) that Dionysus did not forget about his mother, though he never knew her, and longed for her. Therefore, he dared the perilous journey to the netherworld in order to find her. Defying the power of Death to keep her, he won, and took her to Olympus. As mother of a god, although a mortal, herself, she was allowed to dwell among the immortals.

I offer this interpretation: Dionysian ecstasy does not necessarily require the abandonment or forgetting of our human origins (or nature), even while inspiring us to great daring and noble deed. And though mortal, we can be delivered to lofty heights. Our relationship with divine ecstasy can deliver us to a realm of divine-like existence, that is, the dwelling with the divine. Another interpretation is that it is a perilous and daring task for the male to seek out the feminine (which is part of him) from his depths. But, succeeding in this task, his feminine part becomes exalted, as if divine.

Put in terms most mundane, "Wine is bad as well as good. It cheers and warms men's hearts; it also makes them drunk" (Hamilton, 1942, p. 60). "The worship of Dionysus was centered in these two ideas so far apart — of freedom and ecstatic joy and of savage brutality. The God of Wine could give either to his worshipers" (Hamilton, 1942, p. 57). Consider this, as well. Liber, an ancient Italian deity of the vine, worshipped as a fertility god, came to be identified with Dionysus and his Roman counterpart, Bacchus (Funk and Wagnalls, 1984). It is from his name, Liber, that we derive such words as "liberty," "liberation," "liberal," and "libertine." So, again, we see freedom, being set free, not restricted, and licentiousness (indulging desires without restraint) as stemming from the same source.

Although we do not know a lot about the Greek mystery religions, the Eleusinian, the Orphic, the Dionysian, because they did remain mysteries (Campbell, 1990), we do have the mythic material concerning Dionysus. And, importantly, we have the expression of these two competing world views often referred to and so beautifully symbolized by Apollo and Dionysus.

Moving from the mythopoetic to the philosophical, Nietzsche placed himself clearly and strongly on the side of the Dionysian. In *Twilight of the Idols*, he declares himself boldly, "I, the last disciple of the philosopher Dionysus — I, the teacher of the eternal recurrence" (Kaufmann, 1982, p. 563). Nietzsche saw in the Dionysian the very core of the Greek veneration of life. "For it is only in the Dionysian mysteries, in the psychology of the Dionysian state, that the *basic fact* of the Hellenic instinct finds expression — its 'will to life.' ... Saying Yes to life even in its strangest and hardest problems, the will to life rejoicing over its own inexhaustibility even in the very sacrifice of its highest types — *that* is what I call Dionysian" (Kaufmann, 1982, pp. 561-

562). Somewhat earlier, in speaking of the Hellenic instinct, Nietzsche refers to "that wonderful phenomenon which bears the name of Dionysus," and goes on to say that "it is explicable only in terms of an *excess* of force" (Kaufmann, 1982, p. 560).

Thus Spoke Zarathustra, Nietzsche's most popular book, is replete with examples of what Kaufmann terms "Dionysian exhuberance" (Kaufmann, 1982, p. 107). (In fact a strong case could be made that this work is an account of a Dionysian epiphany.) As an example of his regard for passion, Zarathustra speaks the following: "And whether you came from the tribe of the choleric or of the voluptuous or of the fanatic or of the vengeful, in the end all your passions become virtues and all your devils, angels" (Kaufmann, 1982, p. 148).

Joseph Campbell (1990, p. 198) offers a noteworthy summary of the meaning of the Dionysian. "The best discussion, in my opinion, of Dionysos [*sic*] and Apollo is in Nietzsche's *The Birth of Tragedy*, where they are shown in relation to the whole world of the classic arts. Nietzsche writes of Dionysos [*sic*] as the dynamic of time that rolls through all things, destroying old forms and bringing forth new with, what he terms is, an 'indifference to the differences.' In contrast to this is the light world of Apollo and its interest in the exquisite differences of forms, which Nietzsche calls the *principium individuationis*. The power of Dionysos [*sic*] is to ride on the full fury of the life force. That's what he represents. So, the essential message of the rites, apparently, is that of a realization in a properly prepared way of the dynamic of inexhaustible nature which pours its energy into the field of time and with which we are to be in harmony, both in its destructive and in its productive aspects. This is experience of the life power in its full career."

Nietzsche, himself, in his discourse "Toward a psychology of the artist" in *Twilight of the Idols* (Kaufmann, 1982) gives us an especially valuable perspective. "If there is to be art, if there is to be any aesthetic doing and seeing, one physiological condition is indispensable: frenzy. ... In this state one enriches everything out of one's own fullness. ... A man in this state transforms things until they mirror his power — until they are reflections of his perfection. This *having to* transform into perfection is — art" (p. 518). (In reading these pieces which I have strung together, and in the following ones, consider psychotherapy as one of the arts, with the therapist and the person in therapy as co-creators. Add the "art of psychotherapy" to the arts which Nietzsche explicitly addresses — painting, sculpture, poetry, music, acting, dancing.) Nietzsche proceeds to distinguish the Apollonian and Dionysian forces in art. "What is the meaning of the conceptual opposites which I have introduced into aesthetics, *Apollinian* [*sic*] and *Dionysian*, both conceived as kinds of frenzy? The Apollinian [*sic*] frenzy excites the eye above all, so that it gains the power of vision. . . . In the Dionysian state, on the other hand, the whole affective system is excited and enhanced: so that it discharges all its means of expression at once and drives forth simultaneously the power of representation, imitation, transfiguration, transformation, and every kind of mimicking and acting. The essential feature here remains the ease of metamorphosis. . . . It is impossible for the Dionysian type not to understand any suggestion; he does not overlook any sign of an affect; he possesses the instinct of understanding and guessing in the highest degree, just as he commands the art of communication in the highest degree" (pp. 519-520).

Before departing Nietzsche (and keeping the art of psychotherapy still in mind), I want to call attention to one more of his insights. To wit, ". . . all becoming and growing — all that guarantees a future — involves pain" (Kaufmann, 1982, p. 562). Let us not lose sight of this point in its brevity. *Nota bene: all becoming and growing involves pain.*

In her discussion of the Apollonian and Dionysian, within the context of psychotherapy, Karen Horney (Shostrom, 1967) identified the former with mastery and molding, the latter with surrender and drift. To her way of thinking, neither is better or worse, per se. They are two natural human tendencies. No one is completely one or the other, but rather we all lean more toward one or the other, sometimes preferring one, sometimes the other at different times. When manifesting the Apollonian leaning, the person will emphasize being in charge and in control, making things happen as he or she wants, trying to change the environment to suit his or her will. In contrast, the Dionysian leaning becomes manifest in an acceptance and surrender to what is and a "willingness" to be taken away, carried away, to flow with the river that is life. That river may be halcyon or it may be tempestuous, but most often arousing of passion.

At this point we can segue into the thinking of Carl Jung (1970) by mention of his discussion of the principles of "logos" and "eros." The "logos" principle is one of objective interest, putting aside emotional and personal subjective considerations. "Logos," being found both in Greek and Latin, meant the word by which the inward thought is expressed, or the thought itself. It refers to the doctrine of reason or thought as the controlling principle of the universe. Hence, "logic" and "logistic." "Eros," in contrast, comes from the name of the Greek god of love, Cupid for the Romans. Hence, "erotic," pertaining to or prompted by sexual desires, and "cupidity." Therefore the eros principle is one of affective-cum-psychic relatedness, a subjectively emotional mode of experiencing the world. Jung noted that in the Western view, this mode of psychic relatedness is usually seen as "feminine," whereas the logos principle is more often identified with the "masculine" orientation. With origins in the collective unconscious, these archetypes evolved into the psychic structures of anima (the "feminine" within the man) and animus (the "masculine" within the woman). Before leaving Jung's contribution to our understanding of the two world views, I want to offer a summary: The logos principle represents reason and objective interest, it is archetypally "masculine," its structural representation in the psyche of woman is the animus, and the ectopsychic function most related to it is Thinking. The eros principle represents psychic, affectively based relatedness, it is archetypally "feminine," its structural representation in the psyche of man is the anima, and the ectopsychic function most related to it is Feeling. The logos principle is Apollonian. The eros principle is Dionysian.

Writing for the popular audience, Sam Keen (1974) addressed the Apollonian and the Dionysian as the "rational" view and the "cosmic" view, respectively. He emphasized work as valued above play in the rational view, and the opposite value in the cosmic. In addition to this difference in content, work versus play, Keen suggested that in the rational view efficiency is sought, whereas in the cosmic view, it is ecstasy. The two world views can be summarized, as I understand Keen's position, as valuing efficient work (the rational or Apollonian view) or valuing ecstatic play (the cosmic or Dionysian view).

In his popular novel, *Zen and the Art of Motorcycle Maintenance*, Robert Pirsig (1974), too, addresses the Apollonian and Dionysian world views, naming them, respectively, "classical understanding" and "romantic understanding." His book is subtitled "an inquiry into values," and explores classical understanding and romantic understanding through what might well be seen as an allegory. The allegory involves riding and maintaining motorcycles on a long motorcycle journey. As he says, "Although motorcycle riding is romantic, motorcycle maintenance is purely classic" (Pirsig, 1974, p. 67). His exploration derives the following characterization of the classical understanding. Fundamentally, the world is seen as underlying form. From this, the mode of classical understanding proceeds in an orderly fashion using reason and laws or principles. Facts take priority over esthetic considerations, as thought takes priority over feelings in the pursuit of control.

Romantic understanding, for Pirsig, is derived from seeing the world in terms of immediate experience. Thus the mode of romantic understanding tends to be inspirational, imaginative, creative, and intuitive. Feelings and esthetic considerations are given priority over thoughts and facts in the pursuit of experience and intuitive understanding.

Of particular importance for the present essay is an insight offered by Pirsig concerning misunderstandings. He suggests that because persons tend to orient themselves through one of these two modes of understanding, classical *or* romantic, they will have difficulty understanding or appreciating those who orient through the other mode.

The Insight and Expression Polarity in Psychotherapy

We see, then, that my opening quotes of Jack Nicholson and of William Blake reflect two different world views or value systems. Call them what you wish, keeping in mind that each pair of labels hints at a nuance of inflection: Apollonian-Dionysian, Logos-Eros, Rational-Cosmic, Classical-Romantic.

These two world views are manifest, as one might well expect, in the realm of psychotherapy. I suggest the terms "Insight" and "Expression" as the inflections in that realm. So, the Apollonian-Dionysian, Logos-Eros, Rational-Cosmic, Classical-Romantic world views and values are reflected in this microcosm as Insight-Expression psychotherapy views and values.

At this point, a side excursion is called for in the interest of clarifying the above idea of Insight-Expression in psychotherapy. In the 1960s, with a battle waging between behavior therapy and psychoanalysis, Perry London (1964) published a book which he titled *The Modes and Morals of Psychotherapy*. In this book, he distinguished two "modes," calling them "Insight Therapies" (meaning psychoanalysis, primarily) and "Action Therapies" (meaning behavior therapies). His thesis, as I understand him, was that Action Therapies are more appropriate for treating circumscribed symptoms and Insight Therapies are more appropriate for "expansion of consciousness." By way of implying the prescription of appropriate therapy to the problem — symptom or meaning of one's life — London appeared to have reached toward a truce between behavior therapy and psychoanalysis. He acknowledged the efficient control of symptoms such as phobias by means of behavior therapy. And, he acknowledged the legitimacy of exploring issues of meaning through psychoanalysis. He drew the distinction poignantly, and with poetic flair, when he queried rhetorically, "May not men leap from cliffs for other reasons than those for which dogs salivate to bells?" (London, 1964, p. 38).

Now, let us look at what London's writing suggests in light of the two world views. Action Therapies are designed for efficient control of symptoms, a goal oriented task of mastery and molding, based on objective, unadorned technical application of underlying principles ("laws" of learning and conditioning). This is quite clearly a paragon of the Apollonian way.

But, what of Insight Therapies? London (p. 57) emphasized psychoanalysis as a way of raising consciousness. In psychoanalysis the emphasis is on *analyzing*. The taboo of "acting out" is based on the notion that if one acts on one's feelings, this interferes with analyzing their meaning. Not only does the acting out relieve one of the emotion, so it is no longer present for analysis, but psychic energy may be dissipated which could better have been used in the work of analysis. Thus, acting out can be a defense and a resistance. Psychoanalysis values insight, an intellectual task requiring reason. The traditional analyst was to be objective and apply precisely the psychoanalytic rules and techniques. Insight Therapies, as defined by London, are, I submit, more Apollonian than Dionysian. Perhaps not as extreme as Action Therapies, they are, nevertheless, basically an Apollonian approach. Analytic understanding of meaning is, indisputably, of the Logos. (Space does not permit me to garner here all of the evidence for my point. Keep in mind, I am referring to a classical psychoanalysis, not to some of the later developments which are under the rubric of "psychodynamic," or to some eclectic approaches which integrate psychodynamic theory or techniques with expressive therapies.)

Several years ago I was invited to be part of a "think-tank" for the National Institute of Mental Health. Our task was to derive guidelines for the funding of NIMH sponsored research in the "experiential" psychotherapies. Perry London had been chosen to be the moderator. In the course of our discussions we struggled greatly with understanding each other and with agreeing on guidelines, or even agreeing on what experiential psychotherapy is. Looking back, I now see the difficulties as stemming largely from an Apollonian-Dionysian split. The good-will, conscientiousness, and intellectual capability of all the participants was not adequate to overcome the difficulties completely. Most of the participants had, I see now, a strong Apollonian leaning, so to bring forth more Dionysian concerns tended to usher in confusion and frustration. And yet, the more Apollonian participants seemed fascinated with the Dionysian input. My impression is that Perry London, as well as the majority of the participants in the "think-tank," held an implicit Apollonian perspective, consistent with their expertise in Action or Insight Therapies.

Had Perry London been writing just a few years later, he perhaps would have included a third mode of therapy. To be complete, he would have to have included what are now identified as the Expressive Therapies. This mode includes Bioenergetics and other Neo-Reichian therapies (e.g., Core Energetics, Hakomi, Organismic Psychotherapy, Radix), Gestalt therapy, Pesso System Psychomotor therapy, Primal Scream therapy, and Psychodrama. Although some of these were being practiced at the time that London was writing, they really exploded onto the psychotherapy scene in the 1960s and 1970s. At the risk of oversimplification, I would characterize this mode as focusing on facilitating the person in therapy to open to creative and spontaneous expression of feelings.

To reiterate, then, my thesis is that the two competing world views are reflected in the realm of psychotherapy. Action Therapies (i.e., behavior therapies) are radically Apollonian. If we exclude them from our further discussion of *psycho*therapy, we can then see more clearly the dimension of Insight-Expression as the psychotherapy inflection of the Apollonian-Dionysian world views.

Let us now look more closely at the Insight mode of therapy as manifestation of the Apollonian world view. As I noted earlier, London emphasized, using psychoanalysis as his major example, that Insight Therapies have as their focus the raising of consciousness. (The meaning here is not in the sense of "higher" consciousness as used in the context of transpersonal psychology, but rather in the sense of more thorough understanding.) As, too, I noted, the focal activity of psychoanalysis is *analysis*. The purpose of psychoanalytic work is to analyze the life of the analysand, increasing understanding by making functional connections between remembered childhood events and feelings and current feelings, experiences and behaviors. With analysis comes insight (Smith, 1999). Neurotic and characterological symptoms, transference, dreams, and slips of the tongue all are part of the life of the analysand and, as such, are grist for the analytic mill. "Thus, Freud wanted analysands to *remember*, not escape from the unpleasantness of painful memories or the hard work of analysis by 'acting out' their issues" (Smith, 1999, p. 75).

The Insight mode of therapy includes more than psychoanalysis. London, himself, included Client-Centered therapy, making claim that the distinction between interpretation (major tool of the analyst) and reflection (major tool of the Client-Centered therapist) is more apparent than real. "The difference in usage is then a matter of exposing feelings in the proper context. The Freudian requires more interpretive latitude in order to get them to appear in the context of history, while the Rogerian can afford merely to reflect because he will in any case interpret the exposed feeling with no reference to time" (London, 1964, p. 50).

Elsewhere, I have suggested that Cognitive therapies also are of the Insight mode. "If taken in their broader meaning, and not restricted to their technical psychoanalytic meaning, insight, interpretation, and analysis describe much of cognitive therapy as well as the myriad of psychodynamic therapies. The essence is that the therapist is an external translator, tracing things to their source and explaining to the person in therapy. Depending on the proclivities of the therapist, the problems of living reported by the person in therapy may be traced to [i.e., analyzed] childhood events or to irrational beliefs and negative cognitive schemas … such analysis and explanation are seen as *necessary* by psychodynamic and cognitive therapists alike" (Smith, 1999, p. 76).

So, the childhood event, the irrational belief, the negative cognitive schema, the unexposed feeling all constitute the "underlying form," the "unadorned fact," which is to be addressed "reasonably" ("objectively") and "ordered" until "mastered." This is consonant with the Rational, the Classical, the Logos, the Apollonian.

In contrast, the Expressive mode of therapy honors the enactment of one's passion above the understanding of it. The various therapies which can be included under the Expressive rubric differ in the distance they place between the primary importance of expression and the secondary importance of understanding, but all look toward the ecstasy of passionate expression as their forté. They all value spontaneity in the surrender to feelings and immediate experience. All look to personal transformation, the metamorphosis for which Dionysus stands.

In the present writing I have referred to the Apollonian-Dionysian as a polarity or dimension. Horney (Shostrom, 1967), as noted earlier, saw them as two natural human tendencies, with no person being all one or all the other. So, too, it may be best to see Insight therapies and Expressive therapies as the poles of a continuum. Any given therapist may lean more one way or the other, as well, with the degree of leaning somewhat changeable. But for heuristic purposes it is easier, at times, to speak of the poles, not the continuum between. Thus, I identified the Insight mode of therapy as Apollonian and the Expressive mode as Dionysian. Additionally, at the extreme of the Apollonian pole is found the Action mode of therapy. At the extreme of the other pole, beyond the Dionysian lies the Bacchanalian. The Expressive mode, debased, is irresponsible and harmful, as some of us have witnessed, particularly in the excesses of the 1960s and 1970s. If the most extreme of the Expressive mode is Bacchanalian, with impulsive acting out and unbridled eros, what is the most extreme of the Action mode? It is dehumanization through the mechanical, dispassioned application of techniques. In the words of Paul Tillich (1962, p. 653), "A self which has become a matter of calculation and management has ceased to be a self. It has become a thing."

Toward a Resolution of the Polarity of Insight and Expression

"Nothing too much." This was pithy advice of the Sages of Ancient Greece (Kopp, 1971). Applied to our topic, this could suggest not too much insight (meaning insight without expression), and not too much expression (meaning expression without insight). This sage advice is echoed in Aristotle's Doctrine of the Mean, popularly referred to as the "Golden Mean" (Popkin & Stroll, 1956). For Aristotle, this is the way to happiness, acting so as to steer a path between the two extremes. These ancient sources are a call to a resolution of polarities.

Both Insight Therapy and Expressive Therapy offer something of value, both have their forté, as we have already seen. But that valued emphasis, that strong point, may also be a limitation. Through the character of Harry Haller, known as the "Steppenwolf," Herman Hesse (1969, p. 55) demonstrates so clearly for us that "... every strength may become a weakness (and under some circumstances must) ..." The poetic words of Jack Nicholson and of William Blake can now be read again, not just as messages of advocacy, but as messages of illumination. They elucidate "the weakness inherent in the strength" which Hesse addresses. We can paraphrase William Blake, making his point specific to psychotherapy: "Those who have Insight but do not give Expression to it, are creating deadness." For Jack Nicholson's words one might say: "Expression without benefit of Insight — the definition of 'impulsive' behavior — brings chaos to one's life."

We see, then, an emerging integration of Insight and Expression. Expression, the more liberal pole (that is, of *Liber*), animates and enlivens, celebrating aliveness. Insight, its guide, is the conservative pole, slowing the pace and lending security to each animated step. But, too much slowing of the pace may deaden, under the guise of security. "And you all know," Hecate (the lead witch in *Macbeth*) reminds us, "security is mortal's chiefest enemy" (Shakespeare, no year, p. 935).

If we turn, once again, to the mythopoetic, trusting in its metaphorical epistemology, we can be instructed in the relationship of Insight and Expression. The Norse god, Odin, appears in many hypostases including All-father, God of Poetry, God of the Dead, and God of Battle. As a shamanic figure, he was wont to shapeshift, taking on various forms in order to carry out his exploits. The many myths in which he has a part, often a leading role, show him to be passionate and active (Crossley-Holland, 1980).

We learn in the *Prose Edda* (Sturluson, 1954) that two ravens sit on the shoulders of Odin. He sends them out every day to fly over the whole world and return to him, bringing him news of all they see and hear. Their names are Hugin and Munin, meaning "Thought" and "Memory." Thus, we are told that Odin, active and passionate as he is, is informed by thought and memory. That is to say, Odin's Expression has benefit of Insight. Lee Hollander (1962, p. 57) in his translation of *The Poetic Edda*, speaks of Hugin and Munin as "'Thought' and 'Remembrance,' Othin's [*sic*] ravens which bring him intelligence."

At another level of interpretation, we can look to the birds themselves. They are ravens, seen in the Viking world as birds of the battle field. So, by virtue of the mental functions they stand for and the expressive activity they symbolize, they themselves are a metaphor for the bringing together of Insight and Expression.

Let us take the myth further. In *The Poetic Edda* (Hollander, 1962, p. 57) we find the following. "The whole earth over, every day, hover Hugin and Munin; I dread lest Hugin droop in his flight, yet I fear me still more for Munin." Is Odin telling us that he fears the loss of thought, but he fears the loss of memory more? It appears so. This would then suggest that the more conservative function (memory) is of the greater importance in the constituting of guiding intelligence.

The Norse mythology, in summary, appears to offer us a clue to the reconciliation of the polarity of Insight and Expression. To wit, action is best guided when informed by thought *and* memory. Action/Expression, being liberal (i.e., of *Liber*) benefits from the conservative influence of thought and memory/Insight. Memory, being the more conservative, may be the more important component of Insight.

It was this plus Germanic/Norse mythology which served as cultural backdrop to the development of German philosophy. And, a case can be made that it was the nineteenth-century German philosophers, particularly Nietzsche, who provided the philosophical roots for the emerging psychologies of Freud, Jung, Adler, Rank, Reich, and in turn, Perls and Lowen. Of these luminaries, I believe it was Perls who best reflected the Odinic reconciliation of what in the psychotherapy context we call Insight and Expression. But, he did this in a manner which is decidedly Dionysian (Smith, 1991). Perhaps the Dionysian core of the Gestalt approach is best reflected by Arnold Beisser in his expression of the "paradoxical theory of change." Briefly stated, ". . . change occurs when one becomes what he is, not when he tries to become what he is not" (Beisser, 1970, p. 77). There it is, no mastery and control, but rather *the surrender to one's nature*.

Elsewhere, I have dealt in detail with Reich's system of therapy (Smith, 1985) and with Reich's influence on Perls in the development of Gestalt therapy (Smith, 1975, 1985). I will not take space to reiterate, except for specific points which are relevant in the remainder of the present essay.

My own approach to therapy is an integrative one, drawing heavily on the work of Reich and Perls, among others. I have described it in *The Body in Psychotherapy* (Smith, 1985) and in the book which Jeffrey Zeig and

W. Michael Munion co-edited, *What is psychotherapy?* (Smith, 1990). My work is also presented in Richard Sharf's *Theories of counseling and psychotherapy* (1996, 2000).

In *The Body in Psychotherapy* (1985), I offer a model for the description and understanding of psychobiological existence based on need cycles, the cycles of contacting other people and other things in one's world for the satisfaction of needs and the withdrawal which follows. Calling this the Contact/Withdrawal Cycle, I explicate it in terms of natural and of pathological functioning. Space does not allow detail here. Put most briefly, the cycle consists of the arising of a Want, leading to organismic Arousal, which differentiates into Emotion, that calling for Action, which becomes an Interaction with someone or something, which leads to Satisfaction, of the Want. Following this Contact Episode comes Withdrawal until another Want becomes figural, emerging from the background of potential Needs and Preferences. In the pathological form, there is self-interruption of the flow of the cycle through various pathological mechanisms serving to allow an avoidance of the next stage of the cycle.

Erring on the side of brevity, once more, I can summarize the "what," "why," and "how" of psychopathology as follows:

What is psychopathology? Any pattern of habitual self-interruption in the Contact/Withdrawal Cycle.

Why does one choose to self-interrupt? Self-interruptions are in response to a "toxic introject" (an introjected message which forbids full aliveness). The toxic introject consists of a content (what is specifically forbidden — the want, organismic Arousal or excitement, an Emotion, an Action, an Interaction, Satisfaction, Withdrawal, or some combination of these) and a "catastrophic expectation" (a threat that something catastrophic will happen if the voice of the toxic introject is disobeyed). So, the self-interruption is an avoidance of the next (forbidden) stage of the Contact/Withdrawal Cycle.

How can one self-interrupt? Self-interruptions are accomplished through a synergistic combination of four mechanisms: (1) Lowered Arousal through inadequate breathing; (2) Clouded Awareness through several means known in psychoanalysis as ego defense mechanisms; (3) Retroflected Action (Action blocked or inhibited through "body armoring," i.e., chronic muscular tensions); (4) Retroflected Interaction (doing to oneself what one would like to do to the other or what one would like the other to do to one).

It is to the explication of the Contact/Withdrawal Cycle that much of *The Body in Psychotherapy* (Smith, 1985) is devoted. I leave it to the interested reader to consult this source if the details are desired. Hopefully, the overview just given will suffice for the purpose of the present essay.

My inspiration for the Contact/Withdrawal Cycle came primarily from the writings of Fritz Perls. From reading his books and articles, I became familiar with his idea that good contact requires both excitement and awareness. Consider this idea. Without excitement, or we could substitute "passion," contact with the environment will be weak and diminished. Good contact means satisfying contact, contact which satisfies some want. And, it implies action, but not just action per se, action which is interactive with someone or something. So, we have the notion of (passionate) action-interaction.

But the action-interaction sequence most often will miss the target, unless guided. The guide is "awareness." In the context of Gestalt therapy, "awareness" is preferred to the psychoanalytic term "insight." The former incorporates thought, memory, affect, and sensation, with particular emphasis on the senses. (Those of you who have traveled in Gestalt circles are familiar with the saying, "Lose your mind and come to your senses.") "Insight," in contrast emphasizes thought and memory, with particular emphasis on memory.

Awareness is the guide — awareness of one's Want (both need and preference, given options for meeting that need), awareness of Arousal (excitement), awareness of Emotion (passion), awareness of Satisfaction. What is guided is Action-Interaction, the Expressive portion of the Contact Episode. So, we see an intimate link of interdependence between Awareness and Expression.

Erving Polster (1970, p. 70) in his typically thoughtful and clear manner wrote, ". . . knowing the difference between being hungry, angry, or sexually aroused surely is a lengthy step toward knowing what to do. In this interplay between feeling and doing lies the crux of our search for good living." Using the metaphor of the synaptic arc which facilitates union between sensory and motor neurons, he introduced the concept of the "synaptic experience." By this he meant the experience of union between awareness and expression. Furthermore, Polster suggested that some people are more "awareness oriented," some more "action oriented."

I see the "synaptic experience" as a core value in the Gestalt approach, as well as a core concept. In the inimitable style of Zen, with its paradox of simplicity and profundity, a story is told. When a jealous competitor challenged a Priest named Bankei, trying to show that he had no miraculous powers, and holding up yet another priest as greater, Bankei replied, "Perhaps your fox can perform that trick, but that is not the manner of Zen. My miracle is that when I feel hungry I eat and when I feel thirsty I drink" (Reps, no date, p. 68). The real miracle — "consciousness in action" (p. 175).

If we look at Apollo and Bacchus as representing the extremes of the poles, then Dionysus represents a moderated position (relative to Bacchus). As a therapy which follows the Dionysian path (Smith, 1991), Gestalt therapy is, then, not extreme. It is, however, decidedly Dionysian in its emphasis on Expression as pre-eminent.

One of the ways in which Expression is ascendent in the Gestalt approach is illustrated in the Contact/Withdrawal Cycle. There are feedback loops in the cycle such that later steps clarify and enhance earlier steps. "For example, taking action may enhance the felt emotion, or if the action is not appropriate to the emotion, the action may reveal to the person what the actual emotion would be if it were allowed into awareness. It is as if there were a reverberating wave which further enhances previous steps as each new step is taken" (Smith, 1985, p. 31). In practice, this means that often the person in therapy is encouraged to express (Action-Interaction) in a psychodramatic way in the therapy session as a means of discovering or clarifying an underlying Emotion, Arousal or Want. In other words, Awareness may emerge from Expression. As Hugh Prather wrote (1970, no page number), "Sometimes the only way for me to find out what it is I want to do is to go ahead and do something. Then the moment I start to act, my feelings become clear."

Insight therapies, especially more psychoanalytic ones, tend to take the path of: talking → memories (thinking) → feelings. In contrast, an Expressive therapy, such as my body-oriented Gestalt approach, offers the alternative path of: body work → feelings → memories. The body work may consist of a variety of techniques, as discussed in *The Body in Psychotherapy* (Smith, 1985), in addition to psychodramatic expressive work. These techniques include selected body postures, gentle touching, "catalytic touch" (Brown, 1990), directed breathing, Bioenergetic "stress postures" (Lowen & Lowen, 1977), "orgonomic massage" (Reich, 1949), and so forth. The key, here, is that feelings are directly accessed through body experience and expression.

The idea in the Gestalt approach is that Awareness and Expression are themselves two parts of a Gestalt. As parts of a Gestalt, they cannot be fully understood in isolation, but only in their relationship. Speaking wistfully, Barry Stevens (1984, p. 4) asks, "What is it but awareness and acting in accord with circumstances?" Yes, awareness *and* acting, Awareness and Expression. She wrote further, emphasizing the integrity of this Gestalt, "Observation/understanding/action without an intervening period of thought" (Stevens, 1984, p. 85). This same integrity is reflected in Gestalt praxis when Fritz Perls (1998, p. 72) instructs us that "The reintegration of the dissociated parts of the personality is best undertaken by resensitizing and remobilizing the symptoms of orientation and manipulation." He is calling attention to both resensitizing desensitized orientation functions, that is, Awareness, *and* remobilizing frozen Expression. Borrowing from Everett Shostrom (1967), I have suggested to therapists in training with me a simple guide for working with persons in therapy. It can be used as a reminder to facilitate the process of the person in therapy. "*Identify* feeling, *experience* the feeling, *express* the feeling." Again, the Gestalt of Awareness *and* Expression.

In the Gestalt approach, then, we find the resolution of the polarity of Insight and Expression. We need only to translate the more historically bound concept of insight into the more here-and-now focused concept of lived (experienced) Awareness. Awareness and Expression, then, represent two parts of a whole, two parts of a Gestalt. (In the Contact/Withdrawal Cycle, they are further differentiated into smaller constituent parts Want, Arousal, Emotion, Satisfaction and Action, Interaction, respectively.) In spontaneous living, Awareness flows into Expression. They are wed as one.

Awe and Terror in the Experience of the Gestalt of Awareness and Expression

My introduction to body work was at a Summer Workshop of the American Academy of Psychotherapists. Vivian Guze, who had trained with both Fritz Perls and Alexander Lowen, was offering a workshop on Bioenergetics. When she asked for a demonstration volunteer, preferably one who was not experienced with Bioenergetics, I came forward. I was both curious and naive. Vivian asked me to bend backwards over a "breathing stool," a backless bar stool with a rolled up blanket on it, with the center of my back on the mid-point of the stool. Following the instructions of her soft voice, I placed my arms back over my head, letting them dangle, dropped my chin, and made an a-a-a-h-h sound with each exhalation. From time to time, she placed her hand along my sternum and made a firm vibratory motion directed downward into my chest as I exhaled. What I experienced was awesome. I felt a rush of aliveness throughout my body, or more accurately, throughout my whole being. The level of energy which I felt was intense, almost more than I thought I could handle. Vivian's confident and calm voice helped me not to panic, although I had moments of fear as the feeling of energy pulsed in me. My sounds grew louder, perhaps they were screams. Then, Vivian invited me to stand up slowly, and then, once I had my feet solidly under me, once I was well "grounded," to bend forward and with knees slightly bent, allowing my arms and head to hang. This position balanced the previous position of a back bend over the stool. What I noticed when I stood up, finally, was that my vision was unusually clear, colors were very vivid, and my voice, when I spoke, sounded deeper and more resonant than how I remembered it. I felt warm and very good, a rather paradoxical excited calmness. This transformation, occurring in just a few minutes, I later estimated, was dramatic. I was so awed by my experience that I knew I wanted to learn body-oriented psychotherapy. I also knew that I was not ready to pursue this powerful level of work yet. It was fully a year before I began my training in Bioenergetics. During that year I read about the approach and continued in my personal therapy which was Insight oriented.

What is so awesome, so terrifying about waking up, coming alive? In describing my integrative approach, I wrote, "It is the exquisite focus on organism-in-environment *process* which appeals most to me about the Gestalt approach. To this I add the awesome power of the Reichian and neo-Reichian procedures for assessing and facilitating that process" (Smith, 1985, p. ix). Gestalt may be characterized as a therapy which focuses on personal process as that unfolds moment by moment in the here-and-now of the therapy session. In the unfolding of personal process, as reflected in the tracking of the Contact/Withdrawal Cycle, the self-interruption becomes apparent. As the person in therapy flows through a cycle, the usually abrupt self-interruption bespeaks an avoidance. The avoidance is of the next step, the step in the unfolding process which is forbidden by the toxic introject. By bumping into the toxic introject, specifically with confronting the catastrophic expectation, anxiety is aroused. As Perls (1998, p. 90) said in an early session, only more recently published as a paper, "Any emotion that is not developed as emotion will appear as anxiety. It's the blocking of the natural flow of vitality." And, of course, by "not developed" he meant the avoidance of the expression of that emotion. So, moving ahead with natural process, in spite of a catastrophic expectation, can be terrifying. In this context, Erving and Miriam Polster (1973, p. 119) have written that ".... change itself calls forth terror ..." When one has done so and discovered the catastrophe did not ensue, the experience can be awesome.

In the growth toward natural, spontaneous expression there is a particularly troublesome stage which is frequently encountered. In introducing this, the Polsters wrote of four levels of expression: blocked, inhibited, exhibitionistic, and spontaneous. The blocked and inhibited stages are both non-expressive. In the case of the former, the person does not know what he or she wants to express and in the latter, the person knows, but expresses not. The third stage, the exhibitionistic is reached when the person does express what he or she wants, but the expression is new. Not yet fully integrated or assimilated into the personality, expression at the exhibitionistic stage may be awkward. But, as the Polsters (1973, p. 126) pointed out, "... one does not simply and uniformly move into grace from a blocked or inhibited position. ... Some willingness to accept the ... awkward moments is indispensable to growth." I would add that with the awkwardness of the exhibitionistic stage may also come terror.

In words and description more in keeping with the awe and terror of which we are speaking, Wilhelm Reich (1949) posited what he called a "phase of the breakdown of secondary narcissism." Reich suggested that the continuing frustration of natural needs leads to contraction of the body armor (chronic muscular tensions). It is this conflict between inhibited impulses and the inhibiting armor that leads to a secondary narcissism (as contrasted with the primary narcissism which results when the infant cathects her or his own body parts as part-objects of love). In other words, as investment of libido in the outside world is made more difficult or is withdrawn, the energy builds up within, intensifying a secondary narcissism. When the armor, which is the characterological protective mechanism, is loosened or dissolved, there is a temporary condition of helplessness. This is the phase of the breakdown of secondary narcissism. During this phase, the person has strong, freed energy, but with a concomitant lack of "safe" neurotic controls. This phase of therapy is often stormy, with the person feeling terror.

Perls probably borrowed from Reich's phase of the breakdown of secondary narcissism, including the essence of it in his five-layer model of neurosis (Smith, 1975a). Although consistent in his conceptual presentation of the layers of neurosis, he was not always consistent in his numbering of them. Disregarding the numbering, then, the layers emerge as follows (Smith, 1985): Neurosis is characterized by a *cliché layer*, a layer of tokens of meaning. Beneath that is a layer of playing roles, playing "games," a *phony layer*. Next is the *impasse layer*, characterized by the "phobic attitude." At this phobic layer the phobic attitude results in avoidance of contact, and in turn, the feeling of being lost, empty, stuck, and confused. Beneath this is the death layer or *implosive layer* where the person is paralyzed by opposing forces, trying to pull in and hold herself or himself together. If successfully worked through, this implosive layer will unfold into the final layer, the *explosive layer*.

The explosive layer is characterized by authentic experiencing and expression of emotion. The explosion may be into grief, if a loss had not been assimilated, or joy, or anger, or sexual feelings. There is a clear parallel, here, between Reich's phase of the breakdown of secondary narcissism and Perls' progression through the impasse, to implosion, and to explosion. The essence in both cases is the dissolution of organismic core defenses in order to e- merge, after the "walk through hell," with an authentic expression. The im-

~

SCHOPENHAUER, FREUD, AND PROJECTION

"It is a radical deficiency that, in the education of post-Freudian psychotherapists, most students are left illiterate about the humanities." Thus, with a note of seriousness, declared Rollo May (1991, p. 153). Based on my own experience over the past thirty years and more, as a psychotherapist, workshop leader, and professor, I will not only nod to May's opinion, but will paraphrase him, adding particular emphasis as follows. It is a radical deficiency in the education of many psychotherapists that they are left illiterate about *philosophy*. Not only may many psychotherapists be functionally illiterate about the humanities in general, but may be so with respect to philosophy, specifically.

Having made the above contention, the burden is on me to make a case for how a grounding in philosophy is important for a psychotherapist. First of all, let us look at what constitutes a system of psychotherapy. Most easily recognized, each system contains a body of techniques or therapist behaviors. These techniques are the procedures or methods used by a therapist given to that system's approach. These techniques are based on a theory of what invites or brings about growth or healing. This theory comes out of a theory of psychopathology, or what leads to emotional or mental disorder. This theory, in turn, emerges from a more general theory of personality, which may or may not contain a sub-theory of normal development. And, beneath the level of technique and beneath the level of theory, there is yet

From: *Voices*, 38(1), 86-93 (2002).

another level, that of philosophy. It is philosophy which is the foundation of the psychotherapy system. In order to be well understood, a therapy system must be known at its several levels. All too often, I have found, not only students, but practicing therapists identify a particular therapy primarily or exclusively by its techniques. This limited and partial understanding leads to superficiality and misunderstanding.

Philosophy is at the core of psychotherapy. A moment's reflection on some of the traditional topics which have occupied philosophers confirms this. Consider, for instance, epistemology, esthetics, ethics, logic, and metaphysics (in its modern meaning). So whenever we as psychotherapists enter into consideration of questions of evidence and knowing, of harmony and beauty, of proper conduct and the good life, of clear and critical thinking, or of spirit, we enter that realm long occupied by the philosophers.

Let me offer one brief example of what I am proposing. It is an epistemological position which is the core differentia specifica between behavior therapy and existential therapy. At the level of technique, behavioral rehearsal and a Gestalt empty chair dialogue may look identical. (I remember a therapist who approached me following a Gestalt therapy demonstration that I gave at a professional meeting and insisting that what he had just seen me do was behavior therapy!) And, at the level of theory, with the admission of differences in language and differences in emphasis, there may be room for rapprochement. But, behavior therapy is based firmly on strict empirical epistemology, existential therapies on empirical epistemology highly tempered by a metaphorical epistemology. With their respective philosophical cores enucleated, behavior therapy and Gestalt therapy stand far apart!

For the behavior therapist, grounded in a strict empirical epistemology, there is belief in an objectively knowable world. And this objective world of facts can be known only through sensory input, albeit sometimes enhanced by technological devises such as an event counter, a stopwatch, or the various apparatuses for monitoring physiological processes. The tendency is, then, to observe the patient or client, get the facts, and introduce interventions that hold promise of changing the undesirable facts. The patient or client tends to be viewed objectively, with the problem behavior often more the focus than the person manifesting that behavior. The person may be viewed more as a case to be managed or cured, the treatment to be guided by objectively observable facts, and the outcome to be assessed by objective sensory observations.

In contrast, the Gestalt therapist, or any other humanistic or existential therapist, admits of a non-objective reality that receives primary attention. Personal experience is the primary focus, the subjective world of the person in therapy. This private world is best known, although perhaps not with the certainty of objectively knowable facts, through metaphor. It is neither how fast the person's heart is beating, nor how many meters from to the phobic object that the person is willing to approach that is of primary interest, but rather the subjective experience of fear, conveyed through a metaphor such as feeling like a lamb in a den of ravenous lions.

Beyond the fact that as psychotherapists we are in the realm of philosophy, at least implicitly if not explicitly, there are clearly discernible threads linking specific philosophers with various therapies. In the present paper, I will focus on such a thread emanating from Arthur Schopenhauer. I will demonstrate that Schopenhauer conceptualized a phenomenon, later to be termed "projection," antedating Freud by years.

Did Freud know of Schopenhauer's works? Certainly so. In 1914 Freud added a footnote to *The Interpretation of Dreams*, which was published in 1899, but bore the publication date of 1900. "Ferenczi (1912) has proposed an ingenious 'over-interpretation' of the Oedipus myth, based on a passage in one of Schopenhauer's letters" (Freud, 1961, p. 263). Later, in the same volume, Freud quoted Silberer who reported a reverie in which Silberer compared the views of Kant and Schopenhauer concerning time. Somewhat later, in 1925, Freud presented an extract from Schopenhauer's *The World as Will and Idea* in an appendix to "The Resistances to Psychoanalysis" (Rothgeb, 1973).

Henri Ellenberger (1970) stated that "the similarities between certain essential teachings of Schopenhauer and Freud have been shown by Cassirer, Scheler, and particularly by Thomas Mann" (p. 209). "Thomas Mann said that psychoanalytic concepts were Schopenhauer's ideas 'translated from metaphysics into psychology'" (p. 542). Referring to Schopenhauer and Nietzsche, Ellenberger wrote "there cannot be the slightest doubt that Freud's thought echoed theirs" (p. 542). Ellenberger cited Louis S. Granjel as identifying three main points that Schopenhauer and Freud have in common: "an irrationalistic conception of man, the identification of the general life impulse with the sexual instinct, and their radical anthropological pessimism," and continuing with the citation, reported Granjel as writing that "these similarities cannot be explained only in terms of a direct influence of Schopenhauer upon Freud, but also in terms of the similarity in the personalities of these two thinkers" (p. 209). The point is that Granjel saw a direct influence on the part of Schopenhauer on Freud. Additionally, we are told by Ronald Lehrer (1999a) that according to minutes of the Vienna Psychoanalytic Society, Alfred Adler had "once tried to establish a direct line from Schopenhauer, through Marx and Mach to Freud" (p. 230).

How early in his life did Freud become aware of Schopenhauer's philosophy? Early in his career, as is well known, Freud came under the influence of Joseph Breuer, and in the mid-1890s they published accounts of their work together. Lehrer (1999b) wrote that "it is worth noting that in addition to being Freud's friend, Paneth also knew Breuer. He may even have been the person who introduced Freud to Breuer. Breuer, like Paneth . . . probably had at least some general knowledge of aspects of Nietzsche's philosophy and psychology. (He certainly appears to have been familiar, as was Paneth, with Schopenhauer.)" (p. 185). This is suggestive, at least, that Freud was aware of Schopenhauer's works quite early. In contrast to this suggestion, however, it was stated by Lancelot Whyte (1962) that "Freud explained that he avoided reading Schopenhauer and Nietzsche until late in life," quoting Freud as having written, "I was less concerned with priority than with preserving my impartiality" (p. 160).

It is established, then, that Freud was familiar with Schopenhauer's work, and that he was probably influenced by it. How early this influence began and the extent of it may be debated. Regardless of the latter, I find it interesting to compare the two men's way of dealing with the phenomenon which came to be called projection. For, as stated by Christopher Young and Andrew Brook (1994), "there is no definitive way to settle the question of whether Freud read Schopenhauer before, say, 1892 or not, but such evidence as there is makes us wonder" (p. 116).

Schopenhauer's main work, *The World as Will and Idea* was published in 1818. Schopenhauer (1928) begins *The World as Idea* with the dramatic declaration, which serves as a summary of his entire discourse: "The world is my idea." Continuing, he wrote:

> . . . this is a truth which holds good for everything that lives and knows, though man alone can bring it into reflective and abstract consciousness. If he really does this, he has attained to philosophical wisdom. It then becomes clear and certain to him that what he knows is not a sun and an earth, but only an eye that sees a sun, a hand that feels an earth; that the world which surrounds him is there only as idea, i.e., only in relation to something else, the consciousness, which is himself. (Schopenhauer, 1928, p. 3)

To declare that the world is my idea meant to Schopenhauer that whatever is perceived is not something out there, rather it is a change in the body of the perceiver which is an effect of a thing out there. The critical point is this. In ordinary causal perception, the object out there causes a change in a sense organ and then by means of a reverse process this effect is referred back to its cause. It is this second stage of the perceptual process which imparts meaning to the perceived object. Usually, this second stage is unconscious (Jones, 1952). Those who have not, as Schopenhauer so quaintly put it, "attained to philosophical wisdom" do not realize the dual-stage process of perception. The second stage, being unconscious, is not taken into consideration and *perceived attributes are erroneously believed to be intrinsic to the thing itself*.

It follows, therefore, that in perceiving an object in the environment, one knows only that there is an object there, but not what that object is in and of itself. Perception may be veridical only in so far as it identifies the presence of an object, but not veridical as far as any conclusions as to the nature of that object.

Schopenhauer (1928) expressed his view strongly, and with adamantean tone. "No truth therefore is more certain, more independent of all others, and less in need of proof than this, that all that exists for knowledge, and therefore this whole world, is only object in relation to subject, perception of a perceiver, in a word, idea" (p. 3).

The "world as idea" has two fundamental, necessary and inseparable parts. The first is object, the forms of which are space and time. The second part is subject, which, in contrast, is present, entire and undivided in every percipient thing and therefore not in space and time.

Ideas, themselves, are of two types, ideas of perception and abstract ideas. Abstract ideas are concepts, the capacity for which is "reason." It is in reasoning or the production of concepts, Schopenhauer believed, that humans set themselves apart from the non-human animals. The former type of ideas, ideas of perception, are found in all animals, human and non-human.

In his thinking, Schopenhauer (1928) did not mean to imply that the subject and object are in a causal relationship. "It is needful to guard against the grave error of supposing that because perception arises through the knowledge of causality, the relation of subject and object is that of cause and effect. For this relation subsists only between the immediate objects known indirectly, thus always between objects alone" (pp. 14-15).

A problem in Schopenhauer's position, which he fails to address adequately, is that of illusory perception. He admits that illusion may at moments take the place of the real in the idea of perception. But, in his exuberance to show that in the sphere of abstract thought error may reign forever, he fails to pursue illusion in perception. So, he leaves us knowing only that illusion may occur.

With respect to "rational knowledge," Schopenhauer (1928) has this to say.

> Speaking generally, to know rationally (wissen) means to have in the power of the mind, and capable of being reproduced at will, such judgements as have their sufficient ground of knowledge in something outside themselves, i.e., are true.

Thus only abstract cognition is rational knowledge (wissen), which is therefore the result of reason . . . . Rational knowledge (wissen) is therefore abstract consciousness, the permanent possession in concepts of the reason, of what has become known in another way. (Schopenhauer, 1928, p. 38-39)

Reason is necessary for quick conclusions, bold actions, and rapid and sure comprehension, but it may hinder intuitive, direct discovery.

Schopenhauer (1928) wrote of the body as being the framework from which all else is perceived.

In fact, the meaning for which we seek of that world which is present to us only as our idea, or the transition from the world as mere idea of the knowing subject to whatever it may be besides this, would never be found if the investigator himself were nothing more than the pure knowing subject (a winged cherub without a body). But he is himself rooted in that world; he finds himself in it as an *individual*, that is to say, his knowledge, which is the necessary supporter of the whole world as idea, is yet always given through the medium of a body, whose affections are, as we have shown, the starting-point for the understanding in the perception of the world. (Schopenhauer, 1928, p. 63)

Every act of will is, of course, a movement of the body and the body therefore can be called the objectivity of the will.

Schopenhauer (1928) offered a summary of the will and the idea as follows:

I here conclude the second principal division of my exposition, in the hope that, so far as is possible in the case of an entirely new thought, which cannot be quite free from traces of the individuality in which it originated, I have succeeded in conveying to the reader the complete certainty that this world in which we live and have our being is in its whole nature through and through *will*, and at the same time through and through *idea*: That this idea, as such, already presupposes a form, object and subject, is therefore relative; and if we ask what remains if we take away this form, and all those forms which are subordinate to it, and which express the principle of sufficient reason, the answer must be that as something 'toto genere' different from idea this can be nothing but *will*, which is thus properly the thing-in-itself. Everyone finds that he himself is this will, in which the real nature of the world consists, and he also finds that he is the knowing subject, whose idea the whole world is, the world which exists only in relation to his consciousness, as its necessary supporter. (Schopenhauer, 1928, pp. 130-131)

The individual's body is an object among objects, and the one endeavor of knowledge is to find out the relationships among these objects. Only through these relationships with the body does an object gain significance. That is, only insofar as an object is related to one's body, one's will, is it of interest. In this view, Schopenhauer implies a selective perception, a perception which is selective with respect to relation to oneself. What one perceives, then, what one selectively attends to reveals something of oneself. It tells that one is interested and is therefore related to that object.

Schopenhauer seemed very much aware of the influence of one's past on one's current behavior. "Now, objective perception acts with regard to what is remembered just as it would in what is present, if we let it have influence over us, if we surrendered ourselves to it free from will" (Schopenhauer, 1928, p. 165). This seems consistent with projection in its broad sense as Freud came to use the term.

The use of the word "projected" can be found in a 1894 paper by Freud (1963a), "The Justification for Detaching from Neurasthenia a Particular Syndrome: The Anxiety Neurosis."

The psyche develops the affect of anxiety when it feels itself incapable of dealing (by an adequate reaction) with a task (danger) approaching it externally; it develops the neurosis of anxiety when it feels itself unequal to the task of mastering (sexual) excitation arising endogenously. That is to say, *it acts as if it had projected this excitation into the outer world.* (p. 114)

The emphasis in the final line was indicated by Freud in his paper. The important point, here, is that originally Freud used the term "projected" in a strictly pathological sense. The described dynamic involved a distortion of reality, that of regarding an endogenous excitation as if it were an exogenous threat of real danger.

In an 1896 paper, "Further Remarks on the Defense Neuro-Psychoses," Freud (1963b) introduced "projection" as an unconscious mechanism of defense, more specifically as a manner of repressing an intolerable idea which is in painful opposition to the patient's ego. Here is how he explained projection:

It only remains for me now to turn to account what has been learned from this case of paranoia in a comparison between paranoia and the obsessional neurosis. In each of them repression has proved to be the nucleus of the psychical mechanism, and in each of them the repressed content is a sexual experience in childhood. . . . Part of the symptoms again originate in a primary defence — namely, all the delusions of distrust, suspicion and persecution by others. In the obsessional neurosis the initial self-reproach has undergone repression by the formation of the primary symptom: *self-distrust* . . . . In paranoia the reproach is repressed in a manner which may be described as *projection*; by the defence-symptom of distrust directed against others being erected; in this way recognition of the reproach is withheld. (p. 172)

Continuing to trace the evolution of the concept, we can read of a broadened use of the term projection in Freud's 1913 book, *Totem and Taboo* (Freud, 1950).

In the case we have been dealing with, projection served the purpose of dealing with an emotional conflict; and it is employed in the same way in a large number of psychical situations that lead to neurosis. But projection was not created for the purpose of defense; it also occurs where there is no conflict. The projection outwards of internal perceptions is a primitive mechanism, to which, for instance, our sense perceptions are subject, and which therefore normally plays a very large part in determining the form taken by our external world. . . . internal perceptions of emotional and intellective process can be projected outwards in the same way as sense perceptions; they are thus employed for building up the external world, though they should by rights remain part of the internal world. (p. 64)

What we can see in Freud's writing is the evolution of "projection" from a metaphorical descriptor of a process of dealing with an intrapsychic threat in the dynamics of anxiety neurosis (1894), to a metaphorically-derived concept of an ego defense mechanism in paranoia (1896), to a metaphorically-derived general mechanism involved in creating one's experience of the external world (1913). In the first and second steps of this evolution, Freud recognized projection only in pathological context, only in the context of psychic conflict. In the first, it is feeling of sexual excitation which is projected. In the second, it is a thought of self-reproach. Arriving at the third step in the evolution of his thought, Freud recognized projection as operating not only in the realm of conflict but in the conflict-free realm as well. Projection is a general psychological mechanism occurring within and without pathology.

In toto, Freud's evolving position on projection offers a finer grain analysis than does Schopenhauer's view of the world as will and idea. I suggest, however, that the view offered by Schopenhauer nevertheless contributes a valuable perspective for psychotherapists. Schopenhauer suggested a broad perspective, emphasizing the extent to which we project, the extent to which we create our own worlds. Therein he espoused a view which may well bring to mind current work on constructivism. At the same time, he emphasized the influence of memory and here emphasized selective perception. Freud's work with these two themes does in no way replace or vitiate Schopenhauer's, but again, offers a somewhat different perspective at the level of a more fine grained analysis. For example, *transference*, a cornerstone of psychoanalysis, is a specific case of memory influencing current interpersonal perception. *Primal repression*, which Freud distinguished from *repression proper*, is at once an alternative term and an explanatory construct for at least one category of selective perception.

I invite the reader to consider these two men's views, carefully comparing, contrasting, and integrating. To conclude, allow me to share an excerpt from R. K. Gupta (1975), in which he quoted Freud.

> While Schopenhauer may be said to have psychologized philosophy, Freud may be credited with having philosophized psychology. In the process, the two established a solid common ground of interests, ideas, and insights, so much so that Schopenhauer is often credited with having anticipated many of Freud's findings. No wonder, too, that this should be so, for as Freud himself remarks with reference to Schopenhauer, "Why should not a bold thinker have divined something that sober and painstaking investigation of details subsequently confirms?" (p. 728).

~

NOTES ON THE RECOMMENDATION OF BOOKS AND FILMS TO PERSONS IN PSYCHOTHERAPY

As with everything that the therapist may say or do in psychotherapy, the therapist's recommendation of a book or a film may carry meanings not thought of or intended.

First and foremost, material that a therapist recommends comes therapist recommended, and that means, at the very least, that the material is valued by the therapist and, at most, that it may be seen as something to which the therapist has proprietary claim. The person receiving the recommendation may be delighted at the gift of opportunity or may feel the burden of required *home-work*. In the latter case, old issues concerning assigned tasks may be awakened, as well as transference feelings toward the therapist born of a history with parents and teachers. The point is that a recommendation might not be experienced as *just* a recommendation.

It behooves the therapist to be circumspect when recommending a book or a film. For a therapist who is, in terms of what Jung termed the ectopsychic functions, a *thinking* type, a recommendation means a carefully thought-out judgment. For a therapist who is an *intuitive* type, it reflects an insight into the fit of the material to the person in therapy.

Whether perceived through intuitive grasp or judged through careful thinking as a match for the person in therapy, the book or film must be relevant to that person in particular if it is to stand out and elicit careful attention. And, in order to speak to the person in therapy, the material must

From: *Voices*, 41(1), 100-101 (2005).

be relevant in two aspects. First, the *content* of the book or film must address something in the life of the person in therapy that is (or becomes, through the book or film) energized. Secondly, the recommended book or film must be at the appropriate *level*, not so simple that it is uninteresting or an insult to the person's intelligence, and not so recondite that it cannot be grasped or leads the person to feel stupid. In order to be of impact, it must be coterminous with the growing edge of the person in therapy.

It may be of value to define briefly the concept of the *growing edge*. "The growing edge is on the boundary between what is actual and what is potential, between that which is realized and that which is not yet real." (Smith, 1998, p.9). "The growing edge is at the limit to be extended. It is at the cusp of being and becoming" (Smith, 1998, p.11).

Several of the principles of the *growing edge phenomenon* that I have outlined and explored (Smith, 1998) seem important for the present discussion. "Working too far behind the growing edge results in a lack of growth. Spending too much time working at the growing edge without respite results in stagnation (arrest of progress). Forcing beyond the growing edge (attempting increments which are too large) [can result] in a backlash (loss of previous growth). . . . Resumption of growth following a plateau usually reflects a fresh strategy or a new insight. This may appear as a sudden expansive leap in growth" (pp. 18-19). These principles may be of use in the selection of material to recommend to a client for reading or viewing. A thoughtfully selected book or film may well introduce the person in therapy to just that "fresh strategy" or "new insight" that would allow the next growth step.

A final consideration is the match between the type of literature, taken in the broad meaning of the word, and the proclivity of the person in therapy to thinking, feeling, or action. Just as different types of yoga are best prescribed for persons of thought, persons of emotion, and persons inclined toward action (Jnana Yoga, Bhakti Yoga, and Karma Yoga, respectively), different kinds of literature can serve different purposes. Some literature, primarily of the essay type, appeals primarily to thought. Some self-help books are of this kind. Other literature, *les belles letters*, including narrative fiction, poetry, and drama (including film), appeals to emotion, serving less to inform with facts than to inspire or offer the potential for insight by eliciting strong affect. Still other literature, including manuals of various sorts, encourages action through prescribed activity and behavioral practices. This category includes many other self-help books. Thus, we would do well to suggest literature that is best suited to the cognitive, affective, or cognitive inclination of the person in therapy.

To close, I suggest a caveat. To wit, just because I like it or benefitted from it does not mean that the person in therapy with me will, too!

~

NIETZSCHE'S TWO METAPHORS OF AUTHENTICITY

Citing evidence that early Gestalt therapy was influenced by Nietzsche's philosophy, I suggest that Beisser's "paradoxical theory of change" may be a derivative of Nietzsche's biological metaphor for authenticity. Furthermore, I suggest that the integration of Nietzsche's second metaphor for authenticity, that of the artist, would significantly enhance Beisser's theory.

Whether Arnold Beisser was influenced by reading Nietzsche, I do not know. That Gestalt therapy was so influenced is, however, apodictic. In his biography of Frederick Perls, Martin Shepard (1975) described his biographee as having had the benefit of a classical German education. Surely such an education would have included at least some attention to Nietzsche. "A lover of opera, of Mozart and Mahler, he could quote Heine and Rilke to his ladies and Goethe, Schopenhauer, and Nietzsche to his colleagues" (Shepard, 1975, p. 2). Direct evidence is provided by Perls himself. In his first book, *Ego, Hunger, and Aggression*, Perls (1947) alluded to Nietzsche. And, in *Gestalt Therapy Verbatim*, Perls gave credit to Nietzsche for "the idea of the incomplete person" (1969a, p. 27).

Perhaps the most commonly recognized debt that Perls owed to Nietzsche is in his paraphrasing of one of the latter's "Apophthegms and Interludes" from *Beyond Good and Evil* (Nietzsche, no year). Perls wrote as follows: "As Nietzsche said: 'Memory and Pride were fighting. Memory said,

From: *International Gestalt Journal*, 28(2), 25-30 (2005).

'It was like this' and Pride said, 'It couldn't have been like this' — And Memory gives in'" (1969a, p. 42). With only minor changes in the wording, Perls (1969b) also quoted this in his autobiography, *In and Out the Garbage Pail.* "As Nietzsche put it: Memory and Pride were fighting. Memory said 'It was like that,' and Pride said: 'It couldn't have been!' And Memory gave in"(1969b, no page). Compare these quotes from Perls with Nietzsche's apophthegm: "'I did that,' says my memory. 'I could not have done that,' says my pride, and remains inexorable. Eventually — the memory yields" (Nietzsche, no year, p. 73).

The influence of Nietzsche on Gestalt therapy is further suggested as we are told that Paul Goodman was conversant with Nietzsche's work, particularly in reference to art and religion (Stoehr, 1994, p. 157).

Having established the link between Nietzsche and Gestalt therapy, it seems highly likely that Perls, Goodman, and probably other early Gestalt therapists, *possibly* including Beisser were familiar with Nietzsche's two metaphors of authenticity. Such acquaintance could well be a factor in, if not a basis for Beisser's formulation of "The Paradoxical Theory of Change," or at least a readiness for Gestalt therapists to be amiable toward the theory. It is to these metaphors that I will now turn.

Through his meticulous analysis of Nietzsche's work, Jacob Golomb (1999) has identified two apparently contradictory models of authenticity. (Although Nietzsche did not use the term *authenticity* explicitly, Golomb makes a strong case that the term is appropriate in this context.) The first model derives from a biological metaphor, that of a plant actualizing the potential of its seed. To list a plain example, a sunflower seed contains the potential for a sunflower plant. Within an appropriately supportive environment of temperature, soil conditions, sunlight, and moisture, the potential of that seed may be actualized, the potential made actual in the form of the developed sunflower plant.

This potentiality is constituted both of possibility of what may be, and of limitation on what *could* be. The possibility is a fully developed sunflower in all its splendor; the limitation is that this seed may only become a sunflower, and never a rose, a violet, or an orchid. So in Nietzsche's first model, authenticity resides in making manifest an innate nature. It was to this view of authenticity that Nietzsche referred when he wrote of loving one's fate. "My formula for greatness in a human being is *amor fati*: that one wants nothing to be different . . . Not merely bear what is necessary, still less conceal it . . . but *love* it" (Nietzsche quoted from Golomb, 1999, p. 19).

Nietzsche's second model of authenticity, based on a metaphor of the artist, is that of creating oneself, shaping oneself through spontaneous choice. To be authentic in this model is to create freely. It is this model that is echoed by Nietzsche through the voice of Zarathustra: "This is my way; where is yours? — thus I answered those who asked me 'the way.' For the way — that does not exist" (Nietzsche quoted from Golomb, 1999, p. 15).

Nietzsche (1982) continued, expounding this metaphor and at the same time making it more concrete. "*One thing is needful.* 'Giving style' to one's character — a great and rare art" (ibid., p. 98). "In order to give style to one's character, one must recognize all of one's strengths and weaknesses, and then . . . comprehend them in an artistic plan until everything appears as art and reason and even weakness delights the eye" (ibid.). With words that invoke the image of the sculptor or the painter, Nietzsche continued as follows.

> Here a large mass of second nature has been added; there a piece of original nature has been removed: both by long practice and daily labor. Here the ugly which could not be removed is hidden; there it has been reinterpreted and made sublime . . . (Nietzsche, 1982, p. 99)

Keeping these two models (and metaphors) in mind, let us return to Gestalt therapy. Perls may well have had Nietzsche's biological metaphor in mind when he wrote as follows.

> Every individual, every plant, every animal has only one inborn goal — to actualize itself as it is. A rose is a rose is a rose. A rose is not intent to actualize itself as a kangaroo. An elephant is not intent to actualize itself as a bird. (Nietzsche, 1969a, p. 31)

Let us look further to what may be evidence of another connection between this biological metaphor and Gestalt therapy. Elsewhere I have suggested that the Gestalt approach is heavily imbued with a Dionysian world view (Smith, 1991). Of all of the writers who have participated in the explication of this world view (Nietzsche, Jung, Horney, Joseph Campbell, Sam Keen, Robert Pirsig, among them), Horney has most succinctly captured the Dionysian path as one of *surrender and drift.*[*]

---

[*] In order not to lose the present focus, I will resist taking the tangent that would explore the Dionysian world view in detail. I refer the interested reader to chapter four of *The Person of the Therapist* (Smith, 2003).

I suggest that it is just such surrender and drift that was implied by Arnold Beisser when he wrote that "... *change occurs when one becomes what he is, not when he tries to become what he is not*" (1970, p. 77 — italics in original). We might paraphrase Beisser as follows. "Change occurs when one *surrenders* to what he or she is, when one *drifts* with the flow of one's inner being rather than struggling against the current." Is this not congruent with the model of authenticity that derives from Nietzsche's biological metaphor? Is this not the commitment to which Nietzsche challenged us — *amor fati*?

As evident as the congruity between Beisser's (1970) paradoxical theory of change and Nietzsche's biological metaphor for authenticity is, Beisser does not to show affinity for Nietzsche's artist metaphor. This lack of affinity is particularly exposed as Beisser apparently shifted his level of discourse specifically to psychotherapy and sounded the tocsin against any "... coercive attempt by the individual or by another person to change him ..." (ibid., p. 77). In stating that the Gestalt therapist "believes change does not take place by 'trying,' coercion, or persuasion ..." (ibid.), he was speaking against the role of "changer" (ibid.) and was wishing to emphasize that change requires that "... one takes the time and effort to be what he is — to be fully invested in his current positions," that he "... abandons, at least for the moment, what he would like to become and attempts to be what he is" (ibid.). Herein Beisser shifted his paradoxical theory of change from the more general level of actualization of self to the more specific level of the parallel postures of the therapist and the person in therapy that are most promoting of change.

While Nietzsche, too, would surely take a stand against coercion, as we have seen, he is not averse to "long practice and daily labor" in the "rare art of giving style to one's character." Note that Nietzsche placed this personal work in the context of authenticity. Not only did he not mean a process of coercion, he did not mean fakery or the creation of falseness as an outcome. He challenged us, I believe, to something in addition to, and even loftier than acceptance of our innate nature, something more than the wisdom reflected in Beisser's paradoxical theory of change. *Nietzsche, himself, posed a paradoxical theory of change, wherein the paradox is internal to the theory, itself.*

The "tension between Nietzsche's two prescriptions for authentic life," to borrow a phrase from Golomb (1995, p. 120), may be resolved in Heidegger's ontological synthesis, which Golomb rephrased as follows. "Own your Being by *creating* your self and by *appropriating* your heritage. Return to your self and its historicality and accept them anxiously by overcoming the temptation to lose them in the distraction of everydayness" (ibid.). My view of this is that "in creating oneself one is manifesting the artistic mode of authenticity, whereas in appropriating one's heritage one is claiming one's innate nature, thereby honoring the actualization mode of authenticity" (Smith, 2003, p. 85).

In this view, we honor the *Umwelt* of physical and biological reality into which, Heidegger instructed us, we are *thrown*; we honor the *Eigenwelt* of choice and personal meaning; and we avoid falling into the *Mitwelt*, of absorption into the mass through ordinary routine and non-discernment of in-authenticity (Smith, 2003). Shifting to the idiom of Sartre, the challenge is to create ourselves through our choices within the limitations of the *facticité* of our heredity, history, and traditions (Golomb, 1995). And, as Sartre emphasized, this means not only accepting our freedom to choose, but the ineluctability of our making choices.

Beisser, we might say, focused on the appropriation of our heritage, the *facticité* of our being, when he articulated his paradoxical theory of change. I wish to suggest, even to warn, that the Gestalt therapist may be restricted by the purview of Beisser's paradoxical theory of change. Important as it is, this theory is, I believe, incomplete.

"So, to develop depth of personhood, one is well advised not only to actualize one's innate potentials, but to invoke the muses and rhapsodize on oneself, to create a singular self through a unique sequence of spontaneous choices" (Smith, 2003, p. 123).

~

GESTALT ANALOGIES

Appealing primarily to the reader's cognition, expository prose is vulnerable to reductionistic thinking. For this reason, more indirect forms of writing, metaphor in all its faces — kenning, parable, allegory, riddle — has often been preferred by teachers of wisdom. The *analogy* may be experienced as a form that is mid-way between exposition and metaphorical forms, thus giving invitation to blend intuition with thinking. Analogies are used in the present paper to explore the rich theory of the Gestalt approach in its relationship to the philosophical and theoretical systems from which it was created, thereby opening the reader to new levels of possible meaning.

Introduction

One of the most general misunderstandings of the Gestalt approach through the years has been that it is anti-intellectual and lacks well-developed theory. However, anyone who is conversant with the Gestalt literature is keenly aware of a large and compelling body of theory. Perhaps this misunderstanding was reinforced, or even spawned, through a misinterpretation of the now famous Perls quote, "Lose you mind and come to your senses." The Polsters (1973) put the issue in perspective by explaining that "theory and

From: *Norsk Gestalttidsskrift, II*(2), 54-59. (Published in a slightly modified version as Gestaltanalogier. Translated by Synnøve Jørstad) (2005).

knowledge remain suspect, not because of inherent worthlessness, but because of their historic isolation from action" (p. 3). *Nota bene*: It is when theory and knowledge are *isolated from action* that they are not held in high regard in the Gestalt approach. In the extreme, theory and knowledge in such isolation approaches Scholasticism. Completing their perspective, the Polsters stated that "without theoretical orientation, however, action is vulnerable to oversimplified and glib imitativeness — even mimicry — and to the use of the gimmick" (p. 3). Perls (1969), himself, took the position that "the more comprehensive the intellectual support is, the less wobbliness will be encountered in the higher, that is the superimposed levels" (p. 116). In the interest of furthering the intellectual understanding of the theory of the Gestalt approach, and thereby enhancing the intellectual support for this approach in praxis, I propose a study through analogy.

The Nature of an Analogy

Quoting Paracelsus, Sheldon Kopp (1971) wrote that a teacher of vision and truth would do well not to tell ". . . the naked truth. He should use images, allegories, figures of wonderous [sic] speech, or other hidden round about ways" (p. 19). For naked truth, expository prose bald and unadorned, wrote Kopp is liable to "computer-bank reduction" (p. 19). But, "a metaphor is defined as a way of speaking in which one thing is expressed in terms of another, whereby this bringing together throws new light on the character of what is being described" (p. 17). Kopp, although acknowledging that there are technical distinctions between metaphor, similes, and analogies, stated that as a basic way of knowing, and taken in the broad sense, metaphor denotes "any kind of comparison as a basis for the kind of illumination we call poetic" (p. 18). Thus, we may think of the analogy as a type of metaphor. Following Kopp, I suggest that knowing metaphorically (a metaphorical epistemology) does not depend entirely on thinking rationally (a rational epistemology), and not on checking sensory perceptions (an empirical epistemology), but on the "intuitive grasp of situations, in which we are open to the symbolic dimensions of experience, open to the multiple meanings that may all coexist, giving extra shades of meaning to each other" (p. 17).

Perhaps the power of the analogy derives from its lying somewhere between expository prose on the one hand and kenning, parable, and allegory on the other hand, but clinging more closely to the cognitive and not eliciting the affective as surely as do the latter. Perhaps, too, the analogy is akin to the riddle in that there may be a moment of recognition that does not always come immediately upon the reading. The analogy may invite a more or less delayed "aha!" as rational and intuitive processes commingle, synergize, and layers of meaning emerge.

The form that defines an analogy is A : B :: C : D, which is read, "A is to B as C is to D." Thus, an analogy is elegantly succinct, and yet through the form that defines it, carries not redundancy, but nuances that would require much elaboration if one were to spell out the full meaning. A reverberating cycle of meaning may be set up as knowing the relationship of the first and second terms of the analogy (A and B) points to the relationship of the third and fourth (C and D) and vice versa. Some analogies are strong, reflecting equivalence, while others are weaker, reflecting only similarity. Some are tight or precise, others loose or approximate. In some cases the analogy points out a parallel, in other cases the analogy calls attention to a contrast. Layers and aspects of meaning may emerge if one is patient and allows oneself to linger with the analogy, turning it over in one's mind, and perhaps then letting it incubate before addressing it again. Analogies are best read unhurriedly.

Gestalt Analogies

In "The Roots of Gestalt Therapy" (Smith, 1997), I suggested five major sources from which Perls and the other founders of this approach drew, namely Psychoanalysis, Reichian Character Analysis, Existential Philosophy, Gestalt Psychology, and Eastern Religion. It would be expected, therefore, that many analogies could be found between Gestalt therapy and each of these sources. Below, I offer, in turn, Gestalt analogies within each of these five areas. Let us, then, analogize, beginning with an example.

Psychoanalysis

As an example, consider "Top-dog" : Perls :: Harsh superego : Freud. This analogy states that the concept of "Top-dog" stands in relationship to Perls' theory as "Harsh superego" stands in relationship to Freud's. Here are two relationships that in some manner are similar. Pondering this analogy, one may recognize that the similarity is that both top-dog and harsh superego are used by their respective authors to refer to something that stands in opposition to free or unbridled expression of impulses. In a sense, the two concepts are alike. Further consideration, however, reveals that they are not exactly the same, only similar. Top-dog is named for a function (demand for suppression), whereas harsh superego is based on the name of one of the elements of Freud's structural model of the psyche (Id, Ego, Superego). Perls' term, descriptive of a manner of communicating, is more dynamic and implies an "Underdog" with whom to dialogue. So, an internal dialogue that is in or close to one's awareness is implied. For Freud, superego is a partly unconscious structure that interacts with a conscious ego and a mostly unconscious id. So, here, the implication is for an unconscious intra-psychic dynamic involving repression of an instinctual urge. The language, itself, used by each author reveals further difference. "Top-dog" is colloquial and invites quick reference to one's own experience. "Harsh superego," on the other hand, is technical and in order to be understood requires thoughtful reference to a vast and complex underlying theory.

These observations lead to a conclusion that the Gestalt approach, while having similarity to psychoanalysis, emphasizes function over structure, awareness over unconscious processes, values personal experience over theoretical knowledge, and is concerned with impulses themselves rather than underlying instincts. This conclusion comes from my work with the above analogy. At this point I will stop and invite the reader to explore this cognitive/intuitive process of comparing and contrasting the first and second halves of this analogy for him or herself.

For my above example I feel somewhat apologetic. To explain an analogy does violence to it, for it takes away some of the potential for the analogy to invite the "aha!" experience of the reader, him or herself. Certainly an explanation interferes with any delayed "aha!" that may only emerge after lingering with the analogy and turning it over and over in one's own mind. Like a riddle, an analogy may fall flat when its meaning is explained rather than discovered by the person him or herself. As the analogy is explained, it loses its metaphorical quality and becomes a "naked truth." Therefore, I want to invite readers to rely on a co-mingling of their own rational *and* intuitive processes, arriving on their created meanings of the following analogies through a poetic illumination.

Holism : Gestalt therapy :: Psyche : Psychoanalysis

Hunger instinct : Gestalt therapy :: Sexual instinct : Psychoanalysis

Contact boundary disturbance : Gestalt therapy :: Ego mechanism : Psychoanalysis

Awareness : Gestalt therapy :: Memories : Psychoanalysis

Awareness : Gestalt therapy :: Insight : Psychoanalysis

Awareness : Gestalt therapy :: Consciousness : Psychoanalysis

Explosive layer (expression) : Gestalt therapy :: Abreaction/Catharsis : Psychoanalysis

Self-image : Gestalt therapy :: Ego-ideal : Psychoanalysis

At-this-moment-unaware : Gestalt therapy :: Unconscious :
Psychoanalysis
Integration : Gestalt therapy :: Analysis : Psychoanalysis
Toxic introject : Gestalt therapy :: Harsh superego: Psychoanalysis
"Mind-fucking" : Perls :: Intellectualization : Freud
"Bull shit" : Perls :: Rationalization : Freud
"Elephant shit" : Perls :: Intellectualization : Freud
Impatience : Perls :: Positive cathexis : Freud
Dread : Perls :: Negative cathexis : Freud
Figure/ground : Gestalt therapy :: Conscious/unconscious :
Psychoanalysis
Dream as "Royal road to integration" : Perls :: Dream as "Royal road to the
unconscious" : Freud
Support and frustration : Perls :: Interpretation : Freud

Reichian Character Analysis

Impasse phenomenon : Perls :: Phase of the breakdown of secondary
narcissism : Reich
Chronic retroflection of action : Gestalt therapy :: Muscular armor :
Reichian therapy
Frustration : Perls :: Interpretation of character resistances : Reich
Development of self-support : Perls :: Immunization : Reich
Excitement : Gestalt therapy :: Charge : Bioenergetics
Self-support : Gestalt therapy :: Grounding : Bioenergetics
Expression : Gestalt therapy :: Discharge : Bioenergetics

Existential Philosophy

Self-actualization : Perls :: *Amor fati* : Nietzsche

"Chicken shit" : Perls :: Small talk : Heidegger
Self-in-environment : Perls :: Eigenwelt, Mitwelt, Umwelt : Heidegger
Self-in-environment : Perls :: Transcendent ego & facticité : Sartre
Pathological confluence : Perls :: Falling into Mitwelt : Heidegger
Pathological confluence : Perls :: Being-with-others : Sartre
"You are you and I am I . . ." : Perls :: Eigenwelt : Heidegger
"You are you and I am I . . ." : Perls :: Transcendence : Sartre
Eros : Perls :: Logos : Frankl

Gestalt Psychology

Unfinished business : Perls :: Uncompleted task : Zeigarnick
Healthy confluence : Perls :: Homonomy : Angyal

Eastern Religion

Awareness : Gestalt therapy :: Mindfulness : Zen
"As if" existence : Gestalt therapy :: Maya : Zen
Awareness continuum : Gestalt therapy :: Meditation : Zen
Paradoxical theory of change : Beisser :: Law of reversed effort : Watts

~

Projection in Depth

A perusal of the literature demonstrates that the concept of projection has enjoyed a prominent position in Gestalt therapy. Perls went so far as to declare that whatever one thinks one sees in the world or in another person is nothing but projection. Wishing neither to introject the notion that everything is projection, nor to dismiss the statement summarily, an in depth examination of the concept of projection is offered. Perls' early writing is examined and set in the context of Schopenhauer's philosophy, Freud's theory, and Bellak's model of levels of projection, with an overview of projective personality assessment. The solipsistic problem that Perls may have created with his declaration that everything is projection is addressed.

In the course of describing her work with Fritz Perls, Muriel Schiffman (1971), in *Gestalt Self-Therapy*, stated that he had made the pronouncement, "everything is projection" (ibid., p. 5). "In a little while I began to see the startling truth in Fritz's seemingly arbitrary statement," she added (ibid., pp. 5f.). If we take Perls' statement seriously, and do not dismiss it as mere hyperbole for shock value, then we must surely want to understand what he meant, a task that requires that we examine the concept of projection in some depth. Furthermore, consistent with Perls' pronouncement, it is notable that

From: *International Gestalt Journal*, 29(1), 101-128 (2006).

in the early Gestalt therapy literature projection was afforded a very prominent position.

The prominence of the concept of projection in the early canon of Gestalt therapy is apodictic. Note, for instance, that in his book, *Ego Hunger and Aggression*, Perls (1942/1992) devoted two chapters to projection. Again in the classic, *Gestalt Therapy* (Perls, Hefferline, & Goodman, 1951), projection was explored, both in Volume One and in Volume Two. In addition to this extensive handling of projection in his first two books, Perls addressed the concept in a number of early papers. These include a paper entitled "Theory and Technique of Personality Integration" (Perls, 1948/1975) and the paper, "Morality, Ego Boundary and Aggression" (Perls, 1955/1975). There is also a manuscript called "Psychiatry in a New Key" that Perls (1978) is believed to have started in the early 1950s and to have worked on for several years before it eventuated in a book, *The Gestalt Approach & Eye Witness to Therapy* (Perls, 1973). In this work, too, projection is given considerable importance.

Taken together — Perls' bold statement that everything is projection, and the prominence of projection in the early Gestalt literature — we have an over determined impetus for exploring projection in depth.

The World as Will and Idea: Schopenhauer

As a human penchant, the imposition of interpretations on ambiguous forms has been noted for centuries. For example, Leonardo da Vinci, in his *Introduction to the Painter*, wrote of the mark made on a wall from throwing a wet sponge, suggesting that "various experiences can be seen in such a blot, provided one wants to find them in it — human heads, various animals, battles, cliffs, seas, clouds or forests and other things" (Zubin, Eron, & Schumer, 1965, p. 167). He also mentioned the possibility of imagining words in the peal of a bell (ibid.). Such early references notwithstanding, a rich starting point for an in-depth examination of projection is the philosophy of Schopenhauer (Smith, 2002).

The *World as Will and Idea*, Schopenhauer's major work, was published in 1818. Schopenhauer began the division entitled *The World as Idea* with a dramatic declaration that served as a summary of his entire discourse: "The world is my idea." Continuing, he wrote:

> This is a truth which holds good for everything that lives and knows, though man alone can bring it into reflective and abstract consciousness. If he really does this, he has attained to philosophical wisdom. It then becomes clear and certain

to him that what he knows is not a sun and an earth, but only an eye that sees a sun, a hand that feels an earth; that the world which surrounds him is there only as idea, i.e., only in relation to something else, the consciousness, which is himself. (Schopenhauer, 1818/1928, p. 3)

To declare that the world is my idea meant to Schopenhauer that whatever is perceived is not something out there, but is a change in the body of the perceiver which is an effect of a thing out there. Here is the critical point. In ordinary causal perception, the object out there causes a change in a sense organ and then by means of a reverse process this effect is referred back to its cause. This second stage of the perceptual process imparts meaning to the perceived object. Usually, this second stage is unconscious (Jones, 1952). Those who have not, as Schopenhauer so quaintly put it, "attained to philosophical wisdom" do not realize the dual-stage process of perception. The second stage, being unconscious, is not taken into consideration and *perceived attributes are erroneously believed to be intrinsic to the thing itself.*

It follows, therefore, that in perceiving an object in the environment, one knows only that there is an object there, but not what that object is in and of itself. Perception may be veridical only in so far as it identifies the presence of an object, but not veridical as far as any conclusions as to the nature of that object.[*]

Schopenhauer expressed his view strongly, and with adamantine tone.

No truth therefore is more certain, more independent of all others, and less in need of proof than this, that all that exists for knowledge, and therefore this whole world, is only object in relation to subject, perception of a perceiver, in a word, idea. (1818/1928, p. 3)

The "world as idea" has two fundamental, necessary and inseparable parts. The first is object, the forms of which are space and time. The second part is subject, which, in contrast, is present, entire and undivided in every percipient thing and therefore not in space and time.

Ideas, themselves, are of two types, ideas of perception and abstract ideas. Abstract ideas are concepts, the capacity for which is "reason." It is in

---

[*] There are, of course, philosophers who think that even the perception of objects is an interpretation.

reasoning or the production of concepts, Schopenhauer believed, that humans set themselves apart from the non-human animals. The former type of ideas, ideas of perception, are found in all animals, human and non-human.

In his thinking, Schopenhauer did not mean to imply that the subject and object are in a causal relationship.

> It is needful to guard against the grave error of supposing that because perception arises through the knowledge of causality, the relation of subject and object is that of cause and effect. For this relation subsists only between the immediate objects known indirectly, thus always between objects alone. (Schopenhauer, 1818/1928, pp. 14f.).

A problem in Schopenhauer's position, which he fails to address adequately, is that of illusory perception. He admits that illusion may at moments take the place of the real in the idea of perception. But, in his exuberance to show that in the sphere of abstract thought error may reign forever, he fails to pursue illusion in perception. So, he leaves us knowing only that illusion may occur.

With respect to "rational knowledge," Schopenhauer had this to say:

> Speaking generally, to know rationally (wissen) means to have in the power of the mind, and capable of being reproduced at will, such judgments as have their sufficient ground of knowledge in something outside themselves, i.e., are true. Thus only abstract cognition is rational knowledge (Wissen), which is therefore the result of reason . . . . Rational knowledge (Wissen) is therefore abstract consciousness, the permanent possession in concepts of the reason, of what has become known in another way. (Schopenhauer,1818/1928, pp. 38f.)

Reason is necessary for quick conclusions, bold actions, and rapid and sure comprehension, but it may hinder intuitive, direct discovery.

Schopenhauer wrote of the body as being the framework from which all else is perceived.

> In fact, the meaning for which we seek of that world which is present to us only as our idea, or the transition from the world as mere idea of the knowing subject to whatever it may be besides this, would never be found if the investigator

himself were nothing more than the pure knowing subject (a winged cherub without a body). But he is himself rooted in that world; he finds himself in it as an *individual*, that is to say, his knowledge, which is the necessary supporter of the whole world as idea, is yet always given through the medium of a body, whose affections are, as we have shown, the starting-point for the understanding in the perception of the world.Schopenhauer,1818/1928, p. 63 — italics in original)

Every act of will is, of course, a movement of the body and the body therefore can be called the objectivity of the will.

Schopenhauer offered a summary of the will and the idea as follows:

I here conclude the second principal division of my exposition, in the hope that, so far as is possible in the case of an entirely new thought, which cannot be quite free from traces of the individuality in which it originated, I have succeeded in conveying to the reader the complete certainty that this world in which we live and have our being is in its whole nature through and through *will*, and at the same time through and through *idea*: That this idea, as such, already presupposes a form, object and subject, is therefore relative; and if we ask what remains if we take away this form, and all those forms which are subordinate to it, and which express the principle of sufficient reason, the answer must be that as something 'toto genere' different from idea this can be nothing but will, which is thus properly the thing-in-itself. Everyone finds that he himself is this will, in which the real nature of the world consists, and he also finds that he is the knowing subject, whose idea the whole world is, the world which exists only in relation to his consciousness, as its necessary supporter. (Schopenhauer,1818/1928, pp. 130f. — italics in original)

The individual's body is an object among objects, and the one endeavor of knowledge is to find out the relationships among these objects. Only through these relationships with the body does an object gain significance. That is, only insofar as an object is related to one's body, one's will, is it of interest. In this view, Schopenhauer implies a selective perception, a perception which is selective with respect to relation to oneself. What one perceives, then, what one selectively attends to reveals something of oneself. It tells that one is interested and is therefore related to that object.

Schopenhauer also seemed very much aware of the influence of one's past on one's current behavior. "Now, objective perception acts with regard to what is remembered just as it would in what is present, if we let it have influence over us, if we surrendered ourselves to it free from will" (ibid., p. 165). This seems consistent with projection in its broad sense as Freud came to use the term.

Roots in Psychoanalysis: Freud

Did Freud know of Schopenhauer's work? Certainly so. In 1914 Freud added a footnote to *The Interpretation of Dreams*, which was published in 1899, but bore the publication date of 1900. "Ferenczi (1912) has proposed an ingenious 'over-interpretation' of the Oedipus myth, based on a passage in one of Schopenhauer's letters" (Freud, 1900 / 1961, p. 263). Later, in the same volume, Freud quoted Silberer who reported a reverie in which Silberer compared the views of Kant and Schopenhauer concerning time. Somewhat later, in 1925, Freud presented an extract from Schopenhauer's *The World as Will and Idea* in an appendix to "The Resistances to Psychoanalysis" (Rothgeb, 1973).

Henri Ellenberger stated that "the similarities between certain essential teachings of Schopenhauer and Freud have been shown by Cassirer, Scheler, and particularly by Thomas Mann"(1970, p. 209). "Thomas Mann said that psychoanalytic concepts were Schopenhauer's ideas 'translated from metaphysics into psychology'"(ibid., p. 542). Referring to Schopenhauer and Nietzsche, Ellenberger wrote "there cannot be the slightest doubt that Freud's thought echoed theirs" (ibid., p. 542). Additionally, we are told by Ronald Lehrer that according to minutes of the Vienna Psychoanalytic Society, Alfred Adler had " . . . once tried to establish a direct line from Schopenhauer, through Marx and Mach to Freud" (1999a, p. 230).

How early in his life did Freud become aware of Schopenhauer's philosophy? Early in his career, as is well known, Freud came under the influence of Joseph Breuer, and in the mid-1890's they published accounts of their work together. Lehrer wrote that

> It is worth noting that in addition to being Freud's friend, Paneth also knew Breuer. He may even have been the person who introduced Freud to Breuer. Breuer, like Paneth . . . probably had at least some general knowledge of aspects of Nietzsche's philosophy and psychology. (He certainly ap-

pears to have been familiar, as was Paneth, with Schopenhauer.) (Lehrer, 1999b, p. 185)

This is suggestive, at least, that Freud was aware of Schopenhauer's works quite early. In contrast to this suggestion, however, it was stated by Lancelot Whyte that "Freud explained that he avoided reading Schopenhauer and Nietzsche until late in life," quoting Freud as having written, "I was less concerned with priority than with preserving my impartiality" (Whyte, 1962, p. 160).

It is established, then, that Freud was familiar with Schopenhauer's work, and that he was probably influenced by it. How early this influence began and the extent of it may be debated. Regardless of the latter, I find it interesting to compare the two men's way of dealing with the phenomenon which came to be called projection. For, as stated by Christopher Young and Andrew Brook, "there is no definitive way to settle the question of whether Freud read Schopenhauer before, say, 1892 or not, but such evidence as there is makes us wonder" (1994, p. 116).

The use of the word "projected" can be found in a 1894 paper by Freud, "The Justification for Detaching from Neurasthenia a Particular Syndrome: The Anxiety Neurosis."

> The psyche develops the affect of anxiety when it feels itself incapable of dealing (by an adequate reaction) with a task (danger) approaching it externally; it develops the neurosis of anxiety when it feels itself unequal to the task of mastering (sexual) excitation arising endogenously. That is to say, *it acts as if it had projected this excitation into the outer world.* (Freud, 1895 / 1963a, p. 114 — italics in original)

The emphasis in the final line was indicated by Freud, himself, in his paper. The important point to note here is that originally Freud used the term "projected" in a strictly pathological sense. The dynamic that he described involved a distortion of reality, that of regarding an endogenous excitation as if it were an exogenous threat of real danger.

In an 1896 paper, "Further Remarks on the Defense NeuroPsychoses," Freud introduced "projection" as an unconscious mechanism of defense, more specifically as a manner of repressing an intolerable idea which is in painful opposition to the patient's ego. Here is how he explained projection at that time:

> It only remains for me now to turn to account what has been learned from this case of paranoia in a comparison between

paranoia and the obsessional neurosis. In each of them repression has proved to be the nucleus of the psychical mechanism, and in each of them the repressed content is a sexual
experience in childhood. . . . Part of the symptoms again
originate in a primary defence — namely, all the delusions of
distrust, suspicion and persecution by others. In the obsessional neurosis the initial self-reproach has undergone repression by the formation of the primary symptom: self-distrust . . . . In paranoia the reproach is repressed in a manner
which may be described as *projection*; by the defence-symptom *of distrust directed against others* being erected; in this
way recognition of the reproach is withheld. (Freud,
1896/1963b, p. 172 — italics in original)

Continuing to trace the evolution of the concept, we can read of a
broadened use of the term projection in Freud's 1913 book, *Totem and Taboo*:

In the case we have been dealing with, projection served the
purpose of dealing with an emotional conflict; and it is employed in the same way in a large number of psychical situations that lead to projection. But projection was not created
for the purpose of defense; it also occurs where there is no
conflict. The projection outwards of internal perceptions is
a primitive mechanism, to which, for instance, our sense
perceptions are subject, and which therefore normally plays
a very large part in determining the form taken by our external world. . . . internal perceptions of emotional and intellective process can be projected outwards in the same way as
sense perceptions; they are thus employed for building up
the external world, though they should by rights remain part
of the internal world. (Freud, 1913/1950, p. 64)

We can see in Freud's writing the evolution of the concept of "projection" from a metaphorical descriptor of a process for dealing with an
intra-psychic threat in the dynamics of anxiety neurosis (1895), to a metaphorically-derived concept of an ego defense mechanism in paranoia (1896),
to a metaphorically-derived general mechanism involved in creating one's
experience of the external world (1913). In the first and second steps of this
evolution, Freud recognized projection only in pathological context, only in
the context of intra-psychic conflict. In the first, it is the unacceptable feeling

of sexual excitation that is projected. In the second, it is the thought of self-reproach. Arriving at the third step in the evolution of his thought, Freud recognized projection as operating not only in the realm of intra-psychic conflict but in the conflict-free realm as well. Projection thus became in Freud's view a general psychological mechanism that occurs both within and without the realm of psychopathology.

In toto, Freud's evolving position on projection offers a finer grain analysis than does Schopenhauer's view of the world as will and idea. I suggest, however, that the view offered by Schopenhauer nevertheless contributes a valuable perspective.

Schopenhauer suggested a broad perspective, emphasizing the great extent to which we project, and thereby the extent to which we create our own worlds. At the same time, he emphasized the influence of memory and therein emphasized selective perception. Freud's work with these two themes, creation of our own worlds and selective perception, does in no way replace or vitiate Schopenhauer's, but again, offers a somewhat different perspective at the level of a more fine grained analysis. For example, *transference*, a cornerstone of psychoanalysis, is a specific case of memory influencing current interpersonal perception. *Primal repression*, which Freud distinguished from *repression proper*, is at once an alternative term and an explanatory construct for at least one category of selective perception.

Levels of Projection: Bellak

The theory that evolved with Freud suggests an organizing schema for types of projection, although Freud did not, himself, make such a schema explicit. However, Hall and Lindzey (1970), in their discussion of Henry Murray (best remembered for his development of the Thematic Apperception Test in collaboration with Christiana Morgan), discussed his distinction between *complementary projection* and *supplementary projection*. The former term refers to the tendency to perceive or understand one's environment in such a manner as to make it congruent with or to justify one's needs, affects, and impulses. Thus, one's perceptions and understanding *complement* one's needs, feelings, and action tendencies. *Supplementary projection*, in contrast, refers to the case in which one endows objects or persons with attributes that one possesses, but that are personally unacceptable. Complementary projection is concerned, then, with the conflict-free sphere of the ego while supplementary projection is of the sphere of intra-psychic conflict, the realm of psychopathology. Murray clearly drew the distinction between non-pathological projection and pathological projection.

Leopold Bellak (1950), too, made the schema suggested by Freud's work explicit, expanding and refining it. While introducing *apperceptive distortion* as a more general term to replace projection, Bellak retained the term *projection* for two specific types of the more general process. Taking his lead, again from Freud, Bellak noted that Freud had suggested in *Totem and Taboo* that what we project is a product of co-existing perception and memory. Bellak summarized Freud's assumption as being that unconscious memories of percepts influence the perception of contemporary stimuli. In proposing the term *apperception*, Bellak wrote that he liked the definition of the term that had been suggested by C. P. Herbart. Quoting Herbart, Bellak wrote that *apperception* is "the process by which new experience is assimilated to and transformed by the residuum of past experience of any individual to form a new whole. The residuum of past experience is called apperceptive mass" (*ibid.*, p. 11). Defining apperception as a dynamically meaningful interpretation of a perception, and adding that we all distort apperceptively, the distortions differing only in degree, Bellak presented his schema of "Forms of Apperceptive Distortion."

Bellak suggested reserving the term projection for the greatest degrees of apperceptive distortion, explaining such "true projection" as follows.

> We are dealing not only with an ascription of feelings and sentiments which remain unconscious, in the service of defense, but which are unacceptable to the ego and are therefore ascribed to objects of the outside world . . . they *cannot be made conscious* except by special prolonged therapeutic techniques. (Bellak, 1950, p. 13 — italics in original)

From this description of *projection*, Bellak (1950) differentiated a subtype that he termed *inverted projection*. Inverted projection, in keeping with the psychoanalytic theory of paranoia, involves a process of *reaction formation* in which the impulse that is unacceptable to the ego is converted into the opposite. The new impulse is then ascribed to the outside world. Projection, with or without reaction formation, constitutes the first level of apperceptive distortion.

The second level of apperceptive distortion, *simple projection*, can be understood as associative distortion through a transfer of learning, or in more complex situations, the influence of previous images on present ones. What has been learned in one situation may become an expectation that is brought to bear on a new situation, thus giving rise to a distorted perception of the new situation. With such distorted perception, one may experience in the new situation the affect that was aroused in the original situation. The distortion may expose itself as patently subjective or even absurd. *Simple projection* is less rigidly adhered to and less frequently employed than *projection*, and is more easily brought into awareness than is the latter. It is not necessarily of clinical significance, as it is certainly of frequent everyday occurrence.

Bellak's (1950) schema continued with what he termed *sensitization*. The hallmark of sensitization is the overly sensitive perception of existing stimuli. Instead of the creation of an objectively nonexistent percept, in sensitization there is a consensually agreed upon stimulus, but the perception of that stimulus is out of proportion to the stimulus, the reaction being overblown or extreme. Sensitization is akin to *selective vigilance*, a topic of research in perceptual psychology that at one time was very popular. Bellak explained this level of apperceptive distortion as follows: "There is sensitization of awareness (coexistent with unawareness of the process itself and of the existence of the trait within oneself, as inherent in any defensive mechanism) owing to one's own unconsciously operating selectivity and apperceptive distortion" (1950, pp. 16f.). "Sensitization merely means that an object that fits a preformed pattern is more easily perceived than one that does not fit the preformed pattern" (*ibid.*, p. 15).

The next level of Bellak's (1950) schema is *externalization*, at which there is a slightly repressed pattern of images that have an organizing effect on one's perception, and that one can recognize relatively easily.

Finally, in order to anchor his schema, Bellak offered a fifth level, that of *purely cognitive perception.*

> Pure perception is the hypothetical process against which we measure apperceptive distortion of a subjective type, or it is the subjective operationally defined agreement on the meaning of a stimulus with which other interpretations are compared. (Bellak, 1950, p. 17)

Recognizing that the term *apperceptive distortion* is not widely found in the literature and therefore lacks in ease of recognition, I suggest a re-labeling of Bellak's model as one of *projection*. Additionally, I suggest for the sake of conceptual clarity that his category of *projection*, with its sub-category of *inverted projection*, be divided into two categories labeled *pathological projection* and *inverted pathological projection*, respectively. By so doing we can recognize immediately that both of these newly named categories are pathological.

There is a further advantage, as well. Now arranged as follows — *Cognitive Perception, Externalization, Sensitization, Simple Projection, Pathological Projection,* and *Inverted Pathological Projection* — a hierarchical model is created that reflects an *increasing lack of awareness* and *increasing distortion of reality.* This is to say, that as one moves from the beginning to the end of the above list of categories of projection, one is defining processes that reflect less and less awareness on the part of the person employing them, and at the same time, an increasing degree of distortion of the perceived reality.

I submit that Bellak's model, with the minor revisions that I have suggested, provides us with a pragmatic template for a fine-grain analysis of the phenomenon of projection, one that may clarify otherwise clouded understanding of the phenomenon by inviting us to a more precise terminology. By differentiating these six levels, we may gain an invaluable perspective on a given instance of projection, seeing it in relation to the full spectrum of the phenomenon.

Lawrence Abt has suggested several intriguing ideas that can augment our understanding of the above schema. Among them is the following:

> The more structured the stimulus field, the more dependent
> behavior usually is upon the operation of the external factors
> in perception; and, conversely, the greater the vagueness and
> ambiguity of the stimulus field, the greater the opportunity
> for and need of internal factors in perception to operate.
> (Abt, 1950, p. 50)

By "external factors in perception" Abt was referring to "the so-called autochthonous determinants of Gestalt psychology" (*ibid.*, p. 50) that help the individual to organize her or his perceptual world. His latter phrase begs for explication. Allow me to quote from "The Roots of Gestalt Therapy" (Smith, 1976).

> Gestalt psychology deals with "wholes" and the basic data are
> "phenomena." Many of the properties of the whole are
> "emergent," inherent in no single part, but perceived when
> the parts come together. Thus, Gestalt psychology often is
> concerned with "fields" (a dynamic system or whole in which
> a change in any part affects the entire system). Organization
> of the field is in terms of "figure" and "ground." A "good
> form" persists and tends to recur. A "strong form" coheres
> and resists disintegration through analysis or fusion with
> other forms. A "closed form" is both good and strong,
> whereas an "open form" tends toward "closure" by complet-
> ing itself as a good form. Organizations are "stable"; once
> formed they tend to persist or to recur with reinstatement of
> the same situation or the recurrence of a part of that organi-
> zation. "Adjacent" units (in time or in space) and units which

are "similar" in quality tend to combine. Organization tends toward "meaningful objects." Organized object forms tend to be preserved even as stimulus conditions change ("object constancy"). Organization, form, and object character usually depend on "relations of parts, not on the particular characteristics of the parts themselves" (Boring, 1950). The general guiding principle in perception is the "Law of Pragnanz," or the goal-directed tendency to restore cognitive equilibrium after a disequilibrium has occurred in the perceptual field. That is, there is an intention toward a good Gestalt. The "Law of Pragnanz" is served by three closely related processes, according to Wulf: "leveling," or changing the field organization in the direction of symmetry and good distribution; "sharpening," or accentuating of the essential figural elements; and "normalizing," or making the figure clear and simple. (Wolman, 1960) (Smith, 1976, pp. 25f.)

Further implications drawn from discussions by Apt (1950) and Bellak (1950) are that perception is an active, selective process of organization, and the more that such organization is aided by external factors of perception, the more consensual it is likely to be. But, as the ambiguity of the stimulus increases, the perceiving person is invited increasingly to use her or his internal frames of reference. Seen from another perspective, the greater the need of the individual to distort apperceptively, the more pervasive will be such distortion, even in relatively structured perceptual situations.

Projective Methods, Projective Techniques: Frank

Any in-depth exploration of projection would be incomplete without due consideration of projective testing. Let us, then, turn briefly to such consideration, keeping in mind the theoretical context proposed by Apt (1950) and Bellak (1950).

In a now classic article, "Projective Methods for the Study of Personality," published in 1939, Lawrence K. Frank voiced concern about the limitations of the use of group norms and laws in the understanding of the individual. In his words,

Culture provides the socially sanctioned patterns of action, speech, and belief that make group life what we observe; but each individual in that group is a personality who observes those social requirements and uses those patterns idiomatically, with a peculiar personal inflection, accent, emphasis, and intention. (Frank, 1939/1965, p. 3)

As Frank further explained,

What we can observe, then, is the dual process of socialization, involving sufficient conformity in outer conduct to permit participation in the common social world, and *individuation*, involving the progressive establishment of a private world of highly idiosyncratic meaning, significances, and feelings that are more real and compelling than the cultural and physical world. (Frank, 1939/1965, p. 3)

In addition to the concern that paper-and-pencil tests miss the individual's "private world of highly idiosyncratic meaning, significances, and feelings," some clinicians expressed a methodological concern. A major problem that was identified with paper-and-pencil inventories was the contamination of scores by the factor of social desirability. (This issue has been addressed in the construction of many of the paper-and-pencil inventories currently in use.) So it was that some clinicians reasoned that projective techniques, by virtue of their ambiguous nature, held greater promise for ideographic assessment and for tapping into the deeper levels of personality that subjects would not (because of social desirability concerns) or could not (because of repression) reveal. This reasoning was reflected in the publications of Lawrence Frank and Henry Murray. In 1938, in a privately circulated memorandum, Frank first used the term *projective methods*. It was in this same year that Henry Murray introduced the term *projective tests* (Rabin, 1981).

Projective testing is based on the critical assumption that a person is consistent in terms of her or his projection. That is, what is projected in one situation is what is projected in another. Therefore, the projective test is regarded as a *microcosm* of the testee's *macrocosm*. The projections made manifest in and through the testing situation are regarded as the projections that the testee is inclined to in her or his world at large.

The projective instrument, itself, in order to be a good test, must consist of a standardized, ambiguous stimulus that is pregnant with possibilities. By definition, in order to constitute a test, the materials must be standardized. Also, standardization of the stimulus materials is essential for the accumulation of clinical norms against which a given person's responses can be judged.[*] It is the ambiguity of the stimulus materials that issues strong invitation for projection. And, the more involving the task and materials, without critical loss of ambiguity, the more inviting is the task of an increased number of responses.

Reflecting these criteria — standardized, ambiguous stimulus, pregnant with possibilities — a very large number of projective tests has been developed. I will mention, here, several formats with an example of each: Inkblot perception (Rorschach), projective drawings (House-Tree-Person), reproducing and symbolization of geometric forms (Bender Visual-Motor Gestalt Test), selection and arrangement of colored geometric pieces (Lowenfeld Mosaic Test) or colored symbol objects (Kahn Test of Symbol Arrangement), sentence completion (Rotter Incomplete Sentences Blank), story telling techniques (Thematic Apperception Test by Morgan and Murray), and word association (Rapaport, Gill, and Schafer Word List).

In order to emphasize the great number of published projective tests, allow me to add that I know of at least six inkblot tests, eight drawing tests, nine sentence completion tests (in English), and twenty thematic tests. This is but a fraction of the projective tests that have been published or otherwise standardized in terms of directions and materials. Surely, their number is a reflection of the degree of interest in projection.

To conclude this discussion of projective testing, an overview of the rationale for interpretation may be useful. In interpreting the projective material that has been generated by the testee, the clinician must first make careful phenomenological observations of that material. It is these phenomenological observations that are then individually interpreted, generating hypothesis as to meaning. The greater the degree of converging lines of evidence for each hypothesis within and between projective instruments, the greater the certainty that the clinician may have in her or his interpretation.

Certainty is lost as we shift from the observed phenomena to theoretical interpretations based on increasing steps of inference. Therefore, the deeper (more inferential) the interpretation, the more lines of converging evidence we require in order to feel secure with that interpretation. Otherwise stated, certainty of an interpretation is an inverse function of the depth of the interpretation (depth being understood as the number of steps of inference) as well as a direct function of the degree of converging lines of

---

[*] Note that this is a move away from a purely idiomatic approach and a partial concession to the nomothetic.

evidence for that interpretation. Thus, the clinician may come to discover how and what the testee has projected.

Everything Is Projection: Perls — Redux and Explication

Projection has enjoyed a central place in Gestalt theory from the time that Perls' work emerged from classical psychoanalysis. Let us look chronologically to his early writing, then, for his limning of projection.

As mentioned above, in his first book, *Ego, Hunger, and Aggression*, Perls devoted two chapters to projection. It is of note that in the "Introduction to the 1969 Random House Edition" he himself wrote that this book "represents the transition from orthodox psychoanalysis to the Gestalt approach" (1942/1992, p. xv). Near the beginning of his chapter, "Projection," Perls wrote as follows:

> There exists a predifferent stage for which, to my knowledge, no name has yet been coined. One often observes a baby throwing its doll out of a pram. The doll stands for the child itself: "I want to be where the doll is." This emotional (exmovere) stage differentiates later into *expression* and *projection*. A healthy mental metabolism requires development in the direction of expression and not projection. The *healthy character expresses* his emotions and ideas, the *paranoid character projects* them. (Perls, 1942/1992, p. 185)

Clearly, at this point in his thinking, Perls saw projection as a pathological process in contrast to the healthy process of expression. Continuing, Perls identified projection as "essentially an unconscious phenomenon" in which the person "cannot satisfactorily distinguish between the inside and outside world" (ibid.). This latter point concerning the clouding of clear awareness was most likely what he was referring to when he wrote in a 1948 paper entitled "Theory and Technique of Personality Integration" that "in the projection mechanism, desensitization is apparent . . . ." (Perls, 1948/1975, p. 66). Refusing to identify with those projected parts of his own personality, the person visualizes them as being in the outside world, ". . . outside the Ego boundaries and reacts accordingly with aggression" (Perls, 1942/1992, p. 186). Starkly stated, "projections are, in the strictest sense, hallucinations" (ibid., p. 190).

Perls pointed out that "not always is it the outside world ... which serves as a screen for projections; they can also take place *within the personality*" (ibid., p. 187 — italics in original). A stern conscience may be an example. Not simply the result of introjection, such a conscience may reflect the projection of aggression (reproach) onto the conscience. Projection could also be focused on a body part. In addition, Perls noted that rather than expressing an emotion within an actual situation, a memory may be produced whereby that emotion may be projected into the past.

At this early point, Perls discussed projection of guilt generally, and specifically sexual (love) impulses, aggression, and in the case of God, omnipotent wishes. In his chapter on "The Assimilation of Projections," Perls expanded his discussion of projection to *transference* in psychoanalysis.

> The patient often sees something in the analyst which bears a resemblance to important persons of his childhood, but seldom is the image picture of the analyst identical with the original image . . . Every analyst has experienced that the "transferred" image changes in the course of the analysis, and that now this and then that feature of the image comes to the foreground." (Perls, 1942/1992, p. 289)

In addition to his scholarly exposition on projection, Perls included a chapter in *Ego, Hunger, and Aggression* titled "Reality" in which he examined in detail what he termed the "interdependency of the objective and subjective worlds" (*ibid.*, p. 35). Therein, using the example of a farmer, a pilot, a painter, an agronomist, a merchant, and a couple of lovers viewing a cornfield, he showed how the meaning of that common visual stimulus was different for each person. Based on their respective needs and interests, the farmer saw an opportunity to make a living, the pilot a safe landing place, the painter a subject for the canvas, the agronomist a source for scientific data, the merchant a means of making money, and the lovers a private place to be together. Not calling this projection, Perls, nonetheless, acknowledged in this example the selectivity and subjectivity of perception based on personal needs and interests. He did so again in his paper "Theory and Technique of Personality Integration," stating,

> . . . reality *per se* does not exist for the human being . . . . Reality is determined by the individual's specific interests and needs . . . . Whatever is the organism's foremost need makes reality appear as it does. It makes such objects stand out as figures which correspond to diverse needs. It evokes our interest, attention, cathexis or whatever you choose to call it. (Perls, 1948/1975, p. 51)

Also, in this paper, Perls addressed a crucial issue that he identified with the following query. "How is it that some part of a personality which should be experienced as belonging to the personal structure is disowned and treated as belonging to the outside world?" (ibid., p. 64). The answer he gave derives from the childhood state of confluence with the environment. Having not yet developed contact functions fully, the child is not aware of boundaries between self and others, between subject and object, between projection and expression. Thus:

> If the state of confluence does not develop into the ability to make contact, or if by later de-sensitization the boundary is breached, then the infantile projection mechanism remains. Self-expression does not develop, as it presupposes the recognition *and* manipulation of the boundary. With this lack of adequate self-expression, an emotion will not be expressed and disposed of by emotional discharge, but it will be projected and remain in emotional connection with the personality. (Perls, 1948/1975, p. 51 — italics in original)

Perls made a connection between certain projected tendencies and the emotions that may ensue. For instance, he suggested the nexus of projected tendencies to accept and greed, projected tendencies to reject and fear. The paranoid person is connected to her or his persecutor through hate, the religious person to her or his deity through awe.

Perls astutely recognized the relationship between language and projection. The use of passive language, such as "It *occurred* to me," or "I was *struck* by a thought," to paraphrase two of his examples, reflects a projection of initiative and responsibility. In such cases, agency is disowned and attributed elsewhere, often to a vague and ultimately elusive driving force.

In Volume I of *Gestalt Therapy* (Perls et al., 1951), projection is written of as "... putting your own attitude into the other person and then saying that this person *makes* you feel thus and so" (ibid., p. 101 — italics in original). Expanding this statement into fullness, the authors proposed the following.

> A projection is a trait, attitude, feeling, or bit of behavior which actually belongs to your own personality but is not experienced as such; instead, it is attributed to objects or persons in the environment and then experienced as directed *toward* you by them instead of the other way around. (Perls et al., 1951, p. 211 — italics in original)

A careful reading of the above statement will suggest an epistemological problem. Can we accept the phrase "behavior which actually belongs to your personality" at face value? Or must we ask who the authority is who can declare with certainty what *actually* belongs to your personality? Intriguing as the latter question is, it would no doubt lead us into a lengthy philosophical discussion that would take us away from the intended thrust of the present paper. Therefore, I will be content with merely raising the question.

In a manner characteristic of, if not peculiar to *Gestalt Therapy*, the authors offered a compelling explication of the dynamics of:

> This mechanism . . . functions to interrupt mounting excitement of a kind and degree with which the person cannot cope. It seems to require the following: (1) that you be aware of the nature of the impulse involved; but (2) that you interrupt the aggressive approach to the environment which would be necessary for its adequate expression; with the result (3) that you exclude it from the outgoing activities of your "I"; nevertheless, since you are aware that it *does* exist, then (4) it *must* come from outside — notably from a person or persons "in" your environment; and (5) it seems forcibly directed toward you because your "I," without realizing it, is forcibly interrupting your own outwardly directed impulse. (Perls et al., 1951, p.211 — italics in original)

Importantly, Perls et al. take the position that projection is pathological only when inappropriate and chronic and is ". . . useful and healthy when employed temporarily in particular circumstances" (ibid., p. 212). They suggest as an example feeling oneself into a future situation as one plans for it or anticipates it, and then integrates oneself with the projection as one follows through. Or, in sympathy one may feel oneself into the other person, solving one's own problem by solving the other person's. And, artists may alleviate problems by projecting into their work. What makes projection unhealthy ". . . is the structural fixing on some impossible or non-existent object, the loss of awareness, the existence of isolated confluences, and the consequent blocking of integration" (ibid.).

I find the discussion of projection in *Gestalt Therapy* to be impressive. It seems carefully thought out, and although not exhaustive, quite extensive. To explore many of the ramifications presented would take us unnecessarily beyond the ambit of the present paper, so I will suggest only that the interested reader consult that work.

In his paper, "Morality, Ego Boundary and Aggression," Perls (1955/1975) tackled the deconstruction of moral codes. In so doing, as is reflected in the title of his paper, he set out to demonstrate the link between morality and aggression. Although this is the major thrust of his exposition, that is not what is most germane to our focus. However, the role of projection in the construction of a moral code is. In summary,

> Good and bad are responses of the organism. But the label "good" or "bad" is then unfortunately projected onto the stimulus; then, isolated, torn out of context, these labels are organized into codes of conduct, systems of morals, often legalized, and connected with religious cosmologies . . . . . instead of owning up to our experience as ours we project them and throw the responsibility for our own responses onto the stimulus. (ibid., pp. 29f.)

It is, then, that I may say "You are good!" in response to your doing something that I feel good about, something that I like. Conversely, if you do something in response to which I feel bad, something that I do not like, I may say "You are bad!" Having projected my good or bad feeling response onto the other person, I have thereby labeled certain behaviors as good, others as bad, and created an inchoate moral code.

From Schopenhauer to Freud; Freud, to Bellak and Perls

A case could be made that Freud, as he evolved and expanded his conceptualization of projection, refined Schopenhauer's view of the "world as will and idea" (knowingly or unknowingly). Starting specifically with the clinical realm, Freud, in time, expanded his view of projection to include perception more generally. In turn, both Bellak and Perls expanded and refined Freud's conceptualization. Bellak, as we have seen, was highly systematic in his approach, offering a detailed model of levels of projection. Perls, on the other hand, focused carefully on specific parameters of projection.[*]

---

* It would exceed the scope of the present article to include all of the other people who have additionally contributed to the evolution of the concept of projection. I have intentionally been highly selective of whom I have included, picking those persons who form a backdrop from which Perls' position can best be understood.

In his very early writing, circa 1942, Perls set the healthy process of *expression* in opposition to the pathological process of *projection*, an unconscious, hallucinatory process that involves desensitization and is paradigmatic in paranoia. The screen for projection, he wrote, may be not only the outside world, but may include a body part, an inner function such as conscience, or even the past (memory). Content wise, projection is usually of those wishes for which one feels guilty, namely sex and aggression, but may be of omnipotence (in the case of the "god"). Perls also included *transference* in the psychoanalytic setting in his discussion of projection. *Nota bene:* Perls discussed at length the interdependency of objective and subjective worlds, the latter referring to individual needs and interests, but without labeling the subjective world a projection.

In 1948 Perls explicitly added to his discussion of projection the idea that there is no reality per se, thus highlighting the existence and the weight of the subjective worlds. Importantly, too, he now offered an explanation of projection that included lingering childhood confluence with the environment or a later desensitization (loss of acute sensory awareness) as an element in its dynamics. Perls offered examples of linguistic patterns that are commonly found in projection, "it" language in place of "I" language being paradigmatic.

Perls et al., in 1951, wrote of projection as a mechanism for interrupting mounting excitement of a kind and degree with which one cannot cope. That is, expression not allowed may be converted into projection. Traits, attitudes, feelings, and any bit of behavior may be projected, Perls et al. wrote, thus making it explicit that projection is not always pathological. To make this point absolutely clear, Perls et al. stated that projection is pathological only when inappropriate and chronic. Then, in 1955, Perls presented a theory of the etiology of moral codes and systems, even religion, that places projection in a preeminent role.*

We can conclude that Perls, obviously, did not intend *projection* in its narrower sense, that is, in the sense of a strictly pathological process, when he, according to Schiffman (1971, p. 5), stated that "everything is projection." If, however, we understand projection in its wider sense, as in the multi-level model of Bellak, then Perls' statement can be accepted as more than shocking overstatement. And, as we have seen, in his own writing Perls acknowledged a realm of non-pathological projection, even though he did not identify all of

---

* Freud, too, had visited here: "Spirits and demons, as I have shown . . . are only projections of man's own emotional impulses" (Freud, 1913 / 1950, p. 92).

the nuances of Bellak's model. And so, in the present article, we have come full circle, in the process having created, I hope, a strong Gestalt. "I suggest we start with the impossible assumption that whatever we believe we see in another person or in the world is nothing but a projection" (Perls, 1969, p. 67).

A Problem of Solipsism and Its Resolution

When Schopenhauer (1818/1928) declared that the whole world is only an object in relation to a subject, that it is the perception of a perceiver, in a word, "idea," and that perception can only be veridical in its identification of a presence, but not veridical in its conclusions as to the nature of that presence, he invited us into a realm of extreme subjectivity. Perls' declaration that everything is projection could be taken as an invitation or even a prodding into a further step of apparent solipsism. From his statement, one could reason, then, that all I can know is *of* me, and *from* me, and *is* me. My world would then be closed, exclusive, and subjective in the ultimate sense. (If *everything* is my projection, then even Schopenhauer's concession to non-subjectivity — that the identification of a presence can be veridical — may be seen as compromised.)

It appears that Perls may have introduced a philosophical problem when he stated that everything is projection, *the problem of solipsism in the definition of projection*. The resolution of this problem can be found, ironically, within the definition itself. If we look carefully to the expanded definition offered in Bellak's model of the levels of projection, we can see that his *purely cognitive perception* is an escape from the confines of solipsism. It is true that he saw this level as a "hypothetical process" (1950, p. 17). But, if we recognize this level, at once, as both a *projection* and as a basis for a *consensual reality* we can accept Perls' statement without falling into the trap of solipsism. If we admit of perceptions that contain projected consensual elements *and* projected non-consensual elements, then everything is projection, but everything is not *just* a uniquely, individually, subjectively distorted perception!

What I am suggesting is that a perception is a Gestalt made up of elements of which the consensually defined purely cognitive perception is one. Such a perception is not merely a degree of cognitive perception plus some degree of another level of projection, but a Gestalt wherein (forgive my use of the hackneyed axiom) the whole is greater than the sum of its parts. The "external factors in perception" referenced above (Apt, 1950, p. 50), are relevant here. Evidence exists from the experiments of the Gestalt psychologists that there are certain organizing principles that are shared by individuals. Perhaps such "autochthonous determinants" (ibid.) are put in place by virtue of a shared design of nervous systems, then influenced by shared developmental history of exposure to certain categories of perceptual stimuli. We need not be concerned, here, with how this comes about, but only that there is compelling evidence of shared organizing principles. In addition, within a particular culture or subculture there are shared languages and commonly held theories. The vocabulary and the grammar (syntax) of each shared language and analogously the terminologies and the concepts of the theories held in common may offer both possibilities and limitations on the ways that objects and events are perceived. Each particular perception is, then, to a greater or lesser extent consensual, and to a greater or lesser extent my own distortion, rarely, if ever, entirely one or the other.

Ergo, my perception is, indeed, mine. But, it is also, to some degree, shared. Thus, all is projection, if by projection we mean a perceptual Gestalt constituted of elements of consensual cognitive perception, and externalization, sensitization, simple projection, pathological projection, or inverted pathological projection.

~

BEHIND AND BENEATH THE FACES OF FEAR

A Family of Faces of Fear

The multifarious faces of fear, named and written out for the eye to see, surely impress with their number and their nuances of expression. Consider carefully the faces that appear along this spectrum. Freud differentiated *neurotic* or *instinctual anxiety* (focused on the passions of the id), *reality anxiety* or *fear* (focused on dangers in the external world), *moral anxiety* (focused on superego demands), as well as *primary anxiety, signal anxiety,* and *fright,* not to mention *castration anxiety.* Karen Horney contributed *basic anxiety* to the theoretical corpus. Otto Rank appointed *life fear* and *death fear* to a major position in his perspective. In the expression of the psychodynamic thought known as Object Relations-*cum*-Attachment Theory, and echoing such names as Mary Ainsworth and John Bowlby, the identification of *stranger anxiety* and *separation anxiety* were added, along with *insecure attachment* with its far reaching teleological implications. Rollo May focused on *existential anxiety* as a subset of *normal anxiety.* Commonly known, but having lost their close identity with their originators, we recognize *anxiety-attack, panic-attack, free-floating anxiety, psychotic anxiety, depressive anxiety, paranoid or persecutory anxiety,* and of course, *phobia.* Harry Stack Sullivan found particular fascination with *awe, dread, horror,* and *loathing,* the family of *uncanny emotion.* I leave it to the interested reader to study each of these faces and facets *ad libitum.*

From: *Voices,* 43(2), 57-61 (2007).

Return of Childhood Emotion

Although a peculiar nuclear family, that of the *uncanny emotions*, their relationship to the other faces of fear should require no justification. It is in their quality of being eerie, weird, giving the skin chilly, crawling, sensations that they are special, and this peculiar quality derives from their being a replay of primitive anxiety from early childhood. It is the return of the primitive fear or anxiety, Sullivan (1953) informed us, which gives rise to the quality of uncanniness.

Predating Sullivan, in his essay of 1919, "The Uncanny," Freud (1963) suggested that it is rare for adults ever to become free of the morbid anxiety of childhood that was produced by *darkness, silence,* and *solitude.* Familiar experiences of childhood, these have become alien to us. Their return results in some degree of anxiety for most, if not all of us. "The uncanny is nothing else than a hidden, familiar thing that has undergone repression and then emerged from it" (p. 51). The *uncanny* constitutes "certain things within the boundaries of what is *fearful*" (p. 19). Thus, the paradoxical relationship between the familiar and the unfamiliar, *das Heimliche* and das *Unheimliche,* that with which we are at home and that with which we are not.

Consistent with the theme of the uncanny emotions as a return of the infantile, let us look more closely at Horney's *basic anxiety*. Basic anxiety is the experience of "feeling isolated and helpless toward a world potentially hostile" (Horney, 1950, p. 297). This is an ineluctable experience of infancy and childhood, and stands as the prototype for later experiences along the spectrum of anxiety.

Allow me to expatiate by delving into an early childhood memory. In good Gestalt therapy fashion, I will speak in the first person and present tense, leaving this here-and-now perspective only for later explanatory comments.

> I am leaning on a clothesline pole. Its raw wood is gray and weathered. It leans, slightly, and with effort I wiggle it. It is thick and rough to my little hands. I hug it. I cry quietly. I feel so alone, abandoned. I feel a hollowness in my belly. I feel cold, even though it is a warm summer evening, not yet dark. They are gone, leaving me here. I am afraid. Those here seem distant, withdrawn, indifferent. Do they know where I am? Do they like me? Will they take care of me?

Consider the phenomenology of this sojourn in the realm of basic anxiety. I lean, seeking support from the immediate environment that I selected. I attend to the pole, noticing its color, its texture, its size. I relate to the pole by wiggling it. I move toward greater intimacy with the pole by hugging it. Now, in relationship with the pole, I cry. But I cry quietly, not to call the others' attention to myself. Embodying the feeling of being alone and abandoned by my parents, I feel empty and cold. (Interestingly, an older cousin later told me that my father had taken a summer job driving an ice truck. In his jocose mendacity, he made my father the *ice* man. Maybe he saw something, in the same manner as that of the little boy in Hans Christian Andersen's *The Emperor's New Clothes*.) Note the sequence. I am left by my parents. I go away from the people with whom I am left (people who seem unsafe), in favor of an inanimate object (that seems safe).

◆ ◆ ◆

It was not a tree, that I have chosen to hug in my adult life following my exploration of American Indian spirituality. The object I selected was rudely crafted to be in the service of the distaff side. (I never remember my father taking part in the work at the clothesline.) First a lean, then a hug, a progression of intimacy expressing what an informed Gestalt therapist would label as a form of *retroflection of interaction*, I did to myself what I would have liked another (my mother) to do to me. My retroflection of interaction, a *contact boundary disturbance* in the patois of Gestalt therapy, analogous to a *defense mechanism* in psychoanalytic theory, was my response to my experiencing of *basic anxiety*. I felt abandoned, alone, and helpless in a potentially hostile world, and fled said anxiety. Approaching darkness, silence, and solitude attended me, Freud's very model for the primary experience of anxiety. I was and was not at home. Of course, one could conjure up a deeper more classically psychoanalytic interpretation, opining that I sought this phallus-like clothesline pole (designed to serve the women of the household, yet) as the symbolic representation of the father from whom I wanted protection. If one is inclined to multiple levels of interpretation, justified by the principle of *overdeterminism*, this interpretation may be added, with a not unappealing plausibility. The father who protects and the mother who comforts would both, then, be represented in the unconsciously driven solution of basic anxiety. The pole would symbolize a dual, thus redundant embodiment. "Yea, though I walk through the valley of the shadow . . . thy rod and thy staff they comfort me."

Embodiment and the Lived Experience of Fear

Anyone conversant with the body-oriented psychotherapies (Reichian Orgonomy; Neo-Reichian therapies such as Bioenergetics, Core Energetics, Hakomi, the work of Stanley Keleman, or Radix; Malcolm Brown's Organismic Psychotherapy; Pesso System Psychomotor Psychotherapy; and so forth) knows the relationship between breathing and the living of fear, throughout its spectrum. Consider the gasp for air that ushers in fright, the cessation of breathing that accompanies freezing in fear, the rapid, shallow breathing leading to hyperventilation that is a hallmark of a panic-attack. Likewise, reflect on the muscular tetany as one cringes in terror, the tensed muscles as one holds still for fear of detection, the loss of bladder or bowel control that may attend fright. Recall the skipped beat of the heart or the pounding, racing heart that are part of the experiences of fright and lingering fear, respectively. Remember the sensation of sweating palms. Such psychosomatic, or perhaps better termed, organismic phenomena are well studied in the body psychotherapies.

In an earlier piece, I addressed such embodiment in a brief manner, noting the interplay of organismic arousal, organismic support (or lack thereof), catastrophic fantasy, and the interference of breathing that establishes anxiety (Smith, 1992, p. 302).

ANXIETUDE

Excitement growing!
Not enough support.
Imagine the worst.
Gasp! Don't breath!
Anxiety, my old friend.

Eroticizing the Faces of Fear

The suggestion has been proffered in psychoanalytical circles that fear, if eroticized, may be pleasurable (Goldberg, 1977). Weight is certainly lent to this hypothesis by the popularity of the horror genre in film and literature, wherein horror and fright are often wedded to erotic images. Even the most frighteningly gruesome and grisly scenes are tolerated, even requested, when juxtaposed with the presence of Eros.

I am going to suggest that in the hypothesis that *fear, eroticized, becomes pleasure* we can find an inestimably important guideline for therapeutic intervention. If the person experiencing anxiety, wherever on the anxiety spectrum, can eroticize the experience, that experience may be stripped of its anhedonic mien. That is to say, with the ushering in of pleasure, the physiognomy of fear is transformed. *Nota bene*: I am *not* suggesting that any ethical principle or guideline be breached within the therapeutic relationship. Eroticization ≠ Genital Sexualization. By eroticization I mean tapping into the deep and primal pool of pleasure that is in the province of Eros. It is not limited to genital primacy. This is the province not of cupidity (in its obsolete sense), but of love and of passionate involvement. It is related to what Ferenczi spoke of as an "erotic sense of reality" (Smith, 1987). It may be elucidated through meditation on the following analogy. Eros : Logos :: Pathos : Ethos.

How is fear to be eroticized through psychotherapy? The answer to this is enshrouded in the mystery of psychotherapy, itself. It can be conceptualized, but not captured by evoking a factorial model in which the person of the therapist; the personhood of the person-in-therapy; the co-created alliance between the therapist and the person-in-therapy; and the methods, strategies, and techniques employed form the main effects which combine into higher order interaction terms. More than half a century of psychotherapeutic research has yet to parse the statement of this model in a manner that is consensually accepted. Each psychotherapeutic school chooses certain aspects of this model on which to focus and arrogates by depreciating other foci. So, I leave it to the sectarians of psychotherapy to address the question of the "how" of the therapeutic task, and state by way of disclosure that my bias is to invite cognative reframing through body work as an essential aspect of my approach. I stated the following in the description of the workshop ("Psychotherapy from Below") that I offered at the conference of the American Academy of Psychotherapists to be discussed shortly.

Daring to tap into the primal erotic energy that animates us, body-oriented Gestalt therapy is a "psychotherapy from below." It is informed not only by the psychological tradition of Ferenczi, Reich, and Perls, but also by the erotic philosophical tradition of Schopenhauer and Nietzsche and the erotic literary tradition of D. H. Lawrence.

Interestingly, the planning committee of the 2002 Institute and Conference of the American Academy of Psychotherapists held in Washington, DC chose the theme of "Pleasure & Perversity," subtitled "the erotic in psychotherapy." I quote from the conference brochure.

In the development of psychoanalysis, sexuality was the central force in Freud's theory. Subsequent theories have modified, deemphasized, or expanded the centrality of sexuality. Beyond the model of psychosexual development, the sexual exists in the psychotherapeutic work in countless forms, from romantic love to passionate desire. The erotic not only touches every issue that arises in our office — it is what comes from the work.

Or, as David Mann was quoted in this brochure, taken from his book *Psychotherapy: An Erotic Relationship*, "I consider that the erotic pervades most if not all psychoanalytic encounters and is largely a positive and transformational influence." More specifically, "the fundamental nature of the erotic is that it is psychically binding and connects individuals at the most intimate and deepest of levels. The erotic transference therefore, is potentially the most powerful and positive quality in the therapeutic process."

In one of the plenary sessions of this AAP meeting, the opinion was expressed that the choice of this theme was bold, courageous, and of immense importance for our time. There was much resonance with this view.

GESTALT THERAPY AND THE CONCRETIZATION OF NIETZSCHE'S METAPHOR

ABSTRACT

Following a brief acknowledgment of the widespread influence of Nietzsche's philosophy on psychotherapy, I make a specific case for a strong influence on Gestalt therapy. In presenting this case, I focus on Nietzsche's elaborate use of an eating metaphor in his diatribe against those who have not learned to discriminate from the subjective position of "I." Suggesting that Perls was influenced by Nietzsche's metaphor, I examine his explication of the hunger instinct, aggression, and his model of "psycho-dental stages of development." I suggest that the metaphorical approach of Nietzsche and the scholarly essay approach of Perls enhance one another, leading to greater understanding when taken together.

Gestalt Therapy and the Concretization of Nietzsche's Metaphor: Nietzsche's Influence on the Early Luminaries of Psychotherapy

The extent to which a person's ideas are picked up and further developed by others may be a meaningful criterion of that person's genius. Genius may be manifest in the creation of an idea and in its development; when

From: *Gestalt Review*, 11(3), 207-216 (2007).

someone else takes that idea and extends it or applies it, additional evidence accrues. Applying this criterion to Friedrich Nietzsche, one must conclude incredible genius. Even a cursory eye to the indices of books by Freud, Jung, Adler, Rank, Ferenczi, Horney, Reich, Binswanger, May, Laing, Assagioli, and Perls reveals apodictically that all of these luminaries of psychotherapy were influenced by Nietzsche. A moment of reflection surely suggests as a truism, given that Nietzsche is widely cited in the psychotherapy literature, that one journal article can not possibly do justice to the breadth and depth of his influence. This would clearly require volumes, and much more erudition than I command.

Nietzsche and Perls

There are innumerable points in Perls' writing, alone, that are echoes of Nietzsche. Perls does not credit Nietzsche for most, but the similarities are far too strong for anyone conversant with Nietzsche's works to miss. To cite these numerous similarities and explore them would, in itself, constitute a tome. What I willnow do is focus on one of these ideas, and how Perls used and extended it in his development of Gestalt therapy.

First, and by inclusion of examples, I will provide evidence of Perls' familiarity with Nietzsche's writing. In his biography of Perls, Martin Shepard (1976) wrote that Perls had the benefit of a classical German education. "A lover of opera, of Mozart and Mahler, he could quote Heine and Rilke to his ladies and Goethe, Schopenhauer, and Nietzsche to his colleagues" (p. 2). Perls' colleague during the early days of the development of Gestalt therapy, Paul Goodman, not surprisingly was also conversant with Nietzsche's ideas, particularly on art and religion (Stoehr, 1994). In his book *Ego, Hunger, and Aggression*, published first in 1942, Perls (1992) alluded to Nietzsche. Later, in the 1969 publication *Gestalt Therapy Verbatim*, Perls (1971) credited Nietzsche with "the idea of the incomplete person" (p. 30).

No doubt the best-known reference to Nietzsche in Perls' work is his paraphrase of one of the former's apothegems, found in *Beyond Good and Evil* (Nietzsche, n.d.). Perls (1971) wrote:

> As Nietzsche said: "Memory and Pride were fighting. Memory said, 'It was like this' and Pride said, 'It couldn't have been like this' — And Memory gives in." (Perls, 1971, p. 45)

With only minor variation, Perls (1972) quoted this again in his autobiography, *In and Out the Garbage Pail*. Compare this with Nietzsche (n.d.): "'I did that,' says my memory. 'I could not have done that,' says my pride, and remains inexorable. Eventually — the memory yields" (p. 73).

The Central Point: Nietzsche's Metaphor of Eating

I move now to the central point of the present paper, Nietzsche's idea and Perls' extension of it. Nietzsche (1982c) gave voice to Zarathustra, saying:

> Verily, I also do not like those who consider everything good and this world the best. Such men I call the omni-satisfied. Omni-satisfaction, which knows how to taste everything, that is not the best taste. I honor the recalcitrant choosy tongues and stomachs, which have learned to say "I" and "yes" and "no." But to chew and digest everything — that is truly the swine's manner. Always to bray Yea-Yuh — that only the ass has learned, and whoever is of his spirit. (Nietzsche, 1982c, p. 306)

This is the point, at once metaphorical and inchoate. The swine's manner is to eat indiscriminately, to take in most anything without benefit of a discerning taste. By refusing nothing, it accepts all. And, like the swine, the ass babbles "yes, yes." People, Zarathustra points out, can be of this same spirit. They are the omni-satisfied who have not learned to discriminate from the subjective position of "I." They have learned neither to say "yes" willfully, nor "no." Lacking conviction, they assume a chronic passive posture of acceptance of that which comes along, a position that negates active consideration and choice in the nonce.

Nietzsche (1982c), continuing to speak through the voice of Zarathustra, added to his metaphor of eating. In the context of breaking the "old tablets of the pious," breaking "the maxims of those who slander the world," he added, "break this new tablet too. The world-weary hung it up, and the preachers of death, and also the jailers; for behold, it is also an exhortation to bandage" (pp. 317-318). Speaking of the world-weary, the preachers of death, and the jailers, he explains:

Because they learned badly, and the best things not at all, and everything too early and everything too hastily; because they ate badly, therefore they got upset stomachs; for their spirit is an upset stomach which counsels death. For verily, my brothers, the spirit is a stomach. Life is a well of joy; but for those out of whom an upset stomach speaks, which is the father of melancholy, all wells are poisoned. (Nietzsche, 1982c, p. 318)

Read this again, carefully. Feel the wisdom emerge from the poesy, the concept from the metaphor. Herein Nietzsche has articulated the relationship between, as he says, bad eating and its consequences, namely, an upset stomach. On the literal level, this is a relationship known by every schoolboy who has eaten too many green apples. On the metaphorical level, however, the upset stomach symbolizes a spirit betrayed by bad learning; that is, learning that misses what is most important, learning that comes too soon, and learning too hastily gotten. A spirit thus betrayed finds not joy, but melancholy. But, "to gain knowledge is a joy for the lion-willed!" (p. 318). Note: a leonine will has teeth to match.

In *Ecce Homo*, Nietzsche (1982a) again made reference to eating, writing: "Silence is an objection, and swallowing things down necessarily makes for a bad character — it even upsets the digestion. All who remain silent are dyspeptic" (p. 659).

This time, however, as I read him, he departs from the realm of pure metaphor and enters that of the psychosomatic, denying any crude dichotomy of mind and body. He suggests two important and literal relationships. First, he identifies that when one suppresses one's words of objection, one creates indigestion. When one "swallows one's words," as we say, we are keeping within that which needs expression. We are choosing an opposite process, swallowing, to negate the urge to speak out. Although words are not physical matter, the suppression of expression of sound may, indeed, activate the apparatus of swallowing, if only in muscular micro-movements. The unvoiced objection leaves a trace within, a trace with physiological as well as psychological presence. Herein is the nexus of lived language and the lived body.

Second, Nietzsche suggests that personality in its manifestation, if not in its ongoing formation, is affected adversely by the swallowing of one's objections. The suggestion here is one of lack of congruity between what is internal and what is externalized, and such incongruity bespeaks a lack of sincerity, a lack of genuineness, a lack of authenticity. Such lack does violence to "'the will to truth.' . . . 'I will not deceive, not even myself': *and with this we are on the ground of morality*" (Nietzsche, 1982b, p. 449).

The Metaphor of Eating in Perls' First Book

The title of Perls' (1942/1992) first book, *Ego, Hunger and Aggression*, may at once be taken as an echo of Nietzsche's metaphor (and psychosomatic statement) of eating, and a promise for elaboration within the realm of psychotherapy. In his statement of "Intention" at the beginning of the volume, subtitled "A Revision of Freud's Theory and Method," Perls wrote:

> Psychoanalysis stresses the importance of the Unconscious and *the sex instinct*, of the past and of causality, of associations, transference and repressions, but it either underestimates or else neglects the functions of the Ego and of *the hunger instinct*, of the present and of purposiveness, of concentration, spontaneous reactions and retroflection. (Perls, 1942/1992, italics mine; p. xviii].

Following Part One, "Holism and Psychoanalysis," Perls devoted the entirety of Part Two of his book to "Mental Metabolism." In terms of the focus of the present writing, there are several chapters that are particularly germane; namely, "Hunger Instinct," "Mental Food," "Introjection," and "The Pseudo-Metabolism of the Paranoiac Character." The third part, Perls explained,

> . . . is designed to give detailed instructions for a therapeutic technique resulting from the changed theoretical outlook. As avoidance is assumed to be the central symptom of nervous disorders, I have replaced the method of free associations or flight of ideas by that antidote of avoidance — concentration. (Perls, 1942/1992, p. xviii)

Perls titled Part Three "Concentration Therapy," and devoted a chapter to "Concentration on Eating." (The lore in the Gestalt community tells us that Perls' wife, Laura, dissuaded him from continuing to call their form of therapy such, given the connotation of "concentration" at that time.)

By way of introducing the concept of *mental metabolism* and drawing the parallel with eating and digesting food, Perls (1992) quoted his friend Jan C. Smuts. After establishing a psychoanalytic training institute in Cape Town, Fritz and Laura Perls became friends with Smuts, a statesman, soldier, and philosopher, then Premier of South Africa and author of *Holism and Evolution*:

> The Personality, like the organism, is dependent for its continuance on a supply of sustenance, intellectual, social and suchlike, from the environment. But this foreign material, unless properly metabolized and assimilated by the Personality, may injure and even prove fatal to it. Just as organic assimilation is essential to animal growth, so intellectual, moral and social assimilation on the part of the Personality becomes the central fact in its development and self-realization [Perls, 1992, p. 121].

"Psycho-Dental" Stages of Development

Based on his belief that Freud had emphasized the unconscious and the sex instinct, but in so doing had neglected the Ego and the hunger instinct, Perls sought to explicate a developmental model based on dentition to parallel Freud's model of psycho-sexual stages of development. In doing this, Perls (1992) wrote explicitly of "the correlation of mental and dental behavior" (p. 144) and of "the structural similarity of the phases of our food consumption with our mental absorption of the world" (p. 149). In *Ego, Hunger and Aggression*, he stated succinctly: "The different stages in the development of the hunger instinct may be classified as *prenatal* (before birth), *predental* (suckling), *incisor* (biting) and *molar* (biting and chewing) stages" (p. 126). And "The intake of the world shows three different phases: *total introjection, partial introjection* and *assimilation*, corresponding to the suckling, "biteling" [*sic*] and "chewling" [*sic*] phases (the predental, incisor and molar stages)" (p. 151).

This model of *psycho-dental stages of development*, if you will, is rendered most simply in a soliloquy in *In and Out the Garbage Pail* (Perls, 1972, pp. 216-217). Allow me to present this conceptual discussion, further simplified through paraphrasing.

> *Introjection* is an organismic concept. Something is taken in, real or in fantasy. *Aggression* is not a mystical energy, but a

biological energy needed for biting, chewing, and assimilating foreign substance.

Suckling stage: Total introjection. You take in the whole.

Incisor stage: Partial introjection. You take in parts.

Molar stage: Assimilation. Through de-structuring, the material is made available to be made one's own.

The gist of this is that in order for one to be able to assimilate ideas, concepts, ideologies, beliefs, values, or whatever, one must de-structure them through a process analogous to thorough mastication. Such *rumination*, to use a word with a double meaning that serves to enliven the analogy, destroys the wholeness in order to render pieces small enough and altered enough to incorporate (again, the analogy is enlivened with the word *in-corporate*). Or, in the process of rumination, some material may be judged distasteful, even toxic. With rumination, with really *sinking one's teeth into* something and *chewing on it*, one is best able to be discriminating, *swallowing* that which tastes like it can be digested, and spitting out that which *tastes* unwholesome. Discrimination is limited when one bites off chunks but does not chew. Such limited de-structuring makes the material painful to swallow, and leads to mental indigestion. Worse still, in the pre-dental stage of sucking, one is profoundly indiscriminate and vulnerable to swallowing whole material that is devoid of nurturing substance or toxic. Mental food, undigested, can be recognized when it is *regurgitated*, recited with a quality that speaks of a lack of understanding. Simply memorized, it is recited more or less verbatim, often in a voice that sounds mechanical. Or, it may be projected, as is evidenced in the case of paranoia. If one likens the former to vomiting, the latter could be likened to diarrhea. (Recall the once popular and graphically crude phrase, "Don't lay your s--t on me!") One cannot but marvel at the richness of the lived language that ties together the physical and the mental planes of hunger, aggression, rumination, taste, swallowing, digestion, assimilation, regurgitation and toxicity.

The Core Concept of Introjection

As a technical term appropriated from the literature of psychoanalysis, introjection has been given a central role in the theory of Gestalt therapy. It is a core concept, seen at once as the source of psychopathology and as one of the contact boundary disturbances (which are analogous to defense mechanisms of the Ego in psychoanalytic theory). In both of these simultaneous meanings, the term begs expatiation.

In Gestalt therapy theory, psychopathology is seen as stemming from *a toxic introject*. A toxic introject is a message that has been taken in, hence *introject*, and is bio-negative. That is, it is not in support of the aliveness of the person, but rather it is a demand for a lessening of aliveness, hence *toxic*. A toxic introject is comprised of two components. First is the content. The content is the demand, the should or should not. The content may demand that one should not be aware of certain needs or desires, should not become organismically aroused or excited, should not be aware of certain feelings, should not express through certain actions, should not express through certain interactions, should not be aware of the satisfaction of certain needs or desires, or should not withdraw from contact. In other words, the toxic introject demands a self-interruption or multiple self-interruptions in the satisfaction of need cycles.

In my particular formulation of this cycle (Smith, 1985), I have suggested that the cycle consists of the emergence of a need as figural from the ground of potential needs —> organismic arousal (subjectively experienced as excitement) —> differentiation of a specific emotion from that excitement —> bodily action —> making that action interactive with someone or something in the environment that holds promise of fulfilling the need in question —> satisfaction —> withdrawal (until the need in question, now having receded into the background of awareness, emerges once more into awareness as the preeminent need).

The second component of the toxic introject is the *catastrophic expectation* — the expectation that something awful will ensue, should the voice of the toxic introject be disobeyed. This expectation of catastrophe, ushered into awareness by felt anxiety, lends the toxic introject power and insidiousness. Without this component, the toxic introject would be confined to the cognitive realm and, lacking an emotional component, could be resolved on a purely cognitive level. On recognizing the message of should or should not, one could simply and easily choose to ignore it. Toxic introjects often are acquired early in life, when, lacking self-support, the child is dependent on parenting figures and is therefore vulnerable to the threat of the greatest of catastrophes, the loss of parental love.

Thus, introjection as toxic introject is the essence of bad mental metabolism at its worst. A message dis-affirming of full aliveness is swallowed whole or in large part. Dwelling inside, it is yet foreign, unnatural, toxic.

As indicated earlier, introjection refers at the same time to a disturbance at the boundary of contact between a person and her or his environment. Given that a person chooses in response to a toxic introject to interrupt a natural cycle of contact and withdrawal, and given that one traverses such cycles guided by awareness, the clouding of awareness is a means whereby the interruption can be effected. "What do I want?"; "What am I feeling?"; "What do I have to do to get what I want?"; "With whom or with what do I have to do what I have to do in order to get what I want?"; "When am I satisfied and ready to withdraw?" These questions are answered in the realm of awareness.

In order to avoid the anxiety that would attend the disobeying of a toxic introject, one can choose to cloud one's awareness. One way of doing so is to confuse oneself. Awareness can be confused by means of any one of three related strategies — *introjection, projection,* and *confluence.* Introjection, as we have seen, involves taking in another's idea, value, belief, moral guideline, and so forth, and acting on it without having examined it thoroughly and decided whether to incorporate it. An opposite process, projection, involves the frequently inaccurate attribution of an idea, value, belief, moral guideline, and so forth to another when it is something that one holds, oneself. (Obviously, Perls adopted [and adapted] these two concepts from psychoanalytic theory.) Introduced by Perls, confluence refers to the blurring of the Ego boundary so that one does not differentiate *you* and *me* clearly, creating the impression of an *us* only.

The confusion in the case of each of these three strategies is one of ownership or, in a more existential sense, agency. In each case, personal responsibility is denied. When awareness of this existentialum of personal responsibility is lost, we find ourselves in the confusing situation of trying to credit or discredit ourselves for what others do, or credit or discredit others for what we do. In Perls' wry words (1973), "The introjector does as others would like him to do, the projector does unto others what he accuses them of doing to him, the man in pathological confluence doesn't know who is doing what to whom" (pp. 40-41). (It should be noted that there are additional means of clouding awareness having to do with dulling rather than confusing, namely deflection and desensitization. There are also additional strategies for self-interruptions that can be brought to bear at specific points of the cycle of contact and withdrawal, namely retroflected action and retroflected interaction. These additional topics are, however, beyond the scope of the present paper. The interested reader can find thorough discussion in *The Body in Psychotherapy* [E. W. L. Smith, 1985]).

Whether viewed as the source of psychopathology or as a disturbance of the contact boundary, the acquisition of an introject assumes a pre-dental (or in the case of a partial introject, an incisor) level of functioning. Writing developmentally, Perls (1992) noted that with the eruption of incisors comes the ability to attack solid food, and to hurt:

The more the ability to hurt is inhibited and projected, the more will the child develop a fear of being hurt; and this fear of retaliation, in turn, will produce a still greater reluctance to inflict pain. In all such cases an insufficient use of the front teeth is to be found, together with a general inability to get a grip on life, to get one's teeth into a task [p. 125].

In addition, Perls (1992) related the lack of oral aggression, lack of use of the teeth, with impatience, greediness, and the inability to achieve satisfaction. Not wanting to take the requisite time and not wanting to put forth the energy of using the teeth, so to speak, the person functioning at the pre-dental stage will not de-structure the material in question and, having not rendered it assimilable, will find satisfaction elusive.

Return to Nietzsche and the Mythological Tradition

Let us return to the words of Zarathustra (Nietzsche, 1982c) as he speaks of "the world-weary, the preachers of death, and the jailors": "Life is a well of joy; but for those out of whom an upset stomach speaks, which is the father of melancholy, all wells are poisoned" (p. 318). Nietzsche-cum-Zarathustra speaks through metaphor, offering us more than the spoken words themselves. Perls, on the other hand, wrote as a scholarly essayist (and in his later work as a popular essayist) offering clinical insights. In doing so, he was able to synthesize aspects of Nietzsche's work and the work of Smuts into his own clinical perspective. For example:

Introjection — in addition to its occurrence in melancholia, formation of conscience, etc. — is a part of a *paranoiac pseudo metabolism*, and is in every case contrary to the requirements of the personality. . . . *In melancholia . . . the impulse to attack is directed against the introjected object*. It is retroflected from the real food (laziness in using the muscles of the jaw; often hypotenuse of the face muscles) [Perls, 1992, pp. 151-152].

And:

Melancholia is mostly a phase of cyclothymia of the manic-depressive cycle. In the manic period the unsublimated, but dentally inhibited, aggression is not retroflected

-346-

as in melancholia but is directed in all its greediness and with most violent outbursts against the world. A frequent symptom of cyclothymia is dipsomania which is on the one hand a sticking to the "bottle" and on the other a means of self-destruction [p.155].

If we turn, now, to the Northern mythological tradition from which German philosophy and, in turn, psychotherapy arose, we find an intriguing theme, a thread connecting the three:

> Learning and knowledge were not by any means passive activities for the Germanic people. Because acquiring knowledge and acquiring things were so integrally related conceptually, such acquisition is often described and carried out in what seems to us to be a rather violent and disorderly way. Rape and pillage, reason and passion, seem not to have been widely different in impulse or process for these people. Thus the descriptions of "interchange" among worlds are themselves more often than not told in or accompanied by terms of power, domination, and ultimately, destruction. The sharing of information ... is most often a combat in which the "concept" or "knowledge" is contended, wrestled for, and finally won in a purely physical sense [Bauschatz, 1982, p. 128].

The "'interchange' among worlds" refers, of course, to the nine worlds of the Nordic cosmography. These were the worlds inhabited by humans, giants, dwarfs, elves, gods, and goddesses, and the souls of those who did not die courageously. In this universe, knowledge was often gained by means of traversing other worlds, where adventure was certain. I choose the word traversing advisedly, intending it both in the sense of crossing back and forth and in the sense of taking issue against or opposing. Knowledge of other worlds was hard gained, requiring courage, aggressiveness, and struggle. The destruction that often ensued may symbolize for us the de-structuring of concepts in order that they be made assimilable.

As I quoted earlier, Zarathustra (Nietzsche, 1982c) proclaimed that "to gain knowledge is a joy for the lion-willed!" (p. 318). I noted then that a leonine will has teeth to match. "Laughing lions must come!" (Nietzsche, 1982d, p. 395). Thus spake Zarathustra and having heard, thus spake Perls.

~

ART, ARTISTS, AND THE GESTALT APPROACH:
AN INTRODUCTION

Does Gestalt therapy in its theory and praxis have a significant contribution to make to the understanding of the artist and the arts? This is the broad and telling question that I have proposed to address in the present volume. The answer will perhaps unfold in the mind of the reader as the selections of the several authors are read, contemplated, and integrated. But, before attending to the new material, soon to be presented, it is only appropriate to consider the views and theories already published by Gestalt-oriented theorists and therapists. To the overview of this earlier material I now turn.

Gestalt Psychology: Laws of Perception

Looking to one of the roots of the gestalt approach, Gestalt psychology (Emerson & Smith, 1974; Smith, 1997, Wallen, 1970), there are several concepts that are certainly of interest in considering art and artists. Given that these concepts were invented and the underlying natural perceptual phenomena from which they were derived were in some cases discovered by Gestalt *psychologists*, one could argue against their inclusion in a study of the contributions of Gestalt *therapy*. It has been well argued, however, that Gestalt psychology is one of the essential roots of the gestalt approach and that

---

From: *International Gestalt Journal, 30*(2), 1-26 (2007).

these concepts were of great importance to Perls in his early formulations. Such should be evident even from a reading of Perls' early work from the 1940s (e.g., *Ego, Hunger, and Aggression*, 1947/1969/1992) as he departed from classical psychoanalysis.

Before including *learning* within its major focus, Gestalt psychology had its greatest success in the study of *perception* (Smith, 1997). (In fact, its proponents, such as Köhler, came to regard learning as a sub topic of perception. Learning has taken place when one has perceived the appropriate relationships, when one has put together the elements of the learning problem into a Gestalt. Thus, learning is secondary to perception. Learning consists of discovering the correct response, which is dependent on *structuring of the field*, i.e., Gestalt formation. When one has formed the Gestalt, one has sudden *Einsicht* [insight], the *aha!* experience. The proof of *Einsicht* is found in the reproducibility of the behavior and the ability to apply the behavior to new situations.) Therefore, as a psychology of perception, Gestalt psychology's principles and concepts offer perspective and tools for approaching art. A brief review of these principles and tools may be worthwhile at this point.

Using a simple perceptual problem as his example, Ehrenfels published his *Gestaltqualitäten* doctrine in 1890 (Smith, 1997). Consider the perception of a square. The four lines, considered one by one, are the *Fundamente*; the four lines placed at right angles, forming a closed figure, create the *Grundlage*. The quality of *squareness* is the *Gestaltqualitäten*. Ehrenfels' criteria for a Gestalt (*Gestaltqualitäten*) were *superordination* (the whole is greater than the sum of the parts, e.g., the notes form a melody) and *transposibility* (the form can be discerned with different contents, e.g., a given melody can be arranged in several keys). (This Gestalt doctrine is so central to the Gestalt approach that in his autobiography Perls penned a poem in which he paid tribute to Ehrenfels' [written "Ehrenfeld's"] discovery of "The irreducible phenomenon of all Awareness, the one he named. And we still call GESTALT" [Smith, 1997, p. 32]). Little imagination is required to recognize the usefulness of the doctrine of the *Gestaltqualitäten*, including the concepts of *Fundamente, Grundlage, superordination*, and *transposibility* as a tool for analyzing and understanding a painting, a piece of creative writing, or a musical composition.

With the basic data being *phenomena* in and of themselves, Gestalt psychology focuses on *wholes*. As demonstrated in the above example, properties of the whole may be *emergent* when the parts come together, rather than being inherent in the individual parts. Gestalt psychology is therefore concerned with *fields*, or dynamic systems in which a change in any single part affects the entire system. The field, itself is organized in terms of *figure* and *ground*. The Danish psychologist Rubin investigated the figure-ground relationship in visual perception, delineating five distinguishing characteristics. First, the figure has form, while the ground is relatively formless. Second, the ground tends to appear to extend continuously behind the figure and is not interrupted by the figure. Third, the figure is possessed of a quality of *thingness*, whereas the ground has a quality of undifferentiated material. Fourth, the figure appears to be nearer than the ground. And, finally, the figure is more impressive than the ground, better remembered, and more inviting of attributed meaning. In addition, Rubin discovered that upon repeated exposure to a given visual field there is a tendency to perceive the same figure-ground organization. Rubin termed this tendency *figural persistence*. Of further interest is his discovery that when the figure and the ground are reversed, the field tends not to be recognized. Following this seminal work by Rubin, Vernon demonstrated that these several discoveries applied not only to visual perception, but to auditory perception as well. Further, Woodworth and Schlosberg were able to apply these figure-ground phenomena to the understanding of social kinesics by viewing phasic movements as figure and supporting posture as ground (Smith, 1997).

Within this context of figure and ground, a *good form* is one that persists and tends to recur; a *strong form* coheres and resists disintegration through analysis or fusion with other forms; a form that is both good and strong is termed a *closed form*, in contrast to an *open form* that tends toward closure by being completed as a good form. The Gestalt tends to be stable. That is, once formed it tends to persist or to recur if the situation is reinstated, or if a part of that Gestalt recurs. *Fundamente* that are adjacent in time or space, or that are similar in quality tend to combine, with the organization tending to form a meaningful *Grundlage*. Even as stimulus conditions change, the organized object form (*Grundlage*) tends to be preserved. This preservation of the *Grundlage* is known as *object constancy*. Understandably, in the context of what has been discussed above, organization, form, and object character depend on the *relations of parts*, more than on the particular characteristics of the parts themselves (Smith, 1997).

The overall guiding principle in perception, according to the Gestalt psychologists, is the *Law of Pragnanz*, meaning the goal-directed tendency to restore cognitive equilibrium after disequilibrium has occurred in the perceptual field. In other words, to restate something that has been stated above, there is an intention toward a good form, or *good Gestalt*. According to Wulf, the *Law of Pragnanz* is served by three closely related processes that he named *leveling, sharpening,* and *normalizing*. First, *leveling* refers to changing the organization of the field in the direction of symmetry and good distribution. *Sharpening* involves the accentuating of the essential figural elements, and *normalizing* refers to making the Gestalt clear and simple (Smith, 1997). Surely, a working knowledge of the principles of Gestalt psychology provides a rich perspective from which to approach the arts — *belles lettres*, dance, music, painting, sculpture, theater. One of the real strengths of Gestalt psychology is its provision of analytical tools whereby the art object or art performance can be deconstructed and thereby recognized at multiple levels, from the *Fundamente*, to the *Grundlage*, and to the *Gestaltqualität*, without losing sight of the dynamics connecting those levels. These are principles that illuminate each level while relating the levels one to another.

The application of Gestalt psychology to the understanding of art is demonstrated perhaps nowhere more fully than in the work of Rudolf Arnheim. A student of Wertheimer, Arnheim became a prolific writer examining art through the lens of Gestalt psychology and thereby creating a Gestalt theory of esthetics. His many books, the best-known probably being *Art and Visual Perception* (Arnheim, 1954/1974), span decades. A special issue of *Psychology of Aesthetics, Creativity, and the Arts* (Smith, Smith, & Kaufman, 2007), was published in honor of his centenary. I refer the interested reader to this issue. Given that Arnheim was not involved in the development or practice of Gestalt *therapy*, I will not claim his work in my present exploration of Gestalt therapy contributions to the understanding of art and artists. I will leave it to the interested reader to pursue the reading of the book and journal referenced.

Organismic Theory and Art

Following the lead of the Gestalt psychologists, Andras Angyal, Kurt Goldstein, Prescott Lecky, Kurt Lewin, and Abraham Maslow drew heavily on basic Gestalt doctrine and extended it into the realm of personality as a whole. These Organismic Theorists, like their predecessors, were influential in the early formulations of Gestalt therapy. "Although Perls knew Wertheimer, Koffka, Köhler, and Lewin only through their writing, he had direct contact with Goldstein and Gelb. In 1926 Perls worked as an assistant to Goldstein at the Institute for Brain-injured Soldiers" (Smith, 1997, p. 28).

Although there are multiple points at which Organismic Theory can be shown to have had formative influence on Gestalt therapy (Smith, 1997), I will focus in the present writing on those which are most directly relevant to art and artists. To begin, Angyal suggested that the ineluctable tension between the person and her or his environment may lead through successive stages of differentiation and integration to *self-expansion*. Self-expansion has two aspects. The first, *autonomy*, consists of expansion of the organism by assimilation and mastering the environment, that is, *self-determination*. The second aspect, *homonomy*, consists of fitting into the environment and participating in something that is larger than the self — *self-surrender*. Herein the person may submerge the self through union with a social group, with nature, with an omnipotent being. The specific motives that may derive from and thus serve homonomy include desires for love, religious sentiments, patriotism, and of special interest to us in the present context, *esthetic experience*. We see, then, that *Angyal has identified esthetic experience as a motive, a motive that serves self-surrender by allowing one to participate in something that exceeds the ambit of self*. Angyal's perspective should intrigue anyone who has interest in the arts.

Goldstein, under whom, as I have noted earlier, Perls worked, had profound influence on Perls (Smith, 1997). Of the many aspects of Goldstein's organismic theory that were incorporated into early Gestalt therapy, two emerge as relevant to the understanding of art. One is the distinction that Goldstein drew between *concrete* and *abstract* behavior. Concrete behavior is a direct and automatic reaction to the stimulus configuration that one perceives. In contrast to this, abstract behavior involves thinking about the stimulus pattern — what the pattern means, how it can be used, what its conceptual properties are, what its relationship is to other stimulus patterns — and then acting upon the configuration. This distinction is pertinent to understanding audience response to art, as well as to the understanding of the designation of abstract art, itself.

The notion of *self-actualization* was one of Goldstein's major conceptual contributions. In his theory, self-actualization is the sovereign motive of the organism, and all of the apparent drives expressions of this master motive. Self-actualization is the creative trend of human nature whereby the person unfolds his potential into the realm of the actual. The satisfaction of any specific need becomes figural when it is the temporally immediate prerequisite for self-realization of the organism (Smith, 1997). Ergo, artistic creativity would be understood through his theory as being driven by and serving the urge for self-actualization.

Zeigarnik, one of Lewin's students, found when comparing the short-term memory for finished and unfinished tasks that unfinished tasks were better remembered — the Zeigarnik Effect. These results were predicted, based on Lewin's tension system hypothesis (when one undertakes a task, there is a level of tension, that tension being reduced upon task completion). When replicated under conditions where the subject feared failure in the task being performed, interruption of the task resulted in a reversed Zeigarnik Effect (completed tasks were better remembered). Zeigarnik used the covert task of thinking in her research, but another of Lewin's students,

Ovsiankina, extended the work to overt activities and had results that were consistent with those of Zeigarnik. This work formed a basis for Perls' formulation of the dynamic of *unfinished business* (Smith, 1997). This tension system hypothesis-*cum*-dynamic of unfinished business may be found useful in the understanding of the creation of, or performance of art.

For a deeper and more intense study of Gestalt psychology, I recommend the classic by Wolfang Köhler (1947), *Gestalt Psychology*. For a truly profound study, one may choose in addition, *A Source Book of Gestalt Psychology*, edited by Willis D. Ellis (1938/1997), originally published in 1938. This latter volume includes contributions by Goldstein, Lewin, and Zeigarnik, as well as Wertheimer, Gelb, Koffka, Köhler, and Wulf.

For many people, hearing the term *self-actualization* is more likely to elicit the name of Abraham Maslow than that of Kurt Goldstein. His theory of motivation, although similar to that of Goldstein, is more widely recognized. Maslow (1954) introduced a need-based theory of human motivation in which the several needs are arranged hierarchically in terms of priority or potency. As a more potent or prior need is satisfied, the theory suggests, the next need on the hierarchy will emerge and press for satisfaction. In their very popular textbook, *Theories of Personality*, Calvin Hall and Gardner Lindzey (1957) listed Maslow's hierarchical order of the needs from most to least potent as follows: "Physiological needs such as hunger and thirst, safety needs, needs for belongingness and love, esteem needs, needs for self-actualization, cognitive needs such as a thirst for knowledge, and finally aesthetic needs such as the desire for beauty" (p. 326). The feature that I want to emphasize, here, is that there were seven categories of needs listed hierarchically, and that *the aesthetic needs were at the top of the hierarchy*.

In the second edition of their book, published in 1970, Hall and Lindzey (1970) altered their wording as follows. Maslow

> has propounded a theory of human motivation which differentiated between basic needs and metaneeds. The basic needs are those of hunger, affection, security, self-esteem, and the like. Metaneeds are those of justice goodness, beauty, order, unity, and so forth. The basic needs are deficiency needs whereas the metaneeds are growth needs. The basic needs are prepotent over the metaneeds in most cases and are arranged in a hierarchical order. The metaneeds have no hierarchy — they are equally potent — and can be fairly easily substituted for one another. The metaneeds are as instinctive or inherent in man as these basic needs are, and when they are not fulfilled the person may become sick.

These metapathologies consist of such states as alienation, anguish, apathy, and cynicism. (p. 328)

Note that with their revision, aesthetic needs no longer occupied a crowning position in their interpretation of Maslow's model, but were regarded as one of the needs that shared the top rung. Given that Hall and Lindzey's text was the standard for college courses in theories of personality for a decade or more, their interpretations of Maslow's model has likely been more influential than Maslow's own writing.

In writing about esthetic needs, Maslow (1954) suggested that we know even less about these than about other needs, but was convinced that such a need truly exists in *some* individuals. Such people actually "get sick (in special ways) from ugliness, and are cured by beautiful surroundings; they *crave* actively, and their cravings can be satisfied *only* by beauty" (p. 97). Continuing, Maslow wrote that "some evidence of such an impulse is found in every culture and in every age" (p. 97).

Maslow (1954) suggested several differences between higher and lower needs that are of interest for our discussion of art. Whereas he wrote of the basic or lower needs as being arranged in a fairly definite hierarchy based on their relative potency, he saw the needs that constitute self-actualization as being more idiosyncratic. Maslow suggested that "the higher need is a later phyletic or evolutionary development" and that "higher needs are later ontogenetic developments" as well (p. 147). That is to say, the higher the need the more specifically human it is, and the later in the individual's development it will appear. As Maslow quipped, "as for self-actualization, even a Mozart had to wait until he was three or four" (p. 147). Additionally, the higher the need the less imperative it is for survival, the longer its gratification can be postponed, and the more vulnerable the need is to disappearing completely. Consistent with these considerations, higher needs are less easily perceived. Yet, deeper happiness and serenity, and greater richness of the inner life ensue when the higher needs are met. Maslow saw the pursuit and gratification of higher needs as reflecting a trend away from psychopathology, a more healthward trend. As may be obvious, better conditions are required for the fulfillment of the esthetic need than for the satisfaction of lower needs, be these conditions economic, political, or educational.

The extent to which Perls was influenced by Maslow, or Maslow by Perls, is open to debate. As recounted by Walter Truett Anderson (1983), the two men had an acrimonious clash when Maslow came to Esalen in 1966 to discuss his concept of a *being language*. Their conflict emerged as the dominant figure during the weekend conference, highlighted by Perls' calling

Maslow a "sugar-coated fascist," and Maslow's declaring in reference to Perls' unconventional behavior, "This begins to look like sickness!" (pp. 136-137).

As suggested earlier, one could argue that for Gestalt therapy to take credit for insights of Gestalt psychologists constitutes misappropriation. Just because Gestalt psychology constituted a major root of the Gestalt approach to psychotherapy would not, according to this argument, justify crediting the discoveries and theories of the former to its unclaimed offspring. Perls (1969), himself, even admitted that he was never accepted by the academic Gestalt psychologists.

Paul Goodman Addresses Art

Whichever side one may choose in the above argument, it seems very clear that given his early and extensive involvement in its development, the work of Paul Goodman belongs with Gestalt therapy. Situating his work squarely with Gestalt therapy should evoke no argument.

Paul Goodman did not proffer any organized or systematic discussion of art or artists. But, being a recognized and accomplished writer, himself, he sometimes produced essays containing insights into the creative process. In "Designing Pacifist Films" he recognized that, paradoxically, antiwar films may actually predispose their audiences toward war (Goodman, 1961/1977). The gratuitous violence and horror contained in such films, particularly those that are commercially successful, often have a "titillating effect and remain in the soul as excitants and further incitements" (p. 109). Not content to leave his reader or would-be film maker with a possible conundrum, he stated a corollary point. "Factual and analytic handling of images of war can neutralize their pornographic effect" (p. 116). These insights are certainly as relevant today as they were in 1961 when he published this essay.

Writing for a primarily psychoanalytic audience, in 1963 Goodman (1963/1977) offered "The Psychological Revolution and the Writer's Life-View," in which he made the case that every writer must present in her or his writing her or his view of what the world is. Using himself as an example, Goodman indicated that his own writing reflects his seeing life from the perspective of his having assimilated the work of Freud, Sullivan, Reich, Abraham, Rank and Groddeck, thus seeing "the psychosomatic, the fantasy, the unexpressed interpersonal act or avoidance, almost as I see red and blue" (p. 170). It is this "effect of psychological learning on texture and style" (pp. 170-171) that is his major focus. Goodman does, however, also mention that any thorough consideration of the relation of psychoanalysis and literature must also consider the exploration of the psychological meaning of authors and their works, as well as the literary genre of psychologizing, itself. He admitted the value of the two latter topics, but found his interest much keener in the realm of the first mentioned topic. In reference to this first topic, Goodman stated that "as a writer I do not 'apply' the findings of psychology; but I write as I experience, and I have been brought up to experience 'psychologically'" (p. 176). Demonstrating his broad literary background, Goodman presented compelling examples of works that reflect the various aspects of psychological acumen that have come to permeate *naturalism* as a literary style. These aspects included continuity of the life experience from childhood onward; unconscious processes, including the return of the repressed; the continuity of dreams, daydreams, and waking life, as well as errors (slips), fantasy, and wishful thinking; open recognition of sexuality; and attention to character and the psychosomatic expressions thereof.

Tucked away in an essay entitled "On Intellectual Inhibition of Explosive Grief and Anger," Goodman (1962/1977) declared confidently that intelligent, sensitive persons often choose to be artists. An object of beauty can get under habitual intellectual defenses, for the experience of beauty is pre-conceptual. The art object, standing for some tangible lost object, therefore can lead to weeping. The creation of this experience is, according to Goodman, meaningful to the intelligent, sensitive person as artist.

In an apparent mood of self-disclosure, Goodman (1951/1977) wrote "On Being a Writer: An Essay for My Fortieth Birthday." He never published this essay. In the tone of a confession, he wrote that "'wanting to write' has sprung from a physical and emotional discomfort, a vague excitement, the pressure of the accumulation of random thoughts and images, and the command of some unknown speaker" (p. 205). His wont was "not to make a plan, but set going at once on some thought or rhythm that is not impossible, not too irrelevant, not out of the question. This at once proceeds to 'write itself'" (p. 205). Herein, Goodman offered us a glimpse into one path of artistic creativity. As he "slipped into being a writer," as he put it, he "was careful to slip into a something or other that did not prevent a flow of *excitement*" (author's italics) (p. 209). Goodman further explained that he made very little money by writing, for he was "niggardly of enhancing the others or paying attention to their wants" (p. 211), and it is those very things that are required for the creation of a sizable audience. His chief reward for being a writer, Goodman declared, was a sense of justification born from expressing his inner excitement and his responses to the world as he experienced it.

In 1960, *Anvil* magazine queried Goodman as to whether writers were tending to become less concerned with politics. Furthermore, he was asked if the writer is obligated to be politically committed, and if there is any conflict between art and political commitment. In his written response, Goodman (1960/1977) stated that "artists are difficult to summate or manipulate sociologically" (p. 227). As I read this, Goodman was saying that the artist is better understood as an individual, comprehended only idiographically, not in the nomothetic language of group membership. This idiosyncratic focus is necessitated, Goodman suggested, by the tendency of each artist to initiate personally and dwell with her or his close conflicts. I see Goodman's view as consistent with the existential philosophical underpinnings of the Gestalt approach.

It is not surprising, given that Goodman was a writer as well as a pioneer of the Gestalt approach, that he addressed writer's block in detail. Some authors, he wrote, have great difficulty in freely imagining interpersonal relations, experiencing inhibition when trying to invent a dramatic plot with characters. The problem lies in their being unwilling to fill out the (external) situations of their stories with their own (internal) experience. To do so would be too close to their personal reality. That is to say, "their difficulty is in dissociating the events from their own actuality, in imagining that the events might be otherwise or that there might be others" (Goodman, 1952/1977, p. 194). Such writers may "resign" themselves, as Goodman put it, to being lyric poets or theorists. In the case of the poet, Goodman opined that he or she suffers from an inability to lie! That is to say, relying largely on unsought feelings, the poet has difficulty letting go of factual associations to her or his life. In order to avoid the embarrassment of revealing oneself through the interpersonal story, then, the artist tells only her or his feelings, without the events of her or his life. The theorist, holding a "noble superstition of object truth" (p. 197), avoids her or his interpersonal story by writing in impersonal generalities. Sociology, politics, and psychiatry may well be chosen as areas for theorizing, wrote Goodman, for they allow some degree of "practical contact." Interestingly, in both the case of the lyric poet and that of the writer of theory, the block to writing dramatic stories is found to be anchored in what Goodman chose to call superstition. For the former it is the superstitious regard of every factual association as being necessary; for the latter it is a superstitious fidelity to truth.

In his conceptualization, creativity requires a flexible interplay of *imagination*, *perception*, and *proprioception*, or as he expressed this with alternative language, *hallucinations*, *sensation*, and *appetite*, respectively (Goodman, 1952/1977). Lacking such flexibility, imagination may be affixed to the perceived actuality, thereby overdramatizing or over interpreting that actuality. Sensation, itself, may then be obscured by its narrow selectivity. Limited to commentary on the actual, the imagination can be stifled and lose its ability to bring deeper emotions to add spice to actuality. An artist in this predicament is doomed, wrote Goodman, to boredom and loneliness, for he or she cannot dissociate from his or her personal plight. "Where the imagination is bound to the actuality, the world is a prison even without bars" (p. 198). Returning to the lyric poet, Goodman advised that such poets write prose stories, lest their poems incorporate these very stories.

Striking another level of discourse, Goodman (1952/1977) explained that it is because something is being avoided in the actuality that imagination becomes inhibited and fixed to that actuality. "Once they are handling their medium, free artists are characterized by reckless courage," and "once this decision to be frank is made, the other difficulties vanish" (p. 200). But the artist must face the social taboo of self-disclosure and the fear of hurting others, for the author writes what others, as well as the artist him or herself, do not want to hear. "The great hurt that he does is not to the others at all; it is a hurt done to himself, and done to him by others, namely his embarrassment and shame" (p. 200).

In outline fashion, based on the above, Goodman (1952/1977, p. 201) revealed the issues of the four stages of the therapy of a literary inhibition of telling stories:

(1) The inhibition of freely imagining interpersonal relations;
(2) The fixing of the imagination on the actuality;
(3) Experimenting in making the actuality into a story;
(4) Finding something avoided in the actuality, to which the imagination has been fixed.

Goodman (1952/1977) identified a particular type of writer whom he called the "first novelist" (p. 197). Such a writer, perforce young, creates as an act of rebellion and thus as an act of "self appointment as an independent author" (p. 197). As such the first novel is pivotal in this artist's life; it serves as the point of departure into a new life with new relations. Goodman distinguished this "first novelist" from the "man with one book" who, regardless of how many books he writes, in essence writes only his autobiography again and again.

Gestalt Therapy and Art

In addition to their chapter on "Verbalizing and Poetry," an examination of the index to Perls, Hefferline, and Goodman's (1951) *Gestalt Therapy* uncovers an array of references to "art," "music," "painting," and "poetry." The eager reader may be frustrated, however, finding that these references are but ancillary in discussions of topics that are central to Gestalt theory, not an integrated or comprehensive exploration of art *per se*. Tidbits, though they may be, they are nonetheless rich and insightful. Some of these references are to Gestalt *experiments* in which a selection of music or an object of art is focused on in the exploration of *contact*. Although not referenced in the index, the movie or play is similarly suggested as the focus for an experiment in *confluence*.

Moving from the experiment on confluence to a more theoretical discussion, Perls et al. (1951) suggested that the *popularity* of a work of art is largely a function of the ability of that work to create in the audience an illusion of reality that is born of an identification (outside of awareness) with the characters or subject matter. Furthermore, art is of deeper value if it leads one to "a difficult identification, some possibility in yourself different from what is customary in action or wish — a larger vision or a subtler analysis" (p. 122). Since style and technique are of great importance to the artist, awareness of these (i.e., the *how* of the art) allows one to identify more fully with the artist and thereby further share in the joy of her or his creation.

Imbedded in the introduction of an experiment in *projection*, Perls et al. (1951) opined that "imaginative artists alleviate their problems by projecting them into their work" (p. 202).

Perls et al. (1951) noted that there is an internal inconsistency in the view of the artist that is presented in the psychoanalytic literature. On the one hand, the artist is described as spontaneous, and spontaneity is recognized as a hallmark of mental health. On the other hand, the artist is thought of as exceptionally neurotic. In extending this critique of the psychoanalytic view, Perls et al. suggested that the extreme interest in the artist's dreams and on the artist's "conscious calculation," (p. 245) is misplaced. What is more important in understanding the psychology of art is the exploration of the artist's "concentrated sensation" and "playful manipulation of the material medium" (p. 245).

Continuing in this vein of critiquing the traditional psychoanalytic position, Perls et al. (1951) noted that Freud had declared that the method and theory of psychoanalysis could address both the *themes* that artists chose and the *blocks to creativity* that artists experienced. He had done so in the case of his exposition on Leonardo. But, Freud declared further, *creative inspiration* and artistic *technique* were not amenable to psychoanalytic investigation. The former, Freud saw as mysterious; the latter he placed exclusively in the domain of art history and art criticism. (Perls et al., however, credited Otto Rank with standing apart from those psychoanalysts who eschewed any attempt at a comprehensive dealing with art, heaping encomium upon him.) For Perls et al., creative inspiration-*cum*-spontaneity, far from being a mystery from which to turn away, is appropriate as a major focus of psychological investigation. Their position can be summarized as follows:

> To the artist . . . technique, style, is everything: he feels creativity as his natural excitement and his interest in the theme (which he gets from "outside," that is, from the unfinished situations of the past and from the day's events); but the technique is *his* way of forming the real to be more real; it occupies the foreground of his awareness, perception, manipulation. . . . The style is himself, it is what he exhibits and communicates. (p. 395)

Perls et al. (1951) stated succinctly that "the transformation of the apparent or inchoate theme in the material medium *is* the creativity" (author's italics) (p. 395). Thus, they saw no mystery in this creative process. Rather, although it is not something that is fully known beforehand, it is something one *does* and then knows and can discuss. And, this process is not peculiar to art. It is true for any sensory or motor activity, any perception or manipulation that addresses a novel situation and creates a Gestalt of it. The Gestalt that is formed is "explicable but not predictable" (p. 396), be this in the realm of art or not.

From the above, it is clear that Perls et al. (1951) did not fully accept the Crocean idea that the artist's intuition of the whole is what constitutes the creative moment, and the rest of the artist's work is but execution. Not to depreciate the importance of the intuition, the dream, they recognized it as something that adumbrates the entire project. They added, however, that the artist, not fully understanding her or his dream, does not know what he or she intends. "It is the handling of the medium that practically reveals his intention and forces him to realize it" (p. 407).

The error made by psychoanalysts with regard to artistic creativity has two entwined parts. First, according to Perls et al. (1951), they made it mysterious by failing to look for it in the realm of health and good contact. Restricting themselves to the structural model of the psyche, the psychoanalysts eliminated the superego as the source of artistic creativity, for it inhibits and destroys creative expression. Then, by eliminating the ego, which observes and executes, suppresses and defends, but does not originate anything, only the id remained. By definition, then, if artistic creativity is inextricably related to the id, it is mysterious and hidden.

What the artist does, according to Perls et al. (1951), is *make something through the manipulation of a medium, solving a fresh problem that is clarified and refined as the work progresses.* The limited psychoanalytic definition of the ego does not provide for an understanding of this kind of organism-environment contact, imbued with excitement and transformation of material reality. Herein lies the second part of the error of the psychoanalysts in their approach to art — a limited definition of the ego, restricting its normal functioning to the societal average. Artistic creativity thus appears extraordinary, that is, either mysterious or neurotic. And once again, the id must be invoked!

In their exploration of personal growth, Perls et al. (1951) briefly addressed the growth of the artist. Having first explained that with growth there are changes in the kinds of feeling that one experiences, and changes in meaning and relevant objects of persistent feelings, Perls et al. distinguished three types or levels of artists. In so doing, they carefully eschewed implying that in this distinction there is a childish attitude to be overcome or a more mature attitude to be achieved. With these considerations in mind, they identified the artists who play capriciously with their art, assuming no responsibility for the results as they please themselves. These artists are the *dilettantes. Amateur* artists, in contrast, play earnestly with their art. They are responsible to the art, its medium and structure, but feel no need to engage it. There are, then, those artists who are earnest with their art, and are committed to it. These, Perls et al. simply designated as *artists.*

Given, as indicated earlier, that Perls et al. (1951) dedicated a chapter of *Gestalt Therapy* to "Verbalizing and Poetry," one could anticipate that their most thorough handling of the arts within this volume would focus especially on this art form. To begin their explication, they indicated that poetry, not scientific semantics and not silence, is the opposite of *neurotic verbalizing.* Neurotic verbalizing constitutes an isolation of the "verbal personality," and involves the use of a form of speech that is "instead of" rather than "along with" the underlying human powers (p. 320). It may serve as a substitute for authentic living. Good speech is speech that is contactful, drawing energy from and making a structure from *I* (the speaker), *Thou* (the one spoken to), and *It* (the matter spoken about), and these levels "cohere in the present actuality" (p. 322). Poetry, they wrote, is a fine art, and therefore a special case of good speech. But unlike other good speech which is socially instrumental, poetry is in a sense an end in itself. Rather than trying to persuade the listener, entertain the listener, or inform the listener of something, in order to manipulate her or him in the service of solving a problem, the poet solves her or his *own* problem through the handling of the medium of poesy.

> The poet's is the special case where the problem is to solve an "inner conflict" (as Freud said, the art-work replaces the symptom): the poet is concentrating on some unfinished sub vocal speech and its subsequent thoughts; by freely playing with his present words he at last finishes an unfinished verbal scene, he in fact utters the complaint, the denunciation, the declaration of love, the self-reproach, that he should have uttered; now at last he freely draws on the underlying organic need and he finds the words. (p. 323)

In this view, poetry "is speech as an organic problem-solving activity . . . a form of concentration" (Perls et al., 1951, p. 323). In contrast, neurotic verbalizing is an attempt to dissipate energy through speaking, and repeating rather than concentrating on the unfinished situation, thereby suppressing the organic need that underlies the verbalization. With the onus on the poesy itself, comes an emphasis of the "vitality" (p. 324) of the speech. Poetry is by necessity, then, more imagistic, more rhythmic, more precise, and the words more imbued with emotion.

In words laudatory and themselves nearly in verse, Perls et al. (1951) wrote:

> In poetic speech . . . the rhythm is given by pulses of breathing (verses), by the gaits of locomotion and dance (meters), by syllogism, antithesis, or other beats of thought (stanzas and paragraphs), and by the orgastic intensification of feeling (climax), then diminishing into silence. Variety of tone and richness of overtone are the potentiality of ringing in the primitive outcries as occasion arises. (p. 325)

Lest the reader be seduced into taking flight into an overly lofty regard for poetry or the poet, Perls et al. (1951) did include a more tellurian note:

> The problem that the artist does not solve is the one that makes him only an artist . . . unable to use the words also instrumentally in further free acts; and many poets feel the obsessiveness of their art in this respect — finishing a work

they are exhausted, and still have not regained a lost paradise. (p. 326)

Still, not to subduct from the art or the artist, Perls et al. (1951) concluded that the particular "subvocal" problems of the poet *are*, indeed, solved. They cite as evidence that an artist's successive works of art are different in a fundamental way, evidencing a deepening of the art problem. Such deepening may lead the artist to confront those of her or his life problems that cannot be solved solely by means of art. Even though the artist may distort truth in her or his poem, and make of it a symbol for the authentic problem, in the course of creating the poem he or she develops that symbol through "a lively use of his senses, keenly noticing sights, scents, and sounds, and empathizing with, projecting himself into emotional situations, rather than alienating his own feelings and projecting them" (p. 326). Surely, with enlivened senses and more complete contact with her or his emotions, the poet is better equipped to address emergent problems.

Laura Perls: Art and Therapy Are Indivisible

The intimacy of the arts and the Gestalt approach is perhaps nowhere more explicitly emphasized than in the life and work of Laura Perls. With understatement, Bloom (2005) simply declared that "Laura regularly combined references to music and literature with her practice of Gestalt therapy" (p. 19). In an interview with Nijole Kudirka (1992) published in 1982 in *Voices*, Laura revealed the intimate intertwining of the various artistic disciplines that were part of her background, and her professional work. Her extensive experience in the arts, included piano (playing since the age of five), literature ("I don't think there is anything in German literature from the Middle Ages to the modern ones that I haven't read" [p. 87]. She read English, French, Greek, and Latin, in addition to her native German), modern dance (since the age of eight), and reading and writing poetry. These experiences informed her as a person, allowing her to be the therapist that she was. "You use technically what you have available in yourself, through your own experience. I have a lot available, because I have a very wide background and a deeper background than most people have here" (p. 89).

When Kudirka (1992) summarized a portion of their discussion stating, "You feel that therapy is really an art," Laura replied, "I wouldn't make such a division between therapy and art" (p. 89). And so, to Laura, for one to ask what the Gestalt approach has contributed to the understanding of the arts and of artists may be naïve and little more than a tautological question. Once more Kudirka proffered a summarization, this time in the form of an analogy: "As Freud is related to archaeology and history, Gestalt Theory could be seen as related to expressive art" (p. 92). Laura raised no objection. With a bow to Kudirka, I will state her analogy in the following form and suggest that the reader contemplate it, allowing the layers of meaning to unfold:

Archaeology-cum-history : Psychoanalysis :: Expressive Arts : The Gestalt Approach

Joel Latner: Artistic Creativity — Imagination and Abandonment

Using his review of the 2003 publication *Creative License: The Art of Gestalt Therapy* (edited by Spagnuolo Lobb and Amendt-Lyon) as his springboard, Joel Latner (2005) dove into those deep and murky waters of artistic creativity. He concluded, in keeping with core process values of the Gestalt approach, that "creativity is much more than novelty; it centers on imagination and abandon" (p. 67). (In parts of his essay Latner discussed creativity in general, while in other sections he wrote about *artistic* creativity in particular. In my present discussion I will focus on artistic creativity, using what he wrote about it specifically and applying ideas that he presented about creativity in general.) Latner emphasized that *imagination* is perhaps the most essential element in the creation of art. With art, we are touched by the way that the novel material has been shaped through the artist's intentions and the artist's creative intelligence, in terms more poetic, the artist's heart and soul. Therein are we awakened, moved, in ways most miraculous and powerful, as we are invited to a fresh recognition of something the artist shows to us. Beyond this, the artist reveals to her or his audience something of her or his own unique way of being. Reflecting depth of feeling, depth of perception, and depth of comprehension, the artist's work can resonate in us, inviting in us a response that goes beyond the shallow and superficial.

Latner (2000) judged the current version of Gestalt theory (i.e., the theoretical trend since Perls' death to make the ego central) to be inadequate to encompass the elements of artistic creativity — depth, abandon, ineffability, inspiration, imagination. "It is disturbing to realize how inadequate Gestalt theory is to this serious subject" (p. 81). Continuing, Latner identified a tension within Gestalt therapy. On the one hand it is a *therapy*, a praxis intended to invite awareness, clarity, and enlightenment. On the other hand, "at the center of our growing edges, is creativity — a mystery" (p. 81). Not to leave us with no direction for working with this tension, Latner proffered the following: "We have to bracket off our dependence on theory and step away from our concentration on the figure and try to become aware of the vital background: the mysterious and unknowable" (p. 81).

By assuming the phenomenological attitude rather than looking to theory, Latner (2005) reflected on the surely common experience of anyone who has trained in the arts — writing, painting, playing an instrument, dancing, etc. — that one learns by "immersing yourself in the culture of the discipline.... For the most part you imitate — with feeling" (p. 86). Further-more, account after account of artists reveal a similar experience in which their work proceeds from an impulse seemingly unrelated to will, volition, or intention. This experience, in Latner's word, is "dreamlike." "It is the experi-ence of being in the presence of something magically compelling, which is occurring on its own. Yet we recognize it as our own. It is both our own, and not our own" (p. 102). These phenomena — learning an art by immersion and doing, and artistic creation in which one is compelled but not intentional — both bespeak and give evidence of *doing* that is *non-egoically driven*.

In his departure from what he saw as an emphasis on the ego in contemporary Gestalt theory, Latner (2005) called our attention to two terms in classical Gestalt theory (i.e., Perls, Hefferline, and Goodman's [1951] *Gestalt Therapy*) that are relevant to understanding artistic creativity. These are *concern* and the *middle mode*. The former refers to the condition in which we give "ourselves to the figures that emerge and evolve in our lives, putting ourselves at the figure's service" (Latner, 2005, p. 107). As the figure emerges, we participate in it, absorbed and consumed, becoming thus embed-ded in the living field in which we exist. Latner related *concern* to the *I-Thou* relationship, wherein the *I* versus *It* boundary is dissolved, and even *mutual influence* falls short of describing this "pervasive confluence of final conflu-ence" (p. 110).

As for the *middle mode*, Latner (2005) wrote that this term was used by Perls et al. in their discussion of *concern*. The term comes from the study of language syntax in which, in some languages, the *middle voice* stands be-tween *active voice* and *passive voice*, unifying action and receptivity. "Where the middle voice spoke from both sides of the fence of ego-active and id-pass-ive, now it speaks in the center of activity and passivity, inside the experience of being carried along in the material, spiritual and imaginative universe" (p. 113).

In summary, as I read him, Latner (2005) located artistic creativity within the vast, uncharted realm of *imagination*. The method of the artist is one of *abandonment*, a departure from ego-driven intention, volition, and will. The importance of *novelty* pales before these. Through the depth of perception, depth of feeling, and depth of comprehension that artists exhibit in their work, the audience may be awakened and moved beyond that which is shallow and superficial. Latner's views on art and artists are more informed by Perls, Hefferline, and Goodman's *Gestalt Therapy* than by more recent Gestalt theory.

~

LOOSE ENDS, TOO LATE, AND FAREWELL

My name is Might-have-been: I am also called No-more,
Too-late, Farewell.
— Dante Gabriel (*House of Life*, sonnet 97)

Dante Gabriel Rossetti, although embracing mimesis (imitation or realistic representation of nature) and history painting (historical subject matter) on his canvases, was a co-founder of the "Pre-Raphaelite Brotherhood" that rejected Raphael's work as corrupting of art and took inspiration from the primitive masters of the Fifteenth century. His life was further imbued with paradox as evidenced by his interring his unpublished poetry with his wife, only to exhume her body to obtain the poetry for publication seven years later. While his *peinture* exerted a strong influence on the incipient Symbolist movement of the mid to late nineteenth century, his writing, including that which was snatched back from the grave, represented what his critics called the "fleshly school of poetry," because of its strongly erotic overtones (Gibson, 2006; Janson, 1991).

Concern with time and loss was a leitmotiv in Rossetti's work. His magnum opus, reflecting this theme, is a gathering of sonnets published as *The House of Life*. In his alembic of poesy, he attempted to distill some perfect moment as the center to time for which he yearned, and thus regarded the sonnet as "a moment's monument." But alas, a monument is both for preserving a memory and mourning the passing of that very memory. In spite of desperate attempts, recognition of inevitable change and loss prevailed over the elusive perfect moment. Rossetti ended *The House of Life* with an accep-

---

From: *Voices*, 44(3), 86-91 (2008).

tance of time, the awareness of transience and loss, the inevitability of death (Landow, 2000).

I want to take the above selection from Rossetti's sonnet 97 of *The House of Life* as a guide for use in considering the wishes after therapy has ended that one had said or done something different. In making this sonnet our cynosure, I fully realize that the meaning which Rossetti intended is not necessarily the meaning which I find in it. (With a nod to Virginia Satir's simple yet elegant teaching, "The message sent is not necessarily the message received!") But, as with all great art, multiple meanings and levels of meaning may be evoked by the work, each member of its audience participating in this co-creation of meaning. In a word, we interpret.

Might-have-been

To look back on a course of psychotherapy and speculate as to what would have happened if I had not done what I did, if I had not said what I said, or if I had done something that I did not do, or had said something that I did not say, is to skirt the borders of fantasy, if not to sojourn completely within the ambit of that realm. If I say or do something, or not, the unfolding of consequences as time passes may inform me. In some cases, then, the repercussions of my words and actions seem quite clear. (My guess is that really bad repercussions follow mostly extreme behaviors, and that it is in these situations that the behavior-repercussions connection is most clear.) But many times post-dictions are inventions with little evidence from reality. Even in the former case, my speculations are probabilistic and not certain.

Let us look more deeply. Events and their sequelae are embedded in a vast and intricate matrix of circumstance. Events themselves and consequences of those events are but surface markers of the underlying matrix. When we look in retrospect and imagine what *might-have-been*, had I said or did, or did not say or do whatever, we are more often than not limiting our scenario to surface elements. This does not, and cannot take into consideration all of the deeper elements of the matrix and how they would have influenced the unfolding of the real situation. That is to say, by playing a game of *might-have-been* I oversimplify as I show disrespect for the larger context. In most cases, not being omniscient, I cannot know with certainty what might have been, had I acted differently.

To create a fantasy built around a moment of acting differently from what I did, is analogous to Rossetti's attempt to create a "moment's monument." If only I had (not) said or (not) done that, the moment would have been the pivotal point for joyous emergence! But, I cannot know if the fantasy moment would have transformed the situation into a better outcome, or if it would have transmogrified the event into perdition!

Playing the *might-have-been* game is predicated on imagining a better present situation as result of altered past behavior. The game admits of degrees, or course, and in more extreme forms may involve anguishing, with "If only I had . . . " ushering in each paragraph of speculation. The attendant feelings must be unpleasant and disturbing. (Let the single-shot cognitive therapist and emotion-based therapist duel over the primacy of thought or feeling, here. Even the double-barreled cognitive-behavioral therapist may be chivied into this duel.) Debased to this level, the *might-have-been* game is revealed as an inflection of the *perfectionism* game. Implicit in this *curse of perfectionism* is a lack of acceptance of self. (With a nod, this time, to Fritz Perls for the term-cum-concept. Incidentally, he has his six-shooter on his hip, ready to duel over over-simplistic dualism.) There is a lack of full acceptance of myself as I was in the real past. I should have been different. I should have been perfect so that I would have acted perfectly.

Had I been so, something else, something better, *might-have-been*.

No-more

Consider this perspective on the enterprise of psychotherapy, a lesser-taken perspective but one that may hold some advantage: *psychotherapy is a live performing art.* To elaborate this perspective and to clarify it, psychotherapy is not a performing art in the sense of entertainment. Neither is it conducted for the distraction or the amusement of an audience, nor is it engaged in by the therapist or the person in therapy to such an end. It does, however, involve live appearance by the therapist and the person in therapy. And, while theorizing about psychotherapy and conducting research on psychotherapy are scientific endeavors, doing it falls heavily into the realm of art. (I recall that James Bugental [1987] titled one of his books *The Art of the Psychotherapist: How to Develop the Skills That Take Psychotherapy Beyond Science.*).

By way of analogy, we may consider the art of a performance of traditional ballroom dance. Two persons meet at a designated arena, designed to allow and to support the activity, at a designated time. By design a good ballroom has a quality sound system with appropriate music, a floor that is conducive to gliding and sliding, sufficient space, and protection from intruding activities. One of the dancers leads, while the other follows. The leader and follower format is made possible and an esthetic level of performance reached only when the two dancers have learned the dance. Each dance may be viewed in terms of placement on a dimension of correct form-cum-formality. Compare, for instance, the waltz or even disco dancing with free-style dancing.

Turning to one-one-one psychotherapy, we can easily recognize the above analogy. Psychotherapy is conducted at a designated time, in a designated place designed to support the activity. There is a status differential that by tradition asks that the person in therapy come to the place of the therapist, and not the other way around. In addition, by dint of education and training it is the therapist who leads the therapy qua enterprise, and overall. It is the therapist who knows the steps, so to speak. The person in therapy is taught to follow the steps, that is, the procedure, the method, the technique. Some of these steps are more formalized, such as in classical psychoanalysis or systematic desensitization, while others are less so.

As with the dance, the procedure, the method, the technique of psychotherapy exists as an abstraction that can be written about and discussed, and as a concrete lived event. Thus, the paradox, "Psychotherapy exists only as it is given life through the person of a particular therapist, yet psychotherapy exists, like a Platonic Form, apart from the practitioner" (Smith, 2003, p. 21).

(The above analogy could be extended to include group psychotherapy by reflecting on group dances such as the Bunny Hop, the Hokey-Pokey, the Stroll, and the Electric Slide when led by someone. When not, the dance would be analogous to a leaderless or peer group.)

My point is that as a performing art psychotherapy is *live*. Its impact is in the live moment. It is not a performance rehearsed, edited, mixed, dubbed, and recorded in a studio and then presented to the person in therapy in its polished and final version. There is only one take with live performance. It is this spontaneity and this aliveness in the moment that give all live performing arts their special quality.

When psychotherapy is appreciated as a performing art, performed live and not studio-produced, two important implications emerge. First, imperfections born of spontaneity are to be expected. Second, the performance of therapy happens in a transient, moment-by-moment framework, then (as live performance) is *no-more*.

Too-late

Playing the *might-have-been* game, anguishing over "what if," is predicated on a time warp. I can only know, albeit in a probabilistic way, the ripples of my past action through the passage of time. Therefore, to imagine being in the past, but with knowledge that I have in the present, based on information that has only emerged over time, is an existential foul. Harsh judgment of my past based on knowledge that was not available in that past situation is characteristic of a game of torture, and identifies it as such.

All personal power is in the present. This is a statement at once bald and bold. It is so much at the core of the Gestalt approach to psychotherapy that Claudio Naranjo (1970) in his formulation of the nine "implicit moral injunctions of Gestalt therapy" articulated the first two as follows:

(1) Live now. Be concerned with the present rather than with past or future;

(2) Live here. Deal with what is present rather than with what is absent (p. 49).

Naranjo (1970) referred to this as the *hic et nunc* or here-and-now principle, and in his explication connected it with Horace's *carpe diem* and literary work by King Solomon, Ovid, Dante, Johnson, Spencer, Shakespeare, Milton, Dryden, Longfellow, and Omar Khayyam. Published in this same time period, Fritz Perls (1970) opined, "To me, nothing exists except the now. Now = experience = awareness = reality. The past is no more and the future not yet. Only the *now* exists" (p. 14). Consistent with Fritz's opinion, but in her own style, Laura Perls (1997) wrote as follows: "Whatever exists is here and now. The past exists now as memory, nostalgia, regret, resentment, phantasy, legend, history . . . . Gestalt therapy takes its bearing from *what is* here and now, not from what *has been* or what *should be*" (p. 221).

What is done is done. I cannot go back and change the past. The past is dead. So as Rossetti recognized, it is *too-late* for what *might-have-been*.

Farewell

Naranjo (1980) wrote that "Words unsaid and things undone leave a trace in us binding us to the past" (p. 55). This is an elegant, even poetic way of expressing the Zeigarnick effect, a phenomenon with which Perls was familiar from his reading of Lewin, and which he observed in temporally extended form clinically (Smith, 1997).

The Zeigarnik Effect is a phenomenon found when comparing the short-term memory for finished and unfinished tasks. Based on Lewin's tension system hypothesis (when one begins a task there is a high level of tension, that tension being reduced upon task completion), Zeigarnik hypothesized that the unfinished tasks would be remembered better, because of the remaining tension. And, indeed, this is what she found. . . . Whereas Zeigarnik used covert tasks in her research (thinking situations), another of Lewin's students, Ovsiankina found, consistent with Zeigarnik's work, that subjects tend to spontaneously resume interrupted activities when left in a free situation (Smith, 1997, p. 28). . . . Perls extended the notion of completion of unfinished tasks into a long-term model and developed therapy techniques for the finishing of one's "unfinished business" from even the distant past. (p. 32)

We would do well to consider and to take seriously the following instructions that the *brujo* don Juan offered his apprentice Carlos Castaneda (1972).

Think of your death now. . . . It is at arm's length. It may tap you any moment, so really you have no time for crappy thoughts and moods. None of us have time for that. . . . You, on the other hand feel that you are immortal, and the decisions of an immortal man can be canceled or regretted or doubted. In a world where death is the hunter, my friend, there is not time for regrets or doubts.
There is only time for decisions. (pp. 46-47)

Whether the reports by Castaneda of his apprenticeship are fictive or not, the wisdom of don Juan's extensive teachings seems apparent. In the material quoted above we are warned against dwelling on regret or doubt. Therefore, unfinished business is to be finished, loose ends to be tied, allowing us to live in the present.

Gestalt has been at the vanguard of psychotherapy method in offering a technique for finishing unfinished business. Naranjo (1970) named this technique *presentification*, explaining that "this may take the form of an inward attempt to identify with or relive past events or, most often, a reenacting of the scenes with gestural and postural participation as well as verbal exchanges, as in psychodrama" (p. 53). Note the compatibility between his earlier presented *axiological principle* of the here-and-now and the *technique* of bringing unfinished business into this here-and-now psychodramatically. The moral injunctions, on the philosophical plane, and the technique of presentification, on the methodological plane, are closely coordinated.

Although the present article is not the place to offer a vademecum for presentification, I will expand briefly on the method. The core of the method is the creation of a here-and-now experience through psychodramatic acting out of the unfinished situation. Often this psychodrama is enacted using the *empty chair*. The person with whom one has unfinished business is imagined as vividly as possible in the empty chair. When one has a good vivid image of the person in the empty chair, one speaks directly to that person. Although thoughts that define and explain the unfinished situation with which one wants to deal are usually stated, emphasis is placed on expressing *present emotions*, using *first-person statements* in the *present tense*. As much as possible, one tries to feel the emotions genuinely, and express them directly, as if the person in question is present. When done well, when the scene is enacted rather than just acted, the experience is psychologically real. It may be important to express *appreciations*, *regrets*, and *resentments*, all three, even if one begins with awareness of only one or two of these. The idea is to go deeply into oneself, dredging up any unexpressed thoughts and feelings. To aid in making the psychodrama more real, one may involve the body fully, with appropriate postural shifts and gestures. When coaching someone through the psychodrama, I remind the person that the purpose is for her or him to express what has been heretofore unexpressed, and that this is not permission for, or rehearsal for a literal encounter with the other person. Therefore, expressions may be, and may even have to be exaggerated, in order for the psychodrama to have its effect. (Empty chair work can be used as rehearsal for a literal encounter, but that is not the issue with which I am dealing here.) This psychodrama may consist of a monologue, or it may involve a dialogue, with the person switching back and forth between the chairs, enacting both self and other, and keeping a dialogue going until resolution is experienced.

Coaching the empty chair monologue or dialogue well requires considerable sensitivity and skill. The most common error, in my teaching experience, is to end the psychodrama prematurely. It must continue until there is a sense of resolution, until the unfinished business seems finished, until the loose ends are tied, sometime requiring multiple sessions.

Loose ends is another name for *unfinished business*; it is also known as the *incomplete Gestalt*. With effective use of the psychodramatic acting out of the unfinished situation, the ends can be tied up, the business finished, and the Gestalt completed, allowing one to disengage, with a genuine *Farewell*, *Too-Late*, and *No-more* to what *Might-have-been*.

The Two Paths of Gestalt Therapy

In the Preface to *The Body in Psychotherapy* (Smith, 1985) I defined the Gestalt approach as consisting of "a philosophical position, a theory of personality, and a therapeutic style. The philosophical position is basically existential, with emphasis on personal responsibility, choice, and the I—Thou relationship. In addition there is . . . a valuing of awareness and experience of 'what is'. . . . The theory of the Gestalt approach is a holistic one, viewing the person as flowing through homeostatic need cycles (or contact/withdrawal cycles), with the all-encompassing need being self-actualization. The therapeutic style is phenomenological, focusing [on] facilitation of the patient's awareness in the here-and-now. . . . I consider this . . . existential philosophy, this organismic personality theory, and this phenomenological experiential style of working to be the necessary and sufficient conditions to define the Gestalt approach. I don't define the Gestalt approach by techniques. The Gestalt approach is given life by the "person" of the particular therapist. Therefore, there are many styles of Gestalt therapy, each reflecting the 'person' of that therapist/artist" (pp. viii-ix). I went on to say that it is the exquisite focus on organism-in-environment *process* that appeals most to me about the Gestalt approach.

I think it a mistake, as well as a gross oversimplification, to place the burden of definition of Gestalt therapy on the techniques. I see this done, not only by callow graduate students, but by professionals as well. Such definition is an oversimplification in that it relegates the rich philosophical under-

---

Previously unpublished.

pinning and the elegantly complex personality theory of the Gestalt approach to a subaltern role, at best barely implied, at worst ignored completely. This oversimplification is further carried out, albeit more subtly, by shifting the focus from phenomenological process to a list of quasi-reified techniques. If such is the oversimplification, then the mistake is in the violation of the integrity of the Gestalt approach, for the philosophical underpinning, the personality theory, and the phenomenological experiential method constitute a *Gestalt*. Although we can differentiate these three aspects for heuristic purposes, they must be considered as components of an emergent Gestalt if the Gestalt approach is to be comprehended in full and compelling mien.

As I suggested, within the Gestalt approach as I have defined it, there are many styles. Because it is not defined by technique, it lends itself in praxis to creative interpretation.

Therapists, in co-creating a lived event, seem to follow one of two paths in their work with persons in therapy. I base my assertion on my thirty-five years of observing and experiencing many therapists who admitted to Gestalt affiliation. I suggest that (within the context of the Gestalt approach) we call these the *Path of Existential Encounter* and the *Path of Psychodrama*. I turn now to an examining of each, in turn.

In the realm of Existential Encounter, the coin is that of phenomenological observation and comment. On this path, the therapist observes the person in therapy — facial expression, posture, gestures, tone of voice, rate of speech, skin tone, slips of the body, slips of the tongue, and so forth. Content of speech is, of course, attended to, but given secondary attention. (Perls, remember, suggested that content play "second fiddle," only.) The therapist also can observe herself or himself, particularly noting the arising of emotional responses, body sensations, and lines of thought. The therapist can then selectively comment on what he or she has observed, but the comment is based on *phenomenological* observation, that is, what has been observed in its raw form, unadorned by theoretical associations, justification, excuses, or conventions of politeness or propriety. In this manner, the therapist, for her or his part, creates an atmosphere of authenticity. It is in this art of the therapist that selectivity of response is critical.

In exploring the Path of the Existential Encounter, it may be instructive to look to the work of Hellmuth Kaiser. I choose to do so for two reasons, even though he was not a Gestalt therapist as such. First, he and Perls were together in a training seminar led by Wilhelm Reich. In a personal communication, Laura Perls told me that this was around 1933. Both, in the development of their respective therapeutic approaches, were, then, influenced by Reich in his *character analytic* period (Smith, 1975, 1997). The second reason is that Perls (1969), not noted for bandying with professional compliments, commented in his autobiography that Kaiser went on to be a very fine therapist.

Welling (2000), in a scholarly discussion of Kaiser's approach, traced the evolution of psychoanalysis from Freud to Kaiser. In his early psychoanalytic work, Freud focused on *analysis of content*, but by 1914 he was considering the *analysis of resistance* in the analysand. In Welling's view, Reich's *character analysis* was an elaboration of resistance analysis. Reich took the position that it is not *what* the patient says, but *how* the patient says it that is to be interpreted. "Reich argued that character resistance can hinder the classic content analysis, as every content interpretation is distorted by the typical rigid cognitive functioning of the patient's character structure" (p. 58). Consistent resistance analysis became the focus of Kaiser's work. But within this focus, Kaiser did not look to underlying character structure as had Reich. Instead of looking at underlying (character) *structure*, Kaiser demonstrated an increasing emphasis on *function*, that is, on existential authenticity, as reflected and made manifest in style of communication. To wit, Kaiser's thinking evolved from seeing the purpose of therapeutic interventions as being to eliminate resistance in 1934, to the increasing of the sense of responsibility in the patient in 1955, and to the diminishing of duplicity by 1965. As expressed by Allen Enelow and Leta McKinney Adler (1965), what Kaiser termed *resistance analysis* in his early work he came to call *defense analysis*, and finally *duplicity analysis*.

To summarize the above, Kaiser's work evolved from focusing on resistance analysis to defense analysis and then to duplicity analysis. His work focused radically on the *how* of the communication as opposed to the *what*, that is, the *style* rather than the *content*. This focus was derived from Kaiser's work with Reich (Enelow & Adler, 1965). Note, then, that duplicity is revealed in *how* one communicates, in one's *style* of communication, without necessary reference to underlying character.

In the Afterword of his editing of Kaiser's works, *Effective Psychotherapy: The Contribution of Hellmuth Kaiser*, Louis Fierman (1965) stated that Kaiser "identifies the essential ingredient of effective psychotherapy as being the authentic communicative relationship offered to the patient by the therapist. A model for effective psychotherapy can thus be conceptualized as one in which the sole and exclusive concern and interest of the therapist is to maintain a communicative intimacy" (p. 203). In a remarkably tightly packed summary of Kaiser's model, Fierman continued as follows. "The *universal triad* consists of the *universal psychopathology*, the *universal symptom*, and the *universal therapy*. The universal psychopathology is the attempt to create in real life the illusion of the universal fantasy of fusion. The universal symptom is duplicity in communication. The universal therapy is the communicative intimacy offered by the psychotherapist" (p. 207).

The task, now, is to unwrap this tightly wrapped package and thereby allow its meaning to unfold in greater fullness. At the time of Kaiser's writing, the term *neurotic* was used in a much broader sense than is now the case, and so it is within this broader meaning that the universal psychopathology was discussed. The neurotic is, then, one who cannot tolerate the fact of fundamental aloneness. Therefore, the neurotic seeks to deny this basic existential fact. This existential aloneness, anathema to the neurotic, emerges with poignancy under three particular conditions: when one wants something that is not valued by others; when one reaches a conviction which is not supported by authority; or when one makes a decision that is not widely approved (Enelow & Adler, 1965).

In *The Person of the Therapist* (Smith, 2003) I remarked on the similarity between Jean-Paul Sartre's depiction of the *human condition* and Kaiser's *universal psychopathology*, noting however, that there are no references to Sartre in Fierman's volume. Whether Kaiser was influenced by Sartre, or (less likely) that Sartre was influenced by Kaiser, I can not be sure. Kaiser did reside in Paris during the late 1930's, having fled Germany. Perhaps Kaiser was influenced by Heidegger as strongly as was Sartre, lending the two men a common philosophical base. Let us look to Sartre, nonetheless, for explication of the human condition, which in turn may help us to understand the universal psychopathology.

"In Sartre's view, the human condition is constituted of *anguish*, created by the imperative to choose, the angst which comes with choice and responsibility. It is constituted of *despair* over our inability to make the world, including other people, do as we would will, leaving us to deal with only probabilities as to what may happen. It is constituted, also, of a sense of *abandonment*, the situation in which there is no ultimate authority to tell us what to choose" (Smith, 2003, p. 29). Although Sartre's words, here translated, may suggest a certain tone *noir*, the similarity to Kaiser's neurotic is apodictic. Sartre, however, offers us more detail, a finer grain analysis, and at once expands on existential aloneness giving it a dark emotional felt sense.

To return to the theme of the neurotic, in the attempt to deny the existential fact of aloneness, the neurotic tries to avoid personal, that is, *individual* responsibility. For the non-neurotic person there may be comfort in an *illusion of fusion*, the illusion that one is not alone. Such illusion can be created by belonging to a club, an interest group, or a religious organization, by playing on a team, playing in a musical group, or marching in a parade. Through joint activities and through memberships one may create an illusion of fusing with others. While voluntarily engaged in joint activity or while enjoying membership in a group, one is unlikely to experience those conditions that Kaiser identified as those that highlight one's existential aloneness. That is to say, one is likely to experience wanting what others also want, reflecting a shared value; to share in mutual conviction, the group norm being as an authority; and to make joint decisions, thus creating a sense of reference group approval. The neurotic, however, attempts to create in real life this illusion, transforming if not transmogrifying it into a *delusion of fusion*.

The way that the neurotic avoids individual responsibility, according to Kaiser, is through *duplicitous communication*. The neurotic does not stand behind her or his words, so to speak. He or she communicates in a way such as to give himself or herself the feeling that he or she is not responsible his or her words and actions. It is this duplicitous style of communication that creates and maintains the delusion of fusion for the neurotic person. And, this is the universal thread that runs throughout all neurosis. Again, we can turn to Sartre for an added nuance of meaning. Kaiser sees the neurotic as trying to avoid personal responsibility for her or his life by means of duplicitous communication. Sartre would see this as an act of *bad faith*, in his preferred language, *mauvaise foi*.

Kaiser came to see that much of the behavior of patients can be understood as an attempt to merge with the therapist, thus to create an illusion (if not a delusion) of fusion (Fierman, 1965). The therapist's foil is non-duplicitous communication. The therapeutic task is the establishment of non-duplicitous communication with the patient. When the patient experiences non-duplicity on the part of the therapist, and finds that this is safe, he or she can then risk the experiment of being more fully behind his or her own words. With this universal treatment, the universal triad is made complete.

With the universal treatment, non-duplicitous communication on the part of the therapist, established in his model, Kaiser went on to define some essential qualities of a good therapist. First, he or she would be sensitive to duplicity, readily recognizing it in the communication of others. Second, a good therapist would be relatively free from duplicity herself or himself. And third, a good therapist would be one who has the desire to engage in straightforward communication with relatively uncommunicative persons (i.e., neurotics, who tend toward duplicitous communication) (Fierman, 1965). In addition to such definition of the good therapist, Kaiser suggested one guideline within the patient-therapist encounter, "don't withdraw, neither physically nor psychologically" (p. 155). The context for this guideline is "that the conditions for effective psychotherapy can be expressed only in terms of personality characteristics of the therapist, and *not* in rules of what he should do" (p. 160).

"Implicit in the above guidelines is the central importance of personhood. Kaiser was relationship-oriented rather than technique-oriented, and defined a therapeutic process which depends on the personal qualities of the therapist, those being clearly articulated, with the goal being paradoxically, the communicative process itself" (Smith, 2003, p. 31).

By way of completing my discussion of Kaiser's work, and to form a bridge back to Gestalt therapy, I want to offer several analogies for contemplation. A good analogy is elegantly succinct, and yet through the form that defines it, carries not redundancy, but nuances that would require much elaboration if one were to spell out the full meaning. Therefore, I invite you, the reader, to be patient and to think on these.

Illusion of fusion : Kaiser :: Healthy confluence : Perls

Duplicitous communication : Kaiser :: Inauthentic expression : Perls

Delusion of fusion : Kaiser :: Pathological Confluence : Perls

Duplicity analysis : Kaiser :: Confrontation (support & frustration) : Perls

This first path of Gestalt therapy, the *Path of Existential Encounter*, is summarized most succinctly by a phrase used by Jim Simkin — "I and Thou, here-and-now."

If in the first path of Gestalt therapy the therapist is a genuine protagonist, then in the second path, the *Path of Psychodrama*, the therapist is more the coach-cum-director. Perls was instructed by Reich that remembrances, in order to be curative, must be accompanied by the appropriate affect. As Perls (1973), himself, stated, "It is insufficient merely to recall a past incident, one has to *psychodramatically* return to it" (p. 65). This is the basis the Gestalt principle of working in the here-and-now. "So it is not sufficient that a patient remember the traumatic times, but those remembrances must involve the feelings which were felt at those times. With the feelings present, for psychological purposes the patient is reliving the trauma. But now, in the therapeutic setting, we have the possibility of processing the feelings, of allowing the natural process of the contact/withdrawal cycle to take place, thus disempowering the toxic introject and completing a piece of unfinished emotional business from the past" (Smith, 1985, p. 140). Claudio Naranjo (1970) introduced the term *presentification* to refer to the process of bringing memories from the past or fantasies of the future into the experienced present.

Particular practitioners of the Gestalt approach may favor one or the other of the two paths, overall. Or, a therapist may prefer one path with one particular person in therapy, the other path with another. Or, a therapist may move from one path to the other as a course of therapy unfolds with a particular person. The two paths are distinct and yet may intertwine like the two strands of the DNA double helix.

~

Retroflection: Self Relating to Self

The self is a relation which relates itself to its own self . . .
— Søren Kierkegaard
(*The Sickness Unto Death*, 1849, in Bretall,
1973, p. 340.)

Kierkegaard . . . speaks of the relation of the self to the self.
And this is exactly what retroflection . . . is. The communi-
cation does not go from self to other, or from other to self,
but from self to self.
— Frederick S. Perls
(*In and Out the Garbage Pail*, 1969, p. 214.)

If these two quotes are understood in their fullness, my essay is then redundant. As for myself, I require explication, and therefore offer the following as but a footnote to the quotes.

It is made explicit in the above statement by Perls that he was at least aware of Kierkegaard's idea of the self in relation to the self. How extensively he read Kierkegaard, we do not know. He did make another reference in a 1966 paper, writing, "All schools of existentialism emphasize direct experience, but most of them have some conceptual framework: Kierkegaard had

---

Previously unpublished.

his Protestant theology . . . " (Perls, 1975, p. 1). A co-developer of Gestalt therapy, Paul Goodman, too, seemed to be conversant with Kierkegaard's works. As Stoehr (1994) put it, Goodman had a theological view of the psyche, "where Lao-tzu, Buber, and Kierkegaard all leave their tracks" (p. 119). We do, however, know that Perls' prevenient references are reflected in the works of later Gestalt therapists. The Polsters (1973) cited Kierkegaard's description of "complete absorption in God as the deepest unity in life," using this in their discussion of the process of figure-ground formation (p. 44). Baumgardner (1975), in opening her first chapter, wrote:

> Gestalt therapy is a matter of attending to another human being in a way which makes it possible for him to be himself, "grounded in the power which constitutes him," to borrow a phrase from Kierkegaard. Continuing in Kierkegaard's tradition, Gestalt therapy is an existential therapy, concerned with the problems evoked by our dread of accepting responsibility for what we are and what we do. (p. 9)

And, in her essays in Gestalt therapy, Crocker (1999) integrated material from Kierkegaard extensively, writing of the real self that is individualistic, the well-lived life that is uniquely one's own, the fear and trembling concomitant with responsible choices involving moral dilemmas, the bitter sweet that is far better to desire than to obtain, and the ultimate sacrifice of living with a terrible paradox.

Clearly, then, Kierkegaard has left his tracks in Gestalt therapy. The term *retroflection* made its appearance quite early in the Gestalt literature, 1947. "Retroflection means that some function which originally is directed from the individual toward the world, changes its direction and is bent back toward the originator" (Perls, 1992, p. 139.). An apt choice of word this is, for *retro* is Latin for *back* or *backward; flexus* is the past participle of the Latin word *flectere*, meaning to *bend*. Combining the two, we then derive a word to signify *to bend or turn backward* — *retroflex*. The nominal form is, thereby, *retroflexion* or *retroflection*, and in keeping with the latter spelling, the acceptable infinitive verb derives as *to retroflect*.

Implied in retroflection is a splitting of the self into a part that is the *doer* and a part that is *done to*. In addressing the retroflector, Perls, Hefferline, and Goodman (1951) wrote as follows.

He stops directing various energies outward in attempts to manipulate and bring about changes in the environment that will satisfy his needs; instead, he redirects activity inward and *substitutes himself in place of the envi-*

ronment as the target of behavior. To the extent that he does this, he splits his personality into "doer" and "done to" (p. 146).

In Perls' (1992) earlier words, from 1947, "*A genuine retroflection is always based upon such a split personality* and is composed of an active (A) and a passive (P) part" (p. 264). Herein is an echo of Kierkegaard (Bretall, 1973), for in *The Sickness unto Death* he wrote "one would do well to distinguish between the active and the passive self, showing how the self is related to itself when it is active, and how it is related to itself . . . when it is passive" (p. 366).

Continuing, with a focus on the pragmatic, Perls (1992) wrote the following:

> From the practical point of view the most important retroflections are: hatred directed against the self, narcissism, and self-control. Self-destruction is, of course, the most dangerous of all retroflections. Its minor brother is the tendency to repress (repression is retroflected oppression). (p. 269)

In identifying *self-hate, narcissism (self-love)*, and *self-control*, I suggest that Perls actually differentiated three *forms* of retroflection, and that in the interest of conceptual clarity these forms must be distinguished. I will now endeavor to do so. First, however, I want to emphasize that when using the word *practical*, Perls was writing from his perspective as a psychiatrist in the decade of 1940. That is to say, he was identifying the retroflections that he perceived as most relevant to psychotherapy praxis, those that were, and are, of the realm of psychopathology.

In the case of self-hate, the feeling and the accompanying impulse to hurt have been turned back on the self, a straightforward example of Perls' definition of retroflection. The active part of the self has chosen the passive part as the target of its aggression. It is for this reason that it has been said that suicide, in instances wherein it is an expression of self-hate in its most dramatic and extreme mien, is a case of mistaken identity!

Self-love is markedly different, in that two healthy needs are involved, namely, the need *to love* and the need *to be loved*. The passive part of the split self is, again, chosen as the target. But, in this case of pathological self-love, narcissism, there is a double loss. First, insofar as it is the active part of the self that is loving the passive part of the self, the passive part, needing to feel loved by another, is left with a need unfulfilled. Likewise, the active part of the self that needs to love another, insofar as it is loving only the passive part of the self, is left with a need unanswered. Both the active and the passive parts of the self are substitutes from the perspective of the other part that has need of an other, the love given and the love received, therefore, ersatz.

The third form of retroflection, self-control, refers to a greater or a lessor degree of holding back, a block or inhibition of action, respectively. Whereas in self-hate there is a substitution of target (the passive part of the self), and in self-love there is a substitution of target (the passive part of the self) *and* a substitution of the doer (the active part of the self), in the case of self-control the active part of the self is held back, inappropriately transforming it into a more or less passive part. Perls (1992) explained this process in terms of body energy.

We repress vital functions (vegetative energy, as Reich calls their sum) by muscular contractions. The civil war raging in the neurotic organism is mostly waged between the motoric system and unaccepted organismic energies which strive for expression and gratification. The motoric system has to a great extent lost its function as a working, active, world-bound system and, by retroflection, has become the jailor rather than the assistant of important biological needs. Every dissolved symptom means setting free both policeman *and* the prisoner — motoric *and* "vegetative" energies — for the common struggle of life (p. 276).

Another somewhat simpler description was offered by Enright (1970), and although focused on a complete block, can be applied equally to inhibition.

> Retroflection describes the general process of negating, holding back, or balancing the impulse tension by additional, opposing sensorimotor tension.... Since the net result of all this canceled-out muscular tension is zero — no overt movement — there is no particular increase in activity at the contact boundary. (p. 112)

Enright went on to say that Wilhelm Reich's concept of *character armor* or *body armor* corresponds to a chronic retroflection, as just described.

In the two other forms of retroflection, reflected in Perls' identification of self-hate and self-love, the block is not in action, but in *interaction*. In both self-hate and self-love the action is taken. The problem is that the interaction has gone awry. Turning once again to the words of Perls (1992), taken from *Ego, Hunger and Aggression*, we find the following.

> There is not the slightest justification for calling only the sex instinct an object instinct. Aggression is at least as much object-bound as sex, and it can in the same way as love (in

narcissism or in masturbation) have the "Self" as object. They both may become "retroflected." (p. 137)

It is clear, as we have seen, that the essence of retroflected interaction is the absence of any environmental object. The Polsters (1973) added further clarification.

The *retroflector* abandons any attempt to influence his environment by becoming a separate and self-sufficient unit, reinvesting his energy back into an exclusively intrapersonal system and severely restricting the traffic between himself and the environment. (p. 71)

Following Perls' identification of both self-hate and self-love, we can discern two types of retroflection of interaction. Following their discussion of retroflected anger (i.e., self-hate), Perls et al. (1951) noted that "retroflections also include what one *wanted from* others but was unsuccessful in obtaining, with the outcome that now, for want of anyone else to do it, one gives it to himself" (p. 150). This refers, of course, to the pragmatically important retroflection of narcissism or self-love. The Polsters (1973), too, explicitly distinguished the two forms of retroflection of interaction. "Retroflection is a hermaphroditic function wherein the individual turns back against himself what he would like *to do to someone else*, or does to himself what he would like *someone else to do to him*" (p. 82).

In the form of retroflection in which someone does to herself or himself what she or he would like someone else to do to her or him, the paradigm content is love. In manifest form it appears as physical actions such as self-holding, self-patting, self-stroking, self-preening, and masturbation. If we but listen, we may learn something from the realm of mythopoesis. In the myth of Narcissus we are warned, for a prayer was answered by Nemesis, goddess of righteous anger. "May he who loves not others love himself" (Hamilton, 1942, p. 88). Implied in this curse is that if one loves oneself, in that sense for which Narcissus has become eponymous, one will not be able to love others.

In the case of the other type of retroflected interaction, in which one does to oneself what one would like to do to another, the paradigm content is, as we have seen, anger (self-hate). In the verbal realm, this can be recognized by statements such as "I hate myself," "I am mad at myself," or "I could kick myself." More subtle are those phrases that delete the reflexive pronoun, but nevertheless contain derogatory self-referents. For example, one might say, "I'm so dumb," "I'm so clumsy," "Dumb me," or so forth. When manifest non-verbally, retroflected anger may be identified by any act of hurting oneself, sometimes including those acts that may appear to be accidental — scratching oneself, hitting one's self, biting oneself, kicking oneself, cutting oneself, and such. Frequently, these acts are made manifest in such a diminished form that they cause little or no pain or tissue damage. If, however, one exaggerates the scratching, the biting of one's lip, or the striking of one's fist on one's knee, the adumbration is revealed and the meaning emerges dramatically. This subtlety of diminished form did not escape the attention of Perls et al. (1951), for they suggested that even "repeated mistakes or acts of clumsiness are often retroflected annoyance" (p. 167). And, what other is annoyance than a pale anger?

The common core of these three forms of retroflection is the solipsistic relationship of a split self. The self is split and engaged with itself, rather than engaging with an other. Viewed from the pathological perspective, as Perls did, retroflection refers to the mechanisms by which one may block or inhibit need serving actions and interactions with others. The retroflections are, then, to use the Gestalt term, *contact boundary disturbances*. In order to place this term in broader context, I offer an analogy.

Contact boundary disturbances : Gestalt therapy :: Defense mechanisms : Psychoanalysis

The introduction of this new term is no mere semantic bagatelle, for it calls attention to an *inter*-personal meaning, forming a nexus between that and the *intra*-personal focus of the older term.

Each of the three forms of retroflection — retroflection of action, retroflection of interaction in the form of doing to oneself what one would like another to do to one, and retroflection of interaction in the form of doing to oneself what one would like to do to another — become manifest throughout a range of intensity. The first two (retroflection of action and retroflection in the form of doing to oneself what one would like another to do to one) have a normal or healthy zone contained within their range of occurrence. Even though Perls, by way of clinical pragmatism, emphasized the pathological aspects of retroflection, he did acknowledge non-pathological instances of these two forms of retroflection.

With respect to retroflection of action, Perls et al. (1951) identified and explored its positive expression in the following manner. "Retroflection is healthy behavior when it constitutes holding back for the sake of caution in a situation of genuine danger" (p. 212). By way of elaboration, they continued,

Normally, retroflection is the process of reforming oneself, for instance correcting the impractical approach or reconsidering the possibilities of the emotion, making a read-justment as the grounds for further action . . . . And more generally, any act of deliberate self-control during a difficult engagement is retroflection. (p. 455)

"In some situations," Perls et al. stated, on a decidedly serious note, "holding back is necessary, even life-saving . . . . The important question is whether or not the person has *rational grounds* for presently choking off behavior in given circumstances" (p. 147). Furthermore, "it is only when the retroflection is habitual, chronic, out of control, that it is pathological" (p. 147).

Doing to oneself what one would like another to do to one can also be healthy, "provided it does not include trying to gratify for oneself what are genuinely *interpersonal* needs" (Perls et al., 1951, p. 150). I would add, that at times when the need is present, but the other person is not, self-soothing, self-stroking, self-holding, and making love to oneself are entirely appropriate.

The two sides of the coin of this form of retroflection of interaction were astutely juxtaposed by Zinker (1977).

The price he pays — among other things — is that of using his own energy rather than being replenished by another person. His rewards are independence, self-reliance, doing better for himself than another can, privacy, and the development of his individual capacities and talents. (p. 103)

Elsewhere, I have suggested that retroflection of interaction in the paradigmatic form of self-hate, unlike self-love and self-control, lacks healthy expression (Smith, 1986). I see self-hate as unnatural and surely a perversion.

If Perls placed the relationship of self to self in a clinical context, and thus with primary focus on psychopathology, Kierkegaard's context was one more philosophical, with primary focus on spirituality. In the interest of the latter, Kierkegaard seemingly was unconcerned with what Perls and most psychotherapists, myself included, would take as pathological. For instance, in an early journal entry, Kierkegaard (Rohde, 1993) revealed the following.

I have just returned from a party of which I was the life and soul; witty banter flowed from my lips, everyone laughed and admired me — but I came away . . . wanting to shoot myself. (p. 13)

And, "Death and Damnation, I can dissociate from everything else but my own self; I can't even forget myself when I am asleep" (p. 13).

Whether to look upon Kierkegaard's explorations of the relationship of self to self — the self-consumption of despair (Bretall, p. 342), self-annihilation in order to "satiate the hunger of doubt" (p. 100), self-concealment (p. 99), self-love in the right way (pp. 284-290) — through a template of psychopathology or a template of spirituality is ultimately a choice for each serious and discerning reader. Regardless, Kierkegaard honored well the self-knowledge that is fundamental to depth and fulness of personhood. Acknowledging the prerequisite of self-knowledge, he wrote in his journal as follows:

> Being too busy has this result: that an individual very, very rarely is permitted to form a heart: on the other hand, the thinker, the poet, or the religious personality who actually has formed his heart, will never be popular, not because he is difficult, but because it demands quiet and prolonged working with oneself and intimate knowledge of oneself as well as a certain isolation. . . . religious things have to do with a softly murmured soliloquy with oneself. (Rohde, 1993, p. 101)

For it is, as Kierkegaard (Bretall, 1973) declared, "One must know oneself before knowing anything else. . . . It is only after a man has thus understood himself inwardly and has thus seen his way, that life acquires peace and significance . . . " (p. 6).

Thus, from a seed sown by Kierkegaard, and fertilizing it with the energetic perspective of Reich, Perls nurtured a three-leafed cultigen that he named retroflection. In the interest of classificatory clarity, I have suggested that the three leaves described as self-control, self-love and self-hate be recognized as retroflection of action, and two distinct forms of retroflection of interaction, respectively.

> I shall now try to fix a calm gaze upon myself and begin to act in earnest.
> — Søren Kierkegaard
> (*The Journals*, 1835, in Bretall, 1973, p. 6.)

BIBLIOGRAPY

Abt, L. (1950). A theory of projective psychology. In Abt. L. E., & Bellak, L. (Ed.), *Projective Psychology*. New York: Grove

Adam, M. (1976). *Wandering in Eden*. New York: Alfred A. Knopf

Aikin, P. (1979). The participation of neuromuscular activity in perception, emotion and thinking. *Journal of Biological Experience, 1*(2).

American Psychiatric Association. (1952). *Diagnostic and statistical manual: Mental Disorders*. Washington DC: American Psychiatric Association

American Psychiatric Association. (1968). *Diagnostic and statistical manual: Mental Disorders* (2 ed.). Washington DC: American Psychiatric Association

American Psychiatric Association. (1980). *Diagnostic and statistical manual: Mental Disorders* (3 ed.). Washington DC: American Psychiatric Association

Anderson, W. (1983). *The upstart spring: Esalen and the American awakening*. Reading MA: Addison-Wesley

Arnheim, R. (1974). *Art and visual perception*. Berkeley CA: University of California. Original Publication 1954

Atwood, G., & Stolorow, R. (1993). *Faces in a cloud: Intersubjectivity in personality theory*. Northvale NJ: Jason Aronson

Baker, E. (1967). *Man in the trap*. New York: Collier

Baumgardner, P., & Perls, F. (1975). *Gifts from Lake Cowichan/Legacy from Fritz*. Palo Alto CA: Science and Behavior Books

Bauschatz, P. (1982). *The well and the tree: World and time in early Germanic culture*. Amherst: University of Massachusetts

Beahrs, J., & Humiston, K. (1974). Dynamics of experiential therapy. *American Journal of Clinical Hypnosis, 17*(1).

Bean, O. (1971). *Me and the orgone*. New York: St. Martin's Press

Beisser, A. (2006). The paradoxical theory of change. In Fagan, J. & Shepherd, I. (Ed.), *Gestalt therapy now*. Gouldsboro ME: Gestalt Journal

Press. Original Publication 1970: Palo Alto CA, Science and Behavior Books

Bellak, L. (1950). On the problems of the concept of projection. In Abt, L. E., & Bellak, L. (Ed.), *Projective psychology*. New York: Grove

Bierce, A. (1958). *The devil's dictionary*. New York: Dover

Blackham, H. (1959). *Six existentialist thinkers*. New York: Harper Torchbooks

Bloom, D. (2005). Laura Perls in New York City – A community recalls its leader during the centenary of her birth. *International Gestalt Journal*, 28(1), 9-23.

Bretall, R. (Ed.). (1973). *A Kierkegaard anthology*. Princeton NJ: Princeton University

Brown, M. (1990). *The healing touch: An introduction to organismic psychotherapy*. Mendocino CA: Liferythym

Bugental, J. (1971). The humanistic ethic: The individual in psychotherapy as a social change agent. *Journal of Humanistic Psychology*, 11(1), 11-25.

Bugental, J. (1987). *The art of the psychotherapist*. New York: Norton

Bynner, W. (1962). *The way of life according to Lao Tzu*. New York: Capricorn

Campbell, J. (1990). *Transformations of myth through time*. New York: Harper & Row

Capra, F. (1984). *The Tao of physics*. New York: Bantam Books

Castanedo, C. (1972). *Journey to Ixtlan*. New York: Simon and Schuster

Cohn, R. (1970). Therapy in groups: Psychoanalytic, experiential. and Gestalt. In Fagan, J., & Shepherd, I. (Ed.), *Gestalt therapy now*. Gouldsboro ME: The Gestalt Journal Press. Original Publication 1970: Palo Alto CA, Science and Behavior Books

Colgrove, M., Bloomfield, H., & McWilliams, P. . (1976). *How to survive the loss of a love*. New York: Bantam Books

Crocker, S. (1981). Proflection. *The Gestalt Journal*, 4(2), 21.

Crocker, S. (1982). A response to Joel Latner. *The Gestalt Journal*, 5(2), 17.

Crossley-Holland, K. (1980). *The Norse myths*. New York: Pantheon

Das, Ram. (1973). *The only dance there is*. Garden City NY: Anchor/Doubleday

Deikman, A. (1969). Deautomatization and the mystic experience. In Tart, C. (Ed.), *Altered states of consciousness*. New York: John Wiley

Dublin, J. (1972). Language as expression of upright man: toward a phenomenology of language and the lived body. *Journal of Phenomenological Psychology*, 2(2).

Dublin, J. (1981). A Bio-Existential therapy. *Psychotherapy: Theory, Research and Practice*, 18(1), 3-10.

Dublin, J. (1997). Gestalt therapy, existential-Gestalt therapy and/versus 'Perls-ism'. In Smith, E. (Ed.), *The growing edge of Gestalt therapy*. Gouldsboro ME: The Gestalt Journal Press. Original Publication 1976: New York, Brunner/Mazel

Eliade, M. (1964). *Shamanism: Archaic techniques of ecstasy*. Princeton NJ: Princeton University. Original Publication 1951

Ellenberger, H. (1970). *The discovery of the unconscious*. New York: Basic Books

Ellis, W. (1997). *A source book of Gestalt psychology*. Highland NY: The Gestalt Journal Press. Original Publication 1950: Humanities Press, New York

Enelow, A., & Adler, L. (1965). Foreword. In Fierman, L. (Ed.), *Effective psychotherapy: The contribution of Hellmuth Kaiser*. New York: Free Press

Enright, J. (2006). An introduction to gestalt techniques. In Fagan, J., & Shepherd, I. (Ed.), *Gestalt therapy now*. Gouldsboro ME: The Gestalt Journal Press. Original Publication 1970: Palo Alto CA, Science and Behavior Books

Espy, W. (1978). *Thou improper, thou uncommon noun*. New York: Clarkson N. Potter

Fagan, J. (1997). The Gestalt approach as "right lobe" therapy. In Smith, E. (Ed.), *The growing edge of Gestalt therapy*. Gouldsboro ME: Gestalt Journal Press. Original Publication 1976: New York, Brunner/Mazel

Fagan, J. (2003). The importance of Fritz Perls having been. In Smith, E. (Ed.), *Gestalt voices*. Gouldsboro ME: Gestalt Journal Press. Original Publication 1992: Norwood NJ, Ablex

Fagan, J. & Shepherd, I. (Ed.). (2006). *Gestalt therapy now*. Gouldsboro ME: The Gestalt Journal Press.(1970: Palo Alto CA, Science and Behavior Books)

Feng, G. (1972). *Lao Tsu, Tao te ching*. New York: Vintage

Fierman, L. (Ed.). (1965). *Effective psychotherapy: The contribution of Hellmuth Kaiser*. New York: Free Press

Frank, L. (1965). Projective methods for the study of personality. In Murstein, B. (Ed.), *Handbook of projective techniques*. New York: Basic Books. Original Publication 1939

Freud, S. (1959). Inhibitions, symptoms, and anxiety. In Strachey, J. (Ed.), *The standard edition of the complete psychological works of Sigmund Freud* (Vol. 22). London: Hogarth Press. Original Publication 1926

Freud, S. (1959). The ego and the id. In Strachey, J. (Ed.), *The standard edition of the complete psychological works of Sigmund Freud* (Vol. 22). London: Hogarth Press. Original Publication 1926

Freud, S. (1962). *The ego and the id.* New York: Norton. Original Publication 1923

Freud, S. (1963). Further remarks on the defense neuropsychoses. In Rieff, P. (Ed.), *Early psychoanalytic writings*. New York: Collier. Original Publication 1896

Freud, S. (1963). Mourning and melancholia. In Rieff, P. (Ed.), *General psychological theory*. New York: Collier

Freud, S. (1963). The antithetical sense of primal words. In Rieff, P. (Ed.), *Character and culture (The collected papers of Sigmund Freud)*. New York: Collier

Freud, S. (1963). The justification for detaching from neurasthenia a particular syndrome: The anxiety neurosis. In Rieff, P. (Ed.), *Early psychoanalytic writings*. New York: Collier. Original Publication 1894

Freud, S. (1963). The uncanny. In Reiff, P. (Ed.), *Studies in parapsychology*. New York: Collier

Funk & Wagnalls standard dictionary of folklore, mythology, and legend. (1984). New York: Harper & Row

Gibson, M. (2006). *Symbolism*. Köln: Taschen

Goldberg, V. (1977). Horror in art: The good, the mad, and the ugly. *Psychology Today, 11.*

Golomb, J. (1995). *In search of authenticity: From Kierkegaard to Camus*. New York: Routledge

Golomb, J. (1999). Introductory Essay: Nietzsche's "New Psychology" In Golomb, J., & Santaniello, W., & Lehrer, R. (Ed.), *Nietzsche and depth psychology*. Albany: State University of New York Press

Goodman, F. (1990). *Where the spirits ride the wind: Trance journeys and other ecstatic experiences*. Bloomington IN: Indiana University Press

Goodman, P. (1991). On being a writer: An essay for my fortieth birthday. In Stoehr, T. (Ed.), *Nature heals: The psychological essays of Paul*

Goodman. Gouldsboro ME: The Gestalt Journal Press. Original Publication 1977: New York, Free Life Editions

Goodman, P. (1991). On writer's block. In Stoehr, T. (Ed.), *Nature heals: The psychological essays of Paul Goodman.* Gouldsboro ME: The Gestalt Journal Press. Original Publication 1977: New York, Free Life Editions

Goodman, P. (1991). My psychology as a "utopian sociologist". In Stoehr, T. (Ed.), *Nature heals: The psychological essays of Paul Goodman.* Gouldsboro ME: The Gestalt Journal Press. Original Publication 1977: New York, Free Life Editions

Goodman, P. (1991). Designing pacifist films. In Stoehr, T. (Ed.), *Nature heals: The psychological essays of Paul Goodman.* Gouldsboro ME: The Gestalt Journal Press. Original Publication 1977: New York, Free Life Editions

Goodman, P. (1991). On intellectual inhibition of explosive grief and anger. In Stoehr, T. (Ed.), *Nature heals: The psychological essays of Paul Goodman.* Gouldsboro ME: The Gestalt Journal Press. Original Publication 1977: New York, Free Life Editions

Goodman, P. (1991). The psychological revolution and the writer's life-view. In Stoehr, T. (Ed.), *Nature heals: The psychological essays of Paul Goodman.* Gouldsboro ME: The Gestalt Journal Press. Original Publication 1977: New York, Free Life Editions

Gordon, J. (1967). Conclusions. In Gordon, J. (Ed.), *Handbook of. clinical and experimental hypnosis.* New York: MacMillan

Gupta, R. (1975). Freud and Schopenhauer. *Journal of the History of Ideas,* 36(4).

Hall, C., & Lindzey, G. (1957). *Theories of personality.* New York: Wiley

Hall, C., & Lindzey, G. (1970). *Theories of personality* (2nd ed.). New York: Wiley

Hamiton, E. (1942). *Mythology.* New York: Mentor

Hanna, T. (1980). *The body of life.* New York: Knopf

Harman, R. (1982). Gestalt therapy theory: Working at the contact boundaries. *The Gestalt Journal,* 5(1).

Hayakawa, S. (1941). *Language in action.* New York: Harcourt, Brace

Hemmingway, E. (1970). *Islands in the stream.* New York: Charles Scribner's Sons

Hesse, H. (1969). *Steppenwolf.* New York: Bantam Books

Hollander, L. (Translator). (1962). *The poetic edda.* Austin: University of Texas Press

Horney, K. (1950). *Neurosis and human growth.* New York: Norton

Hotchner, A. (1983). *Papa Hemingway.* New York: Quill

Howard, J. (1970). *Please touch.* New York: Dell

Janson, H. (1991). *History of art.* New York: Harry N. Abrams

Jones, W. (1952). *A history of Western philosophy* (Vol. II). New York: Harcourt, Brace, & World

Jung, C. (1968). *Analytical psychology.* New York: Vintage

Jung, C. (1970). *Civilization in transition.* Princeton: Princeton University

Jung, C. (1970). *Aion: researches into the phenomenology of the self.* Princeton: Princeton University

Kaufmann, W. (Ed.). (1982). *The portable Nietzsche.* New York: Viking Penguin

Keen, S. (1974). The cosmic versus the rational. *Psychology Today, 8.*

Kierkegaard, S. (Ed.). (1993). *The diary of Soren Kierkegaard (Edited by Peter Rohde).* Secaucus NJ: Carol

Köhler, W. (1947). *Gestalt psychology.* New York: Liveright

Kopp, S. (1971). *Guru: Metaphors from a psychotherapist.* Palo Alto: Science and Behavior Books

Kopp, S. (1974). *The hanged man.* Palo Alto: Science and Behavior Books

Kudirka, N. (1992). A talk with Laura Perls about the therapist and the artist. In Smith, E. (Ed.), *Gestalt voices.* Gouldsboro ME: The Gestalt Journal Press. Original Publication 1992: Norwood NJ, Ablex

Lambert, M., & Bergin, A. (1994). The effectiveness of psychotherapy. In Bergin, A., & Garfield, S. (Ed.), *Handbook of psychotherapy and behavior change.* New York: Wiley

Landow, G. (2000). Rossetti's concern with time and its loss in *House of life.* Retrieved August 2, 2008, from http://www.victorianweb.org /authors/dgr/dgrseti14.html

Latner, J. (1982). The thresher of time: On love and freedom in Gestalt therapy. *The Gestalt Journal, 5*(1).

Latner, J. (2005). America's protean creativity: Gestalt therapy and creative License – essay and book review. *International Gestalt Journal, 28*(2).

Lehrer, R. . (1999). Adler and Nietzsche. In Golomb, J., & Santaniello, R., & Lehrer, R. (Ed.), *Nietzsche and depth psychology.* New York: State University of New York Press

Lehrer, R. . (1999). Freud and Nietzsche. In Golomb, J., & Santaniello, R., & Lehrer, R. (Ed.), *Nietzsche and depth psychology*. New York: State University of New York Press

Leonard, G. (1975). *The ultimate athlete*. New York: Viking

Levitsky, A., & Perls, F. (1970). The rules and games of Gestalt therapy. In Fagan, J., & Shepherd, I. (Ed.), *Gestalt therapy now*. Gouldsboro ME: The Gestalt Journal Press. Original Publication 1970: Palo Alto CA, Science and Behavior Books

Lewin, K. (1952). *Field theory in social science*. London: Travistock Publications

Lewis, C. S. (1996). *The Screwtape letters*. New York: Touchstone

London, P. (1964). *The modes and morals of psychotherapy*. New York: Holt, Rinehart, and Winston

London, P. (1967). The induction of hypnosis. In Gordon, J. (Ed.), *Handbook of clinical and experimental hypnosis*. New York: MacMillan

Lowen, A. (1975). *Bioenergetics*. New York: Penguin

Lowen, A., & Lowen, L. (1977). *The way to vibrant health*. New York: Harper & Row

Lowen, A. (1980). *Fear of life*. New York: Collier

Ludwig, A. (1969). Altered states of consciousness. In Tart, C. (Ed.), *Altered states of consciousness*. New York: John Wiley

Maslow, A. (1954). *Motivation and personality*. New York: Harper & Row

Maslow, A. (1968). *Toward a psychology of being*. New York: Von Nostrand Reinhold

Naranjo, C. (1970). Present-centeredness: Technique, prescription, and ideal. In Fagan, J., & Shepherd, I. (Ed.), *Gestalt therapy now*. Gouldsboro ME: The Gestalt Journal Press. Original Publication 1970: Palo Alto CA, Science and Behavior Books

Naranjo, C. (1978). Gestalt therapy as a transpersonal approach. *The Gestalt Journal*, 1(2).

Naranjo, C. (1980). *The techniques of Gestalt therapy*. Highland NY: The Gestalt Journal Press

Nietzsche, F. (1966). *Beyond good and evil* (Kaufmann, W., Trans.). New York: Random House. Original Publication 1886

Nietzsche, F. (1982). Ecce homo. In Kaufmann, W. (Ed.), *The portable Nietzsche*. New York: Penguin. Original Publication 1908

Nietzsche, F. (1982). The gay science: Book V. In Kaufmann, W. (Ed.), *The portable Nietzsche*. New York: Penguin. Original Publication 1908

Nietzsche, F. (1982). Thus spoke Zarathustra. In Kaufmann, W. (Ed.), *The portable Nietzsche*. New York: Penguin. Original Publication 1884

Partridge, B. (1960). *A history of orgies*. New York: Bonanza

Pearce, J. (1971). *The crack in the cosmic egg*. New York: Julian Press

Perls, F. (1970). Four lectures. In Fagan, J., & Shepherd, I. (Ed.), *Gestalt therapy now*. Gouldsboro ME: The Gestalt Journal Press. Original Publication 1970: Palo Alto CA, Science and Behavior Books

Perls, F. (1973). *The Gestalt approach and eye witness to therapy*. Ben Lomond CA: Science and Behavior Books

Perls, F., & Baumgardner, P. (1975). *Legacy from Fritz: Gifts from Lake Cowichan*. Palo Alto CA: Science and Behavior Books

Perls, F. (1975). Theory and technique of personality integration. In Stevens, J. (Ed.), *Gestalt is*. Moab UT: Real People Press. Original Publication 1948

Perls, F. (1975). Morality, ego boundary and aggression. In Stevens, J. (Ed.), *Gestalt is*. Moab UT: Real People Press. Original Publication 1955

Perls, F. (1975). Group therapy and human potentialities. In Stevens, J. (Ed.), *Gestalt is*. Moab UT: Real People Press. Original Publication 1966

Perls, F. (1978). Cooper Union Forum — Lecture series The self "Finding self through Gestalt therapy". *The Gestalt Journal*, 1(1).

Perls, F. (1978). Psychiatry in a new key: Part I. *The Gestalt Journal*, 1(1).

Perls, F. (1978). Psychiatry in a new key: Part II. *The Gestalt Journal*, 1(2).

Perls, F. (1992). *Gestalt therapy verbatim*. Gouldsboro ME: The Gestalt Journal Press. Original Publication 1969

Perls, F. (1992). *In and out the garbage pail*. Gouldsboro ME: The Gestalt Journal Press. Original Publication 1969

Perls, F. (1992). *Ego, hunger and aggression*. Gouldsboro ME: The Gestalt Journal Press. Original Publication 1942

Perls, F., Hefferline, R., & Goodman, P. (1994). *Gestalt therapy: Excitement and growth in the human personality*. Highland, New York: The Gestalt Journal Press. Original Publication 1951: New York, Julian Press

Perls, L. (1997). Comment on the new directions. In Smith, E. (Ed.), *The growing edge of Gestalt therapy*. Gouldsboro ME: The Gestalt Journal Press. Original Publication 1976

Perls, F. (1998). The manipulator: A session of Gestalt therapy with Dr. Frederick Perls and group. *The Gestalt Journal, 21(2)*.

Peterson, S. (1971). *A catalog of the ways people grow*. New York: Ballantine Books

Pirsig, R. (9174). *Zen and the art of motorcycle maintenance*. New York: William Morrow

Polkinghorne, D. (1983). *Methodology for the human sciences*. Albany: State University of New York Press

Polster, E. (1970). Sensory functioning in psychotherapy. In Fagan, J., & Shepherd, I. (Ed.), *Gestalt therapy now*. Gouldsboro ME: The Gestalt Journal Press. Original Publication 1970: Palo Alto CA, Science and Behavior Books

Polster, E., & Polster, M. (1973). *Gestalt therapy integrated*. New York: Brunner/Mazel

Popkin, R., & Stroll, A. (1956). *Philosophy made simple*. Garden City NY: Doubleday

Prather, H. (1970). *Notes to myself*. Moab UT: Real People Press

Prather, H. (1972). *I touch the earth, the earth touches me*. Garden City NY: Doubleday

Prather, H. (1977). *Notes on love and courage*. Garden City NY: Doubleday

Rabin, A. (1981). *Assessment with projective techniques*. New York: Springer Publishing

Reich, W. (1942). *The function of the orgasm* (Wolfe, T., Trans.). New York: Orgone Institute Press

Reich, W. (1948). *Listen, little man!* New York: Farrar, Straus and Giroux

Reich, W. (1949). *Character analysis*. New York: Noonday Press

Reps, P. (1971). *Zen flesh, Zen bones*. New York: Penguin

Rieff, P. (1966). *The triumph of the therapeutic*. New York: Harper & Row

Rohde, P. (Ed.). (1993). *The diary of Søren Kierkegaard*. New York: Citadel

Rothgeb, C. (Ed.). (1973). *Abstracts of the standard edition of the complete psychological works of Sigmund Freud*. New York: Jason Aronson

Rycroft, C. (1968). *A critical dictionary of psychoanalysis*. New York: Basic Books

Sabin, F. (1940). *Classical myths that live today*. New York: Burdett

Salzman, L. (1968). *The obsessive personality*. New York: Science House

Schiffman, M. (1972). *Gestalt self therapy and further techniques for personal growth*. Menlo Park, CA: Self Therapy Press

Schoen, S. (1994). *Presence of mind: Roots of a wise psychotherapy*. Gouldsboro ME: The Gestalt Journal Press

Schopenhauer, A. (1928). *The philosophy of Schopenhauer*. New York: Carlton House. Original Publication 1818

Shakespeare, W. (2007). *The complete works of William Shakespeare*. Hertfordshire UK: Wordsworth Editions

Shapiro, D. (1965). *Neurotic styles*. New York: Basic Books

Sharf, R. (1996). *Theories of psychotherapy and counseling*. Belmont CA: Brooks/Cole

Shephard, M. (1975). *Fritz: An intimate portrait of Fritz Perls and Gestalt therapy*. New York: Dutton

Shepherd, I. (1970). Limitations and cautions in the gestalt approach. In Fagan, J., & Shepherd, I. (Ed.), *Gestalt therapy now*. Gouldsboro ME: The Gestalt Journal Press. Original Publication 1970: Palo Alto CA, Science and Behavior Books

Shepherd, I. (1992). Teaching therapy through the lives of the masters: A personal statement. In Smith, E. (Ed.), *Gestalt voices*. Gouldsboro ME: The Gestalt Journal Press

Shor, R. (1969). Three dimensions of hypnotic depth. In Tart, C. (Ed.), *Altered states of consciousness*. New York: John Wiley

Shostrom, Ed. (1967). *Man, the manipulator*. Nashville TN: Abingdon Press

Smith, E. (1975). The role of early Reichian theory in the development of Gestalt therapy. *Psychotherapy: Theory, Research and Practice, 12*(3).

Smith, E. (1975). Altered states of consciousness in Gestalt therapy. Paper presented at the meeting of the Georgia Psychological Association, Atlanta, May, 1973. *Journal of Contemporary Psychotherapy, 7*(1).

Smith, E. (1975). *Presentification of archetypal personifications: A transpersonal way of growth.*

Smith, E. (1978). The impasse phenomenon: A Gestalt therapy experience involving an altered state of consciousness. *The Gestalt Journal, 1*(1).

Smith, E. (1978). Response to Gottsegen, J. and Gottsegen, G. The Issue of Cult Identity. *Voices, 14*(3).

Smith, E. (1979). Seven decision points. *Voices, 15*(3).

Smith, E. (1979). Anxiety – The perverse traveling companion. *Voices, 15*(1).

Smith, E. (1984). Characterological styles of emotional plague behavior. *Energy and Character, 15*(1).

Smith, E. (1985). *The body in psychotherapy.* Jefferson NC: McFarland

Smith, E. (1986). Retroflection: The forms of non-enactment. *The Gestalt Journal, 9*(1).

Smith, E. (1987). Therapists in search of the holy grail. *The Gestalt Journal, 10*(1).

Smith, E. (1988). Self-interruptions in the rhythm of contact and withdrawal. *The Gestalt Journal, 11*(2).

Smith, E. (1989). *Not just pumping iron: On the psychology of lifting weights.* Springfield IL: Charles C. Thomas

Smith, E. (1990). Embodied Gestalt psychotherapy. In Zeig, J., & Munion, W. (Ed.), *What is psychotherapy?* San Francisco: Jossey-Bass

Smith, E. (1990). Exploring confluence. *Journal of Couples Therapy, 1*(1).

Smith, E. (1991). Gestalt, a Dionysian path. *Voices, 14*(2).

Smith, E. (1992). *Gestalt voices.* Gouldsboro ME: The Gestalt Journal Press

Smith, E. (1997). The roots of Gestalt therapy. In Smith, E. (Ed.), *The growing edge of Gestalt therapy.* Gouldsboro ME: The Gestalt Journal Press. Original Publication 1976

Smith, E. (1998). At the cusp of being and becoming: The growing edge phenomenon. *The Gestalt Journal, 21*(2).

Smith, E. (1999). Enactment and awareness in the Gestalt approach. *Voices, 35*(4).

Smith, E. (2002). Schopenhauer, Freud, and projection. *Voices, 38*(1).

Smith, E. (2003). *The person of the therapist.* Jefferson NC: McFarland

Smith, E. (2007). *Sexual aliveness.* Gouldsboro ME: Gestalt Journal Press. Original Publication 1987: Jefferson, NC, McFarland

Spurling, S. (1981). *Tenderfeet and ladyfingers.* New York: Viking

Stevens, J. (1975). *Gestalt is.* Moab UT: Real People Press

Stevens, B. (1984). *Burst out laughing.* Berkeley CA: Celestial Arts

Stevens, B. (2005). *Don't push the river.* Gouldsboro ME: The Gestalt Journal Press. Original Publication 1970

Stoehr, T. (1994). *Here now next: Paul Goodman and the origins of Gestalt therapy.* San Francisco: Jossey-Bass

Sturluson, S. (1954). *Prose Edda* (Young, J., Trans.). Berkeley CA: University of California

Sullivan, H. (1953). The interpersonal theory of psychiatry. In Perry, H., & Gawel, M. (Ed.), *The collected works of Harry Stack Sullivan*. New York: W. W. Norton

Taegel, W. (1990). *The many colored buffalo*. Norwood NJ: Ablex

Tart, C. (1969). *Altered states of consciousness*. New York: John Wiley

Tillich, P. (1952). *The courage to be* (2 ed.). New Haven CT: Yale University Press

Tobin, S. (1971). Saying goodbye. In Stevens, J. (Ed.), *Gestalt is*. Moab UT: Real People Press

Wallen, R. (1970). Gestalt therapy and Gestalt Psychology. In Fagan, J., & Shepherd, I. (Ed.), *Gestalt therapy now*. Gouldsboro ME: The Gestalt Journal Press. Original Publication 1970: Palo Alto CA, Science and Behavior Books

Walther, D. (9176). *Applied kinesology*. Pueblo CO: Systems DC

Welling, H. (2000). On the therapeutic potency of Kaiser's techniques: Some misunderstandings? *Psychotherapy: Theory, Research and Practice, 37*(1).

White, L. (1962). *The unconscious before Freud*. Garden City NY: Anchor/Doubleday

Williams, P. (1973). *Das energi*. New York: Warner

Young, C., & Brook, A. (1994). Schopenhauer and Freud. *International Journal of Psychoanalysis, 75*.

Zinker, J. (1977). *Creative process in Gestalt therapy*. New York: Brunner/Mazel

Zubin, J., & Eron, L., & Schumer, F. (1965). *An experimental approach to projective techniques*. New York: Wiley

Gestalt Therapy on the World Wide Web

The Gestalt Therapy Page is the Internet's oldest and most comprehensive web resource for information, resources, and publications relating to the theory and practice of Gestalt therapy.

Visitors can subscribe to News and Notes, a free email calendar of conferences, training programs, and other events of interest to the worldwide Gestalt therapy community.

The Gestalt Therapy Page includes an on-line store that offers the most comprehensive collection of books and recordings available – many available nowhere else!

Visit today: www.gestalt.org

The Gestalt Journal Press was founded in 1975 and is currently the leading publisher and distributor of books, journals, and educational recordings relating to the theory and practice of Gestalt therapy. Our list of titles includes new editions of all the classic works by Frederick Perls, Laura Perls, Paul Goodman, Ralph Hefferline, and Jan Christiaan Smuts. Our catalog also includes a wide variety of books by contemporary theoreticians and clinicians including Richard Hycner, Lynne Jacobs, Violet Oaklander, Peter Philippson, Erving & Miriam Polster, Edward W. L. Smith, and Gary Yontef.

In 1976, we began publication of The Gestalt Journal (now the International Gestalt Journal), the first professional periodical devoted exclusively to the theory and practice of Gestalt therapy.

Our collection of video and audio recordings features the works of Frederick (Fritz) and Laura Perls, Violet Oaklander, Erving & Miriam Polster, Janie Rhyne, and James Simkin.

The Gestalt Journal Press, in conjunction with the University of California, Santa Barbara, maintains the world's largest archive of Gestalt therapy related materials including original manuscripts and correspondence, published and unpublished, by Gestalt therapy pioneers Frederick & Laura Perls and Paul Goodman. The archives also include more than six thousand hours of audio and video recordings of presentations, panels and interviews dating to early 1961.

Made in the USA
Middletown, DE
08 June 2021